| DEC 3 0 1995 DATE | | | |
|---|---|---|---|
|  |  |  |  |
|  |  |  |  |
|  |  |  |  |
|  |  |  |  |
|  |  |  |  |
|  |  |  |  |
|  |  |  |  |
|  |  |  |  |
|  |  |  |  |

# HEISMEN

**OTHER BOOKS BY DAVE NEWHOUSE**

Rose Bowl Football Since 1902
(With Herb Michelson)
Stein and Day, 1977

The Jim Plunkett Story
Arbor House, 1981

# AFTER THE GLORY

# HEISMEN

## BY
## DAVE NEWHOUSE

### The Sporting News Publishing Co., 1985

Published in the United States by THE SPORTING NEWS Publishing Co., 1212 North Lindbergh Boulevard, St. Louis, Missouri 63132.

*Heisman Memorial Trophy ® and likeness of the actual trophy are registered service marks owned by the Downtown Athletic Club under Registration Numbers 936,853 and 936,852, respectively. "Heisman" and "Heisman Trophy Award" also are service marks owned by the Downtown Athletic Club of New York City, Inc.

Library of Congress Catalog Card Number: 85-14842

ISBN: 0-89204-202-8
10  9  8  7  6  5  4  3  2  1

First Edition

# ACKNOWLEDGMENTS

It was on another anniversary, baseball's 50th All-Star Game at Chicago's Comiskey Park, the site of the first midsummer classic, that Richard Waters, president and chief executive officer of The Sporting News, and Dick Kaegel, then editor of the same publication, asked the question: "Got any new book ideas?"

I had been thinking of a tribute to the Heisman Memorial Trophy in conjunction with its 50th anniversary in 1985. Waters and Kaegel thought the idea had merit and asked for a proposal, thus launching a two-year project.

Without these two men, their interest, faith and confidence, there would be no book. I thank them both. Without the help of others, the book would have been much more difficult to write and not as informative.

With special thanks to:

Editor and publisher Bob Maynard, managing editor Roy Grimm and sports editor Bob Valli of the Oakland Tribune, and general manager Bill Dwyer and program manager Ron Reynolds of radio station KNBR in San Francisco, for giving me the freedom and making it logistically possible to complete the book;

Jim Bainbridge of the Oakland Tribune, without whose research files the book would have suffered;

John Steadman of the Baltimore News-American, for his idea that led to the Foreword;

Sports information directors Larry Kimball of Syracuse, Marvin Homan of Ohio State and Hal Cowan of Oregon State, who went above and beyond, and assistant sports information director Eddie White of Notre Dame, who went even beyond that;

Tim Tessalone and his staff at Southern Cal's sports information office;

Public relations directors Greg Suit of the New Orleans Saints, Greg Aiello and Doug Todd of the Dallas Cowboys, Bob Sprenger of the Kansas City Chiefs, Kevin Byrne and Chuck Fisher of the Cleveland Browns, George Heddleston of the Detroit Lions, L. Budd Thalman of the Buffalo Bills and Bob Rose of the Los Angeles Express;

Chuck DeKeado, Morey Rossin, Bill Glazier, Jon and Ginny Hanifin, Susan Pevear, Jerry Norton, Jay Barrington, Leba Hertz and The 101 Club of Kansas City, for special favors;

The libraries of the Chicago Tribune, the Oregonian and the Oakland Tribune;

Authors Frank Luksa (*Roger Staubach: Time Enough to Win*), Jay Dunn (*The Tigers of Princeton*), Robert C. Gallagher (*Ernie Davis: The Elmira Express*), D.W. Stump (*Kinnick: The Man and the Legend*), Tom Akers (*The Game Breaker*) and Albert B. Gerber (*Bashful Billionaire*);

Ron Smith, director of books and periodicals at The Sporting News, for his patience and thoughtfulness;

Mike Nahrstedt, associate editor at The Sporting News, for his painstaking research, editing and dedication to accuracy;

The New York Times, truly the paper of record;

Finally, Jay, Larry, Clint, Davey, Nile, Tom, Bruce, Frank, Angelo, Les, Doc, Glenn, Johnny, Doak, Leon, Vic, Dick, Billy, John, Alan, Hopalong, Paul, John

David, Pete, Billy, Joe, Ernie, Terry, Roger, John, Mike, Steve, Gary, O.J., Steve, Jim, Pat, Johnny, John, Archie, Tony, Earl, Billy, Charles, George, Marcus, Herschel, Mike and Doug—the men who are the book.

D.N.

The Sporting News also would like to express its sincere gratitude to the Downtown Athletic Club of New York City for allowing the use of the words "Heisman Memorial Trophy" and the likenesses of the trophy, both registered service marks, and for its cooperation and assistance in the production of this book.

# TABLE OF CONTENTS

To Patsy, Chad and Casey,
for their love and understanding.

# FOREWORD

The priest wasn't an athlete. He knew little about sports. He was unaware that the dying man in the hospital room, Bruce Smith, had been a football hero of such magnitude that he was awarded the Heisman Memorial Trophy in 1941 as the outstanding college football player in the United States. The dying man never told him.

The priest knew only that there was something unusual about this 47-year-old man who was terminally ill with cancer. And though their relationship spanned only a few months, the priest was moved in a way that he hasn't been moved before or since.

"It was his humility," said the Rev. William Cantwell, thinking back to his visits with Smith at St. Barnabas Hospital in Minneapolis in the spring of 1967. "I didn't know who he was. I learned from others that he had been a great football player. He never mentioned it. He knew himself. We didn't talk about football much."

Smith had led the University of Minnesota to undefeated seasons and national championships in 1940 and 1941. He was extremely handsome, virtuous, religious and clean-cut in the true all-America sense. He also was a tenacious football player, a halfback who performed at his finest in the most crucial situations, thus prompting his nickname, "The Game Breaker."

Father Cantwell was the parish priest at St. Lawrence Church in Minneapolis, the same city in which Smith had starred as a collegian. Among Father Cantwell's responsibilities was to visit the Catholic patients at St. Barnabas and bring them the sacraments. That is how he met Bruce Smith.

"Even though he was fighting to stay alive, he was a remarkable personality," the priest said, remembering Smith vividly. "He wasn't a frivolous guy, but more of a solid-citizen type, the kind of man you'd be comfortable with. He had charisma and a good mind. We talked about the madness in Vietnam, which was then building up. He was bothered by that."

Father Cantwell hasn't forgotten how Smith never complained even though his life was slowly and painfully ebbing away.

"If it took only courage and guts to beat cancer," he said, "Bruce would still be alive. But cancer is no respecter of persons. Bruce wanted to live, and he wouldn't give up, but he never questioned his dying. He wasn't a whiner: 'Why me? Why me?' I know that same kind of inner strength must have made him successful in football."

The priest was struck as much by Smith's humility as his courage.

"Jesus says: 'He who humbles himself shall be exalted. He who exalts himself shall be humbled,'" Father Cantwell said, quoting the Bible. "Bruce never exalted himself even though it's no small thing to live a humble life. He reminded me of Congressional Medal of Honor winners, who've gone through hell but don't flaunt it. Bruce never tried to tell you how good he was. He was the total opposite of my reaction to later Heisman winners, who *demand* the trophy."

The priest was so taken by Smith that following the humble man's death on August 28, 1967, he sought to have Smith canonized.

St. Bruce.

At no other time has Father Cantwell attempted to have someone canonized. Nor is it an easy matter. "There are thousands of saints throughout history," he said, "but there are only a handful of American-canonized saints."

"The canonization process, he noted, sometimes requires two centuries to complete. Not all saints represent the clergy. Both educators and the uneducated have been canonized. Reformed alcoholics have become saints. But no former American athletes.

"Bruce would be a model for youth," Father Cantwell spoke from St. Peter's Church in Greeley, Colo., where he is serving the Paulist Fathers.

Bruce Smith would seem an example, in fact, for all ages. Father Cantwell uses his observations of Smith's courage at the end of his life to inspire hope among those with equally bleak futures. When he visits cancer victims, he tells them of Smith, who wouldn't quit battling an unrelenting, unconquerable opponent, even after his weight had dropped from a well-padded 235 pounds to a sickly 90.

Father Cantwell once loaned a copy of "The Game Breaker," a biography of Smith, to a St. Peter's parish member who had cancer. "He thanked me afterward," the priest said.

"And it's a true story that Hubert Humphrey read 'The Game Breaker' before he died. He was the boy mayor of Minneapolis, you know, and very familiar with Bruce. Humphrey was a shadow at the end of his life, but he wouldn't give up."

St. Bruce? Is it that unrealistic?

If a reformed alcoholic can be esteemed as someone next to godliness, why not an athlete who faced death with the same strength and humility that he faced life, and who achieved heroism in both?

Why not St. Bruce? Can't saints be heroes, too?

Father Cantwell saw Smith for the last time three months before the Heisman winner died. Smith left the hospital and spent the summer of 1967 with his wife and four children at their Lake Geneva home in Alexandria, Minn., 130 miles northwest of Minneapolis. The priest gave the homily at Smith's funeral.

Smith remained strong in front of his family. When his wife, Gloria, mentioned the possibility of a miracle, Smith said: "I am having my miracle. I will have the summer with my family."

Too weak to move much of that summer, Smith sat on the porch of his lakefront home and watched his two sons play basketball and his two daughters swim and water-ski. But there would be one last burst of Smith's incredible inner strength.

"It was a traumatic summer," Gloria recalled, "because we'd have to take Bruce back and forth to the hospital. On one such trip, the hospital elevator wouldn't work. Bruce was in a wheelchair. His brother Wayne and I decided to make a human seat with our hands and carry Bruce up to the second floor, where we needed to go.

" 'The elevator doesn't work?' Bruce said. 'Get me to the stairs.' We wheeled him over, and he literally ran up two flights of stairs before collapsing. Here was this sick, skinny man. . . . He was really amazing."

When Smith knew the fight was over, he told another priest, "Father, I'd like you to do me a favor."

"Sure, Bruce," the priest replied. "What is it?"

"I'm not afraid to die, and I'm sure there is a heaven," Smith said. "I've fought this cancer, and I've no more strength to give. I wish you would pray that I go soon."

That night, one of Smith's daughters, Bonnie, entered his hospital room and saw her father sitting up in bed. He seemed to be listening. Bonnie then watched him extend his arms toward a painting of Jesus Christ on the opposite wall. "Yes, Father," she heard him say. Bonnie backed out of the room, gasping.

"I don't like to talk about this much," Gloria said, "because it sounds . . . weird. But Bonnie said he wasn't hallucinating. He didn't hallucinate until he went into a coma."

Another religious sign appeared after Smith's death.

"We noticed a white cross of sand in the lake," Gloria said. "We don't have any substantiation of what that means. We saw what we saw. But we had never seen it before."

St. Bruce?

"Oh, goodness gracious. . . . Bruce would be mortified," his widow responded. "He didn't think of himself as a saint. He had a deep, quiet faith, but he plodded along doing what we have to do in life."

Even the mere mention of canonization is unnerving to Gloria. "I've had people make jokes," she said, "things like, 'When are you going to build a shrine in your backyard?' "

Gloria believes the canonization efforts are "hopeless," she said. "I know I won't have to worry about it in my lifetime." However, Gloria concedes that it isn't such an illogical idea, her husband as a saint.

"He was a beautiful gentleman," she said. "Sweet isn't a word that applies to a man, but he was very sweet, a real charmer. Very unassuming, very democratic. . . . He was never a snob. When we'd go out, he would spend time with people who hovered around him, even if they were tipsy. I'm sure he got tired of being who he was, but he never showed it."

St. Bruce?

"Why not?" Gloria agreed, finally. "Everyone is so blase these days. There are very few heroes. And it's difficult to find heroes like Bruce, someone who didn't become sophisticated by all the attention around him.

"Bruce remained an ordinary, humble man. He was a special man."

Smith was the seventh winner of the Heisman Trophy, which marked its 50th anniversary in 1985. In those 50 years, 49 heroes have won the trophy, Archie Griffin having received two. Some of those heroes had saintly qualities, too.

Nile Kinnick of Iowa, who earned the Heisman in 1939, two years before Smith, was a well-rounded, gifted young man who could have achieved almost anything in life. He was killed in World War II.

Ernie Davis of Syracuse, who became the first black to win the Heisman in 1961, died of leukemia 18 months later. Like Smith, he fought death with great determination and dignity.

Not all of the Heisman heroes are dead. Other role models live in the persons of Jay Berwanger of Chicago (the first winner in 1935), Dick Kazmaier of Princeton (1951), Pete Dawkins of Army (1958), Terry Baker of Oregon State (1962), Roger Staubach of Navy (1963), O.J. Simpson of Southern California (1968), Jim

Plunkett of Stanford (1970) and Griffin of Ohio State (1974-75).

But then, a number of Heisman winners seem almost godlike to their legions of worshipers.

On this, the golden anniversary of the Heisman, the author decided to learn what has happened to the men who have won the Heisman, the most famous individual honor in American athletics.

The Oscar of sports.

The intent was to visit the Heisman recipients, but because of time and geographical constraints, it was impossible to interview all 49 in person. So, an arbitrary number of 18 was picked based on the author's intuitions, after fingering down the list, of which winners would make interesting chapters. The other 31 would be treated in capsulized fashion, including those who were playing professional football as of June 1, 1985. The intent of the book is to examine these men's lives *after* football, i.e., *after* the glory.

Two of the in-depth winners (Kinnick and Ernie Davis) and two capsulized winners (Smith and Davey O'Brien, the 1938 recipient from Texas Christian) are dead. In these cases, loved ones, friends, teammates and coaches were contacted.

The 18 men chosen, and the accompanying reasons why:

Jay Berwanger, who started it all off;

Larry Kelley of Yale (1936) and Leon Hart of Notre Dame (1949), the only linemen to win the trophy;

Nile Kinnick, because of his flawless character and aborted life;

Tom Harmon of Michigan (1940), a heroic figure in football and at war;

Doc Blanchard of Army (1945) and Glenn Davis of Army (1946), who formed—as Mr. Inside and Mr. Outside—the most feared backfield combination ever;

Dick Kazmaier, the last of the Ivy League winners;

Paul Hornung of Notre Dame (1956), the playboy;

Pete Dawkins, the second coming of Gen. Douglas MacArthur, only to retire from the military at 45;

Billy Cannon of Louisiana State (1959), a Bayou legend and a successful orthodontist who went to prison for counterfeiting;

Ernie Davis, a great athlete and a gentle man, who died in the bloom of life;

Terry Baker, the first West Coast Heisman winner;

Roger Staubach, the super patriot;

John Huarte of Notre Dame (1964), the biggest Heisman upset winner;

O.J. Simpson, the most visible of Heisman honorees;

Johnny Rodgers of Nebraska (1972), who posed the first moral question involving Heisman voting;

Archie Griffin, the only two-timing Heisman hero.

Fifteen of the 18 men were agreeable; in the cases of Kinnick and Ernie Davis, their families and friends were quite helpful. Only Cannon proved a stumbling block, and understandably so.

Cannon's attorney, Robert L. (Buck) Kleinpeter of Baton Rouge, La., informed the author that Cannon would do no interviews from inside the federal prison at Texarkana, Tex., but that he would accept questions in letter form for Cannon's possible reply. He made no promises.

Seven pages of questions were mailed on August 21, 1984, to Cannon through

Kleinpeter, who a few months later said, "Billy told me he is working on something." On March 29, 1985, Kleinpeter wrote that after speaking to Cannon about answering the questions "on at least 11 occasions," he had come to the conclusion that Cannon would not respond.

However, Johnny Robinson's comments on his former college and professional teammate offer some revealing insights on Cannon's struggle. Those thoughts are recorded in the back of the book.

The Heisman winners are a diverse lot, with a wide range of personalities, interests and aspirations, but if there is one trait common among them, it is their modesty. They found it difficult to talk about, or in some cases even to recall, their heralded accomplishments. In the last 10 years or so, as Father Cantwell pointed out, there have been more athletes lobbying for the Heisman. But after achieving their goal, these same aggressive types, in conversations, demonstrated the same deep sense of pride in having won the trophy as their more reserved predecessors.

And, as a rule, the men who received the Heisman are content in life. Almost all of them have extended their football accomplishments into the private sector. A number of them are quite wealthy, some millionaires. This group doesn't include just those still active as professional football players, several of whom became millionaires immediately upon leaving college. Heisman winners have gone into medicine, law, corporate finance, the military, education, broadcasting, publishing, the movies and private business. Only three became head football coaches—Frank Sinkwich, John David Crow and Steve Spurrier. For the most part, football was a means to an end, a catalyst to additional success that they achieved on their own, without being set up or mollycoddled.

A few Heisman heroes failed along the way, but that's only normal out of 49 men. Those who went downhill, however, put on the skids, redirected their lives and even went on to prosper. It's too early to tell about Billy Cannon.

The greater share of Heisman winners are like Bruce Smith, heroic figures whom parents would want their sons to emulate.

On the trophy's 50th anniversary, it's also a time to reflect on its origin. For instance, who or what was Heisman?

Who, not what. But if not for a disobedient son, the Heisman Trophy might be known as the Bogart Trophy—Bogart as in von Bogart, not Humphrey.

Sometime in the first half of the 19th Century, a man defied his father, a German baron named von Bogart, by marrying a peasant girl from Alsace-Lorraine. The son promptly was disinherited. He flaunted his dispossession by taking the last name of his bride—Heismann. Then they fled to the United States, where the son made a fortune in the oil-barrel business in Pennsylvania. In 1869, his grandson, Johann Wilhelm Heismann, was born in Cleveland. By the time the boy enrolled at Brown University, his name had been altered to John William Heisman.

Young Heisman played tackle for Brown before transferring to Pennsylvania, where he was a two-year letterman. He earned a law degree, then decided he would rather practice football than jurisprudence.

Over the next 36 years (1892-1927), Heisman coached at Oberlin, Akron, Auburn, Clemson, Georgia Tech, Penn, Washington and Jefferson, and Rice. He had a clever mind and was credited with devising or recommending a number of college football innovations, including the direct snap from center, the forward pass, spin plays, the jump shift and the first scoreboard that showed down and yards.

In a 1916 game that simultaneously brought Heisman fame and disgrace, his Georgia Tech team defeated Cumberland College of Lebanon, Tenn., 222-0.

After retiring from coaching, Heisman moved to New York and became the first athletic director of the Downtown Athletic Club of New York City. In 1935, he supported an idea by the club to give an annual award to the best college football player east of the Mississippi River.

The Downtown Athletic Club commissioned sculptor Frank Eliscu to create a trophy. Eliscu used Ed Smith, a New York University football player, as his model. Smith had no idea what he was posing for, and he didn't learn that he was the man on the trophy until almost 50 years later. In its final form, the statue stands 14 inches long, 13½ inches high, 6½ inches wide and weighs 25 pounds.

The initial winner of what was then known as the Downtown Athletic Club Trophy was Berwanger, the multitalented halfback from Chicago's fading football program who was chosen in 1935.

On October 3, 1936, Heisman died of bronchial pneumonia at age 66. In his honor, the Downtown Athletic Club renamed its award the John W. Heisman Memorial Trophy and extended the competition nationwide.

The best football player in the country doesn't necessarily receive the Heisman each season. For one thing, many voters never take the time or have the opportunity to watch the top players in the country perform. In addition, only two ends (Kelley and Hart) have been honored over the first 50 years, and no guards, tackles or centers. This oversight is understandable considering the high visibility of skill-position players, but it is by no means right. Nevertheless, the top linemen in the country generally must be content to compete for their own versions of the Heisman—the Outland Trophy and the Lombardi Award.

The Heisman doesn't reflect a perfect voting system, that's for certain. The Oscar of sports is, at times, as fallible as Hollywood's Oscar, which is not always awarded to the best actor or actress in a particular year. Voting for the two famous trophies is based largely on popularity. The Heisman usually recognizes the most *visible* player in the country, an athlete who has set records and/or is the star of one of the nation's best teams. Similarly, the Oscar generally pays tribute to those involved with *box-office smashes*. Drawing this analogy to a conclusion, the Heisman and the Oscar are alike in that they recognize marquee players.

Despite these drawbacks, the Heisman is good for college football because it focuses attention on the autumn game and creates a sense of energy and anticipation about the season. Before each fall campaign, the question "Who'll win the Heisman?" is every bit as prevalent as "Who's Number 1?" But on a continuing basis, there is nothing more prestigious about college football than the bronzed little man with the straight arm.

And the Heisman is among the rarest of fraternities.

"How many clubs," O.J. Simpson said, "have been in existence for 50 years and have only 49 members?"

Nobody ever expressed it better.

Dave Newhouse
Oakland, Calif.
June 1, 1985

1

# Jay
# Berwanger

*He was The First, which at the time seemed to carry no major significance. Never in his wildest dream did he foresee a trophy becoming his claim to fame. But 50 years later, there it was, the name Jay Berwanger, heading one of the most prestigious lists that chronicles sporting achievements. He was an excellent college football player and student, a sharp businessman in later life and always a warm, friendly man with a quick smile. But more than anything else, Jay Berwanger was The First.*

# Chapter 1

# The beginning
# of a legend

*Lights off, camera, action!*

*The film must be 50 years old, though, surprisingly, it is not grainy. It is the football players who date the film. They scamper across the screen, recreating a game that is barely recognizable today.*

*The two teams line up in tight bunches around the football, a formation that resembles a rugby scrum. Most of the running plays, originating from the single wing, are stymied. Occasionally, a few players run out for passes, but their patterns are not precise, nor are the passes particularly well thrown. The overall play is plodding and brutish, not nearly as swift and wide open as modern-day football.*

*One player on the screen, however, is timeless.*

*Eighty-five yards away from the goal line, he gets the ball at his halfback position and blasts through a small hole at right tackle with the power of a fullback. A defender crashes into his legs, but with the stability of a high-wire walker, he maintains his balance. He wards off another tackler with a straight arm, then cuts to his left, accelerating away from more trouble. He reaches the sideline and turns upfield with sprinter's speed. Two more tacklers converge on him. Cleverly, as if his instincts run on radar, he stops dead in his tracks, and the would-be tacklers fly by, grasping at air.*

*The halfback's exhausting race is not yet run. He cuts back to his right to avoid another tackler, receives a teammate's block near the center of the field and, finally, weaves around two more defenders before reaching the end zone standing up.*

*Who was that back . . . Harmon, Grange, Whizzer White?*

*No. Berwanger.*

It was November 1935. Jay Berwanger felt the first snap of winter as he turned up the collar of his overcoat and walked back to the Psi Upsilon fraternity house after another day of classes at the University of Chicago.

There was much on his mind. He had paperwork to take care of as senior class president. He wanted to fit in some studying before dinner. He already was thinking ahead to graduation the following spring.

Inside the house, he checked his mail and found a telegram.

"It said I had won some trophy," Berwanger recalled, "and that there would be two tickets waiting to take a guest and me to New York. That was about it."

Berwanger received many trophies that fall. He was recognized as the best football player not only in the Midwest, but also in the country. The trophy he prized most at the time, however, was the Silver Football presented to him by the Chicago Tribune as the Most Valuable Player in the Big Ten Conference.

The statue from New York was just one more trophy. It wasn't going to change his life. Not then, anyway.

"It wasn't really a big deal when I got it," he said. "No one at school said anything to me about winning it other than a few congratulations. I was more excited about the trip than the trophy because it was my first flight."

Berwanger took Clark Shaughnessy, his football coach at Chicago, to New York as his guest. They were taken to the top of the Empire State Building. They watched a performance of the Rockettes. They had lunch at the 21 Club.

"We received a private tour of their wine cellar," Berwanger said. "I didn't know much about wine, except for the grape wine and rhubarb wine Dad made on the farm back in Dubuque. That rhubarb wine actually didn't taste too bad.

"My New York hotel room was high up. When I looked out the window, the Statue of Liberty was staring back at me. It was all very exciting for a boy from the Midwest. The only problem was that I got tired of carrying that 60-pound trophy in and out of taxis."

The trophy from New York, which actually weighed 25 pounds, was somewhat of a nuisance once Berwanger returned to the Chicago campus. There wasn't enough room for it in his small living quarters at the fraternity house, so he asked his Aunt Gussie to keep it for him until after graduation.

Gussie said she would, but she had no more idea what to do with it than her nephew. She didn't have a mantelpiece wide enough. The trophy was too big for a coffee table. And Gussie wasn't about to put it on the dining-room table for fear that one of her lady friends, while reaching for one of her homemade biscuits, might get poked in the eye by that arm sticking out from the trophy.

Gussie finally found a use for the trophy in her North Chicago home. Hoping to capture some cool breezes off Lake Michigan, she realized one day that she needed something to keep the front door open. The monstrous trophy from the Downtown Athletic Club did the trick. For the better part of 10 years, that trophy served as Aunt Gussie's doorstop.

Nephew Jay got a kick out of that. "I used to flip my hat over the trophy's arm when I'd come to visit," he said.

So, the trophy from New York became not only a doorstop, but a hat rack as well.

It wasn't until after World War II that Berwanger reclaimed the trophy. Fortunately, it still was in one piece, although Gussie wasn't sure what she would use as a substitute to keep the front door open.

The significance of the trophy from New York wouldn't hit Berwanger until another 15 years had passed, by which time Heisman Memorial Trophy winners were regularly turning their collegiate honors into lucrative professional contracts.

"I never dreamed the Heisman would ever be so important," he said. "Nobody talked about it for 25 years. Then television came on the scene, giving college football more exposure, and it became a big deal that I had won the first one.

"I've said a number of times that the difference between winning the first Heisman in 1935 and winning it now is like the difference between nothing and a million dollars."

John Jacob Berwanger, a blacksmith's son from Dubuque, Ia., would best understand that difference. He grew up in a bare existence, attended college during the Great Depression and started out in business with nothing.

Today he is a millionaire. "A couple of times," he said softly.

The trophy from New York eventually brought him everlasting fame, but it did not create his fortune in the manufacturing world. Berwanger has prospered on his business acumen, not his football reputation.

"Everyone wants to meet the first Heisman winner," he said at his office. "It might get me into some doors I might not otherwise get into. But it won't get me any more business."

At first, winning the Heisman didn't open any doors for him.

Two years after winning the trophy, Berwanger returned to New York on a business trip. He decided to impress a date by taking her to dinner at the 21 Club, even though he hadn't called for a reservation.

"You'll never get in without one," his date warned him during the cab ride to the *tres chic* restaurant.

"Don't worry," Berwanger said confidently. "They treated me pretty well two years ago."

At the front door, they were greeted by a rather stiff, dour maitre d', who inquired coldly, "What time is your reservation?"

Berwanger straightened his tie and mustered his courage. "Well, we don't have one," he replied. "But my name is Jay Berwanger. Two years ago I won the Heisman Trophy—you know, the *Heisman*—and was taken here to lunch. I was just telling my lady friend what a marvelous time we had. . . ."

Berwanger was cut off in midsentence by a glare that only a New York maitre d' can give when his patience has worn thin.

"Jay who?"

Nearly a half-century later, Berwanger laughed about the early impact of the Heisman. "I never did get into the restaurant," he said. "I never saw the girl again, either."

Even if heading the distinguished list of Heisman winners didn't exactly make him a household name back then, there is no question that he deserved it as much as—and perhaps more than—any recipient since.

Berwanger was the epitome of the one-man gang. At the University of Chicago, he called the plays, ran, passed, punted, blocked, played defense, kicked extra points, kicked off, returned punts and kickoffs and played 60 minutes.

He didn't dare leave the field. Chicago had absolutely no chance of winning without him.

In fact, without Berwanger, the football program had virtually no chance of surviving. Four years after he played his last game for Chicago, during which time the Maroons won only one Big Ten game, the school dropped football.

The Maroons competed in the Big Ten, but except for a few years around the turn of the century, they did not dominate their competition. Chicago was interested in national endowments, not national football rankings. At Chicago, academics came first, football second. A distant second. While Minnesota, Purdue, Michigan and Ohio State enrolled future big-time coaches and National Football League stars, Chicago's roster was composed entirely of budding surgeons, economists and corporate executives.

No other Big Ten school emphasized academics over athletics quite as heavily as the eggheadish little university near Chicago's lakefront. While it was not uncommon for Chicago's opponents to turn out 50 to 60 football candidates a year, the Maroons were lucky to get 20.

"We were OK until the players started getting hurt," Berwanger said. "Then we just didn't have the depth to compete."

The Maroons were 11-11-2 during Berwanger's three varsity seasons. Without him, they would have been far worse. Though Shaughnessy was an innovative coach, mixing the single and double wings with the T-formation, Chicago's game plan boiled down to this: If Berwanger could hold the game close, maybe Berwanger could win it.

Opponents knew that to beat Chicago, they just had to beat Berwanger. Predictably, they kept a man on him at all times.

"The game I remember this way was against Purdue," he said. "Every time I got the ball, big Ed Skoronski would hit me. His defensive assignment was to go wherever I went, so we never had anyone to block him. He didn't hurt me, but he bruised me. After the game, the team doctor asked me how I felt. 'Fine, Doc,' I told him, 'but my legs are sore.' He stuck a pin into my legs, about an inch deep, and I never felt it."

Morey Rossin, who played basketball and baseball at Chicago when Berwanger attended college and is his good friend today, hasn't forgotten the tactics Big Ten opponents used against Berwanger.

"Teams had suicide squads that went after Jay," he said. "To get him out of the game meant a cinch win."

Despite that strategy, Berwanger was nearly indestructible. He missed only one game in three seasons, after suffering a knee injury as a junior. But just to be on the safe side, he wore a face mask after breaking his nose as a high school senior and again as a Chicago freshman.

"I was told if I broke it again," Berwanger said, "I wouldn't have any nose left to repair."

The mask was designed by Chicago's team trainer, Wally Bock. It was made out of spring steel and had two bars, one running from the top of Berwanger's helmet to another bar that ran across his mouth. The steel was covered by sponge and leather. The contraption elicited a few chuckles from opponents, who called him "The Man in the Iron Mask," but Berwanger was simply ahead of his time. He may not have been the first football player who ever wore a face mask, but he certainly was close.

Berwanger has another famous distinction—he is the only Heisman recipient who was ever tackled by a future President of the United States.

"Jerry Ford showed me, years later, the scar he has on his cheek from trying to tackle me in the 1934 Chicago-Michigan game," said Berwanger, who scored two touchdowns while leading the Maroons to a 27-0 victory over the Wolverines in Ford's senior year. That game marked the first time Chicago had beaten Michigan since 1919.

Ford hasn't forgotten that game, or Jay Berwanger.

"When I tackled Jay that one time, his heel hit my cheekbone and opened it up three inches," Ford said from his office in Rancho Mirage, Calif., near Palm Springs. "The impact of the tackle stunned the cheek, so it didn't bleed. I didn't even know anything was wrong until I got back to the huddle and one of my teammates said, 'What happened to you?' I went to the sideline, where the cut was taped, and I continued to play. I played the whole game. You didn't come out in those days."

The former President was asked which cheek bears the scar.

"I don't know," he replied. "I think it's the left. Wait a minute."

Ford put down the phone and walked over to a mirror. Fifteen seconds later, he returned to the phone.

"It is the left," he said. "There are so many wrinkles now, you can't see it.

"Whenever I see Jay, I tell him he left a permanent impact on me. He was a big back for those days, about 200 pounds. Big and fast. He was of the same capability of a Tom Harmon . . . a complete ball player.

"Jay was truly a one-man gang. And he was the total offense for Chicago in one of its last best years."

Ford played center and outside right linebacker for Michigan. Though Michigan won only once his senior year, he was selected to play in the East-West Shrine Game in San Francisco and the College All-Star Game in Chicago. Two professional teams, Green Bay and Detroit, made him offers, but Ford elected to attend the Yale Law School, where he helped finance his education by assisting the Elis' football team.

Ford has met a number of Heisman winners. He said he knows Clint Frank and Larry Kelley "intimately" from having coached them at Yale.

"My impression," Ford said, "is that Heisman winners were not only leaders on the football field, but in their communities, and what they've done after (football) is a continuation of their leadership in football."

Berwanger, of course, was the prototype.

He chose to attend Chicago primarily because of its educational reputation. Little did he know that his arrival would signal not only the making of Chicago football history, but also, to a large extent, the end. His first year at the school, 1932, was Amos Alonzo Stagg's last.

One of the great football coaches of all time, and certainly the most durable, Stagg coached at Chicago from 1892-1932. He was seven years older than the game itself, and he invented the T-formation at the turn of the century and pioneered such innovations as the huddle, reverse plays, laterals, end-around runs and unbalanced lines.

After the 1932 season, Chicago was forced to retire Stagg at the mandatory age of 70 and replaced him with Shaughnessy. But Stagg was merely warming up. He became coach at the College of the Pacific in Stockton, Calif., and was national Coach of the Year in 1943 at the sprightly age of 81. He continued to coach in some capacity until he was 98, when he decided it was time to retire. He died four years later.

Stagg Field would become, three seasons after the grand old man for whom it was named had left, the showcase for the first Heisman winner.

Breakaway Jay.

"My strengths were speed and elusiveness," Berwanger said. "A fullback is a brave man. He likes to run over people. A halfback, by nature, has to be a coward. He runs away from others. I had 9.9 speed in the 100-yard dash, so I ran away."

Berwanger was hardly a coward. He dealt out as much punishment as he received. At 6-foot-1 and 195 pounds, he was a deadly tackler. Minnesota was the national champion during Berwanger's college days, and he had 14 tackles against the Gophers in one half in 1934.

But those who watched Berwanger play don't remember him for his defense. They remember the runs.

As a sophomore, he barrelled 65 yards for a touchdown against Dartmouth. As a junior, he returned a kickoff 97 yards to score against Indiana. As a senior, there were so many great runs: A 78-yard kickoff return against Wisconsin, a 49-yard punt runback against Illinois that turned certain defeat into victory, and of course his most remembered run, the one he still has on film, his 85-yard scamper from scrimmage against Ohio State. "That run," Rossin said, "had a little bit of every-thing."

That run also might have persuaded voters to single out Berwanger as the first recipient of the Downtown Athletic Club's trophy for the outstanding college football player in the United States.

Actually, only players on teams east of the Mississippi River were considered for the award in 1935, and only Eastern sportswriters were polled. A year later, when the award was renamed the Heisman Memorial Trophy in honor of legend-ary Coach John W. Heisman, a former director of the Downtown Athletic Club, players nationwide became eligible for the trophy as sportswriters throughout the United States joined the voting process.

But the voting limitations in 1935 do not diminish in the least the value of the Downtown Athletic Club's initial award. Berwanger had plenty of stiff competition among players in the East, including a Monk, a Constable and Shakespeare. Monk Meyer of Army was runner-up in the first Heisman vote, followed by Bill Shake-speare of Notre Dame and Pepper Constable of Princeton.

Though the voting line was drawn to exclude roughly two-thirds of the United States, there was little doubt that Berwanger was the best player in the country. One of his teammates had seen the best in the West, Stanford's Bobby Grayson, and declared that Berwanger was better.

"I played freshman football at Stanford," Omar Fareed said, "before transfer-ring to Chicago. I saw Grayson and the rest of the Vow Boys at Stanford, and none could compare with Berwanger.

"I had played high school ball in Glendale, California, with Ned Bartlett, who immediately went to Chicago. He wrote me a letter and said: 'You won't believe what you see. There isn't a football player living who can compete with Ber-wanger.'

"I was a mediocre high school player. I had no chance to play at Stanford. I knew I could play at Chicago. But I transferred because I knew I could get a better education at Chicago than Stanford."

Fareed played in the same backfield as Berwanger. Bartlett, who also played halfback for the Maroons, hadn't misinformed his high school friend.

"Jay was phenomenal," said Fareed, who lives near Los Angeles and has been the team physician for the U.S. Davis Cup tennis team since the mid-'70s. "He could do everything. On offense alone, he was as great as anyone I've seen. He ran like Hugh McElhenny, with the high-knee action, and he could shift on a dime.

"If he had gone to another school, a powerhouse, he would have done more. There would have been no way to hold him down. We had a minimum of talent at Chicago. Jay was like Marcus Allen and all the great ones wrapped into one. They're darn good, but they had good teammates. Everyone has to get blocking, but Jay got the least of any of them."

Fareed remembers when the vote was taken for team captain of the Chicago football team in 1935. He said half the players were members of Berwanger's fraternity, while the other half belonged to Delta Kappa Epsilon. Despite the split, Berwanger was elected captain unanimously.

"He was a terrific guy," Fareed said. "Still is. If you had a leader like Berwanger, you were always in the game. He was a quiet guy who led by example. If someone missed a block, he never complained. I never heard him chew someone out.

"I just came back from Japan with the Davis Cup team. . . . I work out with John McEnroe. He's a good guy, by the way. He doesn't always behave as we would like. Jay wasn't like that. You'd always get the appropriate remark from him or he wouldn't say anything."

For his part, Berwanger isn't convinced that he would have been a better football player at a college that took football more seriously than did Chicago.

"Because we didn't have a lot of players," he said, "I had to do everything. At these other schools, I would have played offense and defense, but they would have had somebody else kick off and return punts and kickoffs. And you never know, I might have broken a shoulder or leg."

At Chicago, Berwanger had a coach who maximized his versatile skills: Clark Shaughnessy.

Shaughnessy was a football junkie. He must have concluded early in life that he was put on Earth to diagram plays because he turned them out at a feverish pace. He was a master of innovation, devising new formations by the week and sometimes by the day. It was a practical necessity at Chicago, where he didn't have the manpower to stand up to stronger Big Ten teams and therefore had to beat them with strategy. He was fortunate to have intelligent athletes who learned quickly. The 5-10 Fareed, for one, remembers a formation where Shaughnessy tried to hide him behind the center in an attempt to confuse the defense.

After Shaughnessy died, someone went up to his attic and found several trunks filled with football diagrams. There is no knowing how many he actually got around to using.

Berwanger has fond memories of his coach. "He was wonderful for me," Berwanger said. "Shaughnessy was able to see what potential I had. We had eight or nine offensive formations, mostly running, which was my strongest suit."

Back in 1933, when Shaughnessy received the Chicago job, he received Berwanger as well. Dutch, as he was known to his teammates, stood out quickly as a sophomore, when he was named the team's most valuable player. He rushed for 667 yards (3.6 average), completed 11 passes for 219 yards and scored eight touchdowns, including four against Cornell in his varsity debut. He handled the punting, kicked seven extra points and played every minute of five conference games.

Chicago's football roster shrank not only because of injuries, but also test scores.

"Half the players on my freshman team eventually flunked out of Chicago," he said. "At the end of my first academic quarter, Fritz Crisler, then the Princeton coach, told me that after I flunked out of Chicago my freshman year, to phone him collect, and he would get me the train fare to come to Princeton and start over as a freshman."

Berwanger persevered and maintained a C grade average over four years at Chicago. "And I worked like hell for those Cs," he said. They were honest Cs, not gift grades handed out to athletes to ensure their eligibility. Chicago played no favorites, not even if they were All-Americas.

"Because of the system at Chicago, everyone took the same classes," Berwanger pointed out. "You were given the same number during examinations so that favoritism couldn't be shown."

The University of Chicago is one of the great centers of learning in the United States. John D. Rockefeller contributed $35 million to the university, which opened its doors in 1892 and was the first school to establish the quarter system and a department of sociology. More than four dozen Nobel Prize winners have studied, done research or taught at Chicago. The years 1932-42 are regarded by Chicago as its golden era for prestigious graduates, including former U.S. Sen. Charles Percy of Illinois, U.S. Supreme Court Justice John Stevens and the first Heisman Trophy winner.

Berwanger was even more impressive as a junior, when the Maroons won their first four games, including that shutout of Gerald Ford and defending Big Ten champion Michigan, but lost their last four. For the season, Dutch ran for 595 yards (4.3 average), passed for 297 yards, returned 13 kickoffs for 347 yards, scored eight touchdowns and kicked eight extra points. Berwanger made several All-America teams. Fielding H. Yost, coach of Michigan's "point-a-minute" teams of the early 1900s, praised him as the best player in the Big Ten.

He was probably the conference's finest all-around athlete, a versatile trackman with Olympic decathlon potential. Besides the 100, he ran the 120-yard high hurdles (15.6 seconds), the 440 (49.0 seconds), pole vaulted (12-6), high jumped (5-8), broad jumped (24 feet), put the shot (48 feet) and threw the javelin (190 feet).

"I ran against Jesse Owens when he was at Ohio State," he said. "I remember looking at the back of Jesse's shirt." Berwanger never beat Owens, but he did win the Big Ten 100-yard dash title one year.

Berwanger was a one-man gang in track as well as football, placing third in the Kansas Relays decathlon as a senior. He contemplated taking the spring off his senior year to concentrate seriously on the decathlon. Free from academic pressures, he believed he could make the U.S. team that would compete in the 1936 Olympic Games in Berlin.

"Most of my decisions, I had to rely on sound judgment," he said. "I talked with one of the university's vice presidents for three hours on what I should do. He told me it would be difficult for me to come back and get my degree, the times being what they were. He convinced me that a degree from Chicago would be more beneficial to me later on than the Olympic experience."

Berwanger stayed in school and graduated on time. He does not regret his decision. "The degree has meant a lot to me," he said. "Look at the pros today who don't have their degrees. When their football is done, what do they do?"

Berwanger had gone to Chicago for an education, and he meant to complete it. He was extremely popular among the students and faculty. Norman Maclean, an English professor who packed the lecture hall when he recited "Song of Roland," once invited Berwanger to join him at a speakeasy, Hanley's, near campus. They slipped in the back door. Imagine the campus commotion that would have been caused if the school's All-America halfback had been caught drinking in a speakeasy, and with a faculty member! Fortunately, the two of them went unnoticed.

With studies, sports and campus jobs occupying most of his time, young Jay Berwanger had little social life. A fraternity brother with a car—a big status symbol during the Depression—dated a girl at Northwestern, and Berwanger occasionally went along on blind dates. "You didn't date much back then," he said. "Not only didn't I have the time, I didn't have the money."

In his last season of football, Berwanger rushed for 577 yards (4.8 average), passed for 405 yards, scored six touchdowns and converted five extra-point attempts. For the third straight year he performed practically every duty on the field, including kickoffs, kickoff returns and punts. He finished his career at Chicago with an average of 37.3 yards per punt and 25.7 yards per kickoff return. There was nothing he could not do well.

But once again, Berwanger did not get much help from his overmatched teammates. The Maroons lost their 1935 opener against Nebraska, 28-7, before winning their next two games against a pair of small schools, 31-0 over Carroll and 31-6 over Western State Teachers College (now Western Michigan). Purdue shut out Chicago, 19-0, but the Maroons came back with a 13-7 victory over Wisconsin as Berwanger scored every point to lead his teammates to their first conference victory of the season. Two more losses followed, 20-13 to Ohio State and 24-0 to Indiana.

That gave Chicago a 3-4 record entering its season finale against Illinois, which had lost to the Maroons only once in their 12 previous meetings. Berwanger, true to Heisman form, came through with a strong performance in which he virtually beat the Illini single-handedly.

Illinois was leading, 6-0, in the third quarter when Berwanger fielded a punt at the 50-yard line and weaved through tacklers as if they were stationary gates on a slalom course to the 1-yard line. Berwanger called two straight plunges by the fullback, who failed to score. Berwanger then called his own number on third down and dived over the middle of the line and fell into the end zone. With Fareed holding, Berwanger kicked the extra point for a 7-6 victory.

And that was how Berwanger's career ended, holding the game close so that he could win it.

On December 10, 1935, club President Walter L. Conwell presented the first Downtown Athletic Club Trophy to Berwanger, who looked at the bronzed figure and assumed that it had been sculpted in his own image.

The Des Moines Register once had photographed Berwanger in a rehearsed scene, cutting across the lens of the camera, the ball under his left arm, his right arm sticking straight out. Berwanger remembered Chicago's athletic department sending the picture on to the Downtown Athletic Club.

"My first wife said she knew it was me (on the trophy) because my socks were always down around my shoes," he said.

Neither Jay Berwanger nor his late wife, Philomela, had ever heard of Ed Smith, the New York University backfield star who actually had posed for the trophy.

Berwanger launched not only the Heisman, but also the National Football League draft. He was the first player ever drafted by the NFL. The Philadelphia Eagles selected him in 1936, but George Halas of the Chicago Bears, looking for a hometown draw as well as a great player, obtained the signing rights to Berwanger.

Not long afterward, Berwanger happened to run into Papa Bear himself at the Palmer House in Chicago.

"How much money would you like to play for the Bears, Jay?" said Halas, kicking off informal negotiations.

Berwanger had absolutely no interest in professional football. At the time, it offered none of the glamour or monetary gains available today. Berwanger knew there was more money and greater long-range potential in the business world. Besides, Halas was paying his players in IOUs.

"Twenty-five thousand dollars over two years," he told Halas.

Papa Bear looked at Berwanger strangely, stroked his chin and promised that he would get back to him. He never did.

"I gave him a figure I knew he wouldn't agree to," Berwanger said.

What if he had?

"I guess I would have signed."

Berwanger wound up playing for the Inland Steel Co. in a promotional game against the Bears the next summer. He worked out a day, then played three quarters. Tackling Bronko Nagurski "was an experience," he said. Joe Stydahar and Dick Plasman "would take turns hitting me, ricocheting me from one to the other," he added. "Then they both caught me at once, one in the chest and the other in the back, and that was the end."

Berwanger's football career came to a crunching conclusion.

Berwanger started the trend of Heisman winners, in the first 10 years of the award, who went to Hollywood to make a movie. He had a small part in "The Big Game," which starred June Travis (who attended the University of Chicago), Bruce Cabot, Andy Devine and William Frawley, who later starred as Fred Mertz on "I Love Lucy." Other big-name college stars appeared in the film, including Bobby Grayson of Stanford and Gomer Jones of Ohio State.

Berwanger's small part grew smaller as the movie progressed. "We had this scene at the goal line," he said. "I was supposed to slap some guys on the butt and say, 'Come on, boys, get in there and fight.' But I couldn't get my voice down low enough, so they cut it out. They didn't want me to stay in Hollywood."

Berwanger took a sales job after college. He supplemented his income by officiating football games and writing a sports column for the Chicago Daily News. The writing job lasted all of one autumn.

"After a year, I was old," he said, without remorse. "It hadn't been a year since I won the Heisman and the glitter was gone."

When Berwanger learned that his alma mater was considering canceling its football program in 1939, he protested.

"I wasn't in favor of it," he said. "The university president at the time (Robert

M. Hutchins) said the school had several choices. 'We could buy a team,' he said, 'but the Chicago Bears aren't for sale. We could drop down a level or we can drop football altogether.'

"One of (the members of) the board of trustees was adamant that we stay in the Big Ten. I argued with him, saying we should drop out of the conference but play schools more like ourselves—Ivy League universities—and we'd still draw 30,000 to 35,000 at Stagg Field."

Hutchins listened to both sides, then made a decision. "Here we have two experts on college football," Berwanger remembers the university president saying, "and you can't agree what must be done. So we'll drop it entirely."

The Maroons were marooned.

Berwanger became a naval officer during World War II after going through the Navy's flight-training program in several cities. He proved himself to be a top-rate flier by the time he earned his wings in New Orleans.

"Berwanger is as great in the air as he was on the football field," Cmdr. Paul E. Gillespie of the New Orleans training school said then. "He is one of the finest students we've ever had."

There were 21 students in Berwanger's flight class; 11 were killed at war. Berwanger was ready to ship out for combat when the atomic bomb, which had been made possible by research at the Chicago campus, was dropped on Hiroshima, Japan. Not long afterward, Berwanger returned to civilian life.

Berwanger and his family moved into a brick apartment house in Chicago, where he discovered that the foam-rubber business for which he had been a salesman before the war had been closed. He quickly went to work building his own business from scratch.

It was about that time that Berwanger finally rescued his Heisman Trophy from duty as a doorstop.

"What happened," he explained, "was my son, who was 4 at the time, came home from nursery school one day and said, 'Who's Jay Berwanger?' My wife and I looked at each other. It was time to tell him who I was. We got out the scrapbooks. I called Aunt Gussie and got the Heisman Trophy back."

Thirteen years after Berwanger won the Heisman, he made headlines again. In the Rose Bowl game after the 1948 season, Berwanger, a Big Ten official, made a controversial ruling that gave Northwestern a touchdown against California. Art Murakowski, a Northwestern back, fumbled at the California goal line, and the ball was recovered in the end zone by a Cal player. Berwanger, the line judge, signaled touchdown. The Wildcats went on to score one more touchdown and beat the Golden Bears, 20-14.

West Coast sportswriters accused Berwanger of showing bias toward the Big Ten with his call.

"It was my job," Berwanger said in his own defense, "to signal the referee when a player got over the goal line, which I did by putting my fist down. Just as I gave the signal, he (Murakowski) fumbled.

"There was a little chatter from the Cal players at the time, but that was it. But the next day there was a picture in the newspapers taken from the end zone which started the furor.

"I knew I was right. But it wasn't until I got several letters from Cal faculty members that I started to feel better. They were sitting on the goal line and had the same view I did. They wrote me and said I had made the right call."

Jay Berwanger Inc., the business started by the blacksmith's son after the war, now is located at 1245 Warren Ave. in Downers Grove, Ill., a 45-minute drive west of Chicago. Berwanger is the first Heisman winner, but he doesn't advertise it. His name isn't blinking in neon lights outside the building. A "1245" is visible on the front door, nothing more. Very unpretentious, like the man for whom the company is named.

Berwanger is a kind man, a gentle man. He has precious little ego and is not consumed by who he is—the original Heisman hero, the ultrasuccessful businessman.

"I was just fortunate that 1935 was the first year they presented the Heisman, and I won it," he said of his good fortune.

And that's all. Berwanger doesn't feel special being the first. "Other than I get more publicity than the third or fourth winner, no," he said. "I haven't tried to seek publicity."

He coughed. He said he smokes too much, even though he has cut back on cigarettes. He lit up another and leaned back in his chair, the smoke wafting across a large photograph of the Chicago campus that hangs behind his desk.

Berwanger had tired of hero talk. "I've left the day open," he said. "I'll show you around the building, then we'll take a little tour of the campus and have lunch at the Faculty Club."

Jay Berwanger Inc. manufactures plastic and sponge rubber strips for car doors, trunks and farm machinery and distributes nationally. The company keeps a work force of about 20 people in the back of the shop—mainly women from Downers Grove—who cut and glue the materials.

Berwanger stopped by the shop and said hello to each employee. Each responded as if he were a friendly next-door neighbor, not an employer. He obviously is a nice man to have for a boss.

Now in his 70s, Berwanger is in the process of retiring. Through a five-year divesting plan, he believes retirement will be possible by 1988.

He stepped outside into the chill of oncoming winter. Berwanger walks with a steady gait for a man his age. He plays golf to keep in shape, and he tested out well, he said, in a recent physical examination. He has large bags under his eyes and a slight paunch, but he appears to be in good health in spite of his smoking habit, which now is down from a pack a day to 10 cigarettes. His doctor wants him to cut out smoking entirely.

Berwanger drove the gray Buick along back country roads toward Chicago while talking about his family. His three children—two sons and a daughter—are grown. His first wife, a Chicago graduate he married in 1940, passed away. They had been friends of Joe and Jane Temple. Joe Temple had pledged Berwanger into the Psi Upsilon fraternity. After Joe died, Jay and Jane learned in time that they could be more than friends. They were married in 1976.

"I took Jane to her first Heisman alumni dinner right after that," he said, "and told her, 'Now don't be surprised if some pretty ladies come up and ask me to dance.'"

Pretty ladies, that is, who are wives of other Heisman winners. Berwanger is among the best dancers of all the Heisman heroes. He knows more steps, and not only is his body graceful and his footwork superb, but he also has tremendous stamina. He starts dancing when the music starts and doesn't stop until the music ends.

Besides being the first Heisman recipient, Berwanger numbers other "firsts" among his accomplishments, some rather amusing.

In the 1930s, a California restaurant named sandwiches after celebrities. If you wanted a hot pastrami, you asked the waitress for a Fanny Brice. If you preferred ham and American cheese, you ordered a William Randolph Hearst. But if your choice was a hot meatball sandwich, one Jay Berwanger coming up! He was the first and only athlete on the menu.

Berwanger also is the only Heisman honoree to have his photograph taken with two Presidents (John F. Kennedy and Herbert Hoover) and a five-star general (Douglas MacArthur)—all in one pose!

"We were at a big football dinner," Berwanger recalled, "and President Kennedy said to me, 'Jay Berwanger, I remember you. You played rugby with my brother Joe.' After college, I had played rugby for a team from Chicago. We played a match against a team from New York that had Larry Kelley, who won the Heisman the year after I did.

"But I didn't know what to say when the President told me about playing with his brother Joe. Here I had done something in football, and he remembered me for my rugby. And I didn't remember Joe at all!"

Berwanger drove past Oak Brook, where he and Jane live in a condominium. They also have a home in Manzanillo, Mexico, between Acapulco and Puerto Vallarta, where they vacation almost every winter.

Berwanger drove into Chicago's metropolitan sprawl and headed for the Midway. Soon, the Chicago campus appeared—tall, gray buildings, stark in appearance, clustered together. "The nice thing about this campus is that it's concentrated," he said. "In zero weather, that's important."

Berwanger is like an excited college freshman when he gets a chance to show off his alma mater. He pointed out one building where he took geography, another where his business classes were located. He then pulled up his car to an abstract sculpture in an open area. The sculpture sits on the spot where Enrico Fermi, professor of physics at Chicago, and a team of scientists triggered the first artificially produced nuclear chain reaction on December 2, 1942.

"And right there," Berwanger said, pointing to the sculpture, "is where the west stands of Stagg Field used to be."

Not far from where Berwanger split tacklers, Fermi split the atom.

Berwanger drove to the back of the campus, where a portable set of bleachers rests on a stretch of lawn. This is the new 3,000-seat home of the Chicago Maroons, who resumed football at the small-time (Division III) level about 30 years after dropping out of the Big Ten. The Maroons now compete in the Midwest Conference. Instead of Ohio State, Michigan and Purdue, they play Coe, Beloit and Ripon. Berwanger sees the Maroons play when time permits.

It began to snow as Berwanger maneuvered the Buick into a parking spot reserved for him behind the campus alumni office by Rossin, who is retired from the gourmet food and liquor business and works part-time for the university as a

Jay Berwanger, the first Heisman Trophy winner, poses with his Heisman (above) in the Jay Berwanger Trophy Room at the University of Chicago. Berwanger stands near an abstract sculpture (left) that marks the spot where Enrico Fermi, a professor of physics at Chicago, and a team of scientists triggered the first artificially produced nuclear chain reaction in 1942.

fund-raiser. Berwanger has helped him on numerous fund drives.

"Jay has been one of our most loyal alumni," Rossin said. The university showed its appreciation when it presented him the University Alumni Service Medal in 1984.

At the Faculty Club, Berwanger and Rossin counted 10 Nobelists in the room, plus law professor Edward H. Levi, who was U.S. Attorney General from 1975-77, and Norman Maclean, retired from teaching and speakeasies and now an author of short stories.

After lunch, Berwanger and Rossin walked over to Bartlett Hall, entering under a stained-glass window of Rowena presenting a sword to Lancelot. Downsword and to the right is the Jay Berwanger Trophy Room, dedicated in 1978.

Old leather footballs, swelled to the size of pumpkins and dating as far back as 1892, are lined up in glass cases. The shape of the footballs explains why they were so hard to throw and so easy to drop-kick during the sport's adolescence.

Also displayed is a large painting of Stagg, a photograph of Walter Eckersall (an All-America quarterback for Chicago from 1904-06) and certificates noting Berwanger's induction into the College Football Hall of Fame in 1954 and his inclusion on Sports Illustrated's 25-year anniversary All-America team, which honored players whose accomplishments extended beyond the football field.

Pinned to the wall is Berwanger's maroon-and-gray jersey, No. 99, with gray patches on the sides and along the sleeves. "They sprayed stickum on the patches to keep us from fumbling," said Berwanger, a prewar Fred Biletnikoff.

He walked over to, and stopped in front of, the first Heisman Trophy.

His trophy.

He gave it to the university. Right below the droopy socks is a fading inscription: "Presented by the Downtown Athletic Club of New York City to John J. Berwanger, University of Chicago, as the Outstanding Football Player of 1935."

Encased in glass in the trophy room bearing Berwanger's name on the campus he loves, the first trophy from New York is safe from ever being a doorstop again.

# Larry Kelley

*He was a laugher, a leaper and a leprechaun. He performed football magic and caught the romantic fancy of a nation. He was poetry in motion. But Laughing Larry Kelley was more than that. He was a three-sport athlete, a scholar and a colorful personality. He was keeper of the faith, purveyor of enthusiasm and the ever-present silver lining. When football was invented, Larry Kelley was but an idealistic dream.*

# Chapter 2

# A lineman gets last laugh

Laughing Larry Kelley, as seen by himself:

"Things happened to me in my football career, things that didn't happen to others. I guess you could say it was magic because they occurred in unique fashion year after year."

Laughing Larry Kelley, as seen by teammate Clint Frank, another Yale gridiron great:

"As a player," Frank said, "Larry had super spring in his legs, and he was an opportunist. He never played his position because he liked to gamble. Sometimes he goofed, but most of the time he didn't. As a person, Larry has a real bright, keen intellect. And he has a happy sense of life—an Irish sense of life."

And finally, Laughing Larry Kelley, as seen by the pundits of the press, who blended his magical football ways and his leprechaun's view of life into prose and even verse. To wit:

*Oh, somewhere in this favored land the sun is shining bright,*
*New Haven bands are playing, New Haven hearts are light;*
*There victory rockets light the sky, there victory cannons crack,*
*There's even joy in Princeton: Larry Kelley won't be back.*

Especially Princeton. If Kelley used magic on Yale's opponents, he was nothing short of Houdini against Old Nassau.

"I enjoyed beating Princeton more than Harvard," Kelley said. "Princeton people, in my experience, were not gracious winners or gracious losers."

Back in 1934, Kelley's sophomore year at Yale, Princeton was favored by as many as 35 points to beat the Elis. After all, Princeton had dozens of players who were high school captains, and the year before the Tigers had beaten Columbia, which then won the Rose Bowl. They also had a 15-game winning streak in progress. Not only was Princeton's talent and momentum stacked against Yale, but the Elis' own record was an unflattering 3-3. At the tables down at Mory's, a popular New Haven tavern, there was gloom instead of foam in Louie's beer.

It was that Saturday afternoon that the football world first learned of Laughing Larry Kelley—the second Heisman Memorial Trophy winner and one of only two linemen ever to win the award.

Princeton dressed 66 players, while Yale's traveling squad numbered 28. Seventeen might as well have stayed back in New Haven because 11 Yalies played the entire 60 minutes; not one substitution was made. Those sturdy 11, known as Yale's "Iron Men," are enshrined in a picture that hangs in Mory's.

"We used a short punt formation," Kelley recalled of the game's one significant play, which began to unfold when Jerry Roscoe heaved the ball skyward. "I crossed over the middle of the Princeton defenders on a pass pattern, but the pass was 10 feet in the air."

Cameras clicked and the Palmer Stadium crowd gasped as the slender end with No. 19 on his light-blue jersey leaped high to pluck the pass out of the autumn air with one hand near Princeton's 30-yard line. After he came back down to earth, he juggled the ball briefly, then began to run . . . backward. "I don't know why," Kelley recalled.

Sometimes magicians are fooled by their own magic.

"I swung toward the sideline," he continued, "and Bob Train, our other end, came back and blocked the halfback. Their safety, Garry LeVan, had a reputation of never missing a tackle or giving up a touchdown. He came up to tackle me, I stopped, he went by, and I scored."

Kelley's 43-yard touchdown beat Princeton, 7-0, in one of the great upset victories in Yale's century-plus football heritage.

It was learned after the game that Kelley had waltzed into the huddle before his big catch and boldly announced: "Change the signal, quarterback, and give me the ball. A Kelley can do anything."

Well, didn't he say it? It was in the next day's newspapers.

Kelley was brash from the day he entered Yale. "Tell (Ted) Coy and (Pudge) Heffelfinger to move over," the freshman said of the former Eli heroes. "Kelley's going to join them soon."

That was in the papers, too. No one doubted Laughing Larry's self-confidence.

The Tigers waited a year for revenge against Kelley and Yale, and they got it in a big way, 38-7. Kelley scored the Bulldogs' only touchdown—the play officially covered 21 yards even though the pass from Roscoe actually sailed more than 50 yards through the air before reaching Kelley in the corner of the end zone—but that game sticks in his mind for another reason: The "Cousin Kelley Special."

Princeton, on Yale's 9-yard line, had a hunch that Kelley was expecting an end-around play. The Tigers sent left end John Paul Jones to the right and sure enough, Kelley, ever the gambler, left his position to meet Jones. But Princeton fullback Pepper Constable faked the handoff to Jones and tossed a lateral to halfback Jack White, who ran around Kelley's vacant side for a touchdown. The "Cousin Kelley Special" had worked.

One year later, it was Kelley who sought retribution. Princeton zipped out to a 16-0 lead, and it looked like another romp for the Tigers. But Yale surged back, and in the third quarter the Bulldogs were within two, 16-14.

Then, with Yale in control of the ball on its own 40, it was time for a double dose of deja vu. Frank set up to pass near his own 25 and unloaded a bomb. Waiting almost 50 yards downfield to scoop it in was none other than the man who had beaten Princeton on just such a play two years earlier, Laughing Larry Kelley of Yale.

Kelley leaped to make the catch. Returning to turf with ball in hand, he dodged one tackler, then saw just one man between himself and six points: Jack White, whose dash across the goal line the year before had spawned the "Cousin Kelley Special." White was a speedster, and Kelley knew that he would lose if he tried to outrace his opponent to the end zone. He needed Plan B.

Fortunately for the Elis, Kelley's mind was quicker than White's feet.

"Instead of running away from White," Kelley recalled, "I turned toward him and gave him a stiff arm, breaking his cheek and flipping him over. That was my revenge for the 'Kelley Special.' "

Kelley scored, giving the Elis a 20-16 lead, and Yale went on to win, 26-23. A 32-yard Frank-to-Kelley pass helped set up the Elis' winning touchdown.

After that game, Charles E. Parker of the New York World-Telegram called Kelley "one of the most romantic figures the sport has produced."

And J.L. Marks composed a poem that appeared in George Daley's "Sport Talk" column in the New York Herald-Tribune. Here is "Kelley at the Bat," boiled down in size:

> The semipros of Eli played the Tunis pros that day;
> The Rices and the Runyons thought they really shouldn't play,
> For Princeton had a smooth attack that rolled on like a tank
> While Yale had only two sound men, a Kelley and a Frank.
> The game moved on as charted by the experts of the land;
> The Tigers clawed for 16 points, the game was well in hand.
> They kicked poor Kelley around the park and rolled him in the dirt,
> They ran around and over him and almost stole his shirt.
> But still a smile lit Kelley's face, a sweet abiding grin.
> Then Ewart came back with a punt and forthwith did begin
> A most amazing spectacle within the Tigers' lair;
> A pass, a sweep, a buck or two and Kel came up for air.
> A spinner through the Princeton line put Hessberg in the clear
> And someone in the Yale brigade let out a hopeful cheer.
> Frank faded back to Newark and threw the ball a mile,
> An Irishman lit out for home and you could hear him smile.
> A blue streak pierced the autumn air, a Mercury en route,
> He stretched and took the ball in stride, then pushed White in the snoot.
> Gangway for grace and speed and skill! Let genius have its flair!
> A goddess kisses Kelley when the ball is in the air.

But the most memorable of Kelley's many outstanding plays occurred not against Princeton, but Navy. "That was the soccer kick," he said. "People have asked me about it for 40-some years.

"It was a ding-dong battle. I was having a great day covering punts, hurdling guys, making tackles. On one punt, the return man (Sneed Schmidt) saw me coming and he dropped the ball.

"I kicked it 20 yards to their 3, picked it up and went into the end zone. They disallowed the touchdown, but we got the ball on the 3 and Clint Frank scored. We won, 12-7.

"My kick was the only thing in the game the newspapers could write about. And so it started a big thing. People wanted to know: 'Did he kick it intentionally or not?' "

Kelley leaned back in an easy chair in his home in Pensacola, Fla. He took a sip of his third Bloody Mary of the morning and said no more.

Well, did he kick it accidentally, which, until the rule was rewritten after that season, was not cause for a penalty, or was the kick intentional?

"I don't know. I really don't," he said. "He didn't catch the ball, and I couldn't fall on it because I was moving so fast. I think it was a reaction, not something conscious."

The East Coast press would have none of that. Surely, Kelley was up to more wizardry, this Merlin among Ivy League mortals. An accident? No sir, you can't trick us with your Irish smile, Laughing Larry.

The press was familiar with Kelley's deception and bedevilment. Against Brown, he appeared out of nowhere to intercept a pass and return it 54 yards to set up a Yale touchdown. In the same game, Kelley scooped up a blocked punt and ran 33 yards for another score. The next day's headlines read: "Larry Kelley 14, Brown 6."

And that was nearly the truth. The Yale kicker was hurt that day, so Kelley found himself attempting to kick an extra point even though he had never kicked before in a game.

"Five bucks you don't make it!" a Brown player shouted at Kelley as he lined up after his second touchdown for his first and only placement attempt.

"I'll see you after the game to collect!" Kelley shouted back. He made the kick but couldn't find the Brown player afterward.

These quotes, Kelley said, are accurate. But "90 percent of the other things I was supposed to have said was fiction," he declared.

Then the alleged remark to a sportswriter before a Princeton game—"The Yale backfield ought to be good. I'll be playing in it all afternoon"—never actually was made by Kelley?

"I never said that," he replied. "I had a great deal of self-confidence. In fact, immeasurable. But I didn't come on strong, and I didn't go around bragging.

"There were a lot of things taken and interpreted by George Trevor of the New York Sun into good quotes. He was a Yalie and liked to write about us."

What was Laughing Larry Kelley really like?

"Not too serious. Not carefree or smug. In between," he said. "I didn't fit the tradition of Yale athletes. Back then, athletes weren't supposed to say anything. The strong, silent type, you know.

"I may have said some things on the field, but not like you've read. I really cared about winning. I'm like Vince Lombardi: 'Winning is everything.'"

His teammates remember him exactly that way.

"I don't think he ever said anything cutting or nasty," said Frank, who won the Heisman himself as a senior in 1937, a year after Kelley. "But if somebody from the other team made a wisecrack, Larry always had the 'blo-mo,' the right word at the right time, to put him in his place."

"He was no-nonsense when we were playing ball," said Bud Miles, who played fullback for Yale. "Larry was a natural. His athletic ability came easy. But he still worked hard. He was a winner."

Earl C. MacArthur, who coached Kelley in prep school, marveled about him years later: "He was a great lad. I used to watch him and wonder why it was that one Irishman should have so much—looks, wit, personality, physique, ability and brains. He was an amazing boy."

Everything came easily for Laughing Larry Kelley.

"I lived near Larry in college," Frank said. "He'd always have the radio blaring, and he'd be talking to people. He never cracked a book, it seemed, and he got good grades. He was Phi Beta Kappa or damn near."

Damn near. At Yale, a grade average of 80 qualified a student for the dean's list. Eighty-five signified Phi Beta Kappa. Kelley petitioned for Phi Beta Kappa but fell just short.

"When I came to Yale, I wanted to be All-America, captain of the football team and Phi Beta Kappa," Kelley said. "Well, two out of three aren't bad."

Considering his busy schedule, making the dean's list was an accomplishment in itself. Kelley played three sports at Yale—football, basketball and baseball—and he was good at all three. He was the second-leading scorer on the basketball team as a senior, and he hit around .300 most of his college baseball career. On top of all this, he attended 100 banquets, by his count, his senior year. And graduated with honors from Yale.

Kelley's IQ was 140. He carried an academic scholarship through Yale. His sharp, analytical mind could solve problems quickly, in the classroom or on the football field. He occasionally was able to "decode" opponents' offensive signals, enabling him to stop plays before they began.

"At one time, I had an unbelievable sense of direction and balance," he said, "and not just in football. You could put me in a house that I had never been in before, turn off the lights, and I could find my way around the house without bumping into things.

"I once met a girl at a party in Cleveland. She lived eight miles away. After the party, I took her home, although I didn't know the area. Then I drove back to Cleveland, without missing a turn and without a map. I was a smart kid."

Kelley was born in Conneaut, O., the son of an auto engineer. The family moved often, from Conneaut to Erie, Pa., to Chatham, Ontario, to Cleveland and finally to Williamsport, Pa., where Kelley attended high school and impressed others with his academic achievements, not his athletic ability.

"I was a voracious reader," he said. "I wouldn't say I averaged two books a day, but I came close."

Out of 420 students in his high school graduating class, Kelley finished fourth or fifth. He isn't quite sure. He is not vague, however, about his biggest athletic accomplishment. "I caught a pass once," he said. More often than not, he dropped them.

Kelley reached his full height of 6-foot-1½ at Williamsport High, but he weighed only 167 pounds. He started in football "only because a couple of kids quit the team," he said.

He showed more ability at that time as a high jumper and low hurdler. In fact, his high school football coach, Harold Rock, told him, "Well, son, if you expect to see any varsity football games, you'll have to pay your way in."

"Judging from what he saw in high school," Kelley reflected, "he was right."

Not one college recruited Kelley, so he attended prep school at Peddie in Hightstown, N.J. That school became a big part of his life. He added 20 pounds, made all-state in football and finished No. 1 in his class.

Still, not one college sought his football services.

Kelley's football coach at Peddie, MacArthur, was a Yale alumnus, and he pushed Kelley toward New Haven. Because no other school was interested and the Elis did offer a partial academic scholarship, Kelley headed for Connecticut.

He started off on the seventh team in freshman football but quickly moved into a starting position. When the season ended, he was a top varsity candidate and was regarded as one of the finest end prospects at the school in years.

He began his first varsity football season on the bench, but in the second half of the opening game against Columbia he caught a touchdown pass. It was Yale's only score in a 12-6 loss, and it earned Kelley the starting job at right end.

As a sophomore, Kelley established himself as one of the finest ends in the East. He went out for basketball and expected the same success. When the coach wouldn't start him, Kelley quit the team.

"I was a little cocky back then," he admitted later. "I wouldn't go through fraternity hazing because I felt it was childish. I later regretted doing those things."

He rejoined the basketball team as a junior and showed that he was just as magical on the hardwood as on the turf. Against Penn State his senior year, Yale was losing, 31-29, with 36 seconds to play when Kelley sank a long desperation shot to tie the score. Then with 6 seconds left on the clock, Kelley launched a shot that swished through the basket. Yale won, 33-31.

He also played baseball with a theatrical flair. In his final at-bat for Yale—his farewell appearance as an Eli athlete—he smashed a double against Harvard that hit one foot below the top of the fence in deepest center field. He narrowly missed saying goodbye to Yale with a home run.

Certainly he made things happen on his own. But once in a while, as he said, things just happened—like the time when two Harvard defenders went up to knock down a pass but instead tipped it into Kelley's hands for a touchdown.

It's little wonder that sportswriters tripped on their verbs and adjectives in trying to find new and interesting ways to describe Laughing Larry Kelley. Just as his jumps excited college football, Kelley made reporters' stories jump with excitement.

The whole Kelley experience was overwhelming for even Grantland Rice, the Shakespeare of sportswriters, who rhapsodized:

> If you figure they've overplayed fiction
> Where Merriwells rise in the fray,
> Without the least semblance of friction
> And make the star play of the day,
> If you figure such stuff is a breeder
> Of yarns that are foolish or stale—
> Just a moment, I beg of you, reader—
> Shake hands with L. Kelley of Yale.

Mary Ruth Kelley handed the yellowed clipping, kept loose inside a scrapbook, to her husband. She read aloud from another scrapbook entry: "Kelley did more to rekindle interest in Yale's jaded football program the last two years than any individual."

She looked affectionately at the large, white-haired man in the easy chair. "That's my guy," she said.

Once as lean and supple as a jaguar, Kelley now is as big and round as a lovable old bear—which he is. As L. Kelley of Yale, he weighed 195 pounds. As L. Kelley of Pensacola, retired educator, he is 240, plump and content.

"I think I made every All-America team in 1936, including the Boy Scouts' All-America team," he said, leafing through the scrapbook. "They wrote and asked if I was ever a Boy Scout. I wrote back and told them I was. So they picked me. But I only made Life, not Eagle."

Kelley held up a piece of paper, about six inches by eight inches. "Here's something you might be interested in," he said.

It was a Western Union telegram, dated December 1, 1936, 11:56 a.m., New York. It read: "Larry Kelley—Yale University—SPORTSWRITERS AND BROAD-CASTERS HAVE VOTED YOU THE OUTSTANDING FOOTBALL PLAYER IN UNITED STATES FOR NINETEEN THIRTY SIX AND WINNER HEISMAN ME-MORIAL TROPHY GIVEN BY DOWNTOWN ATHLETIC CLUB OF NEW YORK CONGRATULATIONS—W B PRINCE CHAIRMAN TROPHY COMMITTEE."

"I got the telegram telling me that I had won it, and I didn't even know there was such a thing," Kelley said. "It was just another of the honors I had come to expect that year.

"The Heisman wasn't particularly a big thing back then. Anything that young and that new has to get a few years under its belt to become important. I think it rated a small article in the Yale Daily News."

At the Heisman luncheon in New York, Yale Coach Ducky Pond told the audience: "He (Kelley) justly deserved this trophy. He was a great opportunist, a fine leader and a crowd player, one who could always rise to any emergency in a game."

Laughing Larry also had a chance to speak. He began by greeting the Down-town Athletic Club with the words "Fellow Rotarians," which broke up the audi-ence, and then he got serious.

"Football today is a great business," he said, "as great as many of the business-es in which you are engaged. And two things have built it up: the press and the radio."

Imagine if there had been television in that age. Kelley, with his spectacular catches and sparkling wit, might have become the first "media star."

Not long after the Heisman luncheon, Kelley climbed on a train and traveled to San Francisco to play in the East-West Shrine Game. There, 3,000 miles from New Haven, he performed his finest magic act.

In the third quarter of a scoreless game, Kelley caught a key 14-yard pass in the East's most important drive, which ended with a field goal by Princeton's Ken Sandbach. The Yale end also blocked a punt that day.

But the climax of Kelley's performance was yet to come.

"I was on defense when the West threw a pass over my head," he said, still visualizing the play. "It was a pass-lateral play, and when the end (Carl Mulleneaux of Utah State) lateraled the ball to the other end (Leo Deutsch of St. Benedict's), I cut in front of him and intercepted it."

Now you see it, now you don't.

"Then I cut back up the field," he said, *"laughing all the way."*

It was classic Larry Kelley, going out in style. He rambled 18 yards before being tackled at the West 7, and even though the East failed to capitalize on

Kelley's heads-up play, it didn't matter. The East won, 3-0.

After the game, writers had no trouble finding Kelley in the East locker room. A faint aroma of perfume led the sniffing reporters to Kelley, who was reading a scented, lavender-colored letter in female handwriting that had just arrived by special delivery. After reading it, Kelley tore it in small pieces and tossed them casually on the floor.

It was a fitting gesture, because there was a sense of romance about his play. Did it extend beyond the football field?

"We all tried to be (romantics)," Kelley said. "Not all of us succeeded. I don't remember the East-West incident. That one passed me by. Just as well hidden."

Said Bud Miles: "Larry knew where the girls were."

At a banquet after the game, Babe Hollingbery, a West coach, still was upset about the stolen-ball trick and dressed down the great end.

"He grabbed me by the collar and actually shook me," Kelley said. "He told me that I could never play for him because I was so far out of position. He was right, but I told him that's the way I played ball. Today you'd call it 'being yourself.'"

If Kelley couldn't play for Hollingbery at Washington State, he sure could have played for the Detroit Lions of the National Football League. The Lions offered Kelley the handsome sum of $11,000, but he turned them down.

"I didn't want to play pro ball," he said. "It didn't have a very good reputation back then."

The Associated Press reported, however, that Kelley signed a contract on October 20, 1937, to play for the Boston Shamrocks of the old American Football League. According to the story, Kelley had agreed to play in the Shamrocks' upcoming game against the Pittsburgh Americans and had an option for the club's four remaining home games.

"I told them (the Shamrocks) I already had a job, but they said they would fly me up for games and blah, blah, blah," Kelley recalled. "I went up one Sunday to watch a game, but I never played for them, and that's the extent of it."

Branch Rickey of the St. Louis Cardinals offered Kelley a $5,000 bonus to play baseball, guaranteeing him that he would start no lower than the Triple-A level of the minor leagues. And if Kelley didn't pan out as a player, Rickey promised, he could have an administrative job. One good mind recognized another.

Again, Kelley declined.

"I guess I was scared of the major league curveball," he said. "But if you remember, the Cardinals back then didn't use linen handkerchiefs with Pepper Martin and the Dean boys. Baseball was filled with hillbillies, and I wasn't sure I wanted to be a part of it."

Kelley even turned down Hollywood. He was offered $1,500 a week to make a movie of his life, "Kelley of Yale," with none other than Lawrence Morgan Kelley playing himself. With his dark, handsome appearance and charming urbane manner—sort of a cross between Henry Fonda and Cary Grant—Kelley might have done well on the silver screen, at least as well as other college football stars-turned-actors such as Sonny Tufts and Johnny Mack Brown.

But in making that decision, Kelley's supreme confidence in himself bowed to personal pride.

"I didn't think I could do a movie," he said. "Quitting the basketball team that one year, not getting involved with the fraternity . . . I had done enough things I was ashamed of. Otherwise, things I've done, I wanted to be proud of."

Such as his being tapped by the Skull and Bones Society of Yale, an honor that is tantamount to being named the outstanding man in the senior class. And graduating in that same class was Potter Stewart, the U.S. Supreme Court justice.

"If Potter's total life was exposed," Kelley said merrily, "he couldn't get elected dogcatcher. Potter was a hell-raiser in college, but there are professional secrets you don't bare.

"Jerry Ford's, too. Our future President was an assistant line coach at Yale while he attended our law school. He lived in a penthouse over the bank with the basketball coach, who was a rounder. They had a good time."

After graduation, Kelley, Stewart and four others sailed for Europe. "That was the thing to do back then," Kelley said. "We saw all the sights—France, Germany. We had a ball."

Ever the individualist, Kelley grew a beard. "Before it became fashionable," he pointed out.

Then it came time to choose a career. Certainly Laughing Larry Kelley, Yale '37, with his athletic and academic achievements, with that quick mind and clever tongue, would be an asset to any corporation. Not only would it be great public relations for any firm that took him in, but he had the ability to move rapidly up the corporate ladder.

"I had a lot of offers to go to Wall Street," he said. "I didn't have any ambition that way. I didn't care about money.

"I just wanted to teach, coach, work with kids, have a good time. A teaching job opened up at Peddie School, and I took it. I taught math and history and succeeded my old football coach, Earl C. MacArthur. I made $2,000 a year."

Kelley would have made five times that amount starting out on Wall Street, but status wasn't his game. His love was education.

"He loves being with kids," Clint Frank said. "I've run into so many kids over the years who were taught by Larry. There was a great Mr. Chips type of affection for him from his students. He commanded affection, love and esteem. That was his equivalent of being chairman of the board."

While teaching and coaching at Peddie, Kelley met Mary Ruth Becker, a nursing student who grew up in Hightstown.

"We were true loves," she said, "but we didn't marry. The flag was waving."

Mary Ruth joined the Navy during World War II. Kelley tried to join the Navy, too, but was denied entry because of broken eardrums, a football injury. He went to work in an aircraft factory, then was allowed to enter the Navy on his second attempt as a civilian service technician.

After the war he was talked into joining a fabric business with another Yale graduate. Kelley became a vice president and made a good salary until he saw "the handwriting on the wall—foreign competition—and I got out."

The corporate world wasn't for him anyway. He wanted to get back into education, so he took a position at Cheshire Academy in Connecticut as a teacher and senior master (a liaison between faculty and administration). Then Peddie beckoned again, and he took over in 1970 as director of alumni and public relations.

At Peddie, Kelley was reunited with Mary Ruth, who had retired from the Navy and whose first husband had died. Larry's first marriage, which produced no children, ended in divorce.

"We married 40 years later," Mary Ruth said, her face beaming. "Isn't that wonderful?"

After Kelley retired, he and Mary Ruth moved to Pensacola, a seaport on the Gulf of Mexico in northwest Florida. Mary Ruth had been stationed there in the Navy and had enjoyed the climate, which features temperatures in the 80s even in the winter. On just such an afternoon in 1984, Kelley shot a 76 on the golf course. Some of that Kelley magic remains.

From his tropical retreat, the Heisman winner cast daggers toward New Haven.

"I thought Yale went to hell under Kingman Brewster," he said of the Yale president from 1963-77. "He gave in to Black Panther demands. He chickened out. And the school let girls in (in 1969) because of pressure. I don't think every school has to be co-ed. Now they room together. That really bugs me.

"I'm a traditionalist. When I went to school, the architecture was mostly Gothic. They've since built some new buildings: Colonial and—yech!—modern. I believe in the good old days. Back in the '30s, our famous professors were in class. Now they sit in their ivory towers, doing research and writing.

"And why can't Yale live within its means? A teammate of mine, Meredith Scott, wrote a letter that was published in the Yale alumni magazine. The letter said: 'You have just come to us for $300 million to increase your endowment, and I can't afford to send my son to Yale.'

"In other words, what are you doing with your money?"

Kelley's face was red, and not from the Florida sun. He doesn't like what has happened to Yale, the football program included. The 1983 squad went 1-9, the worst season in Yale's history. University President A. Bartlett Giamatti and Athletic Director Frank Ryan de-emphasized football to the point of restricted recruiting. Coaches had to coach two sports, so when was there time to recruit? And for two weeks in the football season, there reportedly wasn't soap in the showers, although Ryan denied that allegation.

Kelley was furious, as were other Yale alumni, until they were assured by Giamatti and Ryan that de-emphasis was being de-emphasized. Those who contributed to the Elis' proud football tradition did not want to see it forsaken. The Elis' 6-3 record in 1984 indicated hope for the future.

While Kelley agreed with his former classmates about the state of the football program, he did not plan to join them anytime soon to discuss the matter.

"I don't do anything I don't enjoy," he said. "That's what keeps me from going to class reunions. Everyone comes back bragging about how well he's doing."

Kelley did not mean to suggest that his wealthy classmates were not enjoying life—"It depends what they measure it (happiness) on," he said—but for himself, material gains were unimportant.

"When we graduated," he said, picking his words carefully, "my college friends were just starting out in the world, trying to make their names. But I had already reached my peak. What could I do after college to top what I had already done?"

Kelley had a place in history at 22. Most Yalies, class of '37, would never catch up.

Although Kelley accepted the Heisman with curiosity, he now is involved in the Heisman process. He served on the Heisman Memorial Trophy Committee in 1983 and corresponds regularly with all the winners, keeping them informed of Heisman activities. Kelley attends Heisman reunions.

"The Heisman didn't mean a lot to me when I got it," he said. "It means a lot to me now because it puts me in the same class as O.J. Simpson, Jay Berwanger, Glenn Davis, Doc Blanchard, Marcus Allen, Herschel Walker and Leon Hart.

"We Heisman winners look at ourselves as immortal. I'm on the downhill, but I'm not looking downhill."

Hart is the only other lineman—he, too, was an end—to win the Heisman Trophy.

"Leon and I have become very close friends," Kelley said. "We are a fraternity within a fraternity. We talk a couple of times a year and huddle together during Heisman week."

Kelley is not irritated that the fraternity membership is two.

"I've reconciled myself to the fact that offensive linemen won't win it anymore," he said. "With quarterbacks and running backs, you've got things you can recognize—rushing yards per game, passing yardage, touchdowns scored. Where does the lineman come in? What are his stats? You can't measure or evaluate him. He doesn't stand out.

"But Leon and I . . . we lonesome ends stick together."

Kelley never was lonesome for a spot in football lore. Thanks to sportswriters, who attributed to him a wide variety of comical remarks—some of which were his, most of which were not—Laughing Larry Kelley of Yale became well known to sports fans.

They recall his alleged words to the Harvard quarterback after stopping a crucial end sweep in a 1934 game: "What kind of judgment do you call that, Haley, trying Kelley's end on fourth down?" And there was the jest he made when teammate Charley Ewart, being questioned by trainer Frank Wandle after taking a nasty hit, jokingly identified himself as Kelley: "Take him out, Frank! The little mug has delusions of grandeur!"

But was this the real Larry Kelley? Was the second winner of the Heisman Trophy football's Fred Allen, a comedian, or was he instead the game's Gaylord Ravenal, a gambler backed up by grace, guile, grit, guts and a grin?

One yellowing article in the scrapbook, this one by Joe Williams of the New York World-Telegram, sheds an unusually perceptive light on Larry Kelley. Three paragraphs in particular nearly leap off the page:

"Many legends have grown up around Mr. Kelley, and, like all legends, they lack reality. He has been called a pop-off, an eccentric and a spotlight guy. That kind of fellow never closes out his college career with the honors and genuine acclaim that have come to this young man.

"The cheap attributes with which Mr. Kelley has been invested in some circles may be traced to inaccurate judgment on the part of his critics. They mistook a lively, healthy, fun-loving nature for something else. To Mr. Kelley, football from

*Laughing Larry Kelley, a few years older and a lot wiser, currently is active in Heisman-related activities and has been known to dress appropriately.*

the beginning was a game—a game to be played up to the hilt but with an adventurous gaiety. This may have made him appear 'different' in the eyes of the crowd, but it was just his native way of doing things.

"I have known Laughing Larry ever since he's been at Yale. Or practically so. I'm probably to blame for some of the indictments that have been returned against him by the more conservative Yales. I started giving publicity to those cracks he was supposed to be uttering down on the playing field. Most of them came to me from the barroom humorists of the Yale Club. They were harmless enough, not without a certain flavor of broad humor and, for all I knew at the time, authentic."

If Williams and the other journalists with vivid imaginations had bothered to check with Kelley about the authenticity of the remarks attributed to him, he would have set them straight. But a legend was in the making—the legend of Laughing Larry Kelley—and it was no time to let facts destroy the myth.

# Nile Kinnick Jr.

*He was a talented football hero and a tribute to the Great American Dream. But too often, the good, they die young. And so it was with Nile C. Kinnick Jr., whose plane, forced to make an emergency landing during World War II, crashed in the Gulf of Paria between Trinidad and Venezuela. The body was never recovered, but the indomitable spirit of Nile Kinnick Jr. lived on, buoyed and nurtured by the hearts and souls that it touched.*

# Chapter 3

# Decades later, his name lives on

He was the most perfect of Heisman heroes.

If not for World War II, there is no telling what he would have become. Perhaps a prominent lawyer, governor of Iowa or a U.S. senator.

But that would be underestimating the man. He might have been a U.S. Supreme Court justice. Or even. . . .

President Nile Clarke Kinnick Jr.

"Some people have mentioned that. I don't take it seriously," Nile Clark Kinnick Sr. said. "But Nile's maternal grandfather was a two-term governor of Iowa. So the roots were there."

Those roots never sprouted to their fullest. On Wednesday, June 2, 1943, Ensign Nile C. Kinnick Jr. was forced to make an emergency landing in his Navy Grumman F-4 in the Gulf of Paria between Trinidad and Venezuela.

His body never was recovered.

Forty years later, on a snowy morning in Omaha, Nile C. Kinnick Sr. pushed himself out of a favorite chair. He put a log in the fireplace, then stepped back as the wood crackled and the flame spread. Feeling his body warmed, he returned to his chair and sat down.

At 90, he had long outlived two of his three sons—Ben, the budding engineer, and Nile Jr., the future government leader or man of the judicial cloth—brothers who were killed 15 months apart in the Great War.

"Yes, it still is a shock," the father said. "But it doesn't come up unless someone starts talking about it."

One war fought, two sons lost, an old man's endless grief.

But the old man does not point fingers, does not wonder why. He accepts the loss of lives, including those of his own flesh and blood, as the noblest of sacrifices for a good cause.

"I feel the same about the prospects of war now," he said, the reflection of the fire dancing in his eyeglasses. "We have to defend ourselves."

Nile Clarke Kinnick Jr. believed in the same principle. Those heartfelt convictions were recorded in a diary he kept during his brief naval career. In his first entry, logged December 3, 1941, the day before he was called to active duty and four days before the Japanese attack on Pearl Harbor, he wrote:

"Tomorrow I report at Kansas City for elimination training. . . . I am looking forward with enthusiasm to this new experience. I am fully aware that this country is on the brink of a shooting war in two oceans and that I might, in a very short while, find myself in the thick of very serious combat work.

"But what should be done can be done, and the best way is always through, not around. Every man whom I've admired in history has willingly and courageously served in his country's armed forces in time of danger. It is not only a duty but an honor to follow their example as best I know how.

"May God give me the courage and ability to so conduct myself in every situation that my country, my family and my friends will be proud of me."

By the fireplace in the Omaha home of Nile Kinnick Sr. sits a Navy kit bag with "Kinnick" stenciled on the side.

"That was the bag that came back with Nile's effects," the father said. "I cut the ends off the bag and used it as a wood carrier. Seemed to be the right thing to do."

He forced a smile. The Kinnicks are practical people, even in the aftermath of tragedy. Kinnick Sr. advised his three sons that practical solutions to complex problems were the wisest course. Even a Navy bag that contained his dead son's belongings could be put to use.

Kinnick Jr. was too practical at times.

"I always taught my boys that whatever job they would undertake, to do the best job possible," the father recalled. "When they shoveled snow off the sidewalk, I told them not to make a path, but to clear the whole walk.

"Nile took exception to that. There was a walk that went from the house to the barn on one of the family farms in Adel, Iowa. Near the barn was a privy. Nile told me that since we no longer kept horses in the barn, not as many people walk to the barn anymore, and wouldn't a smaller path to the privy be all right?"

It wasn't, to the father's way of thinking, but he admired his son's practical, clever head. "Nile always had a bright mind," he said.

Nile Kinnick Jr. didn't win the Heisman Memorial Trophy in 1939 with just a sturdy body, a strong arm and reasonably fast feet. Every coach who ever tutored Kinnick thought of him as a "coach on the field."

He was a single-wing halfback at the University of Iowa from 1937-39. At 5-foot-8 and 167 pounds, he was the second-smallest player to win the Heisman. Only the 1938 Heisman recipient, Texas Christian University's Davey O'Brien, a 5-7, 150-pound quarterback, was less imposing.

"Tough as an iron post," Dr. Eddie Anderson, Iowa's coach, would say of Kinnick. "Slap him in the stomach and he'll break your wrist."

Anderson later called Kinnick the finest player he ever coached. "He took an ordinary (Iowa) team and made it great," he said. "He would have been a sensational T-formation quarterback. He could run, kick and pass and was a superb defensive back. But the big reason he was the greatest—he could win so many games for you."

Kinnick's comeback heroics and stamina were the key factors in Iowa's 6-1-1 record in '39, when the Hawkeyes—those proud overachievers from the Corn Belt —were ranked ninth in the nation and missed the Big Ten Conference championship by percentage points.

But there was so much more to Nile C. Kinnick Jr. than just football prowess. He graduated with Phi Beta Kappa honors from Iowa after serving as president of his senior class. In his freshman year of law school at Iowa, he finished third in his class with a 3.8 grade-point average on a 4.0 scale.

If not for World War II, he probably would have been a Rhodes scholar. He wrote poetry, enjoyed the theater and read incessantly—everything from the great works to best sellers to books on government, taxation and the economy.

He was preparing himself for something greater—leadership—perhaps in the image of his hero, Winston Churchill.

"He is the man in history who has completely caught my fancy and imagination," Kinnick wrote in his diary. "I read his every speech and writing with absorbing interest. . . . He is a man of thought, of action, of resolution, and the man of the hour in the world's greatest crisis."

Kinnick was concerned about the plight of minorities, unlike most Caucasian males his age in the early 1940s. Traveling through the South for the first time, en route to a military assignment in Florida, he was stunned by what he saw.

"Have never seen so many Negroes in my life . . . small unpainted shacks in which they live . . . not infrequently a duplex affair with the Negro family on one side and the domesticated animals on the other . . . what a serious social problem it is—and probably getting worse. I have never seen such poverty in the country before—in the city, yes, but not out on the land. . . .

"The inequities in human relationships are many, but the lot of the Negro is one of the worst . . . kicked from pillar to post, condemned, cussed, ridiculed, accorded no respect, permitted no sense of human dignity. What can be done I don't know. . . . When this war is over the problem is apt to be more difficult than ever. May wisdom, justice, brotherly love guide our steps to the right solution."

Kinnick's compassion for others was genuine, his father said.

"Nile was the most sympathetic boy I ever knew," he said. "In Nile's first or second year of grammar school, a boy in his class couldn't answer the teacher's questions on a lesson. The teacher, who was stern, slapped the boy's hand with a ruler.

"Nile came home crying after school. He told us: 'He couldn't answer the questions because he didn't know them. Why did she have to hit him?' That was the angriest I can ever remember seeing Nile."

Besides compassion, Kinnick Jr. had other qualities that would have held him in good stead in Congress or a court of law.

He was handsome and self-assured.

He had a "neat sense of humor," said his cousin, Louise Clarke Hobbs.

"He had a cheerful disposition," Kinnick Sr. said. "But at the same time, he was serious-minded about serious subjects."

He was eloquent. "Nile never sat down to read anything unless he had a dictionary alongside," said Bob Hobbs, the husband of Louise Hobbs and a close friend of Kinnick's in Omaha, at the University of Iowa and in the Navy. "If he came across a word he didn't know, he would look it up immediately. He attained an articulate expression that was unusual."

Nile C. Kinnick Jr. was virtuous in his everyday life, and he undoubtedly would have conducted himself accordingly in politics after World War II. In his words:

"How can any political candidate be really free and independent in thought and policy when he is dependent on wealthy backers for campaign funds? . . . A great majority of our political and economic troubles arise from lack of candor in our leaders. They try to be too smooth and adroit. They put partisan advantage above conviction. Without self-respect, there can be no character."

Wiley B. Rutledge, a former U.S. Supreme Court justice who had taught at the University of Iowa, wrote this posthumous tribute to Kinnick:

"There is no calculating what he might have done in and for the profession or therefore what it and the nation have lost by his sacrifice. Who knows. . . . He might have been the great scholar and teacher, the pre-eminent advocate, the judicial statesman . . . for generations to come."

Instead, two generations later, an old man looks at a kit bag by the fireplace and remembers.

"Nile wasn't at all self-centered," his father said. "He was very generous. He had this ability I never had: He could buy gifts for his mother that were right every time."

Nile Jr. was reared in a close, loving family. His mother, Frances, had a fine soprano voice and once considered a professional singing career. From his mother, Nile Jr. gained an appreciation for the arts. From his father, he learned Midwestern common sense. Nile Jr. grew up in a home of learning, solid values and shared devotion.

A few days before his death, he wrote to his parents: "This task which lies ahead is adventure as well as duty, and I am anxious to get at it. I feel better in mind and body than I have for 10 years, and am quite certain that I can meet the foe confident and unafraid. . . . Truly we have shared to the full life, love and laughter. Comforted in the knowledge that your thought and prayer go with us every minute, and sure that your faith and courage will never falter no matter the outcome, I bid you au revoir."

Kinnick had no premonition that his life soon would be over; he was not a fatalist. He said "au revoir" because he was in love with language, with learning, with life! He was on a temporary mission, and after the war, he would begin another mission: Civilian service to his country.

"Without question," Kinnick Sr. said, "he would have been in some form of government."

One can only imagine what heights Kinnick would have reached; those who knew him from his boyhood days in Adel have no doubt, though, that he possessed the determination, talent and integrity to achieve whatever goal he put his mind to.

The Kinnicks lived in a large frame house in the center of Adel, a town of 1,500 people (at that time) located 25 miles west of Des Moines and seven miles from Van Meter, the boyhood home of Hall of Fame pitcher Bob Feller. Feller and Kinnick Jr. played on the same Junior Legion baseball team, with Kinnick behind the plate and Feller at third base.

Feller pitched "only when they needed relief," Kinnick Sr. recalled. "No, we weren't aware of his fastball at the time."

Baseball was just one of the many sports in which Kinnick Jr. excelled.

"The Kinnicks had a large yard constantly full of young boys playing football," Louise Hobbs said. "Nile was always in charge.

"He was a very good basketball player. I remember him shooting jump shots when it wasn't popular. He could hang in the air and shoot with two hands over his head.

"Nile wasn't very big, but he was unusually mature. He called all his coaches by their first names, even as a young boy.

"He had this great zeal for striving, but athletics were only one part of him. He had such high ideals. Did you know he was religious? He used his religion to pursue these ideals from a spiritual, unlimited point of view."

Besides their home in town, the Kinnicks bought five farms in the area.

"They bought them, but they would mortgage one farm to buy another," said Mrs. Hobbs, who lived a half-block away from the Kinnicks when young Nile was growing up. "The banks wound up owning them, like they did everything else. This was at the end of the 1920s, when people had no money. They worked for 30 cents an hour and paid one another off in raspberries.

"But Nile put himself through Iowa. He said, 'No one's going to put me through school.' And they didn't. He had such a fantastically strong character."

During the Depression, Nile Kinnick Sr., no longer able to make a living in Adel, moved his family to Omaha, where he eventually worked on the loan committee of the Omaha Federal Land Bank.

Kinnick Jr. emerged as an all-state football and basketball player for the Bunnies of Benson High School in Omaha. He then enrolled at Iowa and became a football sensation his first year on the varsity, as a sophomore, returning a punt 74 yards for a touchdown against Michigan, throwing a 69-yard TD pass against Minnesota, averaging 42.7 yards on 55 punts and being named to the All-Big Ten team. Though the Hawkeyes finished with an embarrassing 1-7 record, comparisons already were being made between Kinnick and an All-America halfback from Colorado, Byron (Whizzer) White, who wore No. 24, the same as Kinnick. And the comparisons were not based only on gridiron achievements—White later became a Supreme Court justice. Many observers saw similar potential in Kinnick.

"The closest likeness to Nile is Byron White," Bob Hobbs agreed. "But if you study their backgrounds and qualifications, Nile certainly had as much going for him as White, and probably more."

As an Iowa sophomore, Kinnick also was second on the basketball team in scoring. He then dropped out of basketball and baseball to improve his grades, even though he didn't receive a C in college until he was a junior.

His junior football season was hampered by an ankle injury, and he made only honorable mention all-conference. However, he survived the year with his humor intact.

"I'm no longer a triple threat," he wrote home after one particularly discouraging game that fall. "They'll say I'm a quadruple threat—run, pass, kick and fumble."

The Hawkeyes finished with a 1-6-1 record, and Coach Irl Tubbs was fired. Succeeding him was Anderson, who directed the Hawkeyes to a complete turnaround his first year in Iowa City.

That '39 season belonged to Iowa's "Iron Men"—Kinnick, Erwin Prasse, Mike Enich, Dick Evans, Ken Pettit, Al Couppee, Max Hawkins, Wally Bergstrom, Charlie Tollefson, Bill Gallagher and Bruno Andruska—all of whom played a full 60 minutes at least one game during the season. The Hawkeyes were short on bodies, but never heart.

Iowa opened that year by demolishing South Dakota, 41-0. Kinnick passed for two touchdowns, ran for three more, including a 65-yard romp, and drop-kicked five conversion points.

In the next game the Hawkeyes faced Indiana, a team Iowa had not beaten in seven matchups since 1921. Kinnick, who scored in the second quarter on a short burst after scampering 55 yards to the Hoosier 3-yard line, directed the Hawkeyes brilliantly as the lead went back and forth. Then late in the fourth quarter, with Indiana ahead, 29-26, Kinnick hit Prasse with a touchdown pass for the third time that day to put the Hawkeyes on top, 32-29.

Michigan and Tom Harmon, the 1940 Heisman winner, were too strong for Iowa one week later as the Wolverines prevailed, 27-7. Kinnick's 71-yard pass to Buzz Dean accounted for the Hawkeyes' only touchdown.

"Kinnick was as tough a competitor as any man I played against," Harmon said years later. "I don't care how bad you had Kinnick down, he came back at you."

Iowa rebounded with a 19-13 upset of Wisconsin. Kinnick again was the star, returning a punt 59 yards (not for a touchdown) and tossing three TD passes, including a 39-yarder to Evans and then a 28-yarder to Bill Green in the fourth quarter that brought the Hawkeyes from behind for the victory.

Afterward, Wisconsin Coach Harry Stuhldreher, one of football's famed Four Horsemen of Notre Dame, said of Kinnick: "You find a player like him once in a generation. Usually when you find a great football player, he is great because he has one exceptional talent. Kinnick is exceptional at everything. In addition, he is a great morale man. He is another coach on the field."

Now even *opposing* coaches were saying it.

Iowa kept rolling with a strange victory over Purdue, 4-0. The Hawkeyes scored two safeties in the fourth quarter, the first by tackling punter Jack Brown in the end zone and the second by blocking a Brown punt and downing the Purdue player who fell on the ball in the end zone.

Next up was Notre Dame. The Fighting Irish hit hard that day, but the fighting Iron Men hit back equally hard. It appeared as if neither team would score without a break, which finally came the Hawkeyes' way late in the first half when they recovered a Notre Dame fumble on the visitors' 4-yard line. The Irish player who fumbled the ball had just intercepted a Kinnick pass in his own end zone and was preparing to lateral to a teammate on his runback when Andruska popped him, forcing the turnover.

Kinnick then improvised by switching halfback positions with Dean. Kinnick took the direct snap from center and headed over right tackle for the goal line.

One Notre Dame tackler stood in his way—briefly. Kinnick's running trademark was to drop his forearm and shoulder just before the point of impact, then drive both up and into the defender. He knocked the Irish tackler into the end zone and followed him in for the touchdown. Kinnick's drop kick made it 7-0.

Notre Dame scored later but failed on the extra point. The Hawkeyes, eight of whom played the entire game, then kept the Irish buried deep in their own territory in the final minutes to lock up a 7-6 victory. It was Kinnick's fifth straight game without a minute's rest.

Iowa's seventh opponent was mighty Minnesota, which had defeated the Hawkeyes' only conqueror, Michigan. The Gopher line outweighed Iowa's by 15 pounds per man, and Minnesota controlled the game for three quarters, 9-0.

The Iron Men forged another comeback. Kinnick threw a pair of passes to Dean, then hit Prasse all alone at the 9-yard line, and Prasse ran to the end zone to complete a 45-yard touchdown play.

Iowa later got the ball back at its 21 and moved the ball downfield, aided in part by a pass-interference penalty. At the Gopher 28, Kinnick went to the air and connected with Green in the end zone for a 13-9 Iowa lead.

That was all the edge the Hawkeyes needed as Kinnick intercepted a Minnesota pass with less than 30 seconds to play. The victory was secure, and the joyful emotions of the Hawkeye faithful poured forth. Des Moines sportswriter Bert McGrane was so deeply moved that he sat for 30 minutes, wiping the tears off his face, before he could write a word.

James S. Kearns of the Chicago Daily News composed this moving description of Iowa's victory celebration:

"There's a golden helmet rising on a human sea across Iowa's football field in the twilight here. Now the helmet rises as wave upon wave of humanity pours onto the field. There's a boy under the helmet, which is shining like a crown upon his head. A golden No. 24 gleams on his slumping, tired shoulders.

"The boy is Nile Clarke Kinnick Jr., who has, just now, risen above all the defenses that could be raised against him. . . . Here was Kinnick at the peak of his great career, leading a frenzied little band of Iowa football players to a victory which was impossible. They couldn't win, but they did."

The victory, in Kinnick's final game at Iowa City, took its toll. Andruska broke his wrist, while Pettit sprained his. Gallagher and Couppee suffered shoulder injuries. Iowa no longer was made of iron, but of gauze, tape and plaster of paris.

Against Northwestern in the season finale, Kinnick tore a shoulder muscle and was forced off the field after having played 402 consecutive minutes out of a possible 420 in the last seven games of that season. Iowa settled for a 7-7 tie, but it had been a great season nonetheless.

It was a great season individually for Kinnick, who set several Hawkeye records that encompassed his offensive, defensive and punting skills. Some of those marks still stand, including most punting yards in a game (731), most punt-return yards in a game (201), most interceptions in a season (eight) and most interceptions in a career (18). He received the Silver Football award from the Chicago Tribune as the Big Ten's Most Valuable Player, and he won the Maxwell Award and the Walter Camp Trophy.

Not long after Kinnick's last game as a Hawkeye, a headline appeared: "Iowa's Kinnick Candidate for Heisman Trophy."

A week later, another headline appeared: "Iowa's Kinnick Wins Heisman Trophy."

Kinnick received 651 points in the Heisman voting, followed by Harmon with 405 and Missouri's Paul Christman with 391.

Kinnick's Heisman acceptance speech was broadcast nationwide. In his memorable closing remarks, he said: "I thank God that I was born to the gridirons of the Middle West and not to the battlefields of Europe. I can say confidently and positively that the football players of this country would much rather fight for the Heisman award than for the Croix de Guerre."

Kinnick was selected to every major All-America team in 1939, and he was named the Associated Press Male Athlete of the Year for 1939, with baseball hero Joe DiMaggio finishing second and boxer Joe Louis third. Select company.

After hearing Kinnick speak at the Touchdown Club dinner in Washington, D.C., Sen. Carter Glass of Virginia said to a friend: "That is an exceptional young man. He will go far."

The Marion (Ia.) Sentinel agreed. In December 1939, the newspaper threw its vote to Kinnick for President—in 1956, the year he would be old enough to run for the office.

The Des Moines Register and Tribune, at about the same time, ran a cartoon showing a young man who bore a likeness to Kinnick sitting on a throne with a hot dog in his hand and a crown on his head. The caption read: "Today's King—Tomorrow's President."

Kinnick played in his last football game as a member of the College All-Stars, who lost to the Green Bay Packers, 45-28, on August 29, 1940. He threw a 56-yard touchdown pass and drop-kicked three extra points.

The now-defunct Brooklyn Dodgers of the National Football League chose Kinnick in the second round of the 1939 draft—he almost certainly would have been selected sooner had he expressed an interest in playing professional football —but he passed up their offer, purposely closing out the sports-hero chapter of his life. It was time to get on with other matters. He enrolled in law school.

Dean Mason Ladd of the University of Iowa Law School, in congratulating Kinnick on his rejection of the NFL, told him, "From my observations and from comments of others, you have the capacity to become a high-class lawyer."

By that time, Kinnick had advanced from campus politics to national politics. He introduced Wendell Willkie, the Republican Party's presidential candidate in 1940, at a program in Iowa Falls, Ia. During Willkie's speech, there were as many "We Want Kinnick" calls as "We Want Willkie."

Kinnick would have been good at kissing babies had he run for office in Iowa; many of the male babies were named Nile. It became a popular name in Iowa after Kinnick won the Heisman and even more so after the war.

Following the Willkie introductory speech and an address to a Young Republican state convention, an Iowa country doctor fired off an angry letter to Kinnick, telling him that he was foolishly risking his popularity with such political venturing.

Kinnick answered the doctor's letter, thanking him for his concern but pointing out that "I am not introducing Mr. Willkie because I expect him to do me any good, but because . . . I expect him to do this country some good. I am addressing the Young Republican state convention not because I think that so doing will boost my prestige, but because I am interested in government and have some ambition in that direction.

"Politics are not very clean, but they should be; politics need integrity and idealism; politics more often than not disillusion those who enter with those ideas. Of that I am fully aware. But that does not alter the situation. . . . I shall proceed as best I can—and whether I lose 50 percent popular favor shall not deter me. . . . I am doing what I think is the thing to do."

The doctor was so taken with Kinnick's letter that he wrote back pledging his vote should Kinnick ever decide to run for public office.

On October 17, 1940, Kinnick registered on campus for the draft. Public office and his law degree would have to wait, as would marriage and a family, both of which he longed for.

Kinnick liked the ladies, and they liked him. He was a smart dresser, an excellent conversationalist and a sensational dancer.

"I must admit," he wrote in his diary, "that there is nothing I enjoy more than the companionship of a beautiful woman who possesses breeding, grace, charm and wit. There have been a few such women in my life but not enough. There may have been a time when I was in love with love—but no more. However, I shall not consider my mortal existence complete until I have loved and won a woman who commands my admiration and respect in every way. It looks as if it will be some time before that comes about. . . ."

A war still had to be fought first. But after that, when the right woman came along, he surely would have written poems to her, for he had the heart of Shelley, if not quite the pen.

Kinnick mailed one of his poems to his youngest brother, George, on December 20, 1942, five days before the last Christmas of his life. It read:

Oh, how I long for Christmas back in Iowa,
Where the landscape is white with snow,
Where the ponds and rivers freeze,
And the north wind is sure to blow.

I want to slam down on my sled,
Cut a figure eight with my skates;
Do all the things I used to do,
Before we began to play for higher stakes.

Race out of the cold in by the fire,
Soon warm before the flickering blaze,
With popcorn to eat and stories to tell,
Who doesn't yearn for those wonderful days?

Christmas without snow and cold is not the same.
It's like a picture without a frame.

If the Downtown Athletic Club ever tapped a Renaissance man, it was Nile C. Kinnick Jr.

"He was way ahead of his contemporaries," Bob Hobbs said, "a most unusual personality. One of the great sorrows is that he didn't go on to live a full life."

At about 10 a.m. June 2, 1943, Kinnick was on a training flight over the Caribbean. Bill Reiter, Nile's best friend in Squadron 16, was flying behind Kinnick when he noticed "quite a bad oil leak in his plane," he later said in a letter to the Kinnicks. "I called him over his radio, gave him the lead and followed him back to the ship. By this time the situation was quite bad, and Nile realized that he would have to make a water landing about four miles ahead of the ship (the Lexington, which was making one of its initial voyages).

"He was calm and efficient throughout and made a perfect wheels-up landing in the water. . . . When I reached the spot, Nile was clear of the plane, but I didn't get any signals from him when I passed over. After circling a few times and marking the spot, I returned to the approaching crash boat and led them to the spot, but by this time there was no evidence left of either the plane or Nile. We searched the area for three hours, planes and ships, but to no avail. . . ."

Reiter, who was killed three months later at Wake Island, was the only eyewitness who said he saw Kinnick in the water. It was speculated that Kinnick, an excellent swimmer, was knocked unconscious when his safety belt failed, was thrown free of the plane and drowned.

"I remember the incident," said Nile C. Kinnick Sr., sitting in his Omaha living room. "We had just moved into a new house on June 1 that Nile never saw. His accident was on the 2nd, and we heard about it on the 3rd.

"I had just enrolled in an evening class at the University of Omaha. . . . I left the office and had just pulled into the parking lot at the university, when there was George waiting for me. He told me the message about Nile had just come in. That was about 5 o'clock.

"I went home to be with Frances. We took it with as much grace as we possibly could. We talked and decided to go on with life as best as possible.

"The next day, there was a conference at the federal land bank. I talked it over with Frances, and we decided that the letter about Nile wouldn't be known publicly yet. So I went to the office to help with the conference. I didn't say a word about Nile, but the word got out anyway. Someone at the conference called me into the middle of the hall to tell me the bad news. I told him I already knew."

What sustained the Kinnicks through the ordeal—strong Midwestern roots?

"That must have been it," the father said. "It didn't break us up to the point where we weren't functioning."

However, Frances Kinnick destroyed all of her son's letters to her not long after his death. "They were such personal letters," the father said, "and she didn't want them to be made public.

"I kept some letters that Nile had written me. And in Frances' desk, after she died (in 1966), I did find some letters written to her by a girl at the University of Iowa who had known Nile. She (Elizabeth Charlton) included a quotation that she received from a law student at Iowa (John Evans). It was about Nile, and what he (Evans) said would closely fit my own reaction."

Evans wrote: "The ways of the Lord truly must be many, and some of them seem hard to understand. Perhaps he refuses to allow his special clay to engage in our bloody little game. And you must admit that something would seem out of proportion if Nile Kinnick were to be decorated and famed for killing, burning and maiming. Perhaps he was jerked in the first quarter because war just wasn't his field. He was intended to be a builder, not a destroyer. He didn't fit. But I still believe that he must have been well on the way to being 'the best damn flier in the Navy'—as we always said he would."

Evans, a Marine, later was a war casualty himself, at Saipan.

And on September 17, 1944, Ben Kinnick, a Marine pilot, was killed over Kavieng, New Ireland, in the Pacific.

Kinnick Sr. said the shock was not as strong in the Kinnick home when the tragic news arrived of another son having died at war. "Ben was married," he said, "so his wife was notified first. And his personal effects were sent to her."

Does he think often of his dead sons?

"Yes," he said, stirring the fire with a poker. "Please, follow me."

He walked down a flight of stairs to his basement. There was a surprising bounce in his step, considering that he was 90 years old. Nile Kinnick Sr. had been an athlete himself, winning two letters each in football and baseball at Iowa State College (now a university). He refuses to let old age deter him from working in the yard or transporting himself around town.

Age also did not prevent him from remarrying after Frances Kinnick died. In 1967, he married Elizabeth Van Meter Lampe, whose husband had died a few years earlier. Elizabeth, a niece on Frances' side of the family, had been a flower girl at Nile and Frances Kinnick's wedding.

Elizabeth Kinnick sat upstairs, crocheting, while Kinnick Sr. rummaged in the basement, finding old family photographs. He held out a coin bearing the profile of Kinnick Jr.—the official coin that is flipped before every Big Ten football game.

There are other visible reminders of Nile C. Kinnick Jr. The football stadium at Iowa was renamed Kinnick Stadium in 1972. Other stadiums were named after him, in Tokyo and at Northwest High School in Omaha. A senior high school in Yokosuka, Japan, was given his name. And a park in Adel bears the name Kinnick-Feller Park.

The father walked up the basement stairs, turned off the light and returned to his living-room chair. He noticed that the fire had gone out. He stared into the fireplace. Twenty seconds of silence passed before he spoke.

"Nile came back to Omaha on a two-week leave in early November," he said. "That was 1942. We went to Adel to see family, then I drove him to Des Moines to put him on the Rock Island train to Iowa City, where he was going to see friends.

"That was the last time I saw him. I was the last member of the family to see him."

Ashes to ashes, dust to dust, an unceremonial burial at sea.

One of Nile C. Kinnick Jr.'s favorite books was A.E. Housman's "A Shropshire Lad," which included the poem "To an Athlete Dying Young." One can only imagine what Kinnick Jr. thought when he read:

> *The time you won your town race.*
> *We chaired you through the marketplace;*
> *Man and boy stood cheering by,*
> *And home we brought you shoulder-high. . . .*
>
> *Smart lad, to slip betimes away*
> *From fields where glory does not stay*
> *And early though the laurel grows*
> *It withers quicker than the rose. . . .*
>
> *Now you will not swell the rout*
> *Of lads that wore their honors out,*
> *Runners whom renown outran*
> *And the name died before the man. . . .*

The legacy of Nile C. Kinnick Jr. is that the man died before the name.

*Nile Kinnick Jr., as photographed in 1942 as an ensign at the U.S. Naval Reserve Air Base in Miami, Fla.*

# Tom Harmon

*From the football fields of the United States to the jungles of South America to the rice fields of China, the legend of Old 98 refused to die. The grim determination and unyielding spirit of Tom Harmon would not allow it. And so it was with color, flair and style that the former Michigan great ran life's gamut, from Heisman winner to war hero to actor to respected sports announcer-personality. The man and his legacy live on.*

# Chapter 4

# Old 98: The man from Michigan

As a football player for the University of Michigan almost a half-century ago, Tom Harmon most often was compared to the legendary Red Grange of Illinois. But when it came to death-defying, real-life adventure, Harmon was the Indiana Jones of Heisman winners.

Harmon hip-faked death twice in seven months during World War II. On the first occasion, he was flying over South America when he was forced to bail out of his plane and his parachute didn't open. Given up for dead, Harmon came sprinting out of the Brazilian jungle six days later. The second incident took place over China when a Japanese Zero shot Harmon's fighter out of the sky. He was lost for 32 days, and his obituary already had been set in type when he turned up again.

The United States' wartime enemies were beginning to discover something that Michigan's gridiron opponents knew all too well: Stopping Old 98 was next to impossible.

Harmon's first scrape with death occurred in April 1943. He was flying a B-25 bomber with the familiar "98," his Wolverines jersey number, and the words "Little Butch," his nickname for his girlfriend, painted on the plane. Two other bombers were accompanying Harmon's plane, which was carrying six crewmen in all, on a route that took them over South America.

"I was at about 20,000 feet when we headed into one of the worst storms I've ever seen," Harmon recalled. "We were bouncing up and down like an elevator. Then we got into some hail that took the paint right off the wings.

"I told the other planes to take a 45-degree turn, but we couldn't snap out of it. We were going down. Somewhere around 5,000 feet I gave the order to bail out. I pushed my co-pilot out of the plane. I got out at 500 feet, but my parachute didn't open.

"I can't tell you what kind of tree it was, but it caught my parachute 90 feet above the ground. If it hadn't, there's no question I would have been killed. I swung over to the trunk of the tree and slid down. The plane hadn't crashed that far from me, but the wreckage was hot and heavy, so I couldn't get near it. I went looking for my buddies but couldn't find them.

"That's when I found the right arm of the engineer, severed just below the elbow. I knew it was the engineer's because he had the Army Air Corps insignia tattooed on his forearm.

"I felt I needed to get help and come back, although I had no idea where I was. I found a compass and a bolo knife I had in my kit, plus a couple of chocolate bars, and headed east (toward the Atlantic coast).

"I was in the middle of a jungle. It was a tangle of vines, stumps and grass, all intertwined. Brush against one of those stumps and it was like someone pulling a razor down your leg. It was hard to walk because the vines and grass would wrap around my legs, pulling me back. And it rained continually the whole time I was there, which meant I was walking in muck and mire, and I'd have to push my way step by step.

"I got to a swamp and pulled out the chocolate, but it was full of maggots, and I had to throw it away. That was all the food I had, and I wouldn't eat the entire time in the jungle, but that didn't bother me. I didn't feel the hunger.

"I had to be careful of drinking water. The swamps were full of disease. My mouth was like cotton most of the time. Three times I found moving streams, followed them to their sources and drank and drank.

"I saw planes flying overhead. I'd scream at them—I must have screamed a thousand Hail Mary's—but they couldn't hear me. I kept going till 5:30 each afternoon, when I'd try to make it to the top of a hill before dark. I'd cut long branches and leaves to make a bed, then cut other branches for a lean-to, to try and keep off the rain. I only slept in snatches before I would wake up shaking from the cold. At 5 each morning I hit the trail again, but my legs were so sore that for the first half-hour, I could hardly move.

"I was wading through a swamp one day when I saw either an alligator or crocodile. I can't tell them apart, but it was about 5 feet long, and it wasn't that far from me. I saw something like a log and pushed it in his direction to chase him away. He flipped his tail and sent the log right back at me. I was scared, but he turned and went off another way. Was I glad!

"The jungle was full of insects. Maggots, mosquitoes, bloodsuckers. I kept pulling bloodsuckers off my body. After the third day, my strength was running down, but I just wanted to get out of there.

"I kept moving east when I stepped into this 'hole' 50 to 60 yards wide. It was about 10 feet deep and covered with weeds and mud. I couldn't swim across it, tread or dog paddle. But I had to cross it, and the only way I could was to go down and push off the bottom. I still had my leather jacket on, but it was confining in all that muck, so I took it off. I left it there, on the bottom of that hole. I went down and pushed off at least 50 times. It took me an hour and a half to get across. My body looked like a prune. I only got halfway out of the water on the other side when I collapsed from exhaustion and fell asleep.

"After I woke up, I started off again. By now I didn't have much patience. I wanted to fight back against the vines. When I thought I had them cut, they'd snap back at me. I'd get mad, but I had to hold my temper. If I had ever lost my head, I'd have never made it out.

"On the sixth day, I came to another swamp. It must have been 10 miles across. It looked that far to me, anyway. I lost heart. I knew I couldn't get across it. I didn't have the strength. So, I decided to take a northeast heading around the swamp.

"That's when I found a green broken bottle. That was the first sign of civilization, and I got excited. When I saw a tree that had definitely been cut by a machete, I really got excited.

"Then I saw a path and it was joyful hysteria. I began running as fast as I possibly could down the path until I came into a clearing. I saw this big (Indian) chieftain with muscles all over him. He looked at me, gave me a Pepsodent smile and said, 'Ah-lo.' "

A day later, the natives delivered him to a U.S. base in Surinam, where officials dispatched the happy news to the Army and his worried parents that he was safe and, considering the circumstances, well. Harmon was the only survivor of the crash. Two other men were reported dead, the other three never found.

"The only things that saved me," Harmon said, "were a deep religious conviction and a pair of strong legs. If it wasn't for the superb conditioning I received at Michigan, I couldn't have made it."

Harmon returned to Florida to regain his health and await reassignment. He was sent to North Africa in late May as a Lightning fighter pilot. Then he left for China to join the 449th Fighter Squadron. On August 26, 1943, he shot down his first Japanese plane in a raid on Hong Kong.

Then on October 30, the day before he was promoted to first lieutenant, Harmon left with seven other P-38s to escort a group of bombers on an attack of a Japanese tin smelter on the Yangtze River.

"The Japanese were waiting for us with everything but the kitchen sink," he said. "The lead plane shouted, 'Six Zeros at 3 o'clock!' We were trapped. It was a dogfight, and the only way out was to fight our way out.

"We got six of theirs (Harmon shot down two Zeros himself), and they got three of ours. I was chasing a Zero between 10,000 and 13,000 feet when I was shot down. A large shell hit the gas primer between my legs and blew my pant legs off. A fire started in the cockpit, and I tried to smother it with my hands. By that time I was in a power dive, heading straight down. I got out somewhere around 5,000 feet, I guess. It's hard to tell at a time like that. My parachute opened and the Zeros were shooting at me. I played dead in the chute, hoping that they would stop shooting. They did, but they kept circling me.

"I'm probably the only pilot who ever bailed out of a plane twice and never touched ground. The first time, it was in a tree. The second time, I landed in a lake. The chute came down over the top of me. The Zeros left, and some Chinese guerrillas rowed out in their sampans and pulled me in.

"Right there on the sampan they gave me a Chinese coolie outfit and told me to put it on. When we got to shore, they smuggled me into a farmhouse. I was badly burned on my face, hands and legs. The Chinese put cold tea on the burns. Doctors told me later that they couldn't have treated the burns any better in a hospital. The only burn marks left on my body from that dogfight are on my legs, and you can barely see them.

"While I was being hidden in the farmhouse, an old Chinese whose name was Wong came by me. He must have been 70, but he spoke English. I grabbed him by the seat of his pants and told him, 'Stay with me.' Soon a Japanese squadron was sighted coming down the road. The Chinese got me out of the farmhouse and hid me inside a hedgerow.

"The Japanese soldiers searched the house, found nothing, then went away. The Chinese came back seven hours later to get me. I couldn't walk because the burns had left me in a state of shock and taken the strength out of my legs, so the Chinese had to carry me on a stretcher made of bamboo and rattan. They were prepared to carry me all the way back to my base, which had to be 350 miles away.

"I had 30 to 40 guerrillas with me, including machine gunners, riflemen and a guerrilla captain. I called them 'Harmon's Army.' On the first day they found they couldn't carry me because I was so much bigger than the rest of them. I was 6-foot-2, 200 pounds, while the average guerrilla was 5-4 to 5-5 and 135 pounds. They had to send out for bigger Chinese.

"Our pattern was to travel by night, hide out by day. Later, I was able to walk. The guerrillas knew exactly where they were going, and they had a pretty good line where the Japanese were. We'd hide out in valleys where the guerrillas knew almost everyone, plus every road in and out of the valley. One day I heard a horn blow. I asked Wong what that meant. He said a woman was coming home from church. Security was that tight.

"Finally, we got to the day when we crossed the Japanese lines. I was really frightened. We came out of the mountains and made it through the lines without any trouble. The guerrillas were used to this.

"We made it to the base. I said to Wong out of gratitude, 'What do you want?' He said, 'Mr. Tom, all I want is some cigarettes.' I went to the PX and got him the biggest box of cigarettes I could find. It had 40 cartons inside. Then I found him a wheelbarrow.

"The last time I saw Wong, he was going back home, pushing his wheelbarrow with the cigarettes inside."

Word was sent back to the United States that Harmon had escaped death again. For his parents, Louis and Rose Harmon, his girlfriend, actress Elyse Knox, and other family members and friends, the news was almost too good to be true, but in characteristic Harmon style, the All-America back had beaten the odds again. He was awarded the Silver Star for bravery in action.

"I don't look upon myself as a war hero," Harmon said in the office of his plush Los Angeles home. "I look at myself as a lucky Irishman who got in, got shot at and got out. Just an ornery Irishman who had a driving will to live and who was going to get back alive, no matter what.

"That comes from sports. That's ingrained. Any athlete worth his salt has that."

Fighting spirit. Thomas Dudley Harmon—otherwise referred to as Harmon of Michigan, Old 98, Tommy or just Tom—always had a fighting spirit.

H.O. (Fritz) Crisler, Harmon's coach at Michigan, called him "the greatest competitor I have ever known."

Crisler spoke those words at a special Mass for Harmon at the St. Mary's Student Chapel on the Michigan campus before word had arrived that Old 98 had hacked his way out of the Brazilian jungle.

"I know Tom too well," Crisler added. "I know what he has always done when the pressure was on him. I've seen his cocksureness and tremendous physical strength, and I just won't believe he's through."

Harmon had a fighting heart to match his spirit. One doesn't break Grange's records, become a two-time consensus All-America and win the Heisman Memorial Trophy with a faint heart.

Harmon never backed away from a challenge from the first day he showed up at high school football practice with a wad of bubble gum in his mouth. He had been quite a bubble-gum blower in his hometown of Gary, Ind. He won a city championship, which earned him a new pair of roller skates. Harmon was so used to having bubble gum in his mouth that he often neglected to take it out.

Doug Kerr, the coach at Horace Mann High School, was instructing his football prospects that first day at practice when he noticed a pink bubble expanding in the back. The coach moved in the direction of the bubble, then told its blower, the freshman Harmon, to turn in his uniform.

"I'm not turning in my uniform," said Harmon, unflinching in the face of authority. "I came out here to play football."

"Oh you did, did you?" the coach said. "We'll see about that."

The coach stuck the cocksure freshman in on kickoff returns against the varsity, then told the older boys to teach him a lesson. Harmon ran through them for a touchdown. The coach said to kick it to Harmon again, and he ran through the would-be tacklers for another touchdown.

"That's how I played varsity ball as a freshman," he explained.

Harmon was so excited before his first game that he arrived at the school long before his teammates. The student manager told him to pick out a uniform from among those lined neatly on the floor. Harmon grabbed the cleanest, newest jersey, pulled it on and ran out on the field to warm up by himself. When he returned, the manager told him to take off the jersey because it belonged to the team's star halfback.

"I went to pick out another jersey," Harmon recalled, "but there was only one left. It was old, tattered, with holes in it."

The jersey's number, which Harmon paid little notice to at the time, was 98. Thus began the legend of Old 98, the name and number that Harmon made famous. Forest Evashevski, his roommate, teammate and lead blocker at Michigan, gave him the nickname.

"At practice," Harmon said, "Evy would say, 'Come on, Old 98, let's get it in gear.' "

While in high school, Harmon attended a college game between the University of Chicago and Purdue. He was struck by the versatile talents of Chicago's Jay Berwanger, who ran, passed, punted, kicked off, kicked placements and returned punts and kickoffs.

"My hero became Berwanger," Harmon said. "I had so much respect for him. He had no help at Chicago. I wanted to become the player he was, a 60-minute man.

"I saw him in a newsreel, receiving the Heisman Trophy. I heard the announcer say that the trophy went to the outstanding college football player in the country. That stuck with me. I've always been goal-oriented, and from that day on, I had my eye on the Heisman."

As a senior at Horace Mann, Harmon led the nation in scoring with 150 points. The offers poured in. Kerr suggested that he go to school at Ann Arbor. And Harmon's three brothers—Bud, a Purdue basketball player; Harold, a Boilermaker track man, and Gene, a Tulane basketball captain—encouraged Tom to enroll at Michigan. End of recruiting.

Michigan had a 4-4 record, its fourth consecutive non-winning season, under Coach Harry Kipke in 1937. Harmon's freshman team scrimmaged the varsity three times, "and we beat the heck out of them each time," he said. Kipke was fired after the season, and Crisler was brought in from Princeton to replace him.

"I had two great coaches in my life," Harmon said. "Kerr taught me the fundamentals of football, and there was no finer coach than Crisler."

Crisler served notice from the start that things would be different for the Wolverines. No longer would the Michigan freshmen beat up on the varsity, nor would the Big Ten Conference (also known as the Western Conference in Harmon's time) have a patsy in Ann Arbor to kick around anymore.

The 1938 season opened with the traditional matchup against Michigan State, which had beaten Michigan the previous four years. In Crisler's first game with the Wolverines, his team silenced the Spartans, 14-0. Coming off the bench, Harmon rushed four times for 27 yards in his varsity debut.

He started the next game and sprinted 59 yards for a touchdown as Michigan manhandled Chicago, 45-7. Evashevski was his key blocker, a service "Evy" would provide unselfishly for Harmon over three autumns.

The only team Crisler and Harmon couldn't figure out during their time together was Minnesota, one of the nation's dominant teams under Coach Bernie Bierman in the 1930s. Harmon had great success against every opponent except the Gophers.

In Old 98's first game against Minnesota, he made a costly fumble that the Gophers turned into a touchdown and a 7-6 victory. The Wolverines barely recovered the following Saturday against Yale, trailing 13-2 at the half before Harmon's passing set up two second-half touchdowns and a 15-13 Michigan win.

Harmon starred again with a 13-yard touchdown run and a 22-yard scoring strike to Evashevski as Illinois fell, 14-0, a week later. Harmon had a minor role against Pennsylvania, but the Wolverines still won, 19-13.

After settling for a scoreless tie with Northwestern, Michigan closed out its season against traditional rival Ohio State, which had held the Wolverines scoreless for the last four years. Harmon scored one touchdown in the second quarter, then intercepted a pass and threw for another touchdown as Michigan defeated the Buckeyes, 18-0, and finished the season at 6-1-1.

Old 98, who had led the team with 708 yards of total offense, was just warming up.

Michigan offered no athletic scholarships at the time, Harmon said, instead helping its student-athletes find summer jobs and part-time work while they were in school. Harmon worked in the Gary steel mills in the summer, making between $200 and $300, from which he paid his $125 tuition. He then supported himself at Michigan by busing dishes at the Phi Gamma Delta fraternity house and running copy for a printer in Ann Arbor.

"That's why I have no feelings for these guys who say they can't study and play football, too," Harmon said. "That's a crock!

"My freshman year at Michigan, I had a Spanish final that I studied for all night long. When they handed me the exam in the morning, I drew a blank. I was petrified. I kept thinking that I was letting down people who believed in me—my family, Doug Kerr—and that I'd have to go back and work in the steel mills. After a half-hour, the fog cleared and I was all right, fortunately. It was a two-hour exam, and I got a B.

"I graduated in four years with a B average, while playing two sports and sometimes three, and working besides. You can do anything you want if you put your mind to it."

Harmon played varsity basketball, leading the team in scoring as a sopho-more, and was on the Michigan track team part of his sophomore year, but he quit from exhaustion—one too many sports on top of his study load and workload.

Four football games stick in Harmon's mind from his days at Michigan. The first was against Iowa his junior year of 1939. The Wolverines had continued their newfound mastery of Michigan State, 26-13, in the opener, then met the "Iron Men" of Iowa and Nile Kinnick, who went on to win the Heisman Trophy that fall.

"I was very interested in that game," Harmon said, "because I knew about Kinnick, and this would give me a chance to compare myself against him."

Harmon, playing tailback in the Wolverines' single-wing offense, scored all of Michigan's points that day in a convincing 27-7 victory, the Hawkeyes' only defeat that season. One of Harmon's touchdowns was a 95-yard interception return of a Kinnick pass.

"Challenge Harmon," Bennie Oosterbaan, Michigan assistant coach, said after the game, "and you'll never beat him."

Harmon's performance catapulted him into the national spotlight. His name was being mentioned in the same sentence—and in the same class—as Grange's.

"He has everything," Crisler said of Old 98. "He's best known as a runner, but I'd say his blocking and defensive work are equally as good. Iowa threatened twice after its lone touchdown, and Harmon stopped them twice.

"He's All-American in quality right now, and he hasn't reached his peak yet. Grange was a great runner, but Harmon has all the qualities of a great player, offensively and defensively."

Michigan pounded poor Chicago, 85-0, even though Crisler played his regulars less than half of the game in a hopeless attempt to hold down the score. Still, Harmon had enough time to score twice on long runs, throw a pair of touchdown passes, kick a field goal and boot three extra points. Chicago dropped its entire football program after the season.

Harmon then rushed for 206 yards and scored 21 points in a 27-7 victory over Yale, but trouble was ahead for Michigan.

"I don't think I ever saw a team as high as Illinois was against us the next week," Harmon said, "and I didn't find out why until much later. Their team captain was Mel Brewer, a guard. His mother died shortly before the game. Bob Zuppke, the Illinois coach, called the team together Friday night in their hotel to try and motivate them, only he couldn't think of anything to say. He kept talking until Brewer stood up and said: 'Coach, could I leave the room? I've got a game to play tomorrow.' Then he left quietly. That was all the motivation Zuppke needed. Illinois was ready to run through the door."

The Illini won, 16-7.

Things didn't improve for Michigan the next week. Minnesota pushed the Wolverines around, 20-7, to take another symbolic swig from the "Little Brown Jug" that Michigan and Minnesota have been battling over since 1909. After pass-ing for Michigan's only touchdown, Harmon place-kicked an extra point in that game, making that the only time he ever scored against the Gophers.

"Minnesota had great teams when we played them, don't get me wrong," Harmon said. "But we were flat down for the second straight week. We were in the toilet."

Never the bashful type, Harmon made the same statement publicly, omitting references to Michigan's plumbing problems. He had a campus radio show, all but guaranteeing that his comments would get back to Minnesota, which never cared for Harmon and delighted in beating him.

*"Oh, ho, ho,*
*Harmon we see;*
*Little brown jughead,*
*We'll beat thee."*

Harmon's most memorable run for Michigan occurred against Pennsylvania as a junior. Those who saw it probably still can't believe it. The run not only defied coaching, it defied logic.

The Wolverines were back on their 37-yard line, locked in a tight game in the third quarter. Harmon started right on an end run but encountered a line of tacklers and ran toward the left sideline. Then he began retreating toward his goal—a coaching no-no. Running backs have been taught since Amos Alonzo Stagg was in the crib not to run backward; it's harder to make yardage going in reverse.

But Harmon of Michigan wasn't a normal running back. He kept running in the wrong direction until he had shed enough Penn tacklers and picked up enough Michigan blockers to start up the right sideline again. He eluded the remaining Quaker defenders and raced uncontested the last 50 yards to the end zone, putting Michigan on top, 13-3.

Though the run officially covered 63 yards, Harmon actually ran well over 100. "He ran it," Crisler quipped, "just like I diagrammed it." He ran it, those in attendance agreed, like Grange.

"My running style was like (Vince) Lombardi said, 'Run to daylight,' " Harmon said. "Every runner has a sixth sense, and I had it. I was a cut-back runner who could go against the grain in a step, which meant I could reverse faster than those trying to tackle me. I had better-than-average speed, running 100 yards in 9.8 seconds in high school, which is moving along pretty good for a big guy.

"I always felt the greatest running back I ever saw was Hugh McElhenny (a professional football Hall of Famer). He could run inside, outside, he could cut on a nickel and he could cut away from you. He ran a lot like I did, only he was bigger. He could put more things together than any back—more than Grange or Glenn Davis."

The Penn game, which the Wolverines won, 19-17, and the 1939 season finale against Ohio State were among Harmon's four most memorable games. The Buckeyes jumped ahead, 14-0, converting two interceptions into touchdowns. The Wolverines came back to tie the game, with Evashevski making a sensational catch of Harmon's pass in the end zone and Old 98 juking 16 yards for a score. The stage was set for a dramatic finish.

With 50 seconds left in the game, Michigan reached Ohio State's 24-yard line. A field goal would break the tie, and Harmon was the Wolverines' placekicker. Crisler sent in instructions to go for the three points, but Evashevski had other ideas.

"Evy and Crisler fought a lot," Harmon said. "Evy was a bright guy, a Phi Beta

Kappa, so he questioned Crisler. Those two were like Custer and the Indians."

Evashevski remembered that the Wolverines had been working on a fake field goal from as far back as spring practice but had never used it. Now would be the perfect time, he decided.

"Evy called the play, and I thought (Fred) Trosko was going to flip," Harmon said. Trosko was the holder on place kicks. He had not had a great day so far, and to think that he now had to run with the ball on the game's most important play—and then face Crisler along with Evashevski if it didn't come off—was more responsibility than he cared to accept.

To Trosko's relief, the fake worked perfectly. Harmon stepped forward and went through his kicking motion, purposely missing the ball. Trosko jumped up and ran behind Harmon for the touchdown. Harmon's extra-point conversion gave the Wolverines a 21-14 victory.

Michigan and Ohio State finished with identical 6-2 records, but the Buckeyes still won the conference championship because only one of its losses was in the Big Ten. Michigan finished tied for fourth with Northwestern. Harmon rushed for 868 yards, passed for 488 and led the nation in scoring with 102 points. He was named a consensus All-America, and he finished second to Kinnick in the Heisman voting.

Crisler certainly must be credited with much of Harmon's success in college, not only as his coach, but also as his fashion designer. If teams were going to tackle Harmon, Crisler determined, they would have to do it legitimately, not by grabbing his shirt. So, Crisler dressed his backs in tear-away jerseys.

"After I finished playing at Michigan, I figured I had scored 12 or 13 touchdowns because of the tear-away," Harmon said. "Sometimes I'd go through four or five a game. I know I used five in my last game against Ohio State."

With visions of the Heisman dancing in his head, Harmon spent the summer of 1940 working as a lifeguard back home in Gary. Each morning before the Lake Michigan beach opened, he trained in the sand, sprinting, cutting, stopping, twisting, jumping and striding. By the end of the summer, Harmon's legs were coiled springs. In three years, this conditioning would save Harmon's life. In 1940, it prepared him for a Heisman Trophy season.

Harmon's first step toward emulating his idol, Berwanger, was cross-country in length: Michigan was playing California in Berkeley. To make the trip, Michigan chartered three planes, which was a unique way to transport athletes at that time.

"The intention was fine," Harmon said of the trip west, "but someone got the great idea of flying over the Grand Canyon. Guys were lying in the aisle, sick as dogs, throwing up all over the place. I had had a brief experience with flying, so I wasn't among them. Tippy Lockard, one of our halfbacks, was on the floor, his eyes crossed, his face as white as his shirt. The stewardess asked Tippy if she could get him anything, and he said, "Hell, no!' "

Harmon always will have that run against Penn to look back on, but as far as spectacular games, nothing compares to his performance in Berkeley on September 28, 1940—his 21st birthday. Right before kickoff, Crisler called Harmon over to the sideline while Evashevski huddled with the rest of the players on the field. "This is Tom's birthday," Evy told his teammates. "Let's give him a present by everybody knocking somebody down."

Old 98 took the kickoff at the 6-yard line, headed up the center of the field, made one of his patented cuts through the right side of the advancing line of tacklers and broke into the clear for a touchdown. Happy birthday, Tommy Harmon!

That run was only for openers. Harmon also returned a Cal punt 70 yards for another touchdown, scored on an eight-yard run and threw a short touchdown pass to Dave Nelson. Michigan won convincingly, 41-0, as Harmon contributed to five touchdowns (scoring four himself) and kicked four extra points. His other touchdown play, scored in the second quarter, brought a coast-to-coast chuckle and made a celebrity out of Harold J. (Bud) Brennan.

Brennan, an ardent Cal fan, was sitting in the end zone that day, a little "stiffo" as he would admit later. The balding, paunchy Brennan was getting fed up with the way Harmon was humiliating the Golden Bears, and he told his buddies, "If Harmon breaks loose again, I'll go out there and tackle him myself."

Sure enough, Harmon took off from scrimmage on third down at Michigan's 14-yard line and set sail around left end for the Cal goal line 86 yards away. Before long he had sidestepped everyone barring his path to the end zone—everyone, that is, except an inebriated Bud Brennan.

"I first saw him from 40 yards away," Harmon recalled, "but I didn't know at the time how many beers he had had or what he was going to do. Then I knew. He came after me at about the 2. I gave him a straight arm and a 'soft leg,' and he went flying. It would have been embarrassing to run through 11 perfectly conditioned athletes and then get tackled by a drunk."

Police escorted Brennan away. After the game, Harmon emerged from the dressing room and saw Brennan still surrounded by Oakland's finest. Harmon asked what was going on, and a policeman replied that they were taking Brennan to jail. Harmon, pointing out that Brennan hadn't harmed anyone, suggested that they let him go. The police agreed.

"Bud never forgot that," Harmon said. "We've seen each other over the years, played together in a golf tournament. He sends me a birthday card and Christmas card every year."

Though not even "12 men" could stop Harmon at Cal, he doesn't include that game among his finest. "It was a spectacular game for me on the surface," he explained, "but we scored so fast that it took the life out of Cal, which was actually a good football team. I just don't think that scoring so many points in a lopsided game is much of a personal accomplishment."

As a follow-up, Harmon scored all of Michigan's points in a 21-14 defeat of Michigan State. Harmon scored 20 more points as Michigan pounded Harvard, 26-0, giving him 69 in three games. Michigan reversed the previous year's loss to Illinois, 28-0, then made it three straight shutouts by whipping Penn, 14-0.

Football historians often write how important Evashevski's blocking was to Harmon, phrasing it in such a manner to indicate that without Evy, Harmon was just another back. Syndicated columnist Henry McLemore attacked that assumption after watching Harmon hammer Penn.

"The way it should read is Tommy Harmon 14, Pennsylvania 0," McLemore wrote, "because it was the Gary Galloper who played poison to the Quakers' ivy and cracked them open like the Liberty Bell. . . . I don't want to belittle Evashevski's value, but Harmon can go with or without him. Evashevski was hurt just before the end of the first half and didn't get back into the game. But Harmon kept rolling just the same. As a matter of fact . . . he ripped off two long runs in which his interference was negligible. He simply ran over the Quakers who stood in his way."

After the game, Harmon noticed a Penn equipment manager cleaning up in the locker room and gave him a new pair of Michigan sweat socks with an "M" monogrammed on the sides. The manager thanked Old 98, then introduced himself as Fred Knox. Harmon probably forgot the name as soon as he heard it, but their paths would cross again in the not-too-distant future.

Harmon's fourth memorable game took place in Minneapolis in his third, and last, attempt at beating Minnesota. The Wolverines were convinced they would win this time, realizing they were faster and quicker than the power-oriented Gophers. On a dry field, Michigan concluded, it would be no contest.

The first clap of thunder erupted at 2 a.m. the day of the game, awakening Harmon and his roommate, Evashevski. They listened in their beds as the rain began to pour. It wouldn't stop. By kickoff, the field was a quagmire. Advantage, Minnesota.

"I had holes you could drive a Mack truck through, but I couldn't get to the end zone because I kept slipping and falling," Harmon said. "There were only six times that year when we didn't score after getting inside the opponents' 10, and four of those were against Minnesota."

Michigan's only touchdown came in the second quarter after fullback Bob Westfall recovered a fumble at the Minnesota 5-yard line. On third down at the 3, Harmon passed to Evashevski in the end zone for the score, but he missed the extra point as his kick sailed just left of the upright.

Minnesota's Bob Paffrath later picked off a Harmon pass in the end zone, giving the Gophers the ball on their own 20. On the next play, Minnesota's Bruce Smith, the 1941 Heisman winner, pushed through a hole at left tackle. Six Wolverines had shots at him in the mud, but Smith eluded everyone and maneuvered 80 yards for the touchdown. Joe Mernik kicked the ball squarely through the uprights for the point after, and Minnesota held on to win, 7-6.

"That still is the most frustrating day of my life," Harmon said.

After the game, Harmon was quoted as saying that Michigan should have won by three touchdowns. In return, the city aldermen of Minneapolis sent Harmon a crate of raspberries "as a token of your three scoreless (no touchdown) years against Minnesota." Three winless years, too.

Minnesota wound up national champion in 1940, which made Harmon feel even worse. "I felt we were the best team in the nation," he said. "To this day, Minnesota hasn't convinced me they were better. . . . I don't like to alibi, but we lost a game in the mud. But print that, and here comes Minnesota after me again."

Crushed by the defeat to the Gophers, Michigan barely mustered enough of an attack to turn back Northwestern, 20-13. The Wolverines then traveled to Ohio State, where Harmon launched a final, successful assault on Grange's records.

Harmon scored the first touchdown of the game on an eight-yard run early in the first quarter to tie Grange's career touchdowns record. He then passed for two scores before tallying two more TDs himself on runs of 18 and six yards. Michigan rolled to a 40-0 victory as Harmon closed out his Wolverine career with three touchdowns and 139 yards rushing in a stunning swan song. The crowd in Columbus gave him a standing ovation when he went to the bench after his last touchdown with 38 seconds left in the game.

Old 98 finished his collegiate career with 33 touchdowns, two more than Grange. Harmon scored 117 points his senior year to lead the nation again. His career totals also included 2,110 yards rushing (5.4 average), 1,300 yards passing (232 attempts, 100 completions, 16 touchdowns), a 39.3-yard punting average, 33 extra-point conversions and two field goals.

At a banquet honoring the Michigan team, Harmon gave his teammates and coaches gold footballs "so that they may never forget the part they played in helping Old 98," he said. Old 98, the jersey, was retired by Michigan.

Harmon was named a consensus All-America for the second straight year, and even better than that, his Heisman wish came true. He piled up 1,303 points, outdistancing Texas A&M fullback John Kimbrough, who received 841. At his Heisman presentation, Harmon told the audience that his parents were his major source of inspiration. Then he shook the hand of his father, a night watchman in Gary, and placed the trophy in front of his mother. "Here's the girl," he said, "who will always keep the trophy—and myself—right."

Harmon won virtually all of the major awards in 1940 and was voted the Associated Press Male Athlete of the Year by a wide margin over Detroit Tigers slugger Hank Greenberg. Old 98 was in great demand at banquets and award ceremonies after that, and he spent much of his last semester of college making appearances all over the country.

Harmon also realized his boyhood dream of playing in the East-West Shrine Game on New Year's Day, 1941, in San Francisco. Along the way, he detoured through Los Angeles to appear on Bing Crosby's radio show. Harmon was introduced to English actor Alan Mowbray, who personally guided him on a tour of a movie studio. They had lunch with Roy Rogers and a pretty blonde actress from Connecticut, Elyse Knox, who was making a movie at that studio.

"She was so real, so honest, so different from anyone I had met in Hollywood at the time," Harmon said.

That same night, actress Gail Patrick invited Harmon to a dinner, with a date if he preferred. Through Mowbray, he obtained Knox's phone number.

Little did he know that the actress was the sister of Fred Knox, the Penn football manager.

"After we had lunch," Harmon said, "Elyse went home and told her mother and brother that she had met some football player. When Fred found out who it was, he mentioned the sweat socks and began showing them how I ran with the football.

"I called Elyse just about that time to invite her to dinner. When she came to the phone, I told her who I was, and she slammed down the phone so hard, I almost busted an eardrum. I thought, 'Boy, did I make an impression!' "

Actually, Harmon had mumbled his name, and the actress had mistaken him for someone else. She called back later to apologize and said she would be glad to join him for dinner. That night, they dined with such celebrities as Amos and Andy and Fibber McGee and Molly. Harmon was star-struck, but only by the star on his arm.

A smitten Harmon left for San Francisco, where his East-West play received mixed reviews. He rushed 16 times for 39 yards (only a 2.4-yard average), threw two touchdown passes (one to Evashevski and the other to Ed Frutig, also a Michigan teammate) and intercepted a pass. The game's hero, however, was Missouri's Paul Christman, who passed the West to a 20-14 victory.

Harmon returned to Michigan, corresponded with Elyse and earned his degree. He returned to Hollywood to play himself in the movie "Harmon of Michigan." He starred with Anita Louise and another unknown actor, Evashevski, and earned $25,000 for two weeks' work. Harmon critiqued his acting ability as "passable" and the movie's plot as "a joke." Harmon went on to make 25 to 30 movies in the years ahead, mainly in bit roles and generally cast as a broadcaster.

The next-to-last game in which Old 98 played as a representative of the University of Michigan was in August 1941 in the College All-Star Game in Chicago. Harmon threw a 22-yard touchdown pass to Minnesota's George Franck to draw the All-Stars temporarily even with the Chicago Bears, but the National Football League champions eventually pulled away for a 37-13 win. He also played for the All-Stars in 1945, when a few non-professionals who had long since left school were invited to play in the game because of the dearth of college talent during the war.

The Bears had made Harmon the No. 1 selection in the 1941 draft, but it turned out to be a wasted pick. Harmon told Bears Owner George Halas that he wanted to pursue a career in broadcasting and therefore would not sign a pro contract. So, Harmon went to work for a Detroit radio station in 1941, broadcasting University of Michigan football games. It was the start of a long, successful career behind a microphone.

That career was interrupted temporarily, however, by two events: World War II and a couple of stints with professional football teams. He agreed to play one game for the New York Americans (previously the Yankees) of the American Football League and had an option for a second game.

"I remember scoring our only touchdown in a 7-7 tie with . . . I can't remember the other team (the Columbus Bulls)," Harmon said of his pro debut on October 19, 1941. "I was beating my guards to the hole and decided this was no place for me."

Harmon, who still was busy with his radio job, decided not to exercise his option, and he joined the Army Air Corps shortly thereafter. With a war on the horizon, many other AFL players enlisted in the armed services, too. The league folded after the season.

Harmon kept in touch with Elyse. "According to Elyse," he said, "when I was lost the two times, she became sick with worry and tension, although I didn't learn this until much later."

After Harmon returned from China following his second ordeal, he took Elyse to dinner, brought out a pair of matching diamond rings and proposed. They were married on August 26, 1944, in the same student chapel on the Michigan campus where the special Mass had been held for Old 98 after his first disappearance. Elyse wore a dress made from the silk parachute Harmon had used when he was shot down over China.

Harmon was promoted to captain while his wife was pregnant with Kristin, their first child. Then a speech Harmon made at the Detroit Athletic Club put him in trouble with the top military brass. There were wartime strikes at the time, and

Harmon spoke out against the unions, who were not happy with his remarks. Neither was the War Department.

"What I told them in the speech," Harmon said, "was that kids overseas already were lacking in supplies. We didn't mind being shot at, but there was no way anyone should keep one bullet away from a kid who is defending his country.

"I was blackballed from that point on. I received a telegram from General H.H. (Hap) Arnold himself, the top man in the Army Air Corps, who told me there was no more need for me to make public appearances. The telegram arrived about an hour before I was to go on with Bing Crosby on Bob Burns' radio show. I had to cancel my appearance."

Tom Harmon, war hero, became persona non grata in the Army Air Corps. Forced into silence, he was serving out his time as a P-38 instructor when a special order was issued from Washington granting early discharges to those who had walked out from behind enemy lines. Harmon got his discharge papers the same day.

After receiving his discharge in August 1945, he resumed his radio career, operating his own nationally broadcast sports program out of Los Angeles. He continued to do that even after signing a pro contract in July 1946 with the Los Angeles Rams, who had obtained his NFL rights from the Bears. Harmon signed a two-year, no-cut contract for $25,000 per season, which he said made him the highest-paid player in the league as he began his short NFL career in 1946.

Despite being slowed by legs that had been burned badly when his plane was downed over China, he still was able to break off some long runs for the Rams, including an 84-yard touchdown sprint that ranked as the longest run from scrimmage in the NFL that year. The Rams, however, played him mainly on defense.

"I was like a square peg in a round hole," he said. "I wasn't a T-formation halfback; I was a single-wing tailback."

Nevertheless, he excelled as a defensive back. He swiped three passes his rookie year, including one that he returned 85 yards for a touchdown, the longest interception return in the NFL that season. He did not endear himself to Coach Adam Walsh, however, when he walked up to him one day and told him the Cardinals' left cornerback could be suckered with a stop-and-go pass. Harmon thought nothing of offering a play that he believed would work, as Crisler had expected and appreciated his players' input at Michigan. But Walsh was offended.

"What are you trying to do, pad your part?" he told Harmon. After that, Harmon played offense less regularly for Walsh, who resigned after a 6-4-1 season.

Harmon was the Rams' best defensive back and punt returner during his two years in Los Angeles. In 1947, he returned a punt a league-high 88 yards for a touchdown against Detroit and intercepted eight passes, including the club's longest pickoff return, a 36-yarder. The club fell to 6-6, and Coach Bob Snyder resigned. Rams Owner Dan Reeves offered Harmon a new three-year, no-cut agreement, but Harmon felt that two NFL seasons and 13 career broken noses were enough punishment. He retired.

Harmon then went into broadcasting full-time. "Sports broadcasting was the only job I ever wanted," he once reflected. "It was the thing I loved because it put me among people I knew and wanted to be with. It has always been my ambition to give to sports fans the tremendous satisfaction that sports have given me."

It didn't take long for Harmon to rise in stature as a sports announcer. He was a pioneer telecaster with KTLA in Los Angeles when that was the only television outlet in the city. Then NBC offered him a job as sports director of its radio network outlet in Los Angeles. In 1949, he took over as sports director for the CBS Pacific Radio Network. Harmon switched to ABC 12 years later, hosting a nightly sports program that was heard on hundreds of stations nationwide. Over the years he has been involved in producing and writing as well as announcing sports talk shows and broadcasts for both radio and TV.

Old 98 has covered the broadcasting gamut—every major college bowl game, baseball, the NCAA Basketball Tournament finals, the Kentucky Derby, the Indianapolis 500, the Olympics, championship fights and even Gaelic football. "That was as wild as anything I've done," he said.

His biggest challenge, however, was broadcasting UCLA football games in the early 1970s. The situation was complicated only because his son, Mark, was the Bruins' quarterback at the time.

"It was the toughest job I ever had in broadcasting," Harmon said. "I kept referring to Mark as 'the quarterback'; I couldn't call him Harmon. I continually caught myself not saying anything over the air because I was watching Mark."

Tom Harmon once was caught in a double quandary because UCLA played Michigan in 1972, Mark's first season as a Bruin after transferring from a junior college, thereby matching Old 98's son against his alma mater. The Wolverines won easily, 26-9.

"The best compliment I had paid to me in broadcasting," he said, "was from people who congratulated me after that game for being so unbiased and straight down the line."

Now in his 60s, Harmon has slowed the maddening pace of four or five sports broadcasts a day, a schedule he maintained for nearly 20 years. He does the Los Angeles Raiders' weekly TV highlights, plus play-by-play coverage of the Raiders' preseason telecasts.

Sitting in his office chair, Harmon yawned. His hair is white, thinning to a wisp on top, but he still looks like an athlete. He stays trim by playing golf and skiing.

Inside his office, Harmon is surrounded by family history. Photographs of his children sit on a shelf above his desk, sharing space with the Heisman Trophy and several other large trophies. National and regional magazine covers of Tom and Elyse, both separately and together, are on the wall along with a "Harmon of Michigan" movie poster. An oil painting by Elyse of Old 98, his nose battered and his jersey torn, hangs over his desk.

Tom and Elyse Harmon have been married for more than 40 years, which, for marriages made in Hollywood, is a tremendous accomplishment. It is sad but true that many marriages between athletes and entertainers, or just between entertainers, are lucky to last one decade, much less four.

"Elyse and I always have been able to work things out," he said. "Our marriage is stronger now than it's ever been. Elyse is as fine a mother as ever came down the pike. We have three children and five grandchildren, and she's there all the time. We had the whole family here for Christmas, and Elyse cooked the whole dinner.

"I wish every guy in the world had a wife like mine. That would cut out all the divorces. She's a beautiful woman who made 45 to 50 movies, but beauty is about her 10th-best attribute."

The Harmons' two daughters have had less success with marriage than their parents. They have been married four times between them. Kris was married only once, to singer Ricky Nelson. The couple had four children before they were divorced in 1982 after 19 years of marriage.

It was only natural that Kris and Ricky would meet. The Harmons were good friends with Ricky's parents, Ozzie and Harriet Nelson. At the time, Ricky and his older brother, David, still were starring on the popular "Ozzie and Harriet" comedy show. But Ricky also was a popular singer and a bobby-socks heartthrob.

"I'm not a judge," Tom Harmon said, "but when you get into the music business, and he's one of the biggest singing stars in the country . . . that's too tough to handle.

"The Nelson family lost a great deal of strength when Ozzie died (in 1975). He was the bellwether of the family. Being a lawyer, Ozzie took care of the family business. After he was gone, Rick fell into the hands of bad management. It affected his marriage.

"Harriet still is at our house all the time. There is no animosity between the families. We just don't see much of Rick anymore."

The Harmons' second daughter, Kelly, has married three times. Her first husband was a General Motors Corp. vice president named John Z. DeLorean. When they married in 1969, he was 44, she 20. They had met when Tom Harmon brought DeLorean home to meet his family after playing together in a golf tournament.

Several years after Kelly had been divorced from DeLorean, an FBI agent visited Tom and Elyse Harmon at their home. DeLorean had been arrested on the charge of selling $24 million in cocaine to undercover FBI agents. Government lawyers contended that the automaker made the sale in an effort to save his faltering car company in Northern Ireland, the gull-winged DeLorean sports car. The FBI agent wanted to know if the Harmons were aware of DeLorean's alleged involvement with cocaine. They were not. DeLorean eventually was acquitted in August 1984 after a five-month trial.

"That had to hurt him more than anything in his life," Harmon said, "failing with his name on his car."

After divorcing DeLorean, Kelly married a Beverly Hills doctor. "That didn't last long, either," her father said. Kelly now is married to Robert L. Miller, the publisher of Sports Illustrated. She models and acts, including a featured role in the short-lived "Bay City Blues" television series.

Mark Harmon never has married. He is an actor who appears frequently on television and is a regular on "St. Elsewhere," a critically acclaimed hospital drama.

"We taught our children to be independent," Harmon said, "to be their own best judge of values. When it came to our daughters' divorces, they did the right thing.

"I've got the three greatest kids in the world. We fight and scratch, but when something happens to any of them, they close ranks in a hurry."

Harmon yawned again. The Heisman Trophy was directly behind him, pointing at the head of its sixth recipient.

"When I think of the trophy," Harmon said, "I think of pride, friendships, responsibility and a very select group of men I'm honored to be a part of. When I've been together with the other winners, I notice a bond that I've never seen anyplace else, an instant undercurrent of respect.

"The Heisman is a great honor to be proud of and responsible for, which I don't think all Heisman winners have been. Not all of them have set a positive image for kids today. I feel Heisman winners have a responsibility to stand up for rules and character points, to make our young athletes look up to them."

Harmon, who remains actively involved with the Heisman process as the Far West sectional representative, is glad to be a part of that heritage. And he is just as glad to be alive to talk about it.

# Doc Blanchard

*He was a crushing blocker and a punishing ballcarrier. He was the power source of an offensive machine that scored almost at will. Doc Blanchard was the blue-collar Mr. Inside of Army fame. He combined gloriously with Mr. Outside, the great Glenn Davis. He helped bring Army to the forefront of college football and then sealed his own spot in history by capturing the sport's highest honor. Doc Blanchard combined 'brute' with 'force' and became one of the most-destructive military weapons of all time.*

# Chapter 5

# The powerful
# Mr. Inside

The thick front door of the oak-shaded home in San Antonio swung open, and there stood a thicker Doc Blanchard, the greatest fullback ever to receive a full scholarship from Uncle Sam.

"Have any trouble getting here?" The words were clear, clipped, direct—a military voice—yet wrapped with mirth and ribboned with a Southern drawl. Rhett Butler, All-America.

Blanchard led the way into the kitchen. At 230 pounds—25 more than his playing weight at West Point—much of Mr. Inside had moved outside.

Blanchard introduced his wife, Jody, whom he met while attending flight school in San Antonio and then married after his graduation. In retirement—Col. Felix A. Blanchard Jr. flew his last Air Force assignment in 1971—they now live on the north side of the south-central Texas city.

"Would you like to talk outside," he said, pointing toward the swimming pool in the backyard, "or inside?"

An easy choice. One talks to Mr. Inside inside.

Blanchard mixed a drink, sat down and lit a cigarette. "How far back do you want to go?" he asked.

The beginning.

That would be December 11, 1924, in McColl, S.C., where Felix Anthony Blanchard Jr. was born. Blanchard Sr., a country doctor who hung his shingle permanently in Bishopville, S.C., 50 miles from McColl, and his wife also had a daughter, Mary Elizabeth, who later would become a gynecologist and obstetrician. But of the two children, Felix Jr. would be called "Doc" first. Tabbed "Little Doc" as a youngster, he later became known simply as "Doc."

It didn't take long for a football to find its way into Blanchard's hands. His father used to place a football in his crib when he was a baby, and Little Doc would clutch the ball happily. When he grew old enough to walk, he often would be seen traipsing around Bishopville with his football tucked under his arm. Sports were a part of Blanchard's life almost from day one.

"I wasn't very much academically inclined—didn't much care," he recalled of his boyhood years. "So I just got by. But I did want to study medicine."

Young Felix was sent to a Catholic boarding school, St. Stanislaus High School in Bay St. Louis, Miss., to prepare for college. He was more interested in sports and girls than grades, however, and it was his football rather than his academic marks that attracted universities across the country.

"I could have gone to most anyplace I wanted, Notre Dame, whatever," he said. The U.S. Military Academy was among the schools hoping to land Blanchard, but the South Carolinian had no inclination at the time to become a cadet.

"I had been in an all-boys school," he explained. "I wasn't interested in going into the military, especially in New York."

He thought of attending Tulane, where his father was a 240-pound fullback for Coach Clark Shaughnessy. "When Felix gets mad," Shaughnessy once said, "he's as good as any fullback who ever lived." In time, the same would be said of his son.

But when Blanchard Sr. became ill, Little Doc decided to enroll at North Carolina, which was closer to home. That way his father could travel to see his home games. In addition, the coach at North Carolina, Jim Tatum, was Blanchard's cousin.

The Tar Heels could not believe their good luck, especially when Blanchard led the freshman squad to the state championship in 1942 and inspired fear among varsity players during scrimmages. "Once he knocked out two varsity tacklers on the same play," said R.A. White, the Tar Heels' freshman trainer. "It got so bad that some of the boys wouldn't even try to tackle him."

Glenn Thistlethwaite, a former coach at Northwestern, once watched Blanchard as a freshman and said: "I have seen all the great fullbacks. This boy will be the greatest."

Blanchard was all but certain to start at fullback for the varsity as a sophomore, but he never made it that far at Chapel Hill. He was drafted in the spring of 1943 and was sent to Army boot camp in Miami.

"The Army asked me what I wanted to do," Blanchard recalled. "I didn't know, so I said tail gunner. That sounded good."

From Miami, Blanchard went to Alabama, Utah and New Mexico for his military training. His football reputation, meanwhile, followed him from base to base until West Point got word.

This time when the Army called, Blanchard snapped to attention. He was all ears.

"Have you ever been to Clovis, New Mexico?" he said in explanation of his sudden change of heart. "Well, I was there all winter, and that was long enough. It was cold, windy and lonely."

Blanchard was happy to be sent to Lafayette College in Easton, Pa., to prepare for the West Point entrance exams. While Blanchard was at Lafayette, however, his father died. Felix Jr. had been close to his father and was deeply grieved by his death, but his memory motivated him to become serious about passing the exams. He became a cadet in the summer of 1944.

"I had the IQ," said Blanchard, who dropped the "Little" from his nickname after his father's death. "I just had to use it."

During World War II, West Point was a recruiting office that "swore in" the finest college football talent in the country. Because of the war, athletes who had lettered at other universities could receive appointments to the Military Academy, where three more seasons of eligibility awaited.

Army was awesome during those years, tallying 27 victories, one tie and no losses from 1944-46, despite the fact that at that time, cadets were forced to finish a four-year curriculum in three years in order to meet the country's need for military officers.

"You went from plebes to sophomore to first class," Blanchard said. "There was no junior class."

It didn't matter. Coach Earl (Red) Blaik had so many great players as it was that he had to divide the team into two squads—plebes-sophomores and first classmen—so that everyone could play.

"Except for the quarterback," Blanchard pointed out. "He stayed in the whole time. Otherwise, we alternated quarters."

Even while rotating squads in 1944, Army produced the most explosive offense ever witnessed in football—college or professional—as the Black Knights of the Hudson averaged 56 points per game, setting an NCAA record that still stands for Division I-A schools.

Before the '44 season, Blanchard was given jersey No. 35 and, because of his plebe status, assigned to the second team. Glenn Davis, a halfback on the second unit, was given No. 41. The numbers didn't mean anything at the time, but over the next three years they became synonymous with the greatest backfield pair in college football history.

Mr. Inside and Mr. Outside.

Blanchard and Davis made their explosive varsity debuts on September 30, 1944, against North Carolina, Blanchard's former school. Davis scored three touchdowns, the shortest play covering 37 yards. Blanchard was equally spectacular. Early in the second quarter, Davis threw a short pass to end Barney Poole, who lateraled to Blanchard. Doc took the ball without missing a step and outran the Tar Heel defenders more than half the length of the field to the end zone. Blanchard had power, but he showed in that first game that he could turn on the speed, too. Army won the game, 46-0.

The Cadets were similarly hard on Brown (59-7), Pittsburgh (69-7), the Coast Guard Academy (76-0), Villanova (83-0), and Pennsylvania (62-7). Army's narrowest victories were 27-7 over Duke and 23-7 over Navy. Its most impressive triumph was a 59-0 thrashing of Notre Dame, which had held the Cadets scoreless since 1938 and had not lost in the rivalry since 1931. But the Black Knights made up for that drought in fine fashion, tallying touchdown after touchdown.

"And the Armies (Cadet fans) were up there in the stands screaming, 'More, more, more!' " Blanchard recalled.

Blanchard didn't score against the Irish, but he left the biggest impression of all the Cadets. A game official couldn't get out of Blanchard's way on a running play and suffered a dislocated elbow and a wrenched knee. Doc was a terror as a blocker, too; he hit John (Tree) Adams, Notre Dame's 6-foot-7 tackle, so hard that Adams flipped over and landed on the back of his neck.

In the next day's article for the New York Times, sportswriter Allison Danzig wrote: "But none of these players was more conspicuous in the victory than was Felix (Doc) Blanchard, the powerful plebe fullback. It was Blanchard who almost invariably made the vital block on the scoring plays. It was Blanchard who sent kickoffs into the end zone, who punted when (quarterback Doug) Kenna was not on the field, who intercepted passes and was even more poisonous on the defense than he was in running with the ball."

After the game, Notre Dame Coach Ed McKeever wired home the message: "Have just seen Superman in the flesh. He wears Number 35 and goes by the name of Blanchard."

And Blanchard was still a plebe!

In the Navy game, Army was hanging precariously to a 9-7 lead in the third quarter when it got the football at its own 48-yard line. It was almost all Blanchard from that point on. He powered around end for 20 yards, then smashed inside repeatedly for small chunks of ground until he hit the end zone standing up on a 10-yard run.

"This is the only man," Army assistant coach Herman Hickman said of Blanchard, "who runs his own interference."

Blanchard scored nine touchdowns in 1944, averaged 5.5 yards per rush and intercepted three passes. He was a consensus All-America along with Davis, and he finished third in the Heisman Memorial Trophy voting behind Ohio State's Les Horvath and Davis. To top it all off, the Cadets won the national championship.

And Mr. Inside and Mr. Outside still had two years left.

Never before or since has there been such a perfect backfield blend of brute strength (Blanchard) and blinding speed (Davis). Army could jab teams with Davis or knock their heads off with Blanchard.

The cumulative totals for Mr. Inside and Mr. Outside over three years of assaulting defenses—3,989 yards rushing, 1,317 yards receiving and 89 touchdowns, not to mention their contributions on defense, punting and kick returns—bear witness to their dominance of the college game. And who knows how big their statistics would have been if Army's games had been somewhat closer and if Blaik had not alternated squads in 1944 and 1945, situations that left Blanchard and Davis on the bench much of the time.

Despite all the praise and honors he received over the years, Blanchard is not caught up in nostalgia. He remembers little about his biggest games, biggest runs and biggest achievements. He even is hazy on his first recollection of Davis.

"Out at practice somewhere," Blanchard said. "We were just out there trying to make the team." Talk about modesty! By the same token, Ford was just trying to survive selling automobiles and Hershey was merely hoping to make it in the chocolate business. Blanchard and Davis made the team, of course, and became friends in the process.

Not that they spent all their time together. Cadets were placed in companies by height, and so the 6-foot Blanchard saw the 5-9½ Davis only for dinner, games and practice, including workouts for the academy's track and field team.

"Our personalities were very different," Blanchard said. "Glenn came out of high school a little naive. He didn't smoke, drink, care about dancing with girls. I don't even know if he even knew how to kiss. You can ask him that."

Blanchard, on the other hand, was experienced in all the above. "I liked a good time," he said. "I had all the vices. I enjoyed living."

"He's a fantastic father," Jody Blanchard said from the kitchen.

"Jody," Blanchard responded in his military voice, "go clean up."

"I think it's fantastic, Doc," Jody replied, not one to be outranked in her own home. "Still a father figure."

"Jody, have you cleaned the bathroom? The bathroom needs cleaning."

Blanchard grinned. Where was he? Oh, Glenn Davis.

"We were closer than just teammates," he continued. "We'd warm up together before games, room together on trips. We never felt like we were in competition with each other because both of us were team-oriented.

"We're still friends, only he's in California and I'm here. He doesn't write; I don't, either. We see each other once in a while at reunions and things. I have the same relationship with Glenn as I do the other (Army) players."

Blanchard doesn't believe in keeping up old relationships just for the sake of keeping them up. But Blanchard and Davis are more than an old relationship. Their names are linked forever in football lore. Isn't that something special?

"That's all in the past," Blanchard said. "If you're not 40 or 50, no one remembers. And there's no reason why they should know."

Blanchard's closest friends these days are, like himself, ex-fighter pilots, a coterie he called "the 'old retireds.' We share a common background."

Blanchard stood and went into the kitchen for another drink. It was late afternoon in November, but the thermometer registered 82 degrees. He returned with his fresh drink and resumed the conversation.

"My favorite play was up over the guard," he said. "One of our guards, John Green or Arthur Gerometta, would knock out the (defensive) guard, someone else would take the end, and that was it. We thought it was something new and exciting."

The 205-pound Blanchard hammered relentlessly at opponents, normally between the tackles, while Davis flew around the flanks as part of Blaik's T-formation offense.

"I was strong in the legs," Blanchard said. "I had good acceleration for my size, good quickness. But I wasn't what you would call a speed guy, like Glenn."

He wasn't a sloth, either, running the 100-yard dash in 10 seconds flat. With that speed and his incredible strength, Mr. Inside was what defensive players call a "load." His opponents would agree that pound for pound, no fullback, dog tags or not, ever hit harder than Doc Blanchard, whether he was carrying the ball, throwing a block or making a crushing tackle. He moved laterally as well as he stormed straight ahead, which helped him become a punishing tackler at linebacker. He also punted and kicked off for the Cadets, and though he was used only occasionally as a pass receiver, he demonstrated good hands and jumping ability, averaging 28.2 yards on 19 catches in three years, including a 68-yard reception against Pitt in 1944.

He was, quite simply, an athlete. He learned quickly, mastered easily. When he decided to go out for the track team because he had a big appetite and wanted to remain on the training table outside football season, he had Davis' twin brother, Ralph, a weight man on the Army track team, teach him to throw the shot put. He had experimented with the shot put in high school but never really worked hard at it. After a brief period of instruction, however, he launched the 16-pound sphere nearly 50 feet to win the event in an Army-Navy dual meet.

But football remained his first love, and behind Blanchard and Davis, Army repeated as national champion in 1945, when Blaik promoted the "Touchdown Twins" to the first string. The Cadets averaged 45.8 points and posted five shutouts while trampling all nine opponents, including a military team based in Louisville (32-0), Wake Forest (54-0), Michigan (28-7), Villanova (54-0), Notre Dame (48-0), Penn (61-0) and Navy (32-13).

Midway through the '45 season, Blanchard and Davis graced the cover of Time magazine. The cutline below the photo, which shows the pair of football stars with mud on their faces, reads: "Junior Davis and Doc Blanchard—They Make

Army's T Boil." The dangerous duo also was featured on the cover of Life magazine a year later.

Against Michigan in 1945, Blanchard blasted his way 68 yards for one touchdown and one yard for another, while Davis sped 70 yards for a score. Michigan freshman Wally Teninga had a chance to return a kickoff for a touchdown, but he had to beat one more tackler. Unfortunately for Teninga, that tackler was Blanchard. Courageously, Teninga put his head down and tried to run over Blanchard. The ball and Teninga sailed out of bounds, although not together. Struggling to his feet, the dazed Teninga said to Wolverines assistant coach Bennie Oosterbaan, "I'll bet he felt that one." Oosterbaan smiled at the youngster. Blanchard had never left his feet.

Doc scored twice in the first quarter against Navy in the traditional season finale. The second touchdown was frightening. A Navy defender, choosing to take on Blanchard in the open field, hit legs of concrete as Blanchard left him in a heap and scampered in for a 17-yard TD run. Then early in the second half, Blanchard intercepted a Navy pass and ran it back 52 yards for six points. He also had returned an interception 52 yards for a TD earlier that year against Wake Forest, and he had a 37-yard pickoff return against Notre Dame.

Blanchard scored 19 touchdowns, averaged 7.1 yards per rush and caught four passes for 166 yards in 1945, his finest season. That performance was not overlooked by the Downtown Athletic Club. After finishing third in the Heisman balloting as a plebe, he won the award in '45, with Davis again finishing second, 860 points to 638. Blanchard was the first junior to win the Heisman, the first athlete to win both the Heisman and the Sullivan Award (the nation's highest honor for an amateur athlete) in the same year and the first football player to receive the Sullivan.

The Heisman and Sullivan awards are displayed side by side on a bookshelf in the Blanchards' living room. Nearby is a smaller trophy with an inscription that reads: "First Place, Doubles Handball, Command Staff School, Montgomery, Ala., 1962."

To Doc, they're just trophies, none of which bears much relevance anymore.

"Winning the Heisman made me feel good inside, but that's about it," he said. "It was the biggest award back then, but it didn't have nearly the impact and prestige it has today. For a long time, my mother kept the Heisman."

"We took it to England," Jody called out from the kitchen.

"We did?" Doc said. "Anyway, I don't know that I sit here and look at it and say, 'That's the Heisman.' I understand the meaningfulness of it, but that was years ago. It's just part of the furniture."

With his senior year at West Point yet to come, Blanchard entered the 1946 season as the first Heisman winner ever to try to repeat his award-winning performance. By 1946, however, Army's two-year joy ride atop the world of college football was ready to come back down to Earth. Opponents that once rolled over and played dead when they faced the Black Knights of the Hudson finally were ready and willing to fight. With the war over and servicemen back in school playing football, it was yesterday's privates vs. tomorrow's lieutenants when civilian teams met Lt. Col. Blaik's Cadets.

Army remained one of the best teams in the country but no longer was invincible. That fact was driven home in the first game of the season when Blanchard was tackled by a Villanova player and tore several knee ligaments. The severity of the injury was such that a lesser player would have been sidelined for the rest of the year, but Blanchard's leg muscles were so strong that he missed only two games. The Cadets beat Villanova (35-0), Oklahoma (21-7) and Cornell (46-21) before Blanchard's return against Michigan.

Blanchard, who no longer could punt or kick off and was not able to practice much after his injury, was held in check by the Wolverines for three quarters that day in Ann Arbor. Then in the final quarter, with the score tied, 13-13, he took control. Surrounded by Wolverines, he leaped to make a 24-yard catch that put the ball near midfield. Davis and Blanchard, who somehow managed to keep his gimpy knee under him, began to pile up yardage and moved the ball to Michigan's 7-yard line for a first down. Blanchard then went outside right tackle on the next play and was hit at the 4. On a bad leg, he carried the tackler into the end zone, and Army won, 20-13.

The Cadets beat Columbia, 48-14, and then Duke and West Virginia by identical 19-0 scores before traveling to Yankee Stadium for their annual matchup with the Fighting Irish. Notre Dame, which had been outscored, 107-0, in its two previous meetings with the Black Knights, was bent on revenge. The unbeaten Irish got even—literally.

"The writers were saying that Army had everybody and Notre Dame had no one," Blanchard recalled. "But in '46, we had only a few guys who played the whole year. I hurt my knee in the first game and didn't do much after that.

"Notre Dame, for having nobody, had Johnny Lujack, George Ratterman and other guys who played in the pros. Well, the game was one, two, three, punt. A real defensive battle. (Notre Dame Coach Frank) Leahy and Blaik thought they were playing each other."

Notre Dame's Emil Sitko fumbled early in the game, giving Army the ball 24 yards from pay dirt. Army then was stopped on downs when Blanchard just missed a first down inside the 15-yard line. Halfback Gerry Cowhig later broke loose for Notre Dame but was dropped at the Cadet 12. The Irish advanced to the 4, where quarterback Johnny Lujack was stopped on a sneak after a one-yard gain. Halfback Bill Gompers ran for the corner on fourth and two, but he was tackled at the 3 and Army took over.

The ball kept changing hands. Army's Arnold Tucker intercepted a pass late in the third quarter and returned it to the Cadet 42, setting up the biggest play of the game. Blanchard blasted around his left and found daylight along the sideline. He appeared headed for a touchdown when Lujack, the only man between Blanchard and six points, stopped him cold after a 21-yard gain. But as hard as both offenses tried, the final score was 0-0. Notre Dame went on to win all of its other games and the national championship. Army, with a 9-0-1 record, was runner-up.

After beating Penn, 34-7, a game later, Army traveled to Philadelphia for a season-ending clash with its rival service academy, Navy. Few people gave Navy a chance, but the Cadets came into the game strained and sprained. Several players were injured, including quarterback Tucker, whose shoulder, knee and ankle were ailing. Blanchard, still nursing his knee, played at less than 200 pounds. "By the time we got to Navy, we were beaten up," Blanchard said.

Nevertheless, Army struck fast and hard. The Cadets scored on a 14-yard run by Davis, a 52-yard sprint by Blanchard and a 26-yard Davis-to-Blanchard pass. At halftime, Army led, 21-6, and Doc finally was looking like his old self again.

"Then we played it cozy, like we were waiting for the final gun to go off, and Navy ran us off the field in the second half," Blanchard said.

The Middies dominated after intermission and scored two touchdowns, although they failed to convert the extra-point attempts. Trailing 21-18, Navy moved to Army's 3-yard line with 90 seconds to play. The Middies were ready to write a major upset and the last, unfitting chapter to the Blanchard-Davis era.

With 100,000 screaming spectators in Philadelphia's Municipal Stadium looking on, Navy plunged toward the goal line twice and was stopped for no gain both times. Navy then was penalized five yards for delay of game. On third down, a pass completion gained three yards to put Navy on the 5, but the clock ran out before the Middies could run a final play. The brave, old Army team escaped with a victory—its 28th consecutive game without a defeat.

Blanchard, despite his injury, still averaged 5.1 yards per rush, caught seven passes for 166 yards, scored 10 touchdowns and finished fourth in the Heisman voting. The winner was Mr. Outside.

"Glenn had the speed and tremendous balance," Blanchard said. "He was so nifty, he just ran by people."

By the time Blanchard finished his West Point days—with 1,666 yards rushing, 38 touchdowns and a bundle of individual honors—he had had his fill of regimented academy life, which he regarded as "a game, one of the things you had to do. I was never very serious about it."

Not surprisingly, he was even less serious about his grades.

"I was at the bottom of the class with Glenn, trying to get by," he said. "Academically, it wasn't a strain. I could do what I wanted to do. I just wasn't interested. I'm more into life the way it is."

With his low scholastic record, Blanchard was given only two options as far as a military career: the infantry or the Army Air Corps. The decision was easy. "I didn't know anything about flying," he said, "but I sure didn't want to walk."

So Blanchard, without any previous inclination to fly, became an Air Force pilot for the next 25 years. But then, everything in Blanchard's life happens that way: naturally, without design. He simply falls into things. He wanted no part of West Point life originally, choosing to attend North Carolina instead. Then the Army drafted him, and because he couldn't stand Clovis, N.M., he went to West Point.

He also wanted to eat well, so he joined the track team and became an outstanding shot putter. He didn't even work that hard to become a three-time consensus All-America, a Heisman Trophy winner, Mr. Inside. "Heck, I was lazy in practice," he admitted. But his abundance of athletic talent overcame his lethargy.

If it hadn't been for the war, Blanchard would have stayed at North Carolina and might have played professional football. Or Doc might have studied medicine.

But because of the war, and because of Clovis, N.M., and because of his poor grades, Blanchard fell into a flying career in which he distinguished himself.

"I was happy with what I was doing (flying)," he said with his customary nonchalance, "so I saw no reason to change. It wasn't a hard choice."

Though Blanchard was committed to Army service, he still was interested in one shot at pro football. He was due 60 days' leave upon his graduation from West Point, and along with Davis and Barney Poole, the Army end, he requested an additional three-month furlough to play in either the National Football League or the All-America Football Conference, which operated from 1946-49. The Pittsburgh Steelers of the NFL and the San Francisco 49ers, then in the AAFC, held Blanchard's draft rights.

"I was going to play for someone who would give me the most money," he said. "We had played for nothing (in college). It would have been nice to make some money."

Secretary of War Robert P. Patterson, however, thought otherwise. He rejected the West Point trio's request, saying that "the War Department cannot favorably consider granting extended leave of absence for engaging in private enterprise . . . any other decision would be inimical to the best interests of the service."

Congressman Abe McGregor Goff of Idaho declared that the three had no more right to make money outside the military than "the lowliest unheralded private. . . . Blanchard, Davis and Poole ought to remember the draftees who faced combat dangers and hardships in Europe and the Pacific while, safe on the Hudson, they were enjoying a military education at public expense."

So, Blanchard's hopes of playing professionally were shot down, although Davis and Poole later played in the NFL (Poole also played in the AAFC) after serving their required three years' duty. Blanchard and Davis did use their two-month leave for profit, however, playing themselves in the movie "Spirit of West Point." The film did not meet with rave reviews.

"No need for lengthy explanations about a film called 'Spirit of West Point,' starring Glenn Davis and Doc Blanchard," a critic wrote in a two-paragraph review for the New York Times. "It is a typical low-budget job which trades on the brilliant reputations of the Army's great football pair. Glenn and Doc show up at West Point, absorb the traditions of the place, get on the team and face the pitfalls —mainly math—of a cadet's career. Intercut with these dramatized experiences are flashbacks to the home life of the two and a generous assortment of news pictures of Army games in which the duo played.

"For those who are nuts about football, these newsreel reminiscenses are worthwhile. And with the juvenile trade, the shots of West Point and the rah-rah atmosphere will likely score. Furthermore, we will say this for the makers: They haven't loaded the story with slush about sweethearts, but rather have kept it in a fairly factual, masculine vein. However, Messrs. Davis and Blanchard—Mr. Inside and Mr. Outside—are no threats when it comes to acting before the camera, and the supporting cast is no great help. It is strictly a teen-ager's drama that is showing on the Victoria's screen."

Blanchard doesn't kid himself about the quality of the movie, but he did enjoy making it.

"It was a fun kind of time," Blanchard said of his brief cinematic career. "Ask Glenn. No, I'll tell you. You could imagine what it would be like for two kids just out of West Point to be in Hollywood with an automobile and a lot of money.

"We were very self-conscious about our acting. We had a drama coach, but he told us we were getting worse by the day. He quit after a week. On a scale of one to

10 (one being perfect), my acting was a 10. I never went to see the damn movie. But I did see it years later on late-late-night TV. I wouldn't watch it again."

Blanchard returned to the kitchen for refills. When he came back, the conversation changed to his three children—two daughters and a son, Tony, who played tight end at North Carolina in the late 1960s—and six grandchildren.

"My family does mean a lot to me," he said. "I was writing my boy when you arrived. We're very family-oriented."

"And our kids think Doc is the greatest," Jody chimed in from the kitchen.

"Jody!" Blanchard called out. "Have you cleaned the bathroom yet?"

"Well, they do."

"Jody!"

Blanchard enjoyed his years in the Air Force, and though he can't remember his runs for Army, he can break down 25 years of Air Force duty into years and even months by the planes he flew—P-51, F-80, F-84, F-94, T-33 (trainer), F-100, F-105, F-4 and C-130.

Flying the latest and fastest jets at speeds of 900 mph "wasn't frightening to me," the retired pilot said. "Chuck Yeager had tested the planes (F-100), so I knew there wasn't any problem."

Except for that day in 1959 over the English village. Blanchard, then operations officer for the 77th Tactical Fighter Squadron at Wethersfield Air Base near London, was approaching the base in his F-100 when, the Associated Press reported, the fire warning light flashed.

Normal procedure would have been "for the pilot to parachute out of the plane," the wire report said. "But Blanchard saw below a Sussex village with children playing in the street and mothers pushing baby carriages. The Air Force said Blanchard realized an abandoned plane could plunge into the village, decided to stay with the blazing craft and made a perfect landing. Firemen extinguished the fire."

An Air Force spokesman said: "Nobody would have blamed Major Blanchard if he (had) ejected himself. He had to choose between life and a very possible unlife. In a split second, his cockpit was filled with smoke. . . . He decided to stick with it. It was one of the finest flying jobs I ever saw."

Blanchard, who was awarded a citation for bravery, played down the incident.

"They've got to say those things to give you a medal," he said. "What happened was the fire light went on, the oil pressure was zero, so I called a guy in the tower and said, 'Do you see any smoke coming out?' And he said, 'Yeah, there's smoke coming out the back end.' The oil line had ruptured, and it was shooting oil on the motor.

"I didn't look down and see all those mothers and kids on the streets of Essex or whatever. I was close to the field and I landed. It was easier to land than parachute. It wasn't that big a deal."

Again, the voice from the kitchen.

"He's very modest."

"Jody, if you're done with the bathroom, you can start on the kitchen."

"That's why I love him."

"Jody!"

Blanchard sighed. The bathrooms and kitchen in the Blanchard house were spotless, certainly in no need of serious cleaning, but he enjoys playing operations officer in his own home. He doesn't walk around with a white glove, however, fingering for dust. He doesn't hold inspection daily. He barks out orders, but he doesn't mean them. What he does, in the presence of company, is attempt to hide the modesty that Jody tries to reveal.

Blanchard wouldn't even begin to know how to brag about himself. For one thing, he's just not that type of person. For another, he can't remember much about his past exploits anyway. He doesn't think in terms of individual accomplishments. He played the game of football effortlessly and expertly as part of a team, just as he later would fly perfect missions into the teeth of the enemy over Southeast Asia.

He was decorated for both football and flying. But in Doc's words—words he lives by, words that best capture this humble man, words that could serve as his epitaph—"It wasn't that big a deal."

During World War II, Blanchard was running over tacklers for Army. During the Korean conflict, he was stationed in Alaska. At 43, he finally found himself at war, in Vietnam. Sent to Thailand in January 1968, he flew 113 missions in the F-105, 84 over North Vietnam. He stayed there for a year.

"In Air Force policy, everyone got one trip over there before anyone went again, so all the pilots were old," he explained. "They just put your name on a list and away you went."

Back home, many U.S. citizens were criticizing the government for the United States' role in the war. Crowds protested the loss of American lives in Southeast Asia, claiming that the United States could neither win nor help win the war and could only lose in the face of international embarrassment.

"There never was any question in my mind whether it was right or wrong being over there," Blanchard said. "It was the national policy, and I supported the policy. That's what I did, and I went."

Blanchard was an honorable soldier, and the military honored him upon his return, awarding him the Distinguished Flying Cross.

"You stay a year and survive, and they've got to give you something," he said in his typical modest way. He made it sound so routine, so unheroic.

"You go over, drop bombs, shoot guns, then come back to the base," he said. "It's all in a day's work."

He was never shot down. "Only the bad ones get shot down," he said, although he admitted that he was not immune to fear. "A guy that is dropping bombs and getting shot at . . . if he isn't scared, he's crazy."

Blanchard approached his flying missions the same way he approached his gridiron contests—calmly and instinctively.

"The military teaches you how to react under pressure," Blanchard said. "If you do things enough times, you don't feel the pressure."

You just climb into the cockpit, hit the runway, and every day, every mission, the game of F-105 roulette continues. How many chances, how many chambers? Is there a bullet, and in which chamber? Point the gun at your head, fly-boy, and pull the trigger. One mission . . . 10 . . . 25 . . . 50 . . . 75 . . . 100 . . . 113. You win, fly-boy. You can go home.

"Who knows whose name is on the golden BB?" Blanchard said philosophically. "It's like athletics. You go and do the best you can and that's all you can do."

After each mission, Blanchard would go back to the officers' barracks and look at family pictures. Across the ocean, his wife would do likewise, then get down on her knees. "Jody said she prayed a lot, and that was the reason I came back," he said.

He returned in 1969, and two years later, Blanchard "woke up one morning and said I'd retire." And that was it. No planning, no hesitation.

"It wasn't a question of getting out of the service to do something else," he explained. "I really hadn't planned to do anything."

But once again he fell into something. Six weeks after retiring from the Air Force he was offered a job as commandant at the New Mexico Military Institute. He stayed two years, decided that was plenty, then retired again, permanently.

He hasn't been doing much since.

"Just cleaning the pool and cutting grass," he said, obviously savoring the leisurely life of retirement. "And I'm still trying to learn how to play golf."

More modesty—he shoots in the 80s. In addition, the College Football Hall of Fame fullback enjoys riding his big Honda motorcycle and watching football on television, though he tires of announcers "telling me what I already know."

Blanchard lives contentedly off his Air Force retirement and "some investments." Too contentedly, perhaps, considering his rotund size, which he does not plan to do anything about.

"I ain't going to jog," he said. "I'm going to clap for the young girls who go by in the morning."

Blanchard's weight always has had a tendency, like his Air Force career, to soar. He weighed 222 pounds his freshman year at North Carolina before Blaik honed him into greatness.

New York sportswriter Tim Cohane wrote a poem teasing Blanchard about his build while simultaneously pointing out the reluctant respect West Point first classmen were forced to give the plebe, who already was a hero. The poem, "At Ease, Mister," hangs in Blanchard's home. It reads, in part:

> The "beast detail" will see to it that Felix won't get fat,
> And sometimes mathematics may have Felix on the mat.
> You have to be a man, my lad, that first year at the Point.
> The commandant's pet cat's your only equal in the joint. . . .
> For it's "Mister Dumbjohn, pass the milk! Don't eat until you're told!"
> And, maybe, you don't get the meat until it's kind of cold.
> But when it's Navy, Notre Dame or Penn on Saturday,
> Oh it's "Thank you, Mister Blanchard! You blocked well on that last play!
> . . ."
> Oh it's "Mister Dumbjohn this and that. Hey Mister, on your toes!"
> But it's "Thank you, Mister Blanchard" when the football whistle blows.
> When the football whistle blows, my lad, when the football whistle blows,
> Oh it's "Thank you, Mister Blanchard" when the football whistle blows.

Cohane co-authored with Blaik "You Have to Pay the Price: The Red Blaik Story." Inside Blanchard's copy, Blaik wrote: "To Doc Blanchard: The best—with respect and affection. Earl Red Blaik (no quotation marks around Red)."

"He (Blaik) was way ahead of his time in everything he did," Blanchard said. "Blaik was a real fundamentalist, extremely intelligent. If the defense stayed in one set, he'd hurt them.

"He had an outstanding coaching staff—Herman Hickman, Andy Gustafson, Stu Holcomb, Bob Woodruff. But Blaik had the players, too. No matter how good a coach you are, you're not going to win without the players. Well, maybe one game."

Blaik was more of a coach to his players than a friend, his former star fullback said. "He's not really an outgoing person, not the kind of guy you get to know very well," Blanchard said. "He's just an old Scot."

Blanchard coached briefly under Blaik in the 1950s, scouting opponents by flying himself to their games and getting in his required flying hours at the same time. He was the junior varsity coach in 1951 when Vince Lombardi was an assistant coach for the varsity team.

"We lived next door to Vince and Marie," he recalled. "He was a funny guy, a crazy noodle-bender. Marie was a fun person, too. Vince was competitive, but I didn't see the greatness in him then. You can say that Doc was not very perceptive in those days."

The near-greats and the greats attended Army football practices. One day, Blaik called his coaches together and introduced them to Gen. Douglas MacArthur.

"A year later," Blanchard said, "MacArthur came back, walked up to all of us—there were eight to 10 coaches—and remembered every one of us by our first and last names. That's something I'll never forget."

Nearly 40 years after being an Army plebe, Blanchard attended a football reunion at West Point. The campus atmosphere had changed drastically.

"It was more strict when I was there," he commented. " 'Look at that,' Blaik said, 'they have girls here every day.' I said, 'Yeah, we had girls here once a week and thought that was enough.' "

Female cadets. Times indeed have changed at West Point. Today's cadets wear civilian clothes on the academy grounds while leaving for or returning from a weekend pass or furlough. Today's cadets are allowed to have visitors more regularly. And today's cadets, Blanchard was shocked to learn, can drink alcohol with their meals off-base (if they are at least 19, the legal drinking age in New York).

"If we got caught drinking," Blanchard remembered, "we'd be put in confinement and not allowed to leave our rooms for nine months. My first year at the academy, we couldn't go home for Christmas. We couldn't even go off the post! You could go to Flirtation Walk, but if you got caught kissing. . . . But you can't expect kids today to be like they were 40 years ago."

Forty years have not changed Blanchard, other than physically. There lives inside him a kid who, even though he is in his 60s, still enjoys a high-speed ride on his motorcycle. "I ride it to where I happen to be going," he said happily.

As the conversation wound down, Doc Blanchard, the happy-go-lucky country boy who rarely did anything by design, offered this summation of his life.

"For the last line of your story," he said, "you could say, 'Life has been good to him, and he's grateful.' "

*Former Army great Doc Blanchard, a little bigger and not quite as strong as during his 1940s playing days, relaxes with his Heisman Trophy at his San Antonio, Tex., home.*

# 6

# Glenn Davis

*He was the white-collar half of Army's dynamic 1940s running tandem. While teammate and friend Doc Blanchard softened up opposing defenses on the inside, the speedy Glenn Davis would make them pay outside. He was poetry in motion. He brought grace and style to an otherwise forceful offensive machine. Glenn Davis ran like the wind and blew away defenses with an elusive agility unmatched in college football.*

# Chapter 6

# The elusive Mr. Outside

When Glenn Davis went to Hollywood to turn his touchdowns into taxable income, he traded glamour for glamour. As Davis later discovered, it was not an equitable exchange.

The origins of that trade-off go back to 1947, when Davis and another unskilled actor, Doc Blanchard, visited Filmland to play themselves in a movie. The two had just completed their educations at West Point, which included three seasons of All-America acclaim and one Heisman Memorial Trophy apiece. Hollywood knew it wasn't getting Olivier and Barrymore but nevertheless agreed to pay Davis and Blanchard each $25,000 and 5 percent of the profits to film "Spirit of West Point." The two second lieutenants made more money on that 60-day furlough wearing pancake makeup then generals who had just led our country through war had made in a year. Rank, it seems, doesn't always have its privileges.

According to the script, Blanchard and Davis met for the first time in an Army scrimmage. Davis shot through a hole in the line and was slammed down with a hard tackle by Blanchard, who said, "Hi, I'm Blanchard." Davis replied, "Hi, I'm Davis." It wasn't exactly "Here's looking at you, kid," but the director shouted, "Print it!"

"That's not the way we really met—it was at practice, and I can't remember how it happened—but 99 percent of the movie was fiction," Davis said.

While Davis was re-enacting this dramatized version of his first 22 years, a real-life accident occurred, altering the course of his next few years.

"Later in the film, Blanchard was to punt to me," he explained. "I was to catch it, fake a reverse, then cut upfield and run for a touchdown. But when I made the cut, I tore the ligament and cartilage in my right knee."

After the knee gave out again while fielding a punt in practice before an all-star game a few weeks later, Davis underwent surgery. The cartilage was removed, but the ligament was left alone. "The doctors didn't do anything to the ligament because, in those days, they couldn't," Davis said.

After three years of military duty, Davis resumed his football career, which had brought him plenty of glamour during his four years at the U.S. Military Academy and, he hoped, would continue to do so in the National Football League. It wasn't the glamour that he craved; he simply loved to play football.

But by the time he showed up for his first season with the Los Angeles Rams, his knee injury and the three-year layoff from football had left him basically a one-legged player. He spent two years with the Rams before retiring. "I was as good a football player as a senior in high school as I was with the Rams," he said.

So, the injury he suffered in 1947 thwarted his pro football ambitions. But he discovered another form of glamour in Los Angeles: Hollywood's high society.

One of the extras on "Spirit of West Point" was Hubie Kerns, a track and field star at Southern California who was married to Elizabeth Taylor's makeup girl. When Davis came home on leave in 1948, Kerns arranged a blind date between Davis, then 23 and a national hero, and Taylor, a 16-year-old whose film career was just starting to blossom.

"Elizabeth was a nice person," Davis said. "Naive. That's hard to say now, but she was. We had a lot of fun together, I think.

"Her mother had a great influence on her. Her mother pushed her children. If she hadn't been so pushy, Elizabeth would have been a happier person.

"We'd go out on dates and her mother would do things like tip off a Hollywood reporter that we'd be at some place. Or she would call Hedda Hopper to say that she had received a telegram from Elizabeth saying that things had heated up between us."

Gossip columnists circulated rumors that Glenn and Liz were engaged, and suddenly the mild-mannered football star was caught up in the Hollywood glitter. "I wasn't engaged to her," Davis insisted years later. "I was in Korea and she was in Italy making a movie when that story came out. We dated for three months, that's all."

When the relationship ended, Davis wasn't crushed. "Not at all," he said. "Elizabeth was a lovely person, a nice person. She had a lot of nice friends. I haven't seen her in 30 years, but I've gotten messages from her from people I know who've seen her at parties. Things like, 'Oh, be sure to say hello to Glenn.'

"I've followed her career, sympathized with all the mistakes she's made. Not in her career, but in her personal life."

In February 1951, when Davis was 26, he made what he now considers a mistake in his own life by marrying actress Terry Moore. Their marriage lasted, for all practical purposes, less time than it took Moore to make a movie or Davis to play a football season.

"It was two dark months of my life," he said, wincing. "I knew I had made a mistake 20 minutes after we were married. I knew it even before, but we had sent out the invitations, the announcement had been made. . . . What do you do, walk out?

"I worked for an oil company, Indian Royalty, in Lubbock, Texas, at the time. I didn't have a title, but I was like assistant to the president. Anyway, Terry and I went on our honeymoon, came back to Lubbock for two weeks, then she left for L.A. to make a movie. She never came back."

They were divorced about a year later. Moore married twice more after Davis, those marriages ending in divorce as well. She dropped from the public eye in the 1960s, then reappeared in 1984 at the age of 55, posing nude in Playboy magazine and authoring the book "The Beauty and the Billionaire," which was based largely on her relationship with Howard Hughes. In her book, Moore said she married Hughes but never divorced him before marrying Davis, which would have made her a bigamist.

Davis doesn't believe that story for a moment.

"That's a crock!" he charged. "She was never married to the guy. They were on a cruise and they had the captain of the yacht marry them, no marriage license or nothing."

Moore contends she and Hughes were married in 1949 aboard a cabin cruiser off San Diego. Hughes, a reclusive billionaire with widespread business interests, including many in Hollywood, died in 1976, and since then dozens of wills have been presented by people laying claim to part of his vast estate. In its pictorial, Playboy referred to Moore as "Hollywood's most public widow" and supported its argument that she and Hughes had been married by pointing out that a cash settlement had been reached between Moore and the Hughes estate.

Lloyd Shearer, who once wrote a movie script for Hughes, views that settlement differently. "Tired of her persistent claims against the Hughes estate, its (the estate's) lawyers settled $390,000, or what one lawyer termed 'nuisance settlement money,' on the actress," he wrote in a 1984 copyrighted Parade magazine article. Shearer also wrote that Moore does not have "a shred of legal evidence" to prove that she and Hughes ever wed.

Albert B. Gerber, who wrote an unauthorized biography on Hughes (weren't they all?) titled "Bashful Billionaire," also attacks Moore's contention that she and Hughes ever were husband and wife. Gerber writes: "To get publicity for themselves or for other personal reasons, many of the young ladies babbled about potential marriages to Hughes. Terry Moore temporized, 'I don't know whether I'll marry him or not. I have to wait until after my own divorce from Glenn Davis is final.'"

Davis, for his part, believes that his ex-wife concocted the Hughes widow scenario strictly for the money. Her book, according to Playboy, brought her a six-figure advance from the publisher, and 10 nude or partially clothed photos in the magazine certainly couldn't hurt book sales.

"I saw the pictures," Davis said, shaking his head in disgust. "I didn't read her book, and I don't want to. She's a kook!"

Davis sipped a cup of coffee. It was a Sunday afternoon in Los Angeles at the Wilshire Country Club, where Davis is a weekend golfer with a five handicap. On television, a playoff battle was developing between golfers Craig Stadler and Lanny Wadkins in the 1985 Bob Hope Desert Classic. Davis glanced at the TV screen, then summarized the Hollywood period of his life.

"The mistake was due in part to my naiveness," he said. "I was the kind of guy who dated one girl all the way through high school and West Point. Doris Hanawalt."

If not for World War II, Davis might have married Doris Hanawalt instead of Terry Moore.

"Doris was from a very religious family that attended the Church of the Brethren in La Verne, California, where I grew up," he explained. "When the war broke out, all three of her brothers were conscientious objectors, and rightfully so. Doris and her brothers spent the war at a Civilian Conservation Corps camp in the mountains. With my being at West Point and all . . . that was the thing that came between us."

Davis was extremely shy as a young man, and nothing much has changed. "There's not enough money in the world to make me speak at a banquet," he said. He also was naive when he ventured into Hollywood, which, if given the chance, swallows up or at least changes those types. Davis lost his naivete at great emotional sacrifice.

"I asked myself at the time," he recalled, "if this kind of life was for me. I said that it was not."

So, Davis left Tinseltown after his football-playing days were over and went to Houston, where he eventually joined an oil-business partnership. "Me and another guy put leases together and basically worked together in the oil exploration business," Davis said.

In 1952, Davis went on another blind date, where he met Harriet Lancaster, the widow of a serviceman killed in World War II. Her son was 7 when she married Davis in April 1953. Glenn and Harriet have been happily married ever since and have a son of their own, Ralph, who was named after Glenn's father and twin brother. Davis went to work for the Los Angeles Times in 1954, and now he and his son both work for the newspaper, Glenn as special events director, a position he has held since 1960, and Ralph in the creative graphics department.

"With my job," Glenn Davis said, "I just go from one event to the other."

Davis' office puts on a number of charity events: Grand Prix auto races, indoor track and field meets, football games, award banquets and, occasionally, rock concerts. The Times sponsored the Los Angeles stop on the Jacksons' 1984 "Victory Tour," which produced $200,000 for the newspaper's charity fund after filling Dodger Stadium six nights. The Times also sponsored the 1984 U.S. Olympic Track and Field Trials, which netted $250,000 for the charity fund. More than $15 million has been raised for the fund over the last 35 years, all of which has gone toward youth-oriented programs in Southern California.

Davis works for the same newspaper that first gave him widespread attention for his athletic talents. That exposure and those talents, which were manifested in one incredible series of plays in a high school football game, landed him in "Ripley's Believe It or Not" while he was still a teen-ager.

It happened when Bonita High School, located 35 miles east of Los Angeles in La Verne, beat South Pasadena High in the 1942 California Interscholastic Federation championship playoffs. On three consecutive downs, Davis threw touchdown passes to receivers (including one to his brother Ralph), but all three plays were nullified by penalties. So finally, with the ball by this time back around midfield, Davis faked a pass on the next play, kept the ball himself and ran it in for a touchdown. That one stood, and the six points counted toward his total of 236 points scored in his senior season. The Bearcats went on to win the CIF championship, and Davis was a unanimous choice as the CIF Player of the Year.

Dave Price, an end on that team and the son of Bonita's coach, John Price, remembers being amazed by Davis' many talents on the football field. "He was the greatest running back of that day and maybe of all time until he hurt his knee," Price said. "Then he wasn't the same runner. He was the most explosive starter, with the most acceleration when he needed it, of any runner I've ever seen. He was . . . a good passer, too."

Glenn was born on December 26, 1924, a few minutes after his twin brother and three years to the day after his sister. Glenn and Ralph were fraternal, not identical, twins. Ralph grew to be an inch taller and 10 pounds heavier than Glenn, who is 5-foot-9½ and weighed 170 pounds during his West Point career.

Glenn and his brother and sister grew up in a home situated in an orange grove in La Verne. In those days, Southern California was a citrus paradise. Davis' father, a bank manager, owned hundreds of orange and lemon trees on about 15 acres of land.

It was a picturesque setting, one that Davis was not anxious to leave. He and his brother had their sights set on Southern Cal, where they planned to attend classes on the Navy's V-12 program, which would put them through school in return for a service commitment upon their graduation.

But instead of joining the Navy, Davis was destined to defeat it. Army Coach Earl (Red) Blaik had a friend who frequently vacationed in Southern California and kept tabs on top high school prospects in the area, and this friend wrote Blaik about Glenn Davis.

Years later, Blaik said that those who saw Davis play in high school "told me he was the best halfback in the United States, including all the college backs."

When West Point showed an interest in Glenn, he was flattered. He admired Army's football program and educational reputation, and he liked the idea of receiving an officer's commission upon graduation when, for all he knew, a war might still be raging. But he agreed to score touchdowns for Army on one condition—that his brother be included in the package. Voila! The Davis twins were on their way east.

"We left high school two months before graduating," Glenn recalled, "to go back and study for exams in order to enter the academy on—I still remember the exact date—July 6, 1943."

On the train trip from California to New York, the twins met Clark Shaughnessy, who had taken Stanford to the 1941 Rose Bowl with some newfangled thing called the T-formation. Shaughnessy told the twins to keep an eye on a big fullback who had begun to make a name for himself at North Carolina. "He's really something," Shaughnessy added. That was the first time Glenn Davis had heard of Doc Blanchard.

Without a doubt, Davis is among the finest—if not *the* finest—natural athletes ever to attend the U.S. Military Academy. He lettered in football, basketball, baseball and track and field, both indoor and outdoor.

Every cadet at the time was required to participate in a 10-event physical fitness test that included chin-ups, sit-ups and the vertical jump, standing broad jump, softball throw and 300-yard run. Before Davis' arrival at West Point, the academy record in the test was 865 points out of a possible 1,000. Davis scored 926½.

Football was Davis' most celebrated sport, but not necessarily his best. He was a major league prospect in baseball as a center fielder. Brooklyn Dodgers General Manager Branch Rickey, who watched Davis play on several occasions while the Dodgers trained in a West Point field house, once offered Davis a blank contract to fill in whatever amount he believed was fair. "He probably knew when he made the offer that I couldn't accept it," Davis said. "He knew I was a cadet and I had four years of service ahead of me." Nevertheless, a dozen other major league teams pursued him as well.

"I turned them down, basically, because I would have been 26 when I started baseball, and that's not too smart," Davis said. "In those days, guys in baseball didn't go to college, so they would have had nearly 10 years' experience on me by the time I got out of the military."

Davis also was a good basketball player at the Point, earning one letter. He competed only sporadically in track because of baseball, but he had the ability to be a world-class sprinter or decathlon man with the right kind of training.

An example of how busy athletics kept Davis was the day in May 1947 when he competed against Navy in two different sports. First he played in the Army-Navy baseball game, collecting two singles, two walks, two runs scored and a stolen base in the Cadets' 8-4 loss. Blanchard then drove Davis to the track meet, the only outdoor meet in which Davis ever competed for Army. He quickly laced on a pair of shoes, then tied the West Point record by winning the 100-yard dash in 9.7 seconds and broke the academy mark by winning the 220-yard dash in 20.9 seconds. Army won that dual meet.

"I could have run 9.4 (in the 100) if I had trained," he said.

The West Point physical education staff, naturally biased but logical in its thinking, was convinced that the United States had never produced a better all-around athlete than Davis.

"There are words to describe how good an athlete Doc Blanchard was," said University of Houston football Coach Bill Yeoman, a plebe linebacker at Army in 1946, Davis' last year of football, "but there aren't words to describe how good Glenn Davis was. He's still the most phenomenal athlete I ever saw."

Generally forgotten among Davis' collegiate accomplishments was his plebe year of 1943, when he wore No. 34 (he changed to 41 the next season), scored eight touchdowns and ranked seventh in the nation in total offense. That also was when Davis, a youthful-looking plebe on the '43 varsity team, earned the nickname "Junior."

Davis ran 82 yards for one of his touchdowns in a 52-0 shutout of Columbia in 1943, but what he remembers most about that year was fumbling three times and falling victim to an embarrassing case of ball pilferage against Notre Dame as Army lost, 26-0.

"I got away on an off-tackle run and went 30 yards when someone wracked my arm, knocking the ball up," he recalled. "(Notre Dame's) Creighton Miller caught it and ran" 34 yards to the Army 5-yard line.

"Later on," he continued, "I took a pitchout, only the ball was behind me, and as I reached back to grab it, Jim White, their tackle, took it out of my hands." That play near the Army goal line set up a Notre Dame touchdown, and a Davis fumble in the fourth quarter led to the Irish's final score.

"Well," Davis said of that game, "you could have imagined how I felt. Afterward, Creighton Miller made it a point to tell me: 'Kid, don't feel too badly about today. You'll win a lot of football games.' I sure respected Miller for doing that."

Miller, of course, was right; Davis and the Cadets would win a lot of games. In fact, as an Army halfback, Davis never lost to Notre Dame again, and after his plebe season, he never lost to any team again.

Davis' toughest challenge from that point on was not in athletics, but academics. Specifically, mathematics.

"Coming from high school to West Point is a big jump," Davis explained. "My brother and I weren't prepared academically, and I played every sport besides."

Bonita High was no scholastic training ground for the academy's rigorous schedule. Davis came off the practice field at 5:45 p.m., and after showering and dressing, he'd return to his room for 30 minutes of study before supper formation.

At 7:15, he was back in his room, prepared to study until "lights out" at 10:30. But he'd frequently fall asleep over his books by 8 p.m., and Dick Walterhouse, his roommate and Army halfback and extra-point specialist, would put him into bed and set the alarm for 4 a.m. Davis would get up and study math until reveille at 5:50. In the classroom, he was groggy from lack of sleep and couldn't concentrate on the math professor's lecture.

By midseason of his plebe year, Davis was receiving special tutoring. While the rest of the Army team was seeing Philadelphia and New York on the evenings after the Pennsylvania and Notre Dame games, Davis was being tutored on math back at the academy. Finally, Blaik excused him from practice so he could study more. In December, he flunked math, and in keeping with academy policy, Davis was expelled from West Point.

A dispirited Davis returned home and enrolled in a four-month math class at the Webb School for Boys, a prep school in Southern California. The Webb course was less advanced than the one at West Point, and it gave him a chance to learn some of the material that a majority of his classmates already had learned at other colleges before transferring to the academy. When he applied for and was granted readmission to West Point in the summer of 1944, he was better qualified to tackle the academy a second time. This time he conquered the math. But why would he put himself through such agony again?

"A certain amount of pride," he said. "I made up my mind I wanted to go to the academy, and I wasn't going to change. And my brother was there."

By the time Davis returned to West Point for another year as a plebe, the big fullback Shaughnessy had spoken about had arrived as well. Soon afterward, Davis and Blanchard were united in the most famous second-string backfield ever assembled.

It may seem odd that such talented players as Davis and Blanchard were assigned to the second team, especially when one can look back and see that they both were named consensus All-Americas that season. But the war created a unique situation. Many young men who were interested in both a commission and a college education wisely chose to let the government pay for both, and so the service academies, notably Army, were inundated with the best football players in the country. Blaik was happy to be blessed with all that talent, but it was difficult for him to allot playing time to all the deserving players. So, he did what any Army officer would do under the circumstances: He platooned. According to rank, Davis and Blanchard were assigned to the second platoon.

The starting backfield, which consisted of first classmen Doug Kenna, Max Minor, Dale Hall and Bobby Dobbs, was a star-studded group in its own right. But it merely represented the appetizer before the main course of Davis and Blanchard was served.

The two usually didn't enter a game until late in the first quarter or at the start of the second quarter, and they rarely stayed in the game for more than 30 minutes. That's about all the time they needed to finish off an opponent.

In the 1944 season opener against North Carolina, a game he can't even remember, Davis scored on touchdown runs of 73 and 37 yards and caught a pass and ran 38 yards for a score as Army won, 46-0. He scored three times apiece against Brown, Villanova, Pennsylvania and Notre Dame, too. In their 59-0 humiliation of Notre Dame, the Cadets scored more points than they had tallied against the Fighting Irish in the previous 15 years combined.

By that time, Davis and Blanchard were drawing a great deal of attention, and newspapermen had a heyday waxing eloquent over the twosome's exploits over the next three years. Sportswriter George Trevor of the New York Sun is credited with naming Blanchard "Mr. Inside" and Davis "Mr. Outside." It also was Trevor who wrote, "Ashes to ashes, dust to dust; if Blanchard doesn't get you, Davis must."

Mr. Outside's reaction to Trevor's clever, enduring epithet: "It was just another nickname to go on you. We had so many great players in 1944 and '45 that . . . none of us thought we were anything special."

As a group, the Cadets were, well, unbeatable. Even Navy, which in 1944 had a team worth its salt, too, paled in comparison. The Army-Navy game that year was shifted from Annapolis to Baltimore's Municipal Stadium to accommodate a larger crowd, and more than 66,000 fans contributed to the sale of war bonds by buying tickets to the game.

Army was leading after three quarters, 9-7, when Davis intercepted a pass at his own 28-yard line and twisted his way back to his 48 before being tackled. Blanchard then pounded his way into the end zone for a 16-7 lead. On the next Army series, Davis iced a 23-7 victory with "The California Special," a play Blaik designed to take advantage of what he called Davis' "unlimited gearshifts." Davis took a quick pitch from quarterback Tom Lombardo and cut outside right end. Davis swung to the sideline and shifted into a succession of rapidly increasing gears, outrunning everyone 50 yards to the end zone.

After the game, Blaik said, "The nation's Number 1 football team has beaten the nation's Number 2 football team." There was no argument. Army had completed its first unbeaten, untied season since 1916 to win the national championship. It was the first of three years that Davis and Blanchard were named consensus All-Americas.

Davis was the nation's leading scorer with 20 touchdowns, and he rushed for 667 yards on 58 carries, giving him a stunning 11.5-yard average. Ohio State's Les Horvath won the Heisman in 1944, but Davis became only the second sophomore to finish second in the Heisman voting. (Notre Dame's Angelo Bertelli was runner-up as a sophomore in 1941.)

While the nation lauded Mr. Outside and Mr. Inside for their derring-do, the celebrated players themselves were unaware of most of the attention. Despite their fame, they were treated much like the other cadets. Academy life has a way of keeping people humble.

"You got up every morning at 5:50, and you're tested every day," Davis said. "You had to test proficiently each week or you didn't play. Even if you flunked military photography and drawing, a fairly easy course, you didn't play Saturday. We had enough to think about just trying to survive.

"Another thing, too. The newspaper didn't drop on your porch every morning. We didn't know much about what was going on in the world."

Davis and Blanchard weren't cut out for academy life, although Blanchard adapted more easily. Doc probably figured, in his good-natured Dixie way, that West Point had been like this for years for some good but unknown reason, that he wasn't going to change it and that he might as well just ride it out as best he could.

Junior, on the other hand, fought the system. Davis didn't mind taking a brace—an academy ritual of snapping to attention with shoulders thrown back, chin tucked, stomach sucked—but he thoroughly disliked telling others to brace.

"When I became a first classman, I didn't dish out the discipline to underclassmen," he said. "I didn't go out and try to look for someone doing wrong. Everyone was giving the plebes a hard enough time as it was, and they could do without me."

On one occasion, the football team was taking a train back to the academy from New York City after the 1946 Navy game. First classman Davis stood up to give his seat to Yeoman, a weary plebe. Yeoman refused, knowing that plebes don't take upperclassmen's seats. "Oh, come on," Davis said, standing up and pushing Yeoman into the seat, "sit down."

Years later, Yeoman still recalls the incident, although he thinks Davis may have made that kind gesture in jest because of some good play the plebe had made in that day's game. Nevertheless, such thoughtfulness was par for the course with Davis, he said.

"He was just a super guy, a warm person," Yeoman said. "He represented the Heisman award in its finest fashion."

Davis wasn't the stuff, however, of which generals are made. He was too kind, too naive, too amused by it all. On room inspections he clowned around, especially if he knew which cadet was inspecting. One day it was Lombardo, his backfield mate but a first classman. Davis and Walterhouse greeted Lombardo with grins.

"Hit the deck for 20 (push-ups)," commanded Lombardo, who was accompanied by another first classman and therefore could not go easy on his younger friends. Davis and Walterhouse, along with a third roommate who wasn't an athlete, obeyed. When they finished, Davis and Walterhouse stood up, still grinning. "Hit the deck for 30," Lombardo ordered. The third roommate threw a nervous glance at Davis and Walterhouse. By the time the push-up count had reached 50, the roomie's look had changed from anxiety to anger. When the count reached 110, he simply looked exhausted. Lombardo finally called off the push-up punishment. The non-athlete, who was on the verge of collapse, didn't speak to his roommates for days.

Army's football team again was invincible in 1945. Barney Poole and Hank Foldberg were the ends, Tex Coulter and Al Nemetz the tackles, John Green and Arthur Gerometta the guards and Ug Fuson the center. Davis and Blanchard now were starters along with Shorty McWilliams, a Mississippi State transfer, and quarterback Arnold Tucker, whose sharp passing made the Black Knights more dangerous than ever.

The Cadets crushed everyone on their schedule. By the fourth quarter of Army's 48-0 victory over Notre Dame, Davis had three touchdowns and Blanchard two. Blaik pulled them from the game and, as the oft-repeated story goes, Davis threw down his helmet in disgust and said to his coach, "Heck, Colonel, I want to play football and you're not giving me a chance."

Davis denies ever making that remark. "I never spoke that way to Colonel Blaik in my life," he said. "We had two teams that were practically equal. We were quite content to let Colonel Blaik run the team."

Davis made the most of his playing time. He duplicated his 11.5-yard rushing average of the year before (this time on 82 carries) and scored 18 touchdowns, including one on an 87-yard run and another on a 77-yard sprint. He went 48 yards and 24 yards for touchdowns as Army defeated Navy, 32-13, to wrap up a second straight perfect season and another national championship.

"I don't think anyone can make that kind of yardage without someone blocking for him," he said of his frequent long runs, which included 27 touchdowns on plays of 37 yards or more in his career. "But when you get past the line of scrimmage, it's your own ability.

"Andy Gustafson, our backfield coach, used to yell at his backs as they ran through the line, 'Cut back, cut back!' I can hear him saying that even now. One of Blaik's favorite plays was to start me off right tackle, to get the defense moving that way, then have me cut back to my left, get to the sideline and try to outrun everyone to the end zone.

"But like I said, out in the open it's just instincts, a straight arm and keep your balance. I had good quickness, but I relied on my speed. I also had a longer stride than most players my size. We had fast players back then, but I'd normally be the fastest guy on the field."

Mr. Outside ran with the wind, free and spirited, like a deer. Mr. Inside ran like an angry wolf, with other wolves attacking his flanks.

"I stood behind Doc in the huddle," Davis recalled. "I'd look at his shins and they were chewed up. I'd look at mine and they were as smooth as a baby's bottom.

"Doc was an absolute bull. His calves at West Point were bigger than my thighs. There wasn't anything he couldn't do. He was an exceptionally good pass receiver, a tremendous defensive player. I can't remember when he didn't kick off over the goal line. And not only could he run over you, he had the speed to go at you, then cut and go around you."

In 1945, Davis was the Heisman runner-up for the second straight year, this time to Blanchard. Together that fall they had scored 223 of Army's 412 points.

Some key losses and an opening-game injury to Blanchard, who sat out two games and played at less than full speed thereafter, meant that the 1946 Army team lacked the manpower to dominate teams as it had the previous two years. McWilliams, who transferred back to Mississippi State, was gone from the '45 backfield, and the strength of the line—Coulter, Green and Nemetz—had left, too. In addition, Army's opponents were stronger than before because the war was over and hundreds of football stars were back in college. Army's dominance had a year left to run—if it could hold on that long.

The Cadets' first big test came in the fourth week of the season when they took a 3-0 record to Michigan. Many sportswriters were predicting Army's first loss since the last game of the '43 season.

Early in the game, Tucker was injured. He stayed in the game, but the bulk of his passing chores fell on Davis, who thus became the focal point of Michigan's defensive attack. Davis, with the weight of West Point on his small shoulders, was primed for his finest hour.

"I didn't think I had that good a game, but as time goes on, things get better," he said.

Michigan scored first to take a 7-0 lead, one of the few times a Davis-Blanchard team ever trailed. The Wolverines and college football fans everywhere were waiting to see how the Black Knights of the Hudson would respond. They had their answer in a wink.

Late in the first quarter, Davis found a hole at right tackle at the Army 43-yard line and shot through. Hearing Gustafson shouting at him in his mind, Davis cut back, but three Wolverines were waiting for him. It takes more than three of anything to tackle a mongoose, though, and Davis escaped their clutches and flew down the sideline. There was one man left to beat, Paul White, who appeared to have Davis trapped along the sideline at the 10. Junior faked toward the middle, and White bit just long enough for Davis to squirm between the defender and the chalk for the touchdown.

Davis had tied the score, but he wasn't through yet. Near the end of the first half, Army faced a third-and-23 situation at the Michigan 31. Tucker took the ball from center and handed it to Davis. He lost control of the ball, but somehow it bounced back into his hands. In one motion he whirled and threw toward substitute end Bob Folsom, the future mayor of Dallas, who made a remarkable diving catch with his feet in the end zone and his body stretched beyond it.

Michigan came out smoking in the second half and tied the score, 13-13, but the Wolverines did not tally again despite several strong threats. Blanchard scored the winning touchdown as Army survived its stiffest challenge in three years, 20-13. Davis ran and passed at will and intercepted two passes. Blaik called it Junior's greatest game.

A week later, Army clobbered Columbia, 48-14. Coach Lou Little of Columbia was asked to analyze the game. "He (Davis) is the best runner I've ever seen," he said, "with all due apologies to others who have played the game."

Little's comments came at a football writers' luncheon in New York. Steve Owen, then coach of the New York Giants of the National Football League, was in attendance and agreed with Little's assessment of Davis.

"How does he compare with Red Grange?" a writer asked Owen.

"He runs lots faster than Grange," Owen responded. "Lots faster. . . . I played with Grange (in the same league). He was one of our greatest backs in the whole country. But this kid has a little edge. Speed and ability to cut. Davis can run right up to you and break a square corner on you. He just flies."

Army was strong in 1946, but Notre Dame was stronger. The Cadets were closing out an era, the Irish launching one. They met November 9 in what was billed the "Game of the Century" at Yankee Stadium before a capacity crowd of 74,000. "If Yankee Stadium had a million seats," Army Athletic Director Biff Jones said at the time, "we would still fill it for this game."

Many of the Notre Dame players, recently returned from the war, were 23 or older. Fullback Jim Mello was 25 and had played for Great Lakes Naval Training Station *against* Notre Dame. Halfback Gerry Cowhig had played with Mello at Notre Dame in 1942. Quarterback Johnny Lujack had scored against Army in 1943.

How does one beat a team with all these great players as well as Emil Sitko, George Connor, Jim Martin, Bill Fischer and Terry Brennan, just to name a few? If you're Army Coach Red Blaik, you sit on the ball and don't try anything daring.

"It was an awful game," Davis said. "We played so conservatively. The game was tightly played. No passing. Three yards and a cloud of dust."

Fortunately for Army, Notre Dame Coach Frank Leahy was equally conservative. The game, which should have been called the "Shame of the Century," ended in a scoreless tie. But Notre Dame came away with the "victory" because the Irish, who allowed only 24 points during an 8-0-1 season, went on to win the national championship. Army, which surrendered 80 points overall, finished second with a 9-0-1 record. The Cadets' final game against Navy persuaded the pollsters to vote for Notre Dame.

"We were favored by seven touchdowns on the betting line," Davis said of his final Army-Navy game. He was exaggerating somewhat, but the game was supposed to be a cakewalk for the Cadets.

For one half, it appeared the bettors were right. Army jumped to a 21-6 lead as Davis threw to Blanchard for a touchdown and Mr. Outside and Mr. Inside each ran one in themselves. Davis also stopped a Middie drive with a leaping, one-handed interception.

Army's offense was not heard from again. Navy seized control of the game and began to narrow the Cadets' lead. Suddenly, Army's edge was only three points, 21-18, but the score could have been tied if Navy had converted its three extra-point attempts. In the closing minutes, the Middies were driving toward another touchdown and a staggering upset, but Army stood tall inside its 5-yard line to stop Navy as time expired. The Black Knights' greatest era was complete: Army never lost a football game with Davis and Blanchard, who had played every minute of their last game, as teammates.

On his third try, Davis won the Heisman Trophy with 792 points. Georgia's Charlie Trippi was second with 435 points, followed by Notre Dame's Lujack (379) and Army's Blanchard (267) and Tucker (257). Davis was named the Associated Press Male Athlete of the Year over such notable competition as boxer Joe Louis, golfer Ben Hogan and baseball greats Stan Musial, Ted Williams and Bob Feller.

Davis' 1946 statistics were less impressive than those from the previous two years, but that was partly because of Blanchard's injury, which allowed defenses to key on Davis. Thus, he averaged 5.8 yards per carry—still a highly respectable mark—which brought his career average *down* to 8.3 yards per carry. That figure still ranks as a major-college record (minimum 300 rushes). In his four-year Army career, Davis rushed for 2,957 yards, passed for 1,172 more and scored 59 touchdowns.

If not for Blanchard, whose presence certainly divided some Heisman voters' opinions about who was the best football player at Army, Davis might have won two Heismans. Or by the same token, if not for Davis, Blanchard might have won two. Undoubtedly, they complemented each other beautifully. "I don't think there was ever a pair like them," Blaik said.

As for speed, natural ability and an innate sense of running with the football, Blaik believes Davis was "as fine as anything you'll see today. And I've seen all of them, going back to Grange."

Was Mr. Outside the best that ever was, the Roy Hobbs of running backs?

"I never think about it," Davis said. "I know it may sound peculiar, but when I played at Army, we never thought who was better, who had the best rushing average, who scored the most touchdowns. Whoever got the credit, no one cared.

"In our day, we didn't brag on ourselves. Today, everybody has to tell you how good they are. Muhammad Ali, who was Cassius Clay back then, changed all that. He told everyone he was the greatest instead of standing on his record. I know it was to hype the gate, but players today have no modesty."

Davis checked the TV screen again. Stadler, off the right side of the fairway, was facing a shot that would require him to hit out of deep grass. Two feet in front of his ball sat a giant tumbleweed. Stadler swung, blasting the ball, some grass and the tumbleweed onto the fairway. Davis smiled. Strength admiring strength.

"Glenn's very strong," Blaik said. "You ever see him hit a golf ball? He whales it."

Davis kept distinguished company at West Point, not only as the academy's best all-around athlete, but also as one of its worst students.

"If you wore a star on your coat when you graduated," he said, "that meant you were in the top 5 percent of the class academically. I know two guys with stars who didn't make general. My friend Hank Emerson, who was right down there with me at the bottom of the class, became a three-star general. Alexander Haig was a classmate of mine, and he wasn't a star student, either.

"But Haig became a four-star general and Secretary of State because he had good sense—well, not always good sense," Davis said, laughing. "I was in 'The Area' with him many times. If you had more than 20 demerits, you had to march at 120 paces a minute for an hour with a rifle on your shoulder. Haig liked to sneak out of the barracks at night and go to Highland Falls. Occasionally he'd get caught. He was a fun-loving guy."

Out of the 1947 West Point graduating class of 310 cadets, Davis ranked 305th, Blanchard 296th. But the number wasn't what concerned Davis. "The best accomplishment of mine," he said, "the thing I'm most proud of, is graduating from West Point."

Unfortunately for Davis, his graduation coincided with a torrent of negative newspaper publicity that came down hard on him, Blanchard and Poole. The three cadets wanted to play professional football after learning that some teams were interested in them. Tony Morabito, owner of the San Francisco 49ers of the All-America Football Conference, offered Davis and Blanchard $140,000 each over three years. "I still have the contract at home," Davis said. It was never signed.

Blanchard, Davis and another Army player went to Maj. Gen. Maxwell D. Taylor, superintendent of the academy, with a proposal. "We told him that if the Army would give us a leave of absence each year to play pro football," Davis said, "we would sign an agreement to stay 20 years in the service. He went to the War Department, then came back and told us we had a deal."

When the media found out about the agreement, columnists and then congressmen fired poisoned darts at the three "slackers" and the War Department. The deal was pulled off the table. Blanchard and Davis signed a film deal instead, made their undistinguished movie, then went their separate ways, Blanchard to flight school, Davis into the infantry.

The press continued its attacks on Davis for the next three years after hearing rumors that he tried to resign his commission several times before his three-year commitment was complete. (In 1949, the Army ruled that West Point graduates could resign their commissions after three years of service rather than four.) When it was learned that Davis had used his leave in 1948 to train with the Los Angeles Rams and even play in an exhibition game, the press increased its assaults. Davis was portrayed as the frivolous soldier, one who on top of everything else was dating Elizabeth Taylor. He became a perfect foil for the fourth estate.

Davis was sent to Korea for one year. "Our job was to secure the 38th parallel," he said. "We weren't in combat, just skirmishes. The war broke out three months after I left. But my memories of Korea are awful, especially the 'honey carts.' Koreans saved human wastes. They'd sell them to the guy who brought around the honey cart, and he'd sell them to the farmer as fertilizer. The odor over there smelled like the devil."

Davis' athletic ability, always his ace in the hole, provided his reassignment papers out of Korea. He and another lieutenant formed a regiment basketball team in Korea that won the Far East Army tournament. This team then went to Fort Dix, N.J., for the Army's worldwide basketball finals. Soon afterward, Davis was assigned to West Point to coach the 1949 plebe team's backfield.

While Davis was back at the academy, another report circulated that he had used Blaik's influence to keep from returning to Korea and that he was leaning on his old coach to get him out of the Army early in order to play for the Rams.

Columnist Robert Ruark was among those who assailed Mr. Outside. "Several of Mr. Davis' former teammates are dead as a result of fulfillment of duty in the current little squabble in Korea. It must seem a touch odd to Mr. Davis, who beat one war as an athlete and seems likely to beat another as an athlete. And he is a professional fighter, too, by education and training. . . . I cannot buy Mr. Davis, the unwilling professional warrior."

Dan Parker of the New York Mirror was among the minority of journalists sympathetic to Davis. "Let's face the issue squarely," Parker wrote. "The Army enrolled Davis for his athletic prowess, not because he looked like a General Grant in the bud. He played his role well and has now put in two years of soldiering. . . . Why doesn't the War Department give the boy his release and let him cash in on the great talent which he gave to West Point in exchange for an education."

The Associated Press reported in December 1947 that a second request by Davis to resign from the service had been denied. But Davis said the reporters who wrote that he was trying to quit the Army early were wrong. "I never asked to resign my commission prematurely," he said. "The only time I put in for my retirement was when I was at Fort Monroe, Virginia, when my three years were up. That's not premature."

Blaik said he can't recall ever talking to Davis about resigning his commission early. Both Blaik and Davis said they believe the negative publicity stemmed back to 1947, when Davis and Blanchard attempted to sign with the 49ers.

"You have to remember, they were encouraged to do it," Blaik said. "There was this oil man in Los Angeles who was close to President Truman. He was putting all kinds of pressure on the President to get Glenn and Doc out of the service. Truman was all for it, so was General Taylor and the War Department, but the press came out vehemently against these two youngsters.

"When the cards were down, the writers were unaware of what was going on and made no effort to find out. It was absolutely unfair. The pressure on Glenn was so great, you can't think in terms of what he thought. As far as I'm concerned, you can't fault either Doc or Glenn."

By the time Davis signed with the Rams in 1950, he was nearly 26 and had not played a full season of football since 1946. But the Rams, realizing the magic of his name, made Davis the team's highest-paid player at $25,000. It was money, as it turned out, that could have been put to better use.

"Laying off three years," Davis said, "it was almost impossible to come back. As a running back, you have to use your legs, and for three years I didn't really train. It's different in the case of Roger Staubach (who served a four-year Navy commitment after college) because he's a quarterback, and it's easier to condition an arm."

Davis' right knee never completely healed after being injured while filming "Spirit of West Point," so his leg was taped from ankle to hip, taking away its flexibility. "It got so that when I ran to my right, I had to cut off my right leg, and you can't fake anyone that way," he said. "Here, I'll show you."

Davis pulled up a pant leg. He flexed the muscles in his right leg, and the knee moved a quarter of an inch out of joint.

"I threw my knee out so many times with the Rams," he said, "it wouldn't swell any more."

Davis played mainly on guts in his two years with Los Angeles. He made the Pro Bowl his rookie season after leading the Rams with a 4.7-yard rushing average, catching 42 passes for 592 yards, scoring seven touchdowns and passing for two more.

Davis was at his best in big games. The Rams and the Chicago Bears, who tied for the National Conference lead at the end of the 1950 regular season, had to meet in a December 17 playoff game. In the first quarter, Davis cut through the line, veered back and raced 63 yards into the end zone. A holding call nullified the touchdown, but that play made Chicago's defense begin looking for the run, which opened things up for quarterback Bob Waterfield, who passed Los Angeles to a 24-14 victory.

On the first play from scrimmage in the 1950 championship game against the Cleveland Browns, Waterfield connected with Davis on an 82-yard pass play for a touchdown. The Browns won the game, however, on Lou Groza's late field goal, 30-28.

Davis' injuries mounted his second year. He pulled muscles, and his Achilles tendon was so sore he "could hardly move," he said. Mr. Outside scored only two touchdowns all year. In the 1951 NFL championship game, he lost six yards on six carries and gained 10 yards on three receptions. The Rams beat the Browns without him, 24-17.

Davis retired and went into the petroleum business full time. But the desire to play football lingered. Against the advice of friends, he sold his oil partnerships in Texas for another shot with the Rams in 1953. It was a struggle in courage and futility. His knee would give out after a hard tackle in practice, but he'd get up, say nothing and limp back to the huddle. He finally called it quits, however, after an exhibition game against the Philadelphia Eagles on September 12, 1953. By then the injuries and the limited use of his right leg had just made it too much trouble to play.

Davis went to work for the Los Angeles Times and, in six years, advanced to his current position as special events director. The modest Heisman winner prefers to work quietly and effectively behind the scenes, having no desire to be a celebrity. Roone Arledge of ABC discovered Davis' shyness back in the 1960s when

*Glenn Davis, one of the major forces behind Army's offensive machines of the mid-1940s, prefers to keep a low profile in his position with the Los Angeles Times.*

he contacted him about being a television commentator for college football broadcasts.

"I told him that wasn't my bag," Davis recalled, "but he made a point of setting up an interview. We set up a noon appointment, but when he didn't show up at noon, I left. I just didn't want to do that interview. Arledge got there at 12:10, and my secretary told him I had gone to lunch. He said to her, 'He must have been pretty hungry.' "

Davis had eaten only a salad for lunch at the Wilshire Country Club. "I'm carrying too much weight," he said. Davis was a chubby 195 pounds in January 1985 but was trying to get down to 180. To help matters, he was giving his body a "free month," meaning no alcohol.

It was getting late in the day. Davis watched Stadler run out of miracle shots off the fairway as Wadkins sank a 20-foot birdie putt on the fifth extra hole to win the Desert Classic. It was time for Junior to get back home, pick up Harriet and get back to the club for a 6:30 p.m. dinner reservation. Davis is a prompt person, perhaps because of his West Point training and the three years he spent in the Army. The regimen has spilled over into his civilian life.

"I get up in the morning, and in 25 minutes I've shaved, showered and gotten ready to go to work," he said. "I'm also a very neat person. I pick up my clothes. You won't see much debris on my desk. Of course, others at work say that's because I don't do much."

Walking out of the country club and into the sunshine, passers-by were not blinded by the reflection off his white loafers because there was none. No more spit shines, soldier?

"I've got one of those electric things," he said. "You just stick your shoes underneath, push a button and it's all done for you. But I do own polish."

★          ★          ★

*Col. Earl (Red) Blaik, now nearly 90 years old, lives in Colorado Springs, Colo. The colonel also has a condominium in Las Vegas, where he was reached for an interview in 1985. He sounded alert and healthy over the telephone. "When you get to my age, you don't think of health," he said. "So, you want to know about Blanchard and Davis.*

*"Doc had a marvelous physique and was extremely fast. He could have played halfback. Did you know that Glenn could kick? He told us that one day and we laughed. He kicked one through from 35 yards, then backed up five yards and kicked it through again. I saw Tucker throw him a pass that he put one hand on and juggled for 10 yards before he pulled it in. Amazing.*

*"I still have the greatest affection for them, as athletes and as men. If the Heisman Trophy winners were all like those two, it would be great for football. You have to be satisfied that when you talked to Doc and Glenn, you talked to the best. When you saw them play, you saw the best.*

*"Who was the best of the two? I never separate them. They were so good, people couldn't believe it."*

# Leon
# Hart

*He was bigger, stronger and faster than most of the ends he competed against. He was a perfect blend of power and finesse. Leon Hart was a major reason why the Fighting Irish were undefeated during his four years at Notre Dame. Whether blocking, rushing a quarterback or catching a pass, he presented major problems for opponents. When the prototype football player was designed, Leon Hart was the model. He was an offensive explosion just waiting to be set off.*

# Chapter 7

# The end
# of the rainbow

Leon Hart is, quite possibly, this nation's biggest conservationist, both in size and in heart. He is trying to save what he believes is a true national resource.

The sport of football.

The autumn game has fallen into the harmful hands of big business, which college and professional football have become, thereby polluting, Hart contends, the natural beauty and very essence of the game his football forefathers wrought, nurtured and watched grow.

The erosion process began, as Hart sees it, with the advent of two-platoon football in the late 1940s. For Hart, the game has decayed ever since. Hart's quest is to remove single-platoon football from the list of extinct species and return it to its roots, when the game was played on a surface you mowed, not sewed.

Hart will fight for his cause as long as there is a glimmer of hope, and he believes there is. He will preach at a moment's notice to anyone who will listen, even if the audience is one, which often is the case.

"There is only one rules change needed to get this game back to where it was," Hart said, "and that is if you leave the game in one quarter, you can't come back until the next quarter. That would get rid of the platoon system.

"What's wrong with the game today is that it's played by specialists who are trained not to make mistakes. When they don't make mistakes, nothing happens. It's a boring game."

A look of disgust crossed Hart's face. He shoved the pipe back into his mouth and hit the gas pedal harder, and the large gray sedan with the "N.D. #1" license plates accelerated through the Michigan countryside.

"Knute Rockne said if they keep changing the rules, they'll drive the little guy out of football," Hart continued. "The 60-minute game benefits the little guy because he has more energy than the big guy. Rockne was right. What's the little guy doing today? He's playing soccer.

"Football games used to be won in the fourth quarter by the best-conditioned team. You can't build stamina playing double platoon. What are you playing, 10 minutes?"

Dairy farms and small houses sitting on blocks dotted the green landscape of the northern tip of Michigan's lower peninsula as Hart whizzed by on the rural highway.

"Free substitution is ruining the game," he roared on, his mind racing as fast as the car's engine. "Notre Dame played Alabama in a bowl game. Alabama used 70 men, Notre Dame 35. What kind of football is that—you have more players than the other side?

"What's wrong with 11 men against 11 men? There's nothing wrong with Carnegie Tech beating Notre Dame once in a while. The way it is now, the worst athlete on the field is the quarterback. What does he do but throw the ball? He doesn't even call the plays.

"So, you're left with a game where the development of players' charisma has ceased. There are no players of charisma anymore—the triple-threat backs, the 60-minute men."

Carnegie Tech now is known as Carnegie-Mellon and hasn't played Notre Dame or big-time football in years. Hart was told that, perhaps, he is living in the past, that the good old days are gone for good, and that film comparisons suggest that old-time football really wasn't any better than the brand of football being played today.

Hart countered with a conversation he had had with Benny Friedman, Michigan's great quarterback of the 1920s.

"Benny told me, 'Leon, they don't know what they don't know,'" Hart said. "It's true. Today's players don't know the game the way it was intended to be played. So they don't know what they're talking about. I've thought a lot about what Benny said. That's a wise old saying."

Another old-timer, not as old as Friedman but older than Hart, had laughingly forewarned the author about Hart's soap-box oratories on football.

"Ask Leon what he thinks about the game today," Larry Kelley had said. "He'll give you an earful."

Kelley and Hart: The only linemen ever to win the Heisman Memorial Trophy in its 50-year existence, Kelley in 1936, Hart in 1949. Both played end, which means that no center, guard or tackle ever has won the Heisman. Kelley and Hart believe none ever will.

"I'd like to see a (interior) lineman win it," Hart said, "but he doesn't have a track to run on. The offensive back has the statistics that you read in the newspaper.

"There's only one way a lineman could win the Heisman, and that's to play both ways. But the game is set up so that can't happen. The offense practices on one side of the field, the defense on the other. And they don't speak (to each other). They watch films separately. I don't think any publicity department can sell a lineman unless he plays both ways. Otherwise, he doesn't have the exposure."

Hart played both ways for Notre Dame in 1949, the year when rules changes made two-platoon football more common than ever before. (The double platoon was abolished four years later before gradually making a complete comeback by 1965.) He continued to play both ways in his early years with the Detroit Lions of the National Football League. He blames the pro game, in part, for the contamination of the college game.

"The pros have become the NPSPCL—the National Push-Shove Pass-Catch League," he said. "They get the biggest guys they can find, who push and shove one another around—blocking is a forgotten art—while others play catch. *That's* the pro influence you hear so much about, but the colleges are trying to do the same thing."

The road's surface changed from pavement to pebbles after Hart turned off the highway onto back roads. It's a 40-minute drive from the Pellston, Mich., airport to Mullett Lake, but only if one knows the tendencies of the Michigan State Police, which Hart obviously does.

"What I'm discussing with you is the nucleus of football's problem, and not the cosmetics that others use," he said, turning down a narrow driveway. "We've got to put stamina back in the game—and that one rules change would do it."

College football's one-man Sierra Club ended his exhortations, at least for the moment. He parked the car in front of the A-frame house on the edge of Mullett Lake, located just below the Straits of Mackinac, which join Lake Michigan and Lake Huron.

Hart opened the car door and stepped out into nature. Red pines, white pines, birches. A lake that stretches north as far as the eye can see.

After inspecting the dock, Hart led the way to the A-frame. He wore a blue polo shirt and walking shorts, which revealed his huge arms and thick, muscular legs. Hart is even more massive now than he was in 1949, when he became the largest man ever to win the Heisman, a distinction he still holds. He was 6-foot-5, 252 pounds then; he weighs 280 now.

But though he is gray, middle-aged and soft in the middle, he moved with the gait of a less-heavy, younger man. The athlete that was Leon Hart still can be sensed today.

"Lois?" he called out, entering the wooden A-frame. Lois Newyahr Hart, his wife since February 17, 1950, was preparing a lunch of cold cuts, potato salad, coleslaw, iced tea and chocolate chip cookies. They had been high school sweethearts in the most storybook of Heisman birthplaces, Turtle Creek, Pa., which, Hart said proudly, is not close to Pittsburgh. Just the opposite. "Pittsburgh is 13 miles *from* Turtle Creek," he said.

Leon and Lois were married his senior year at Notre Dame. They have six children (a girl and five boys), including a son, Kevin, who was a three-year letterman at tight end for the Fighting Irish in the late 1970s. Lois is a tiny woman. Standing next to her husband, Hart to Hart, she is dwarfed.

The A-frame is their second home, a weekend getaway also used for summer vacations. The Harts live in Birmingham, Mich., a Detroit suburb, where Leon has his offices. "Leon Hart Industries" consists of a tire business that manufactures tire-balancing material for trucks, a paint business that specifically produces a rust-control primer, and a third venture—the distribution of a light bulb that lasts 60,000 hours and is guaranteed for four years.

When asked if he was a millionaire, Hart laughed and said: "No, I'm rich in other ways. I have eight grandchildren."

Lois Hart proudly showed off some crochet work. It wasn't hers, though; it was her husband's. Showing that he had aesthetic as well as athletic talent, he was rug-hooking an artist's version of the A-frame. A spot on the living-room wall was reserved for the creation upon its completion.

After lunch, Hart moved onto the deck to take in the early-afternoon sun and a lovely view of Mullett Lake. It was a perfect setting in which to think about his past.

Turtle Creek is a mill town, he said. He remembers a drugstore and a poolroom in the center of town but little else. "You'd like to make it romantic," he said, "but . . . no. However, the people there were the salt of the earth."

Hart inherited his size from his father, a 6-3 plasterworker. Leon's parents divorced when he was 8, and his father died several years after Leon had retired from pro football without ever having enjoyed his only child from that marriage.

"I had no real relationship with my father," Hart said. "He got a seat behind our bench when the Lions played in Pittsburgh. He wanted to see me, but I couldn't do it knowing the devastation it would mean to my mother."

His mother remarried, and Hart was reared by his stepfather, a dollar-an-hour crane repairman in Turtle Creek Valley.

At 14, Hart received his first taste of steel-mill life. He recalled his mother saying: "Son, you go to work in the steel mill, so you'll know what hard work is. Then when you go to college, you'll study harder."

Hart spent two summers in high school working in a steel mill, and that experience, as his mother had predicted, had a positive effect on his academics. He had a B grade average in high school, where mathematics was his strong point, a strength that fit in well with his college major, engineering. He also excelled in athletics, winning 10 letters while playing football, basketball, baseball and track. By his senior year, he had grown to 6-5 and 225 pounds. No steel town would hold this scholar-athlete back.

He visited campuses at Pittsburgh, Tennessee, Pennsylvania, Columbia, Virginia Military Institute and Notre Dame. In most instances, he was interested in seeing the school, not enrolling. "You've got to understand," he said, "to get out of that valley, it was like another world."

But once he saw Notre Dame, the kid from Turtle Creek was sold.

"Notre Dame did a lousy job of recruiting me," he said. "But when you want to go someplace, you go. Have you ever been to Notre Dame? Notre Dame (the school itself) is the best recruiter, not the football."

Other recruits who were less interested in the campus' architecture and ambience than Hart chose Notre Dame for another compelling reason: Frank Leahy.

"He was the greatest man I ever met," Hart said. "I was afraid of him, so was everyone. But we worshiped the ground he walked on."

For the next hour, Hart talked exclusively of Notre Dame football, although it really was a remembrance of Leahy, the self-driven coach who was to the Fighting Irish in the postwar era what Knute Rockne had been in the Roaring '20s.

"Leahy's philosophy of life," Hart said, rising to his feet as if some spiritual force had lifted him and then whispered words in his ear, "was, 'Nothing of everlasting value can be achieved without desire, hard work, loyalty, self-discipline and deprivation.' "

Having spread the Leahy credo for another generation to hear, Hart sat back down. He'll never forget the man—or the deprivation.

"He worked us to death," Hart said. "We gave our blood in practice. . . . We'd get up at 6 a.m. and run around two lakes, St. Mary's and St. Joseph's, about 10 miles all together. Then we'd have breakfast. We'd practice from 9 a.m. to noon and again from 3 to 6 p.m. If you dropped a pass, it was 10 laps."

Or if Leahy got a notion in his head, it was 10 laps.

"I was walking in one day after practice," Hart recalled, "and Leahy said, 'Leon, how do you feel?' I said, 'I feel tired.' He said, 'Take 10 laps.'

"The next day after practice, Leahy said, 'Leon, how do you feel?' I remembered the day before, so I said, 'I feel great.' He said, 'Take 10 laps.'

"The very next day, Leahy said, 'Leon, how do you feel?' I looked at him and said, 'Coach, how do you want me to feel?' He laughed and let me go in."

Notre Dame was overflowing with talent after World War II, a fact that became evident when the Irish held Army, which was riding a 25-game winning streak and had won the national championship the previous two years, to a scoreless tie in 1946. That game also is notable in that four past or future Heisman winners were on the field and in uniform at the same time, though only three played: Doc Blanchard and Glenn Davis for Army and Johnny Lujack for Notre Dame. Hart, a 17-year-old freshman, just missed getting into the game.

"Ernie Zalejski and I were called to the sideline," he said. "If (Arnold) Tucker punted for Army, we were going in. But he kept the ball and ran for a first down. After that, Leahy forgot all about us."

Though the game ended in a tie, it was a victory of sorts for the Irish, who had been clobbered, 59-0 and 48-0, in their last two games against the Cadets. The Irish won their other eight games that year, outscoring their opponents, 271-24, and finished the season as the top-ranked team in the country.

The wartime suspension of the three-year eligibility rule had not yet been lifted in 1946, and Hart earned the first of his four varsity letters as a freshman member of that '46 national championship team. He caught five passes for 107 yards and one touchdown, a modest beginning to be sure, but, coupled with his tough defensive play—a fine example is the crushing blow he delivered on Purdue halfback John Galvin, who was attempting to pass but instead bobbled the ball into the hands of a Notre Dame player who then scampered seven yards into the end zone—it was a good indication of greater things to come.

Notre Dame never lost a game while Leon Hart wore an Irish uniform. The Irish went 36-0-2 and won three national championships during Hart's four years in South Bend, Ind. Of course, Hart was surrounded by a number of outstanding players, including several consensus All-Americas like himself: quarterbacks Lujack and Bob Williams, fullback Emil (Red) Sitko, guard Bill Fischer and tackle George Connor. Tackles Jim Martin and Ziggy Czarobski, guards John Mastrangelo and Marty Wendell and center George Strohmeyer also attained All-America status during Hart's tenure at Notre Dame.

"We were really good," Hart said. "We knew we were going to win. It was just by how much.

"No one was in the condition we were. We had formations we never used—a double-T, two quarterbacks under center. One would get the ball, both would spin out. Only half our team knew what was going on. But we were a hard team to scout because we were so diversified. We had audibles the pros didn't even use.

"But the three biggest things we had going for us were stamina, effort and ability. Leahy would tell us, 'Oh, lads, make the opponents want to sit up in the stands with their parents.' "

Leahy's message obviously got through to his players. The Irish posted a perfect 9-0 record in 1947 and won their second consecutive national title. Hart had nine receptions for 147 yards and three touchdowns. In addition to his pass-catching ability, Hart proved himself to be an outstanding blocker and defensive rusher, and he was named to his first All-America team as a sophomore.

Don Doll, a Southern California letterman in 1944 and 1946-48, remembers those powerhouse teams at Notre Dame, especially the 1947 squad.

"That was the greatest team I played against on any level," Doll said, including in that assessment the pro teams he faced in six years with the Lions, Redskins and Rams. "When you move up (to the pros), you move up with good people. I never saw a club that was better drilled."

Doll hasn't forgotten Leon Hart.

"In one game, I bounced off him twice on the same play," the former Trojan said. "Hart caught a curl pass, and I hit him in the thighs. He knocked me to the ground. The play kept going to where I got another shot at him, and I hit him in the thighs again. Obviously that was the wrong spot because he knocked me down again.

"You see movies of those Notre Dame teams, and Hart and Jim Martin just bulge in their uniforms. Hart's muscles popped out everywhere. What I remember most about him was his size and ability to catch the ball."

Doll weighed 170 pounds at Southern Cal. Imagine him trying to tackle an *end* who outweighed him by more than 80 pounds, an end who, by his senior season, was the largest starter on the team—including the interior linemen.

But Hart was no lummox.

"Leahy told me: 'A big man is clumsy, but a graceful big man is like a gazelle. Work on your coordination,'" Hart said. "But what do you do? I didn't know how to improve my coordination. I already had very fast reactions for a big man. It was God's gift to me that I had coordination and speed."

Not only was Hart bigger, stronger and often faster than the ends he played across from, but he also was meaner.

"Leahy would tell us, 'I want the 11 most savage men to play for me,'" Hart said, "so we growled coming out of the huddle."

The Irish bullied their way over their first nine opponents in 1948, Hart's junior season, before traveling to Los Angeles for a season-ending clash with Southern Cal, which already had lost three games that year. Hart remembers Doll's performance in that game.

"Don Doll kept punting the ball inside our 5," Hart said. "His punting that day almost did us in."

Those punts gave Notre Dame terrible field position for the entire first quarter, but that was not the worst of its problems. The Irish had a severe case of butterfingers, fumbling the ball away six times, including the opening kickoff. But the Irish defense held tough, and the game went into the second quarter with no score.

Early in the second quarter, with Notre Dame at the Southern Cal 45-yard line, quarterback Frank Tripucka faded back to pass. Tripucka spotted Hart open inside the 40 and launched a perfect strike to the big end. Hart hauled it in and immediately was hit high and hard by Jay Roundy of the Trojans. Amazingly, Hart maintained his balance and took off for the goal line. About half a dozen Trojans tried to bring Hart down—some more than once—but the stubborn lineman shook them all off. Hart scored, and thanks to his incredible personal effort, the Irish led, 7-0, at the half.

Tripucka was injured on the last play of the half, and sophomore quarterback Bob Williams took over for the Irish. The third quarter was a defensive struggle, however, and the score still was 7-0 with 15 minutes left to play.

Then the tide turned for the Trojans. Following a Jack Kirby interception of a pass by Williams late in the third quarter, Southern Cal drove down to the Irish 1-yard line. Fullback Bill Martin carried it over from there, and suddenly the game was tied. Martin scored again on a three-yard run with less than 3 minutes left to play, and with the extra point Southern Cal had a 14-7 lead.

But the luck of the Irish had not yet run out. Halfback Bill Gay took the ensuing kickoff at the Notre Dame 1-yard line and raced 87 yards downfield before being tackled by Doll. A pass-interference call in the end zone moved the ball to the 1, setting up a short touchdown plunge by Sitko. Steve Oracko added the extra point, tying the game at 14-14 with 35 seconds left.

Oracko then booted an onside kick and recovered it himself on the Southern Cal 48. There was time left for one last drive to the end zone, but Leahy instructed his team to run out the clock, the same decision that caused a national furor in 1966 when Ara Parseghian told Notre Dame to sit on the ball as time expired in the famous 10-10 game with Michigan State.

"Leahy gave the word to Sitko," Hart recalled, "who then joined the huddle and said: 'The old man says to run out the clock. And if you guys do, I'll never play with you again.'

"We started to move the ball, then called our last timeout. We went to the sideline to see Leahy. He looked at the clock and said, 'Oh my God, I thought we were ahead.' He had forgotten the score. We almost won the game but ran out of time. Afterward, as we were leaving the stadium, there was an earthquake. We thought, 'Oh no, the Lord is mad at us.' "

The earthquake didn't inflict any major damage on the teams or the fans at the game, but the tie with Southern Cal did. It cost the Irish the national championship as unbeaten and untied Michigan was elevated to the top spot. Notre Dame wound up No. 2 in the polls.

Despite that disappointment, Notre Dame still had a 28-game unbeaten string that extended back to December 1, 1945, as the Fighting Irish prepared for the 1949 season. Hart, who had caught 16 passes for 231 yards and four touchdowns as a junior and had impressed sportswriters and fans with his all-around tremendous play, by then was considered one of the top college football players in the country. Los Angeles Times sportswriter Braven Dyer, who could not think of enough good things to say about Hart after the 1948 Notre Dame-Southern Cal tie, once wrote about Hart: "Of all the college ends I've seen since 1919, Hart is the greatest. Without him, Notre Dame never could have escaped defeat that afternoon (against the Trojans)."

Hart had his best year ever as a senior as he led the Irish to nine victories in their first nine games. All that stood between Notre Dame and its third national championship in the last four years was a December 3 game in Dallas against Southern Methodist. The Mustangs, with 1948 Heisman recipient Doak Walker on the bench much of the season, were 5-3-1 entering the contest and appeared to be little match for the mighty Irish—especially without Walker.

But like the year before, the season had a thrilling finish. With Hart playing much of the game at fullback, a position he occasionally played in order to confuse defenses, the Irish stormed out to a 13-0 halftime lead. Southern Methodist made its move in the second half, however, led by halfback Kyle Rote, who looked every bit as good as Walker and scored three touchdowns, the last one tying the game, 20-20, in the fourth quarter.

Notre Dame mounted one last scoring drive and went on top, 27-20. That proved to be the final score as a tough Irish defense, led by Hart's bruising hits on Mustang passers, halted Southern Methodist's final drive of the game.

The Irish had averted a disaster, and they had their third national championship in the postwar years. "You are my greatest team," Leahy said in the locker room after the game. "God bless you every one."

It was a stunning accomplishment, especially considering that the biggest star of those four teams from 1946-49 also was a legitimate student-athlete. Hart graduated in four years with a degree in mechanical engineering and a B average despite the fact that Leahy, for all his sermonizing on values, tried to get his classes changed.

"Leahy used to tell us, 'Lads, you're not to miss practice unless your parents died or you died,'" Hart said. "He wanted to get my afternoon labs changed because I couldn't get to practice some days until very late. But the university wouldn't hear of it. You were at Notre Dame to study."

Leahy bowed to university pressure. He was so consumed by football that it became not only his livelihood, but also his life.

"Leahy lived and breathed football," Hart said. "He wouldn't leave campus. I don't think his family gained from that, or him. I also don't think that kind of devotion is necessary, but to each his own."

Leahy would stop at nothing to win. Against Iowa in 1953, he ordered a Notre Dame player to fake an injury in order to stop the clock at the end of the first half. With time left for one more play, the Irish scored. A similar ploy in the fourth quarter gave Notre Dame time to score a tying touchdown with 6 seconds left. Leahy's tactic was perceived as scandalous. Sportswriters and football fans everywhere wondered what kind of sportsmanship was being taught at Notre Dame. Notre Dame wondered, too.

Leahy established an .864 winning percentage in two years at Boston College and 11 years at Notre Dame, which is second in college football history only to Rockne's .881. But it was not enough to make the Notre Dame administration overlook some of his questionable methods, including his recruiting procedures. Leahy's popularity with school officials decreased in his last few years in South Bend because they were worried that the school's football program had become, of all things, too strong. Leahy—overworked, under fire and suffering from a severe illness—retired after the 1953 season. He died of a variety of ailments in 1973.

But the old coach's memory burned brightly when Notre Dame's 1949 national champions held their 35-year reunion in 1984. Hart was in charge of the event.

"I put on the invitations what Leahy used to say to us about practice, that we were not to miss it unless our parents died or we died," he said. "Out of 75 on that team, 53 showed up. And seven had died.

"We had the reunion at Notre Dame the weekend of the Air Force game (a 21-7 Notre Dame loss). The only cheer Notre Dame got that day was when the '49 team was introduced. It was the only time I've ever heard the Notre Dame student body count down the clock and boo when the game ended."

Dark clouds had formed over Mullett Lake. It began to rain softly.

"This will pass over," Hart promised. "Feel how warm it is. It should be really nice tonight. I'm planning to take the boat out."

Hart went back inside and re-lit his pipe. He sat down on a couch and then was told of an old piece of newsreel footage that showed him dragging four or five tacklers for what seemed like 20 yards before scoring a touchdown. It was an incredible display of strength and determination that left audiences gasping.

"That must have been the 1948 USC game, the tie," Hart guessed. "I caught a pass and ran about 30 yards for a touchdown. But I don't think they (the tacklers) were hanging on me. You carry two guys for five yards, then 10 years later it's four guys for 20 yards. Twenty years later, it's eight guys for 40 yards. Thirty years later, it's the whole team for 100."

Despite Hart's modesty, the fact remains that he was an enormously blessed athlete with the power to run right over opponents.

"Leon was such a big, strong fellow," Judge Gus Cifelli, 48th State District Court, Bloomfield Hills, Mich., said of his teammate at Notre Dame and later with the Lions. "He was bigger than his contemporaries at his position. He was so overwhelming.

"But he had a lot of dedication—he really was a hard worker—and above-average intelligence, which showed in his scholastic work. He learned things quickly on the football field and applied them quickly. Our coach (Leahy) saw that potential, and he pushed Leon every day."

An example was the game against North Carolina at Yankee Stadium in 1949. At halftime the score was 6-6. Leahy burst into the locker room and immediately laid into Hart.

"Leon Hart, Leon Hart," the coach said, "you do not deserve to represent Our Lady. . . .Will someone give Leon 76 cents for meal money and let him start hitchhiking for home right now? I see absolutely no need for his mortal soul.

"Let us now bow our heads and pray to Our Lady for forgiveness, for we have disgraced her terribly."

Notre Dame then disgraced North Carolina, 42-6, as a fired-up Hart led his team's comeback. He directly contributed two points with a crunching blow on Dick Bunting that popped the ball 20 yards backward into the end zone for a safety.

Hart led Irish receivers that year with 19 catches and five touchdowns. Two teammates exceeded his 257 yards in receptions, but Hart was the team's most versatile—as well as most valuable—athlete. He also played fullback, rushing 18 times for 73 yards (4.1 average), returned kickoffs and played superb defense.

Shortly after the 1949 season, Hart was handed a telegram from New York. He read it, then took it to assistant coach John Druze and asked, "What's the Heisman?"

Hart was a decisive winner with 995 points. Charlie (Choo Choo) Justice, North Carolina's great halfback, was a distant second with 272, followed by Southern Methodist's Walker with 229. Both Walker and Justice were hobbled by injuries during the 1949 season.

Hart was the leading vote-getter for the Heisman in every section of the country. "The reason I won was exposure," he explained. "In 1949, the platoon system was coming in, and only two guys at Notre Dame, Martin and myself, stayed on the field the whole time. I also was team co-captain and called the defensive signals.

"It was the first year, too, that partial television came in. The trunk lines were laid across the country, so Notre Dame was on television every week. We were also undefeated (10-0) and national champions. Charlie Justice was a heck of a player, but he didn't have the same exposure. And he was injured when we played North Carolina."

Hart received as much exposure from playing fullback, however, as from his weekly TV appearances. "The only reason I was at fullback was to get defenses to collapse," he said.

And it worked. Defenses, aware of how difficult it was to drag down the huge back, would converge at the middle of the line when they saw Hart get the handoff. But what they saw, they didn't always get.

"We had this one play," Hart said, "where I would plunge into the line. Sitko would line up in my spot at right end. But it would be a fake to me, and Sitko would come around, take the ball and run around the other end, where there was no one to stop him."

Hart was an overwhelming choice as the Associated Press Male Athlete of the Year for 1949. Jackie Robinson, the National League's Most Valuable Player, and Sammy Snead, golf's leading money winner that year, were among the athletes who received fewer votes than Hart.

Hollywood heard about Hart's hulking, handsome features, read his press clippings and brought him west for a 10-day screen test for a part in "Quo Vadis," a movie about Emperor Nero.

"They originally approached me to wrestle the bull," Hart said, "then decided to test me for the lead. I think Buddy Baer, the old boxer, got the part of the bull-wrestler.

"My trouble was remembering the lines and looking at the girl at the same time. They didn't like the way I kissed, either, so they told me to go over in a corner and practice kissing with actress Julie Adams. I brought along a friend, Father Jim Doll, that day. I asked him if he thought it was all right for me to be kissing a girl like that.

"He told me, 'Art for art's sake, Leon.' "

Hart didn't get the part. Eight years later he tested for a television pilot, "Brock Callaghan," which chronicled the adventures of a retired pro football player who becomes a private detective. But Hart wanted 100 percent of the residuals, and someone else got the part. The pilot was shown, but it didn't fly, and that was the end of "Brock Callaghan."

After his collegiate career ended at Notre Dame, Hart played in the East-West Shrine Game in San Francisco. He was a tank on offense as he played his normal end position and some fullback. Cornell's Hillary Chollet connected with Hart on a 66-yard touchdown pass, with Hart running the final 25 yards and knocking over Don Paul of Washington State and Lindy Berry of Texas Christian on his way to the end zone. But on defense, Hart was disappointing. The West team was aware of Hart's hulkish size and strength but found him surprisingly easy to block. Fullback Dick McKissack of Southern Methodist knocked him down several times. Even Eddie LeBaron, the 5-8, 165-pound College of the Pacific quarterback, took Hart off his feet. The East had no trouble winning, though, 28-6.

The Lions drafted Hart as a bonus pick after the 1949 season, but it took considerable haggling before they secured his rights. At that time, three teams from the defunct All-America Football Conference were being absorbed by the NFL, and the owners were unsure about how to apportion the college football talent. Hart became the Lions' property after evidence was presented that he had been contacted in South Bend before the draft and had agreed to play for Detroit.

Thus began Hart's somewhat successful, often stormy eight-year relationship with the Lions. During that time, Detroit won three NFL championships. In 1951, when Hart caught 35 passes for 544 yards and 12 touchdowns and made two interceptions, he was named an all-league end on both offense and defense. It was only his second season in the pros, but it also was his best. After 1951, Hart never dominated the pro game the way he had dominated the college game.

"I think he was a better college player," said Don Doll, Hart's teammate on the Lions from 1950-52. "A lot of people expected more out of him because of the Heisman Trophy. And he was the highest-paid player on the team, or close to it.

"But when you get to a different level, you find athletes who are your equal or better. Leon had other competition in the league at tight end, like Pete Pihos of the Eagles."

Thurman McGraw, a Lions tackle from 1950-54, made a similar observation. "Leon had great ability," he said. "I don't know if he used all of it, because he was so damn great. He could have been better if he had worked harder. That's not unusual with players who are talented like that. With them, it comes so damn easy."

Hart doesn't see it that way. He said much of the reason for his lack of greater success as a professional was that he didn't get along with the Lions' colorful quarterback, Bobby Layne, who played both football and merrymaker with equal aplomb, often one right after the other.

"It's pretty well known that Layne and I weren't the best of friends," Hart said. "I had no admiration for the way he lived or acted. I simply had no admiration for the guy."

Hart said there were two elements on the team—a Southern element and a Northern element. Layne, a Texan who played for the Longhorns as a collegian, represented this alleged Southern faction, while Hart, of course, belonged to the Northern camp. According to Hart and some of his teammates, that geographic split caused some problems.

Gus Cifelli played with Hart at Notre Dame and then with the Lions from 1950-52, when Layne's favorite receivers were Texans like himself: Cloyce Box of West Texas State and Doak Walker, a high school teammate of Layne's in Dallas.

"I don't have the same impression (about Hart's NFL career) as Doll," Cifelli said. "Leon was as great a pro player as he was a college player, within the relationship of the two situations. He would have been known as a greater pro player if the political climate were different.

"Leon would be wide open on passes, screaming for the ball. You could see it on film. But Bobby favored the Southern boys."

As Hart's career as a Lion progressed, he gradually lost favor with his teammates and coaches. A couple of newspaper stories in late October 1957 carried accusations by Detroit coaches and players—who asked that their names not be used—that Hart had been "dogging it." One player complained: "Why should we knock ourselves out 12 games a season when this guy loafs around for all but two or three games a year and gets a lot of money?"

In one story, Hart called attention to a hamstring muscle he tore several days after the Lions' exhibition opener with Cleveland. "Anyone who knows anything at all about a hamstring muscle knows it takes time to heal," he told a reporter. "I've reinjured it three times trying to press myself back into shape to play. That's my biggest mistake. I just haven't been able to go at full speed, and I'm as sorry as anyone else about that."

The following spring, Nick Kerbawy, the Lions' general manager, was quoted in a Detroit newspaper as saying that Hart "definitely is a morale problem as far as the club is concerned. . . . I would put myself in a tight situation with the other players if I signed him (to a 1958 contract)."

Two Detroit coaches, again anonymous, expressed open resentment toward Hart in the same article, and one threatened to resign if Hart showed up at the next training camp.

In April 1958, Hart retired at the young age of 29. He went out with dignity, refusing to throw back the stones that had been cast at him by Lions coaches, players and club officials. "Mr. (Edwin J.) Anderson (the team owner) and I discussed all this controversy business and thrashed out all the hearsay and innuendoes," Hart said simply. "As far as I'm concerned, all the writings are just personal opinions and designed to discredit me."

His experience with the Lions, however, has embittered him, perhaps for life. Years later at his lakefront retreat, Hart seemed hurt that anyone would question his desire to play football. To combat another hamstring injury earlier in his pro career, he had played with the inner tube of a tire—a tractor tire—wrapped around his leg. And he said he never "dogged it."

"The Notre Dame years were the most important of my life," he said. "I'm not enamored with professional sports. . . . I loved to play football, but pro football tore it out of me."

Hart's years with the Lions clearly were not his best or his happiest, be that a result of injuries, disgruntled teammates or whatever. So, don't expect Leon Hart to organize a reunion of any of those Detroit championship teams of the 1950s, as he did with Notre Dame's 1949 team.

"Pro football is not a profession," he said. "As an engineer, the longer you're in it, your value increases. In pro football, the longer you're in it, your value decreases. . . . Pro football is a business, and you're the laborer."

The pro football business is much more profitable these days, but Hart detects only greed and selfishness among the benefiting players. He cites the National Football League Players Association, formed long after Hart retired, which signed a pension package with the NFL with one stipulation: No one who played in the NFL before 1959 would qualify for a pension.

Hart was so angered by that snub that he helped start the National Football League Alumni organization in 1967. Hart said that he had acquired affidavits from two NFL owners who said the original intention of the NFLPA was to extend the pension one year backward each time it was extended one year forward. That proposal, Hart claimed, was scrapped.

"We wound up suing the NFLPA and NFL (in 1972)," Hart said. "The suit was thrown out of court (in 1975) because there was no basis of action.

"The current NFL players turn me off completely."

Still, it's interesting to note that Hart would fight to get pensions—when he doesn't need the money himself—for players of his era, including those Detroit Lions who, in Hart's estimation, contributed to his premature retirement from football. He fought that battle—unsuccessfully, as it turned out—as an act of principle, not forgiveness.

The rain had stopped at Mullett Lake. At his retreat, Hart was far away from those pro football days, far from the media spotlight. He quietly enjoyed the peace and serenity of his home in the country. "Sometimes you're so busy with all the necessary things in life," he said, "that you don't have time for the important things."

And Mullett Lake is important to Hart, almost as important as his family, his work and his alma mater.

"I never even brought the Heisman Trophy home from New York," he said. "I gave it to Notre Dame. I felt the university earned it and the team. The *team* was the national champion."

Hart cherishes those days at Notre Dame, the same way he cherishes the idea of today's youngsters learning to play football the way it originally was meant to be played: 11 men vs. 11 men for 60 minutes.

"If college administrations look at it economically—the economics of playing football with 90 players on scholarship—if the costs keep increasing, that will prompt it (the return of single-platoon football)," Hart said.

This football conservationist's sincere optimism is admirable, but it's hard to believe that there really is much hope for his cause. As college football's ability to produce revenue has grown, so has the need for a school to field the best team it can find. As a result, the two-way player has gone from being an endangered species to an extinct one.

And a lineman winning the Heisman again? It's possible—more so than the return of the single platoon—but don't hold your breath. The voters still pay more attention to running backs and quarterbacks than the other players on the field, simply because they are the most visible.

Leon Hart, for all we know, may very well be the last of a dying breed.

*Leon Hart, a big man for Notre Dame during the late 1940s, now is successful as a businessman in Birmingham, Mich.*

# Dick Kazmaier

*He was dashing, dazzling and remarkable, a pick-your-adjective athlete. Yet he was far from the pride of Old Nassau. Dick Kazmaier was just another Princeton student on a campus that tolerated its athletes. Still, he was special. He captured America's fancy on the football field and then broke its heart by refusing to turn professional. He was as Ivy as the league he represented and, like that league, part of a vanishing breed.*

# Chapter 8

# The last
# Ivy Leaguer

Outside, an early-evening snow dusted the maples, oaks, hemlocks and pines in the quaint, historic town where the Minutemen had turned back the British two centuries before, helping to sound the call to revolution that would sever the 3,400-mile trans-Atlantic umbilical cord between Great Britain and her Colonies.

Inside, Richard W. Kazmaier Jr., a wealthy businessman, and his wife rested on a sofa in their attractive home in Concord, Mass., enjoying glasses of wine in front of a fire.

Across the room, on a bookshelf near the fireplace, a bronzed football player extended a straight arm in the direction of the couple's kitchen. The businessman once ran like that himself, side-stepping and stiff-arming, back when he was the last of a vanishing, or vanished, breed.

Richard W. Kazmaier Jr. is none other than Dashing Dick Kazmaier or Dazzling Dick Kazmaier or Remarkable Richard Kazmaier—numerous adjectives were used to describe this heroic figure from Princeton—the last Ivy Leaguer and the last single-wing player to win the Heisman Memorial Trophy.

Kazmaier is a symbol of another era, and the trophy on the shelf serves as a monument to both the man and his example.

"It was an academically fostered and inspired experience," he said of his Ivy years. "Football just happened to come along nicely."

Princeton never produced a finer football player than Kazmaier, which is a statement that stretches the imagination, considering that Princeton played in the very first college football game, in 1869 against Rutgers in New Brunswick, N.J.

Kazmaier twice was an All-America, once by consensus. He led the country in total offense in his Heisman year of 1951, when Princeton and a few other Ivy football teams were competitive nationally and not members of a "gentleman's club," which is what Ivy League football amounts to today. Kazmaier twice led Princeton into the Top 10 of the major national polls. And he is the only son of Nassau to receive the Heisman.

The Ivy Group, which the league was called at the time, "celebrated" his Heisman accomplishment by de-emphasizing football. The following year, the eight Ivy presidents voted to drop spring football and to ban the participation of Ivy teams in bowl games and Ivy players in all-star games.

The Ivy League arrived in 1954, both in name and with a new attitude that it would cease playing a major-college schedule. Two years later, the league began round-robin scheduling. The Ivies now play at the NCAA Division I-AA level, a notch below the major powers, from whose ranks a Heisman winner is picked each autumn.

Unless there is an unforeseeable change in Ivy policy, Dick Kazmaier will be the last Heisman honoree from that cluster of high-education, high-brow learning institutions.

"Ed Marinaro came as close to winning the Heisman as anyone from an Ivy school since I've played, and as close as anyone will ever come, in my opinion," Kazmaier said of the Cornell fullback who was the Heisman runner-up in 1971. "If Marinaro couldn't have won with his outstanding multiple years, then it's almost an impossibility for an Ivy League athlete to win."

Kazmaier would rather keep it that way than have the Ivy League lower its elevated academic standards in order to achieve higher ratings in athletics. Some universities have chosen that crooked path and paid the price. As an example, Tulane tried to combine academic and athletic excellence but was prompted to the realization that things had gotten out of hand when it became embroiled in a point-shaving and recruiting scandal in 1985. The result was the elimination of men's basketball at Tulane—and national shame.

Oh, Kazmaier might like the Ivy League to bring back spring practice, but "if you take Ivy League football, which is a part of the whole academic environment, and compare it to major-college football today, which in many instances is a separate entity from the rest of the university, then the Ivy League role is preferable," he said.

When Kazmaier was a triple-threat tailback, winning national honors, football was third on his list of priorities. His education came first, followed by the friends he made at Princeton. Those same priorities, in the same order, likely exist for most Ivy League student-athletes today, more than three decades after Kazmaier made his mark. But he suspects, and properly so, that football no longer is third in the minds of numerous major-college athletes.

"College sports are now distorted," he said. "They are heavily focused on the monetary aspects of sports, primarily because of television.

"I've seen television interviews with some of the big names in college football, Bernie Kosar of Miami (Florida) University and Doug Flutie of nearby Boston College. Why are they being interviewed? Because they are television football stars. They make money for their universities. It's a total distortion."

Football was competitive when Kazmaier was in college, but the competition was on the field, not at the negotiating table, where schools bid to get the largest slice of the television pie. Nowadays, a coach's image is established by how well he looks in front of a TV camera as well as a chalkboard.

"When I played football, television was in its infancy," Kazmaier said nostalgically. "It didn't have the influence it has today."

The accent still was on the classroom. The student-athlete was Saturday's hero, not Tuesday night's TV special. On Tuesday night, as well as other weekday nights, he was studying.

Princeton's reaction to its first and only Heisman typified the attitude of the times: The school played down the event.

"I was told in the dean's office that I had won it," Kazmaier said. "There was no press conference, not many interviews that I can remember. They (reporters) would have had a hard time finding me. The university wouldn't give out my whereabouts."

The school's attitude—which would be thought of as unusual or refreshing in more recent times, depending on one's perspective—was that the Heisman was a nice trophy, but it must not interrupt the academic process.

Television is directly responsible for making the Heisman presentations a national event in recent years, complete with Hollywood stars. What do Elliott Gould and Leslie Uggams, two of the hosts of the 1977 Heisman proceedings, know about the wishbone offense and prevent defenses? Doesn't matter. It's show biz football, baby doll.

In Kazmaier's time, the Heisman ceremony was more homey, and the Heisman recipient wasn't a national celebrity. In Kazmaier's case, he wasn't even a campus celebrity.

"I didn't experience that kind of recognition as much as other people on other campuses," he said. "I was into the Princeton environment. I was part of everything that every other student did—socially, academically, athletically."

To help finance his education—Princeton picked up only part of the tab—Kazmaier, a native of Maumee, O., waited on tables and drove a laundry truck. An Ohio sportswriter who visited Princeton to write a feature story on the local boy who had made good found the All-America tailback delivering tuxedos. Some campus hero.

It is not uncommon in the television age of college football to have athletes compensated for campus jobs they haven't fulfilled. Football stars who are paid for cutting grass on the practice field often have no idea where the lawn mower is kept. Basketball players who receive checks for supposedly sweeping the gymnasium have yet to push a broom. So much for the educational experience.

The Ivy League is an anachronism, treating athletes as students, with the latter designation considered more important. At Princeton, Kazmaier was not allowed to slide by. He was not catered to, pampered or protected. His Heisman gave him no more chance to succeed than any other Princeton student. Twice in college, Kazmaier lost his scholarship when his grade-point average slipped beneath the steep minimum. In each instance, he took out interest-bearing loans to continue his education.

"Studying was hard for me all the way through college," he said. "Maumee High School doesn't prepare you to compete against students from big schools in the East and independents who know how to study."

But in academics as well as athletics, Kazmaier found ways to succeed. He received a 1 grade (the maximum score on a scale of 1-7) on his thesis and a 1- on his comprehensive examinations to graduate with departmental honors in psychology.

On November 19, 1951, Kazmaier appeared on the cover of Time magazine. This distinction, rare among college heroes, was a tribute to Kazmaier, but also education.

"Richard William Kazmaier," the Time author wrote, "is already one of the nation's best football players. He is also a reminder, in a somewhat fetid atmosphere that has gathered around the pseudo-amateurs of U.S. sports, that winning football is not the monopoly of huge hired hands taking snap courses in football foundries. In a day when most backfields average 180 pounds, he is a slender 5-11, 171 pounds. He is a senior at a small university (3,000) that does not buy football teams. At Princeton he has a scholarship just as 42 percent of his teammates (and 40 percent of all Princeton undergraduates). He is an above-average student majoring in psychology. He has no intention of using football as a passport to a professional athletic career."

Kazmaier was the last Heisman winner from a school other than a military academy to turn his back on a professional football career. The Chicago Bears, knowing Kazmaier's attitude before the National Football League's college draft, made him their 15th selection anyway. George Halas, the Bears' owner and coach, believed he could convince Kazmaier to change his mind, but Kazmaier had it all worked out logically and wasn't about to budge even when confronted by one as persuasive as Papa Bear.

"One of the reasons I didn't play (in the NFL) was that I had the best experience you could possibly have (in college)," he said. "We (Princeton) ended up on top. I was on top in the sense that I had won every award I could have. What more could I possibly gain?

"Another reason why I turned down the Bears was economics. One of the NFL's top draft choices my senior year was Frank Gifford. He signed with the New York Giants for $7,500 a year, which was a tremendous salary in those days.

"At that time, Harvard business school graduates were making better than $9,000 a year to start. So I thought my chances would be better to start off in business. My dream was to work for J.P. Morgan in New York."

Kazmaier did work for J.P. Morgan between his first and second years of graduate school at Harvard. After serving in the Navy, he launched a business career that eventually led to his first purchase of an entire company—Marksman Products, the maker of slingshots and air guns—in 1969. "Not a very erudite product," he said of Marksman, which he still owns.

In 1970, Kazmaier began working briefly for the Kendall Co., which manufactures hospital and health-care products. Then on May 1, 1975, he formed Kazmaier Associates of Concord, Mass., giving the Boston area, in terms of sports names, a Kaz as well as a Yaz.

Kazmaier Associates is a fast-growing consulting business in the field of sports, recreation and leisure. The company has subsidiaries dealing with the sales, marketing and distribution of various kinds of sports equipment in all 50 states and 11 other countries.

"One of the reasons I went to work for myself," Kazmaier said, "was because I didn't want someone telling me I had to retire at a certain age. I want to play golf and fish more, but I don't want to give up my business. I'll go on with it as long as I'm able to function. The whole thing keeps you going, and positive thinking helps you with illnesses that crop up later in life."

Between 1977 and 1981, Kazmaier had surgery on each knee. "I never had my knees injured in football," he said, "but they say that injuries show up later in age." His knees haven't restricted his mobility, though, and Kazmaier remains the picture of health. Although his hair has turned white, he is reasonably trim for a middle-aged athlete.

He brought refilled glasses of wine for himself and his wife, Patti, put a fresh log on the fire, then checked his watch. "I better call the Colonial Inn for dinner," he said. "Patti, do you want to go?"

His wife said she'd rather not because of a cold she was battling. Kazmaier left the room, made his phone call, then settled back on the sofa while the firelight danced on the bronzed trophy on the shelf.

"I can't say that I'm not glad to have won the Heisman," he said, "but it's not as significant a date in my life as other things, such as my education at Princeton and my family, both of which are more important."

Patti Kazmaier met Dick after he had graduated from Princeton, and she knew nothing about his athletic accomplishments. She knows him mainly as Dick Kazmaier, successful businessman and father, so her attitude is understandable when asked what thoughts cross her mind when she studies the Heisman.

"(Whether) to dust it or not," she said, smiling wryly.

Kazmaier was amused by his wife's comment and grinned. He said the trophy across the living room was his third Heisman. The first he gave to his father, who in turn gave it to Princeton. Kazmaier Jr. asked the Downtown Athletic Club for a second trophy, but it arrived with the hand broken off. He ordered another trophy, the one on the shelf, which cost him $1,000. The Heisman isn't cheap, but it's priceless.

Kazmaier's father had been a football player who captained the University of Toledo team in 1925. Kazmaier Sr. later became an assistant plant superintendent at Libby-Owens Ford in Toledo, while his son was a five-sport letterman at Maumee High School—quarterback on the football team, shortstop on the baseball team, high scorer (23 points per game) on the basketball team, fastest man (10.3 seconds in the 100-yard dash) on the track team and No. 2 man (middle 80s) on the golf team.

Young Kazmaier was approached by 25 colleges, including Columbia, the U.S. Military Academy, Princeton and a number of Midwest schools, including Toledo, just up the road from Maumee. Two Princeton alumni living in Toledo encouraged Kazmaier to attend Old Nassau. One of the men was Henry Dodge, class of 1932, plant manager of Libby-Owens Ford. The other was A. Gilmore Flues, class of 1926, a Toledo lawyer who later became assistant secretary of defense.

"If a man like that is interested in you," Kazmaier Sr. advised his son in regard to Flues, "that's enough."

So, Princeton received one of the top three schoolboy backs in the state of Ohio in 1947. The others were Vic Janowicz of Elyria, the 1950 Heisman winner at Ohio State, and Carmen Cozza of Parma, who later distinguished himself as Yale's football coach.

Still, Princeton welcomed Kazmaier with folded arms. "Fine boy," the university's admissions officer wrote after his first meeting with Kazmaier. "Excellent (high school) record. But too small to play college football."

Kazmaier's thin, 5-foot-11, 155-pound frame was hardly imposing, to be sure. His freshman football season was nothing spectacular—he had better success in basketball that year, when he led the freshman team in scoring—and varsity football Coach Charlie Caldwell was reluctant, at first, to play him.

But three games into the 1949 season, Kazmaier broke off touchdown runs of 43 and 55 yards against Pennsylvania. Although Princeton lost, 14-13, Caldwell realized he had discovered something special in the thin sophomore from Ohio. Kazmaier didn't play full time that year, so worried was Caldwell about his brittle appearance, but he led the Ivy Group in total offense with 1,155 yards. Princeton's 6-3 record was its best since 1939.

"I got by with speed my first year," Kazmaier said. "I became a thinking, good football player as a junior."

Kazmaier also played basketball as a sophomore, although he spent most of his time on the bench. It was not until his junior year, when he played only the last half of the season, that he earned a basketball letter. Kazmaier had the talent to participate in such spring sports as baseball, track and lacrosse, but he decided—at the insistence of his coaches—to devote his springs entirely to studying.

By his junior year, Kazmaier had increased in size to 171 pounds, his top weight in college. "I was light, but not as light as 170 pounds would be today," he said. "We didn't have but three or four players over 200 pounds. People just weren't as big in those days."

Despite Kazmaier's size and Princeton's customary low profile on a national scale, both the player and the team established themselves as heavyweights in 1950. While running the single-wing option to perfection, Kazmaier led the Tigers to a 66-0 drubbing of Williams, a 34-0 defeat of Brown and a 27-0 upset of Cornell. The junior tailback also threw three touchdown passes and ran for another in a 34-28 victory over Rutgers, unleashed 65-yard and 13-yard scoring runs as well as 50-yard and 15-yard TD passes in a 63-26 embarrassment of Harvard, and ran for one touchdown and threw for three more in a satisfying 47-12 triumph over Yale.

Princeton was 8-0 entering its final game against Dartmouth when Hurricane Flora rolled in off the Atlantic. Many schools postponed football games, but Princeton and Dartmouth, for reasons known only to them, decided to play in the face of pouring rain and 75-mph winds that rushed in from the open end of Princeton's Palmer Stadium. "It was colder than hell," Kazmaier recalled.

The tarpaulin blew off the field, which became a sea of mud by kickoff. The referee couldn't put the ball on the field between downs because it would float away, and so he handed it to the centers before each wet, gooey snap.

Both teams elected not to punt for the most part after Kazmaier punted early in the game and the ball flew back over his head. The longest upwind punt of the day was a 15-yarder by Kazmaier, but both teams generally kicked the ball only with the wind at their backs. When moving against the wind, they usually ran the ball on fourth down—even with big yardage to go for a first down, of which there were only nine in the game (six by Princeton).

Though 31,000 people had bought tickets for the game, only 5,000 football die-hards showed up. They were rewarded for their bravery with real honest-to-sod touchdowns—all of which were scored downwind. Dartmouth drew first mud, 7-0. But Kazmaier sloshed 37 yards for a Princeton score that made it 7-6 (a bad center snap foiled the Tigers' extra-point attempt).

Kazmaier later broke loose again, trekking 23 yards through the East Coast's biggest mud pie to the Dartmouth 5-yard line. Fullback Jack Davison carried it across in three tries, Kazmaier scored on the conversion run to give him seven points in a hurricane and Princeton won, 13-7, for its first undefeated season since 1935.

Kazmaier finished the season with 707 yards rushing, 665 yards passing and 15 TD completions and made a number of All-America squads along with Princeton center Redmond Finney and tackle Holland Donan. The Tigers won the Big Three championship (by beating Yale and Harvard) and the Lambert Trophy, which is awarded to the best team in the East. Princeton was ranked No. 6 nationally by the Associated Press and No. 8 by the United Press.

"We were about like a Penn State is today," Kazmaier said. "The best teams in the East back then were Princeton, Penn and Cornell. The Ivy Group wasn't as strong a group as other conferences. But the top two, three Ivy teams were as strong as the top two, three teams in any conference."

However, it is doubtful that Princeton could have played powerhouse teams week in and week out. Even the Tigers' coach admitted as much. "Our schedule is easy, hard, easy, hard," Caldwell said. "In the Big Ten, for example, it's boom, boom, boom! We haven't the depth to stand that."

Caldwell, who died of cancer seven years later, was named the American Football Coaches Association Coach of the Year in 1950. "Charlie was a master technician, a master scholar, a modest, motivational person," Kazmaier said. "Our success was his masterful ability plus a lot of intelligent talent."

Making it all work was Dick Kazmaier, the bright, light, handsome, modest and dynamic "little man with the big stuff," as an AP editor described him.

Kazmaier wasn't the best pure runner or passer or punter in the country, but his all-around skills were blended perfectly in the single wing. He was, in fact, devastating on the option play.

"If I had gone to Michigan or Ohio State, I would have been a (T-formation) quarterback," he said. "If you liked to run, pass, be versatile—take advantage of people—the single wing was made for you. I could run and pass, and I could quick-kick. I averaged 37 yards a punt (actually 36.2), which wasn't stupendous, but it was good in those days. I also punted the ball out of bounds a lot. Charlie was death on punt runbacks.

"The principle of the single wing was power blocking around the ends and tackles. But Charlie made it a passing offense through men in motion and flankers. Every passing play, we started in motion. I'd take the snap facing to the side, take a couple of steps, stop and throw the ball. Literally, the opponent couldn't tell what we were going to do."

Caldwell designed the "42 series" (Kazmaier wore No. 42) left and right to take advantage of Kazmaier's versatility. When it appeared that he would pass, he ran. When it seemed as if he would run, he passed. When defenses were thoroughly confused, he quick-kicked.

"He runs 'light,' with a nice forward lean," Princeton backfield coach Judd Timm said of Kazmaier's ballcarrying style. "If he wants to slow down to pick up a blocker, he just straightens up a bit."

And though he didn't weigh much, Kazmaier wasn't timid.

"I could hit and bounce off; I didn't hesitate going into anybody," he said. "I guess my strengths were leverage, balance and speed. I was fast—the fastest player on the team or close to it. I've seen (1976 Heisman winner) Tony Dorsett on TV. He's not overly big by today's standards, but he runs into crowds without being hurt. It's not how big you are, but how you do it."

Before the 1951 season, Princeton was given little chance in the East. With Kazmaier as the only returning starter on offense and just 15 of 40 lettermen back overall, Princeton was expected to finish below Army, Navy, Cornell and Penn in the East.

The Tigers quickly went to work to prove the prognosticators wrong by hammering New York University in the opener, 54-20. The pollsters yawned. New York is a basketball school, they carped. Just wait until Princeton plays Navy and Penn.

Old Nassau faced Navy one week later, and the Tigers had to deal with sticky, 90-degree weather as well as a tough group of Midshipmen. Behind Kazmaier's two touchdown passes, Princeton jumped out to a 17-0 halftime lead. The heat and humidity began to take their toll on the Tigers in the second half, however, as Navy rallied for 20 points. Kazmaier threw his third TD pass of the day early in the fourth quarter, and Princeton barely hung on to win, 24-20.

Penn was Princeton's third opponent, and the Tigers prevailed again, 13-7, as Kazmaier threw a 31-yard pass to Frank McPhee for the winning touchdown. The pollsters were intrigued by Princeton's feistiness but still unimpressed. A 60-7 bombardment of Lafayette did little to change their minds. The French know nothing about American football, they quipped. Cornell was next up for Princeton, and the undefeated Big Red would be an even bigger test for the Tigers than Navy and Penn, it was forecast.

Certainly this matchup, billed by Allison Danzig of the New York Times as "the game of the day the country over," would decide the Lambert Trophy and bring a national ranking to the surviving team.

But the game delivered much more than that. The greatest football player in Princeton history put on the greatest individual performance in Princeton history and led the Tigers to the greatest victory in Princeton history.

How Dazzling Dick passed that day in Palmer Stadium. How Dashing Dick ran. And oh, how Remarkable Richard was a one-man wrecking crew against the men from high above Cayuga's waters. He was involved in five of the Tigers' touchdowns, including three on passes of 45, 33 and four yards and two on runs of three yards, the second one following a 50-yard sprint on a reverse play. He amassed 360 yards of offense, completing 15 of 17 passes for 236 yards and rushing for another 124 yards. He accounted for 70 percent of Princeton's offense—his total far exceeded that of the entire Cornell backfield—prompting Cornell Coach Lefty James to call him "the greatest back I've ever seen." By the time the final gun sounded, proud Cornell was bruised, bewildered and beaten, 53-15.

Pollsters grabbed the phones, sportswriters searched for words and magazine editors looked for Princeton, N.J., on the map.

Danzig called Kazmaier's dazzling performance "one of the greatest passing exhibitions seen on any gridiron since the introduction of the pass in 1906." And former Boston Globe sports editor Jerry Nason, writing 15 years later, said: "I had observed Cagle and Booth, Blanchard and Davis, the magnificent Clint Frank, Bertelli at his best, Gilmer, Sinkwich, Harmon—but never Grange. Yet Kazmaier of October 27, 1951, stands more sharply etched against the backdrop of time than any. Possibly never in the history of intercollegiate football had one player so conclusively imposed his will upon an outstanding opponent as Kaz did that afternoon."

Kazmaier's football career peaked with the Cornell game, but it didn't end there. In fact, the game of which he is proudest occurred a week later against Brown. Snow and mud took away Princeton's passing game, but Kazmaier sloshed for 262 yards and had touchdown runs of 13 and 61 yards in a 12-0 triumph. "My gosh, Kaz is black and blue all over," Princeton trainer Eddie Zanfrini exclaimed after the game. Zanfrini later was largely responsible for making sure that no Princeton football player ever wore Kazmaier's number (42). Princeton does not officially retire jersey numbers, but thanks to men like Zanfrini, who believe in preserving greatness, No. 42 has remained off limits. The same thing happened— with the same number—when a young basketball player named Bill Bradley left the Princeton campus.

Princeton went on to thrash Harvard, 54-13, and Yale, 27-0, in 1951, thereby wrapping up an unprecedented fifth consecutive Big Three championship.

Kazmaier's final game for Princeton, however, turned into a national controversy. The Tigers beat Dartmouth, 13-0, for a school-record 22nd straight victory, but Kazmaier's head was too fuzzy to remember most of the game.

The slender tailback had just released a 14-yard pass to Leonard Lyons at the visitors' 3-yard line, setting up Old Nassau's first touchdown, when a Dartmouth lineman, George Rambour, crashed into him. Kazmaier was helped off the field with a broken nose and a concussion. Except for a token appearance in the last minute of the game, his college career in a Princeton uniform was over.

Rambour contended that he had leaped in an attempt to knock down the pass and accidentally struck Kazmaier. But Kazmaier's teammates, believing Dartmouth had resorted to illegal tactics to get their leader out of the game, sought revenge. The game turned into a donnybrook as 12 men from both teams had to be helped off the field because of injuries. Dartmouth backup quarterback Jim Miller broke his leg.

Charges and counter-charges were hurled between the two campuses, but Kazmaier to this day refuses to comment on whether his injuries might have been inflicted intentionally.

"Who can prove something like that?" he said. "I've never discussed that kind of thing publicly. I never will."

Princeton was ranked sixth by both national wire-service polls after the season, while the supposed Eastern powers—Army, Navy, Cornell and Penn—finished at 2-7, 2-6-1, 6-3 and 5-4, respectively. Kazmaier led the nation in total offense with 1,827 yards—861 rushing and 966 passing. He averaged 5.8 yards per rush and completed 62.6 percent of his passes, the best accuracy mark in the nation. Over three years and 27 games he collected 4,354 offensive yards and either passed or ran for 54 touchdowns, an average of two per game.

After leading Princeton to its second consecutive perfect season and compiling his own incredible statistics, which were especially remarkable considering that the pass was a relatively minor aspect of the college game at that time, Kazmaier walked away with the Heisman Trophy. He received 1,777 points, the most in Heisman history up to that point. Hank Lauricella of Tennessee was a distant second with 424 points, and Babe Parilli of Kentucky was third with 344.

Kazmaier's career at Princeton ended in the injury-filled Dartmouth game, but his collegiate career was not yet over. In December 1951 he played in the East-West Shrine Game in San Francisco. The East squad, coached by Michigan State's Biggie Munn, primarily used a wing-T offense along with an occasional single-wing setup, but Kazmaier performed admirably in the new formation. He fired a second-quarter touchdown pass as the East edged the West, 15-14.

After the game, East quarterback Al Dorow of Michigan State said that Kazmaier wasn't good enough to start at his school. Kazmaier's reaction to Dorow's publicized put-down hasn't changed in 30-plus years. "I learned long ago not to get into a debate," he said. "That's his opinion, and he's entitled to it."

But could he have started for Michigan State?

"I have no idea," he said. "Two weeks after we beat Cornell my senior year, Cornell beat Michigan, which was runner-up in the Big Ten (the Wolverines actually finished fourth). My junior year, we beat Navy, and Navy upset Army, the Number 1-ranked team in the country at the time. So it's an academic decision."

The Heisman voters were not the only observers enthralled with Kazmaier. He received the Maxwell Award and the Walter Camp Memorial Trophy. He also was voted the Back of the Year by both major wire services and was named the AP Male Athlete of the Year over an illustrious field that included Ben Hogan, Stan Musial, Bob Mathias, Jersey Joe Walcott and Otto Graham.

Kazmaier's football career finished on a high note. But the music in his life didn't begin until he met Patti Hoffmann.

Patti was from Perrysburg, O., just across the Maumee River from Maumee. She was a lifeguard at a local swimming pool the summer after her graduation from high school and Kazmaier's graduation from Princeton.

"Someone said, 'Guess who's at the pool? Dick Kazmaier, the football player,'" Patti recalled, sitting on the sofa and sipping wine. "I said, 'He doesn't look like one.' The next day, my cousin said Dick wanted to meet me. We met through the fence, he asked for a date, and I said no. I had to work early the next day. Then we did go out for a date, a movie.

"My older sister heard that I had gone out with Dick and told me, 'Keep dating him, Patti, until I get home to meet him.' People would tell me, 'My gosh, Patti, you're dating an All-America.' And I'd say, 'Yeah, I guess.'"

On that note, an attraction grew between the big-time football star from Princeton and the small-town lifeguard from Perrysburg.

"Dick's mother called me a young Amazon," Patti said, smiling at her husband. "I was a bit leery when he asked me out. Then I found out this All-America mystique, all the publicity, it just didn't seem to fit the individual."

Said Kazmaier: "Although I had left home and gone off to the big Eastern school, I still had the same values of small town and family that Patti had. She wasn't naive. But she was sweet and cute."

Kazmaier returned to the East to attend Harvard that fall, and the following summer Dick and Patti were married in what constitutes, in terms of time spent together, a whirlwind romance. "It still is," Kazmaier said proudly.

The Heisman winner is as proud of his six daughters as he is of his wife, and he rattled off their birth dates quickly, from memory, beginning with Michele in 1954 and continuing with Kimberley (1955), Susan (1959), Kathy (1961), Patricia (1962) and Kristen (1965). "I have a good numerical, quantitative, analytical mind," he said. In short, he is a nut for relevant numbers.

His own birth date is easy: November 23, 1930. His wedding date is no sweat: June 20, 1953. As for his wife's birth date, he said, "I know it, but it's not publishable," then gave the birth dates of his three granddaughters.

Though he has no sons, his girls all inherited some of his athletic talent.

Michele and Susan participated in track, while Kimberley played basketball and tennis. Kathy was an ice hockey goalie at the University of New Hampshire, and Patricia was a defenseman for the Princeton hockey team. Kristen is an equestrian.

"When we moved to Concord, there was no women's hockey," Patti Kazmaier said. "We had street hockey. When Patricia and Kathy saw that, they got excited. Dick outfitted them, and I didn't know whether to laugh or cry.

"One day, Patricia got hit with a tennis ball—that's what they used in street hockey—and came into the house crying. I thought it was getting too rough for the girls to be playing hockey with boys, and I suggested to Patricia that she ought not play the game anymore. She said, 'No, I want a mask.' "

The Kazmaier women went to a variety of colleges in the Northeast. Michele attended Mt. Holyoke in South Hadley, Mass., while Kathy and Kristen went to New Hampshire. Kimberley, Susan and Patricia, meanwhile, decided to follow in their father's footsteps: They went to Princeton.

"When Princeton first admitted girls," Patti said, "Dick's reaction was: 'What are they doing down there? They don't have the facilities.' When we took Kimberley down to visit the Princeton campus, Dick said, 'There are boys across the hall!' He was shocked."

Dick looked at his wife thoughtfully. "I've mellowed," he said.

The small-town values Dick and Patti learned in Ohio two generations ago are either being overlooked or thought of as obsolete today. That makes it hard on parents who want to instill their children with good values, yet allow them to live their own lives with a minimum of parental interference. A certain amount of adjustment is required, and Kazmaier has found it more difficult to adjust than his wife.

"I tell my daughters we didn't live together before we were married," Patti said. "We talk about everything. You have to deal with change. People are afraid of change."

"I'm inflexible in principles and values," Kazmaier said, "but I'm flexible in how you deal with them. I've changed. I'm still changing. I'm trying to take all the things in the modern world and subscribe them to my daughters.

"If I asked my daughters to live within the principles and values I subscribe to, it would be a difficult process. They're not all living with them now. So I have to wait for the evolution, to where those same values, which I believe are ensconced in them, will rule their lives."

"I don't ask that of them," Patti said. "I want them to be free thinkers and productive human beings. If they want to live with someone, that's their business as long as they're happy and they have a God."

"Those are values and principles," her husband said gently. "We're not saying anything differently."

Patti wasn't satisfied. "You expect more of them," she said, her voice more strained than argumentative. "I might let them go and stand on their own two feet more."

"I love my daughters," he said protectively.

Kazmaier checked his watch again. "We had better go if we're going to make our reservation," he said to his guest. "Patti, you sure you wouldn't like to come?"

*The women in Dick Kazmaier's life include (left to right) daughters Patricia and Susan, wife Patti and daughters Michele, Kathy and Kristen. The youngest member of Kazmaier's family photo is granddaughter Jessica, Michele's daughter. Missing from the photo is Kazmaier's daughter Kimberley.*

She hadn't changed her mind, preferring the warmth of the fire to the chill of approaching winter.

Kazmaier drove his 1979 Cadillac toward town, tracing, in effect, our nation's birth—Paul Revere's famous ride, the courageous Minutemen at the old North Bridge and the shot heard 'round the world. Two centuries later, Concord appears as a living, breathing post card from the files of Currier & Ives. A single white candle is visible in the windows of most homes, a local tradition at Christmastime. Snowflakes flutter down gently. The village atmosphere is so quiet, so peaceful and undisturbed, one must listen hard to hear the first cries of democracy.

The Colonial Inn originally was built in 1716. Over lobster, Kazmaier made a confession. There were two incidents during his undergraduate days at Princeton, he admitted, when he broke away from proper ethics for a student-athlete.

"When I was a freshman," he said, "I got my hair cut at this barber shop where there were betting cards. I would bet on Princeton's varsity (Kazmaier played on the freshman team at the time) to win. I bet only a dollar or two, which was big money for me. I was doing it out of innocence until a friend told me to stop before I got in trouble with the NCAA.

"When I was a senior, some parents in town wanted their sons to have the experience of working with a varsity football player. So the captain of the team and myself spent time with youngsters, showing them how to throw a football, demonstrating proper football techniques. We were getting $25 apiece per visit. Then the athletic director at Princeton called us in and told us we should stop doing this because the NCAA had a rule that you couldn't make money from the sport you were playing.

"I was fortunate," Kazmaier said in retrospect, "that I was always in a place where there was a conscience, an environment where people play by the rules.

Now we have an environment where rules are obviated and ignored.

"I read an editorial recently where 'young athletes should know better.' It had to do with college student-athletes who get themselves into academic and athletic difficulty. But nothing in the editorial was said about the coaches and administrators who help create those difficulties.

"When I was a college freshman, we didn't have drugs. I didn't drink, at least during the season. (Kazmaier told Time in 1951 that he enjoyed a few beers with his friends, "though I get stinko on four.") Many athletes today don't have the benefits I had growing up. They're getting drugs thrust upon them. It's a difficult environment with no easy solutions."

It was getting late. The guest signed for the dinner, and Kazmaier agreed to stop by the inn in the morning for further interviewing on his way to a business meeting.

Over breakfast, Kazmaier mentioned that he makes many speeches as president of the National Football Foundation and Hall of Fame, a position he has held since 1974, and as special adviser to the President's Council on Physical Fitness and Sports. The topic of his talks often pertains to spreading commercialization in amateur athletics, especially that caused by television's growing influence, and the resulting dilemma of maintaining, or restoring, purity in college sports.

"The reason I stay involved with the foundation is because we have a scholar-athlete program," he said, "where the focus is on students of a high caliber, students who are leaders in football and in their communities. I don't know of another group that focuses on scholar-athletes other than academic All-America teams."

He emphasized that the NFFHF is not fighting a lost cause, that college athletics will not necessarily be swept up and carried off in a wave of immorality. Nevertheless, the question remains: When will athletes be students again?

"It's happening in 400 (non-Division I) schools," Kazmaier pointed out. "It's the 70 to 100 (Division I) schools where it's not happening, although I know there are some schools within this group that are trying to do it the right way (without cheating)."

Kazmaier then disclosed that the NFFHF has decided to take action against violations of the student-athlete concept. Beginning in the 21st Century, when its new law takes effect, the foundation will induct no players into its College Football Hall of Fame unless they are college graduates.

This action poses somewhat of a dichotomy because there are already members of this Hall of Fame who did not complete their degrees. Kazmaier, who was inducted in 1966, estimates that 20 to 25 percent of the enshrined players are not college graduates. But his attitude, as well as the foundation's, is better late than never.

"We're sending messages to the colleges," Kazmaier said, "that if you bring kids on campus, make sure they get a degree."

The guest charged the breakfast to his room, as he had done with dinner the night before. Kazmaier said he had to make a phone call and left the table for a few minutes. He returned, shook hands and left for his meeting.

An hour later, when the guest went to the front desk to pay for the meals and a night's lodging, he was told, "Mr. Kazmaier has taken care of it."

Dick Kazmaier, still dazzling after all these years.

# Paul Hornung

*He played football like the devil and then partied even harder. He attacked life and courted the ladies with the same gusto that made him one of the top collegiate and professional football players in the country. Paul Hornung was Notre Dame's Golden Boy and Green Bay's lovable rapscallion. He made hearts throb, bodies ache and faces smile. He brought a flamboyant style to a stodgy profession and carved his own colorful niche in football history.*

# Chapter 9

# A Casanova in cleats

*"I was talking to someone about reincarnation," Paul Hornung was saying. "He asked me whom I'd like to be in my next life. I laughed. 'Are you crazy?' I told him. 'Paul Hornung. It hasn't been too bad so far.' "*

The Golden Boy's hair is silver.

It had to happen eventually. Paul Hornung will be 50 on his next birthday, two days before Christmas, 1985, although the fact that he is a yuletide child would seem an anachronism. It appears, given his hedonistic zest for living, that he was born smack-dab in the middle of Mardi Gras. You can almost picture him grabbing a baby bottle of warm milk laced with Jack Daniel's and crawling off with the cutest little thing in diapers he could find.

As for Christmas, Hornung can live with the connection, even though the bar action was usually slow Christmas nights. But hey, he isn't a Grinch. Hornung has always thought silver bells were nice. He just thought Southern belles were nicer.

Actually, he loved them all—Southern, Northern, Eastern, Western—or as many ladies as he could manage in the time that he had. His motto was, "Never get married in the morning, 'cause you never know who you'll meet that night." And the nights were never long enough.

Life had a golden glow for Hornung back then, but that glow now is a smoldering ember. The good times no longer roll, at least not as fast and out of control. The Golden Boy has found his golden girl: Angela Cerelli Hornung.

Paul Hornung, married? The hunk! Palpitating female hearts from the Golden Gate to Gotham will need to be resuscitated once the word is spread.

Not that Hornung has been hiding the news. He married Angela in 1979, and now he's practically domesticated. He holds hands in public, keeps regular hours and attacks the art galleries with the same vigor with which he once attacked the clubs at night, looking for new conquests. With Max.

The Golden Boy's lifestyle has grayed around the temples, too. Around midnight, when the evening once was young for Hornung, his day is ending and his eyelids get heavy. "When Ted Koppel goes off," he said, "I'm asleep."

Another legend destroyed. Hornung's married. Broadway Joe Namath's married. Where are the playboys of yesteryear? Who's left among the great curfew-breakers if Hornung himself, the master bed-check manipulator, goes beddy-bye before the door flings open and the coach's flashlight is aimed?

"The image is over. The days of screwing around are over," Hornung declared. "Hopefully they are, anyway. I know one thing. I don't want to go back on the streets anymore."

Hornung once moved by streetlight. He and Max. Early to bed and early to rise didn't make either of them healthy, wealthy and wise. They pulled off that hat trick by staying out late and getting home when they could. Both are millionaires today.

Hornung and Max McGee still see each other, though not as frequently as during their hell-raising days in Green Bay. Hornung lives in Louisville, while McGee divides his time between Minneapolis and Phoenix. He is married now, too—another good-times guy off the streets.

"Sometimes Max and me will get together for three, four days in Phoenix to play golf," Hornung said. "We'll have a few drinks, have dinner, then an after-dinner drink. Around 11:30, I'll look at Max, Max looks at me and . . ."

It's time to carouse, for old-times' sake?

". . . it's time to go to sleep," Hornung continued. "I'm not in condition anymore. Everything in life is a habit. I used to have bad habits. Now I have good habits."

Imagine Casanova as a Trappist monk. Picture Valentino as a guru on a mountaintop. Now think of Hornung the homebody, washing dishes and taking out the trash. He has yet to break a dish, although he broke many a heart in his freewheeling past. Whichever his choice of dishes, ceramic or dynamic, it takes practice, practice, practice.

When it came to breaking hearts, Hornung got plenty of practice, as the Miller Lite people recognized when they cast him in one of their celebrity commercials opposite a limousine and a shapely pair of legs. Hornung said he first discovered girls—or did they first discover him?—his junior year at Flaget High School in Louisville, Ky. At Notre Dame, he already was dating starlets and models while his classmates were dating coeds at St. Mary's College for women.

"It was like a three-, four-mile walk from the Notre Dame campus to St. Mary's," he said. "You'd meet your date, catch a bus to the movie, take a bus back to St. Mary's, then walk the three, four miles back to Notre Dame.

"Back in college, to find a girl with a car was better than finding a pretty girl. Finding a pretty girl with a car was like being in heaven."

Leave it to Hornung to move from heaven to paradise.

"I dated older girls, around 28 or 29, who had a car and an apartment," he said. "That made it easier."

Green Bay would prove to be an even greater challenge. "When I got there, Green Bay was the Siberia of sports," he recalled. "I hated Green Bay then."

It took awhile, but he and Max turned Siberia into the Garden of Eden. Hornung arrived in Green Bay in 1957, the same year McGee returned to the Packers after two years in the military. "We had the same m.o.," Hornung said. "We liked to seduce women, we liked to spend money, we liked a good time."

The two musketeers cut a swath through the most delightful assortment of women in Wisconsin and beyond. Tales of their escapades were the talk of Green Bay and the Packers' camp.

"Hornung!" a beleaguered Vince Lombardi bellowed at his star halfback after he had been fined for sneaking in from yet another all-night adventure. "What do you want to be, a football player or a playboy?"

"A playboy!" Hornung bellowed back. He probably was overstating the point because he also once said, "I would rather score a touchdown on any particular day than make love to the prettiest girl in the United States."

He did plenty of both. Between Hornung and McGee, their fines were enough to pay for the Packers' team party at the end of the season. They each were good for about $1,500 a year.

"One of the reasons it cost us so much," Hornung said, "was Lombardi's stubbornness. We'd be at training camp for three weeks at a time without a break. That's inhuman. Then Lombardi would let the married guys go home for a night, while the single guys like Max and me would have to stay in camp.

"When I first heard about that, I went up to Lombardi and told him I wanted the night off, too. He said no. I said: 'Look, you're letting the married guys go home and sleep with their wives. I'm 28, and I've got my needs, too. Now I want a night off or I'm going out anyway.'

"That made Lombardi livid. He said, 'You're not going out.' I said to him, 'What do I have to do to get a night off, get married?' He said, 'That would be the best thing for you.' About that time, I started to laugh. So did Lombardi.

"Well, Max and I sneaked out that night. We got two girls from Green Bay to meet us. Max went back to camp at 6 in the morning, but I stayed at the motel. Then Max called. 'We've been caught,' he said. 'I'm coming to get you.'

"We showed up for a meeting that morning. When Lombardi saw me coming in the door, you could see the Italian rising in him. 'Hornung!' he screamed. 'Hornung! You're . . . you're . . . you're unbelievable!' "

Hornung even made it difficult for Lombardi to sleep. Once at 3 a.m., the phone rang in the Lombardi home. The coach sat up instantly. "Oh, my God," he said, "what's happened to Hornung now?" His wife, Marie, looked at her husband incredulously. "It could be your own son that something has happened to," she said, "and the only thing you think about is Hornung."

Lombardi had a strict team rule: Anyone found drinking *at* a bar counter (as opposed to just drinking *in* a bar) was fined $500. No questions asked.

"Lombardi used to ask me where the good restaurants were around the league," Hornung said. "He really didn't know, so I would give him some names. I told him about the Red Carpet in Chicago.

"The next year we're in Chicago, and I've got this date with this pretty little stewardess. We go to the Red Carpet, but we're told our table isn't quite ready. The restaurant has this small bar with a couch and about four bar stools. I wasn't going to sit on a couch, so we sat at the bar waiting for our table.

"I couldn't have been there a minute when Lombardi and his party walked in. He saw me and screamed: 'Hornung! You're fined $500! You're suspended!' Marie tried to calm him down, but he was out of control.

"Before we played the Bears the next day, he told me, 'Hornung, you're starting, but you better have a good game.' I did and we won.

"The next week . . . Lombardi pulled me aside and said: 'You were right and I was wrong about the Red Carpet. I'm going to cut your fine to $250.'

"I told him, 'No, you cut it down to nothing or you leave it at $500.' He said, 'OK, it's $500,' and he walked off. I wanted him to admit a mistake, but he couldn't do it. His stubbornness wouldn't let him."

Hornung and McGee would wring Lombardi's patience until it was dry, but they occasionally brought out his humor. McGee was fined $500 after he was caught sneaking out of training camp one night. He went out the next night, got caught again and was fined $1,000 by Lombardi. At a team meeting the next day, Lombardi told McGee: "If you go out tonight, it's $1,500. And if you can find someone worth that much money, take me along."

McGee and Hornung were a team within a team. "Max had been married and divorced by the time I met him," Hornung said. "I came from a glamorous college career, but no one knew Max from a load of coal. Max (a Packers receiver) was from White Oak, Texas, and played at Tulane. He isn't good-looking, but girls would fall in love with him because he was honest and had a great personality."

The Golden Boy was good-looking on top of being honest and personable.

"I've always been very honest with girls," he said. "I never promised anyone a rose garden when I was 18 or 28. I didn't ask anything seriously from them, and they didn't expect anything seriously from me in the way of a relationship."

For the most part, all Hornung had to do was snap his fingers. "Oh, yeah," he said. "A lot of women.

"I didn't grow up in a period of promiscuity. In the 1950s, 'scoring' was kissing, and 'making out' was necking. I had to fight for sex.

"I never went for the groupies. I dated a lot of starlets. I don't want to mention any names because that doesn't do any good. I can't remember half their names anyway. But they were as interested in their careers as I was in mine. I showed them a good time. I was charming, but I made sure it never got serious. It was like, 'When I get back into town, I'd like to give you a call.' "

For many years, Hornung made sure that his relationships did not develop to the point of marriage.

"I never wanted to settle down early, for several reasons," Hornung said. "I was always traveling, not just football, but year-round, doing endorsements. It was a rat race.

"The professional athlete's life isn't conducive to marriage anyway. I didn't want to get married until I knew I wasn't going to fool around on the road. I was having too much fun, besides, and didn't want to stop. I never lit long enough to get serious."

When Hornung was young, with gold still in his hair as well as his smile, life seemed to him a giant air balloon that had ascended, and the world was at his feet. Written across the balloon was the philosophy of Bobby Layne: "I'd like to run out of breath and money at the same time." Those were words Hornung thought he could live by.

The balloon ride is over, and Hornung has his feet on the ground these days. He looks back upon a half-century of life with amusement and gratitude. "If I could put anything on my tombstone," he said, "it would be: 'Paul Hornung went through life on a scholarship, and he earned it.' "

The Golden Boy has sat in the lap of luxury ever since he discovered he could market his All-America talent and Southern charm into big dollars. He drove a white Cadillac when he was a Green Bay rookie, and he drives one today. Only Hornung fills the driver's seat more amply these days as his stomach now resembles that of an aging satyr. He stopped smoking a few years ago, he explained, and his weight shot up to 260, or 55 pounds more than his playing weight at Notre Dame. He has dieted off 10 pounds and hopes to lose more.

He drove the Cadillac around Louisville, pointing out a few examples of his growing financial empire. He stopped in front of a vacant warehouse that he and business partner Frank Metts bought and sold for conversion into office space and a restaurant. Hornung next pulled up in front of what once was a Durkee's Foods plant and now is Louisville Edible Oil Products, another Hornung-Metts acquisition. Lenny Lyles, a former Baltimore Colts defensive back, joined Hornung and Metts in another venture, the development of some real estate into a shopping center.

Hornung then wheeled the white Cadillac into the driveway of a Seagram's plant, the liquor company's main distillery in the United States. "We can buy this place for $4 million, then sell three-quarters of it for $5 million," he said before joining Metts, a longtime family friend, on an hour inspection tour of the plant. Afterward, Metts drove off in a Rolls-Royce he had picked up for $85,000 in Monaco, while Hornung headed in the direction of the Audubon Country Club.

"People say to me when they see me in town, 'Paul, when did you move back to Louisville?' " he said. "I tell them, 'I've never left.' Except for school and football, and a year and a half I spent working in New Orleans, I've always lived here. I can't walk down the street in New York and Los Angeles without being stopped. But here, I'm no big deal. No one bothers me. I'll never leave Louisville. This is home."

Hornung is the picture of wealth. "I'm doing pretty good," he said with the smile that could—and often did—disarm entire harems. "I'm vice president of a real-estate trust with assets over $18 million. Besides the properties I own with Frank, I've got interest in a soybean refinery.

"I've only really gotten interested in making money the last four years. A lot of it has to do with settling down and getting serious about the future. I owe a lot of it to Frank, whom my uncle started in business years ago. Frank is a hard worker; no one can outwork him. He lives for this kind of thing. Anyway, my plan is to retire in five years. You can put down that I'm worth more than $4 million."

Some scholarship.

Hornung drove into the country club, where he "fools around" with golf. "If Paul had concentrated on golf," Notre Dame Athletic Director Edward (Moose) Krause said back when Hornung was with the Packers, "he'd be another Arnold Palmer. If he had concentrated on the violin, he'd be another Heifetz. If he had concentrated on his studies, he could have graduated cum laude. Paul can do anything. He was *the* most outstanding prospect I've seen at Notre Dame—in football, basketball and baseball. He's a natural."

Hornung ordered a salad for lunch in the club, then, on second thought, decided to chance his diet by also ordering a bowl of chili. He then dug into his life story.

He is Paul Vernon Hornung, the same as his father. But having the same name was the closest they would ever be as father and son. Young Paul was an only child. When he was a baby, the family moved from Louisville to New York after his father was promoted to vice president of an insurance company.

"My dad was a big, good-looking man who got into a fast crowd and began to drink," he recalled. "He became an alcoholic. My parents separated because of the drinking, and my mom brought me back to Louisville when I was 1. My dad lost his job and came back here, too. After the divorce, he couldn't stop the drinking and basically worked his way down in the company.

"I saw him once a week while I was growing up. He always had the presence of mind to remain sober around me. He never saw me play any sports."

Paul was reared by his mother, Loretta, whom he lovingly describes as a "tough little lady. We used to rent the front room of people's homes to live in. My mom scrimped and saved until she finally got a good job with the government, which she kept for 30 years." Loretta Hornung was the personnel director for the U.S. Army medical depot in Louisville. With the money she made, she was able to afford an apartment for herself and Paul.

At Flaget High, Hornung became the best prep athlete in Kentucky in 1952-53 and was named all-state in football and all-district in basketball. He led the football team to the state championship. He set a tournament record with 32 points in a basketball game. He pitched a no-hitter in baseball, "but I lost, 13-12," he said. He had a strong pitching arm, but he hadn't learned how to harness his power.

Hornung excelled in the classroom, too. Academically, he was ranked in the top 20 in a graduating class of about 250 students. It was his athletic prowess, however, that about three dozen colleges coveted.

The recruiting fight narrowed down to Kentucky and Notre Dame. The Fighting Irish won the battle even though their scouts had never seen Hornung play in person. They recruited him strictly on game films.

But in the final analysis, it was a mother's love that won out. "She was the main reason I went to Notre Dame," he said. "She was a strict Catholic."

Hornung's decision was taken hard by Kentucky football Coach Paul (Bear) Bryant. "He told me years later the reason he left Kentucky (for Texas A&M) was because he couldn't recruit me," Hornung said. The Bear probably was exaggerating; actually, he left Lexington in large part because he was tired of playing second banana to Kentucky basketball Coach Adolph Rupp. But Hornung's choice of Notre Dame did depress Bryant, who had gone so far as to bring Kentucky Gov. Lawrence Wetherby to Paul's home for a visit with his mother.

Religion aside, it would have been hard for Hornung to turn down Frank Leahy, the most influential college coach in the country. "How many other coaches do you know who seconded the nomination of a president?" Hornung asked. "Leahy seconded Eisenhower's in 1956."

Leahy, who retired after the 1953 season, when Paul was a freshman, later came out in support of Hornung as "the finest football player I've ever seen." That's a mouthful coming from a man who had coached George Connor and Leon Hart, and against Glenn Davis and Doc Blanchard. Yet none of these athletes was more versatile than Hornung.

"Paul is one of two players I thought could have played every position," Charlie Callahan, Notre Dame's sports information director at the time, said years later. "The other was Johnny Lujack. But Paul was bigger than Lujack, around 205, and could have played guard and tackle in that time."

The image of the Golden Boy began with the varsity-alumni game, a brutal Notre Dame tradition, in the spring of Hornung's freshman year. He threw three touchdown passes as the varsity won, 49-26.

"Tommy Fitzgerald, a sportswriter from Louisville, gave me the name," he said. "He had come up to South Bend to cover that game. Afterward, he wrote something like, 'Against the backdrop of the Golden Dome, a golden boy emerged today....'"

Despite that strong showing, the quarterback job was taken Hornung's sophomore year. Two seniors, Ralph Guglielmi and Tom Carey, were ahead of him. Coach Terry Brennan, who replaced Leahy in 1954, wanted to play the 6-foot-2 Hornung somewhere, so he asked him what he thought about fullback.

"Fine," said Hornung, who had never played the position before. "Just so I can play."

Brennan sent Hornung over to take part in a blocking drill. Wandering over later, Brennan found Hornung cut about the face. The coach asked if he had learned anything.

"Sure," Hornung said. "You hit them before they hit you."

Brennan never got over that. "I've sung Paul's praises for years," said Brennan, who now is in the investment business in Chicago. "He has had some adverse publicity, but he was nothing but a fine young man. A good guy. He worked as hard in practice as he did in games. He was one of the best athletes who ever played. We used him at safety, quarterback, left halfback and fullback. If you had 11 guys with Hornung's attitude, you'd never lose."

As a sophomore, Hornung backed up fullback Don Schaefer, the team's leading rusher, while playing some quarterback. He rushed 23 times for 159 yards (6.9 average) and completed five of 19 passes for 36 yards. He also played defense for the first time in his life and intercepted three passes, one of which he returned 70 yards before being tackled just shy of the North Carolina goal line.

Brennan remembers that game against the Tar Heels. "Paul broke loose (on the pickoff return) and was tackled from behind," he said. "We always kidded Paul about that."

Hornung wasn't a long-distance runner. He was at his best in short bursts. Irish halfback Aubrey Lewis, a track sprinter who could run 100 yards in 9.8 seconds, provided a good test of that. "Over 40 yards, I'd finish a step behind Aubrey," Hornung said. "Over 100 yards, he'd beat me by about seven yards. But nobody else on the team could beat me at 40."

Notre Dame missed a national championship that year by losing only to Purdue, 27-14. "Lenny Dawson went nuts that day," Hornung recalled. "That was his first big game as a Purdue quarterback."

In addition to winning his first football letter as a sophomore, Hornung earned a monogram in basketball, playing 10 games for the varsity and averaging 6.1 points per game. That was the last year he played basketball for the Irish.

The Irish were national contenders in football again in 1955, Hornung's junior year. Hornung was the regular quarterback and, halfway through the season, was generally considered the nation's best. Dawson and John Brodie of Stanford were better passers, but no college quarterback was a better all-around athlete than Hornung.

Notre Dame shut out its first three opponents, scoring 17 points against Southern Methodist, 19 against Indiana and 14 against Miami of Florida. In those three games, the Golden Boy ran for two touchdowns, passed for three more, kicked a 38-yard field goal and intercepted a pass. The Fighting Irish then took their 3-0 record and No. 1 national ranking to East Lansing, Mich.

"Before the Michigan State game," Hornung said, "Duffy Daugherty, their coach, said I was the toughest player he ever had to defense against." Daugherty did his homework well, however, and the Spartans won, 21-7.

Hornung and Notre Dame defeated Dawson and Purdue, 22-7, then beat Navy, 21-7. "That was the game where I made All-America," he said. "It was either me or George Welsh of Navy, and I had a big day." Hornung scored one touchdown, passed 15 yards for another and intercepted two passes against the Middies. Notre Dame then buried Pennsylvania, 46-14, and North Carolina, 27-7.

Every great player has a signature game, and for Hornung it was the Iowa game his junior year. The Hawkeyes scored with about 10 minutes left to lead, 14-7. Hornung returned the ensuing kickoff 23 yards to the Irish 38-yard line. He then directed a five-play scoring drive on which he completed three of four passes. The last one officially was a 17-yard touchdown throw to halfback Jim Morse in the end zone, but Hornung, under heavy pressure, had retreated to the 40-yard line before releasing the football. He kicked the extra point to make it 14-14.

With less than 5 minutes remaining, Notre Dame got the ball back. Hornung threw a 35-yard pass to Morse that put the Irish at the Hawkeye 9. A 15-yard penalty eventually set them back to the 18, but Hornung calmly kicked a 28-yard field goal with 2:15 to play, and the Irish won, 17-14. Hornung was carried off the field by teammates and fans. "It was a wonderful feeling," he said.

One week later, Hornung passed and ran for 354 yards, the single-game total-offense high of the collegiate season, although Notre Dame lost to Southern Cal, 42-20.

Hornung completed 46 of 103 passes for 743 yards and nine touchdowns in 1955. He also was intercepted 10 times, however, or once in about every 10 attempts. "Paul's got to improve his passing," Brennan said. Hornung rushed for 472 yards (5.1 average) and scored six touchdowns, five extra points and two field goals. On defense, he picked off five passes and recovered two fumbles.

"Back then," he said, "I thought I was the best damn safety who ever played." He was a sure tackler, among the best on the team. "Paul didn't mind sticking his nose in there," Brennan said.

Hornung led the Irish to an 8-2 record as he personally came through in the clutch on 36 third- and fourth-down situations by producing a first down or a touchdown. The Golden Boy finished fourth nationally in total offense with 1,215 yards.

"I won the Heisman as a senior because of my junior year," he said. "No question about it."

That trophy was won under great duress. Almost everyone graduated from the 1955 team. Only a handful of seniors were back, including Hornung and Morse. The bulk of the team was sophomores.

"Before the season, we were picked fifth in the country," Hornung recalled. "We weren't that good. In fact, I knew it was going to be a tough season, but I didn't think it was going to be that bad!"

Southern Methodist scored in the waning moments of the opener to win, 19-13. Notre Dame rebounded against Indiana, 20-6, but that was only a lull in the storm. The Irish lost their next five games, including three consecutive weeks at home. Wherever he was, Knute Rockne must have been covering his face with his hands.

Purdue handled the Irish, 28-14, before Michigan State crushed them, 47-14, and Oklahoma embarrassed them, 40-0. The Sooners game was nationally televised. On one play Oklahoma's All-America linebacker, Jerry Tubbs, met Hornung at the line and drove him completely off the television screen.

"We were running the split-T," Hornung said, "which was basically a quarterback option system, and the first thing you did was hit Hornung. I got hit every play whether I had the ball or not."

Notre Dame, in 1956, was a football team named Hornung. He ran, passed, punted, kicked off, kicked placements, caught passes, returned punts and kickoffs and played defense. To stop Notre Dame, you stopped Hornung.

The Golden Boy, even in defeat, was never more heroic. After the fourth week of the season, when he made a touchdown-saving tackle against Michigan State, he played with a dislocated left thumb. He dislocated the right thumb with three games to go.

Navy continued the assault against the Irish with a 33-7 victory. Pittsburgh was only slightly more kind, 26-13. Notre Dame was clearly overmatched. No Gipper speeches could have saved this team, even if the Gipper had made them himself.

The situation upset Hornung, but he wasn't torn with grief. That's not his personality. He was doing the best he could week after week, and if it wasn't enough, why sweat it?

"I hear athletes say," Hornung said after gulping down his bowl of chili at the Audubon Country Club, "that they only care about their performances if the team wins. That's the lyingest fallacy in sports. If a guy scores six touchdowns and rushes for 200 yards, then says he doesn't care about his stats because the team lost, that's b.s. You're paid by your performance. Even in college. You're on scholarship, which means you're getting a $25,000 education for free.

"If I scored five touchdowns and we lost, I still felt good. I wanted to win, too. But if you have a great day, did your best, you can't feel bad."

But if Hornung played badly and the team lost, no one else had the right to feel worse then he did, in Hornung's opinion. "I fumbled four (actually three) times against the Bears (in 1959) and we lost," he said. "When I got back to the locker room, one of my teammates was crying. I wanted to punch him in the mouth. I lost the game and he's crying. They had to get me away from him."

Angelo Bertelli, who became Notre Dame's first Heisman winner in 1943, witnessed the '56 season and the terrible hardship Hornung was under. "He'd go back to pass," Bertelli said, "and either have to hurry his throw off-balance or run with it. Most of the time, he ran."

Because it was too painful for Hornung to handle center snaps with two disjointed thumbs, the Golden Boy moved from quarterback to left halfback and fullback for the last four games of the season. But despite his injuries, he scored every point as Notre Dame defeated North Carolina, 21-14, in his last home game for the Fighting Irish. Hornung rushed for all three touchdowns, the last one coming with 1:16 left in the game, and kicked three extra points to lead the Irish to only their second victory of the year.

Notre Dame was demolished by Iowa, 48-8, a week later but came back to give heavily favored Southern Cal a tough time before bowing, 28-20. In his final appearance for the Irish, Hornung kept Notre Dame in the game with a 95-yard kickoff return for a touchdown and his only three pass receptions in college.

The Irish nose-dived from 8-2 to 2-8 in the span of 12 months. Sportswriter Red

Smith wrote of that team: "(They) overwhelmed two opponents, underwhelmed eight and whelmed none." It was the worst season in Notre Dame history up to that point. Well, the school didn't win a game in its first football season, 1887, but Captain Henry Luhn's boys played only one game. The team had no coach that year and was known as the Notre Dame Catholics.

Other 1956 humiliations: 130 points were the fewest a Notre Dame team had scored since 1939, and 289 points were the most it has ever surrendered. It certainly wasn't the kind of team that could have been expected to produce a Heisman Memorial Trophy winner.

"I had stopped talking about the Heisman after the second game," Hornung said.

The 1956 Heisman candidates constituted one of the best fields ever assembled. The voters had a difficult selection to make among Jim Brown of Syracuse, Jim Parker of Ohio State, Ron Kramer and Terry Barr of Michigan, Jon Arnett of Southern Cal, Tommy McDonald and Jerry Tubbs of Oklahoma, Johnny Majors of Tennessee, John David Crow of Texas A&M (then a junior), Clarence Peaks of Michigan State, Kenny Ploen of Iowa, Dawson and Brodie. Most of those players were consensus All-Americas in 1956. Hornung wasn't, making that the only time a Heisman winner did not earn consensus All-America honors the year he won the Heisman.

Hornung moved a finger down that list. "All-Pro, All-Pro, All-Pro, All-Pro, All-Pro, All-Pro, All-Pro, All-Pro," he said beside the names of Hornung, Crow, Brown, Kramer, Dawson, Brodie, Parker and Arnett.

"You've got the player of all time in Brown," he said, "the prototype of the tight end in Kramer and possibly the best lineman ever in Parker."

What were Hornung's selling points against such impressive opposition? "As a passer, I was fair," he said, "but as a runner I excelled. No quarterback in the country could run with the football as well as I could."

Hornung had the statistics: 917 yards passing (59 of 111), 420 yards rushing (4.5 average), 559 yards in punt and kickoff returns (including a school-record 496 yards on kickoff returns), 59 yards on two interception returns and 26 yards on three pass receptions. That adds up to 1,981 yards, 1,337 of which gave him a second-place finish among the nation's total offense leaders. He came through 31 times on third and fourth down. He played 50 minutes per game, accounted for more than half of Notre Dame's scoring, intercepted two passes, broke up seven more and made 55 tackles. No one could blame Hornung for Notre Dame's horrible season.

On a December afternoon that year, Hornung found an athletic department student aide waiting for him outside his classroom. "Follow me. You're wanted in the athletic department," the aide said without elaboration. Hornung followed him across campus to Callahan's office. Without looking up from his desk, Callahan handed the phone to Hornung and said, "Here, tell your mother you just won the Heisman Trophy."

Classy.

A shocked Hornung not only had won the Heisman, but he also had become the only player from a losing team ever to receive college football's most prestigious award. Jay Berwanger of the University of Chicago, the first Heisman winner in 1935, played on a non-winning team that was 4-4. But 2-8, that's *really* losing.

"I think I got a sympathy vote," Hornung said. "Jimmy Cannon, the great sportswriter, showed me a poll a few years later where I was the most publicized college football player of the 1950s. It helps to be a Notre Dame quarterback. If you were a quarterback back then, you went to Notre Dame."

There are two schools of thought on why Hornung won: A divided camp in Norman, Okla., and the Notre Dame mystique.

Joe Doyle, then sports editor of the South Bend Tribune, voted for McDonald, not Hornung. "Paul had more raw talent than anyone who ever played, but Oklahoma had beaten Notre Dame that year, 40-0," Doyle explained. "Right after I sent in my ballot, the Oklahoma sports information director sent out a wire that the Oklahoma coaches felt Tubbs was their best player. This split the Oklahoma vote."

The final Heisman tally showed Hornung with 1,066 points, followed closely by Majors with 994. Then, back to back, came McDonald with 973 and Tubbs with 724. Together, the two Sooners totaled 1,697 points. They had, indeed, spread the vote. Brown finished fifth with 561. Kramer had 518, Brodie 281, Parker 248, Ploen 150 and Arnett 128 to round out the top 10.

Callahan, now retired in Bradenton, Fla., is convinced that Hornung won the Heisman on his natural ability, not the Notre Dame image.

"I wasn't surprised Paul won, for two reasons," the former publicist said. "I thought he was the greatest football player in the country. And the pros had a thing they called the bonus pick back then. Green Bay had the pick, and they had made it clear that they were going to take Paul. That pretty well said Paul *was* the best player in the country."

There were no promotional campaigns built around the Heisman in the 1950s. "You didn't label someone as our 'Heisman possibility,'" Callahan said. "The coaches didn't approve of it. Late in the season, if you could get a story into the Associated Press, United Press or International News Service, it helped. But you did that with everybody you thought had the possibility of making All-America."

Hornung appeared in Sports Illustrated and had additional exposure because Notre Dame was on national and regional television several times. The Golden Boy was interviewed infrequently, however, because during that era, the coach was the primary source of information on an athlete.

"Myron Cope of Pittsburgh interviewed Paul," Callahan said, "then told me Paul was a better interview than any coach he had talked to."

The split Heisman vote theory involving McDonald and Tubbs makes the most sense, but that doesn't necessarily mean that if one of them had been injured for the Sooners, the other one would have gotten the injured player's vote and, in turn, the trophy. That player's vote could have gone to Hornung, for all we know. Or it could have been spread around evenly.

As for the Notre Dame mystique, if there is such an invisible animal, it is doubtful that it was so strong that it, alone, elevated a player on a 2-8 team to the pinnacle of college football. A player in such a dismal situation would have to have something going for him besides his school's reputation. After all, Hornung is the only player off a bad Irish team to win the Heisman. All of the other five Notre Dame Heisman winners played on teams that were recognized as national champions by at least one organization. The combined record of those five Heisman recipients' teams is 46-2-1.

The split vote and mystique theories have merit, but they are not the main reasons why Hornung won the trophy. In short, he simply was the most talented college football player in the country.

Hornung won some other football honors as a senior such as the Walter Camp Trophy, which is given by the Washington (D.C.) Touchdown Club to the outstanding college back of the year, and the back of the game award in the Hula Bowl. But the Heisman dinner was his proudest moment.

"It was my mother's dinner," he said. "The trophy was more hers than mine. She did a great job of raising me all by herself. She's a wonderful woman.

"My speech was about my mother, but mostly a thank you. I told them the trophy was a complete surprise—the natural, superfluous repertoire that athletes give. They don't have the guts to say, 'I earned it.' "

Why didn't Paul Hornung? "Not at 21," he said. "You just take the trophy and go on down the road."

The Heisman experience sticks in his mind for another reason. It offered him his first limousine ride.

The party was only beginning.

The general consensus at Notre Dame was that Hornung would get to the Hall of Fame if Hollywood didn't get him first. At Friday-night pep rallies, he often was introduced as "the best-looking player to ever play for Notre Dame." After he broke his nose in a game against Purdue, a teammate teased, "You'll never get to Hollywood now."

Hollywood did call. Though Hornung had no thespian experience, he looked like a "star," which in Hollywood is just as important. With curly blond hair, a tall, proud head, clear green eyes, a dimple in his cheek and Elvis lips that women find sensuous, Hornung looked like a young Greek god. Hollywood offered him a seven-year contract under the stipulation that he not play football. He turned it down.

"Can you imagine living year-round in Beverly Hills?" he said. "That would kill you!"

Hornung did appear in the TV series "My Sister Eileen" a few years later. His Packer teammates nicknamed him Eileen. After his career ended, he played a lumberjack in the 1968 movie "The Devil's Brigade," in which he had five speaking lines. As recently as 1984, he was offered a bit part as a tennis coach. "Now, do I look like a tennis coach?" Hornung said in all his frank plumpness. He rejected the part.

Football, not films, is what Hornung had in mind in 1957 when he graduated from the Notre Dame School of Commerce with an 82 grade-point average (B), three points shy of making the dean's list. He signed a three-year, $15,000-per-season contract (plus a $3,000 bonus) with Green Bay, which hadn't had a winning season since 1947.

Lisle Blackbourn was the Packers' coach in 1957, and he played Hornung at quarterback, halfback, fullback and, sometimes, not at all. Hornung would find out on game day where he would be playing. If it was quarterback, Blackbourn restricted him to short-yardage situations and a handful of routine plays.

The highly touted rookie was failing to settle in at any one position, and then he did not play much in several games after ripping ankle tendons. Suddenly, the unproven Heisman winner was on the bench, and doubts surfaced about Hornung's ability to make it in the pros—especially in Green Bay, where the population runs small and the feelings deep.

"In Green Bay, because of its size, everyone knows what everyone else is doing," Hornung said. "When the Packers lost, the players would throw parties in the locker room so no one would know about it. That wasn't my m.o. I held my head high, win or lose. I've always been like that.

"After one game that I didn't play in because I was hurt, I had a date with this pretty little girl. We went to meet Max and his date at this bar. I walked in and three guys got on me. One said, 'Hey, Hornung, you can't play football, but you can sure play with the women.' I took a swing, but I had this big overcoat on, and I missed. The three guys jumped me and were beating the hell out of me when my date ran into the next room to get Max."

Hornung's date found McGee. "Max! Max!" she pleaded. "Paul's getting beat up! Come help!"

"Aw," McGee replied, "Paul can handle it himself."

Blackbourn was fired after a 3-9 season, and popular assistant coach Ray (Scooter) McLean was elevated to succeed him. Things grew worse, for the Packers and for Hornung, a man still without a position.

"Max and I were in a bar one night," he said, "and these motorcycle guys came up and stood right next to me. One of them looked me right in the eye and said, 'McGee, you're full of crap.' Max nudged me from the other side and said, 'You going to let them say that about you, Max?' "

It may have been the only good laugh Hornung had all year. The Packers finished at 1-10-1, their worst record ever, and McLean resigned just before he was fired. The announcement then came that a New York Giants assistant coach had been named head coach and general manager of the Packers.

That was the first Hornung had heard of Vince Lombardi.

"I got a call one day," he recalled. "It was Lombardi. He said, 'Hornung, you're going to be my left halfback or you're not going to make it in Green Bay.' I told him: 'Good, I'm happy. I just want to play.' "

The Packers' party boy once again emerged as the Golden Boy, rushing for 681 yards (4.5 average) and leading the National Football League in scoring with 94 points. The Pack *was* back with a 7-5 record as Lombardi was unanimously voted NFL Coach of the Year.

Green Bay improved to 8-4 in 1960, which turned out to be the Golden Boy's golden season. He scored an astonishing 176 points in a 12-game season on 15 touchdowns, 15 of 28 field-goal tries and 41 of 41 extra-point attempts.

Hornung's total of 176 points remains a pro football record even though the NFL now plays 16 regular-season games. It's possible the record may never be broken because there are no more combination men—running backs who double as place-kickers. To pass Hornung, a back must score 30 touchdowns.

"Truthfully," Hornung said, "I don't think there ever was anyone who was a better all-around pro football player than I was. That's just my feeling."

Hornung has narrow, sloping shoulders that prompted his Packer teammates to call him "Goat Shoulders." As torsos go, he was no Hercules. "My strength was from the hips on down," Hornung said. "I was a smart football player. Good instincts. I knew how to cut, when to cut."

Green Bay end Bob Long said of Hornung, "Inside the 10-yard line, he was probably the finest football player I've ever seen."

The Golden Boy's quickness and cutting ability enabled him to power through tackles. Hornung and fullback Jim Taylor, whose weight of 215 pounds was identical to Hornung's as a pro, popularized the "Green Bay Sweep," football's catch phrase of the 1960s. Other teams began to employ a big-back offense because of the Packers' success, but without the same results. That's because no other team had two backs like Taylor and Hornung.

The Packers reached the NFL championship game in the 1960 season but lost to Philadelphia, 17-13. Green Bay improved to 11-3 in '61 as Hornung again led the NFL with 146 points, including 33 in one game against Baltimore, a Packer record.

He was available to the Packers only on weekends after November 14, when he was called to military duty along with end Boyd Dowler and linebacker Ray Nitschke. In the league title game, Hornung scored 19 points as Green Bay thrashed New York, 37-0. Hornung received All-Pro and Pro Bowl honors for the second straight year and was named The Sporting News' NFL Player of the Year.

Lombardi, who had changed the Packers from the NFL's worst team to the best in the amazingly short span of three years, was called a genius, even though he didn't become a head coach above the high school level until he was 45. For some geniuses, it takes longer.

"Lombardi had the biggest ego in the world, but it wasn't materialistic," Hornung said. "He was all for the team. His stubbornness made him great, but only because we won. If we didn't win, he would have been fighting it tooth and nail.

"We all had a fear of Lombardi. But his greatest coaching was in teaching and knowing his personnel. He didn't have a Jim Brown or Gale Sayers in the backfield. You've got to coach a Hornung and a Taylor. Elijah Pitts is an absolute example of Lombardi's teaching ability. When Pitts came to us, he was a marginal player. Because of Lombardi, he became a respectable NFL running back."

Hornung became Lombardi's whipping boy, not only out of frustration with his late-night antics, but by design.

"Lombardi couldn't get on Bart (Starr) in public because he knew Bart was too sensitive to take it," Hornung said. "Lombardi couldn't get on Taylor because they had a money problem the last three, four years. So Lombardi used me. He knew he could get on me because I could take it. And then he'd tell me, 'Besides, you need it.' "

Though the Italian in Lombardi would rise often and spit out like the waters at the Trevi Fountain following the latest Hornung escapade, he held a deep affection for the Golden Boy.

"My dad loved him," said Lombardi's son, Vince, now president and general manager of the Oakland Invaders of the United States Football League. "Maybe because Paul was, I don't know, all the things my dad wished he could be but couldn't—flamboyant, loose, devil-may-care. While my dad found it frustrating the way Paul lived, he admired the way he could pull it off."

Hornung was a ladies' man, but it's often overlooked that he was just as much a man's man.

"He truly was the leader of that football team," young Vince Lombardi said of the Packer dynasty. "When Dowler, Nitschke and Hornung were in the service, the other players were asking: 'Is Paul coming back? When is Paul coming back?' They were genuinely concerned.

"Paul wasn't just a guy with a ball under his arm. He passed, ran, kicked, blocked your socks off—he did everything. And he got better in the big games.

"He's the kind of guy who, if you were losing by two points with 2 minutes left back on your 20, would walk into a huddle and say, 'Hey, guys, just get me close and I'll get you the field goal.' And he would. Come Sunday, he produced."

When Hornung was tackled, he characteristically pushed his shoulder pads back into place before rejoining the huddle. It was a practical necessity because of his drooping shoulders, but to the casual fan his manner exuded confidence, perhaps a bit of braggadocio, and seemed to speak for all the Packers: Go ahead, knock us down, give us your best shot. But it isn't good enough.

Hornung's highest salary in Green Bay was $75,000. "Lombardi told me he would never pay me as much money as Starr because I made more money in the off-season through endorsements," he said. "But we always had a handshake on $10,000 if I ever needed it." Given Hornung's lifestyle, he usually did, and Lombardi was a man of his word.

The Packers were 13-1 in 1962. Hornung's play was limited because of injuries, but he scored 74 points and the Packers beat the Giants for the second straight year in the NFL championship game, 16-7. Jerry Kramer, not Hornung, kicked three field goals for the Packers.

In 1963, scandal rocked the NFL. A 10-month league investigation showed that Hornung and Detroit Lions tackle Alex Karras were among a group of identified players who had been betting on NFL games.

Commissioner Pete Rozelle said Hornung had become friendly with a San Francisco businessman in 1956 while he was practicing for the East-West Shrine Game. Rozelle stated that Hornung had "frequent" telephone conversations with the businessman during 1957-58 and used him to place bets on pro and college games in 1959. In several instances, Rozelle said, Hornung's bets reached $500. The commissioner went on to say that Hornung continued to bet on games in 1960-61 but stopped during the 1962 preseason. In one season, Rozelle said, Hornung made $1,500, but he broke about even the other years.

The scandal broke after Karras admitted in a taped television interview that he bet on games. "If Karras had kept his mouth shut," Hornung reflected, "he never would have been caught." Nor, in Hornung's mind, would he have been caught. Karras later said he never "bet more than a pack of cigarettes or a couple of cigars and only with close friends, and never with bookmakers."

Rozelle didn't buy the explanation. He suspended Hornung and Karras indefinitely. Five other players, all from the Lions, were fined $2,000 each for betting on games in which they were not involved. Rozelle also fined the Lions $4,000 as a team.

"I did wrong," Hornung said penitently at the time. "I should be penalized. I just have to stay with it."

The league's gambling problem went beyond seven players. Hornung knew of a number of players, including some of the NFL's biggest stars, who bet on games while he was playing. But he wouldn't snitch.

"I told Pete or the FBI people who were investigating, I can't remember which, that I would answer any question truthfully about myself, but I wouldn't talk about anyone else," Hornung said. "When you go through something like this, your butt's on the line. It's stand up and be counted."

Hornung was wrong to place bets, although he maintains that when he bet on the Packers, it was always to win. "And I never played less than my hardest," he said. But he became a fall guy, along with Karras, for his own sins as well as the sins of others. Rozelle reinstated the two All-Pros 11 months later.

The problem of NFL players gambling didn't die with Hornung and Karras. In 1983, Rozelle suspended Colts quarterback Art Schlichter indefinitely after it was revealed that the former Ohio State star had lost an estimated $389,000 to Maryland bookmakers. The suspension was lifted 13 months later.

Hornung, knowing what pain Schlichter must have been feeling, tried to contact Rozelle to see if he could be of any help to the quarterback. But the commissioner's office didn't call back. "I'd rather trust gamblers than most of the businessmen I know when it comes to paying off debts," Hornung said. "Gamblers are notorious that way.

"The gambling code is that you must pay off or you won't gamble for long. If a gambler owes you money, you'll get paid. Of if they go broke and find some money later on, you'll get paid then. Most of the gambling people I've met are honorable."

Hornung said he no longer bets on football. Just the horses. "I lost money overall on football," he said. "But I don't lose on the horses.

"I like to gamble. You grow up in Kentucky and you gamble. This is a thoroughbred state. I was betting on horses when I was 13. I made $140 working as an usher on Derby Day when I was 14."

Hornung has owned or shared ownership in several racehorses, including one that ran in the Wood Memorial. He has 12 seats reserved for every Kentucky Derby and invites friends from all over the country to attend. One year, 20 friends came to watch the Run for the Roses—in 12 seats. "We stormed the gate," Hornung said.

Among his friends is Barney Shapiro, the San Francisco businessman who placed the bets that got Hornung into trouble in the first place.

"Barney's the best guy in the world," Hornung said. "He wasn't a professional gambler. He invented the blackjack slot machine. He has the greatest collection of slot machines you've ever seen."

Dump the relationship because Shapiro contributed to his suspension? Not Hornung. Once he picks someone as a friend, he is extremely loyal.

Hornung has many admirable qualities. He is bluntly honest, almost to a fault. "Paul is totally honest," said young Vince Lombardi, "and that honesty has gotten him into trouble."

Hornung doesn't hide his feelings. He will say what has to be said, whether it hurts others or himself. Conversely, if he feels he is one of the best football players who ever received a scholarship, and he does, he'll tell you without being asked. Some would take that as a sign of conceit.

"I'm not conceited," Hornung said. "I am very confident. Athletes are vain. They're brought up that way. I'm vain, too, but I don't wear it on my sleeve. I know how to handle it. I'm very well-liked. There's no question I've been a leader everywhere I've been."

Or as Dizzy Dean once said, "It ain't braggin' if you can do it."

After being reinstated, Hornung didn't do it as well. He scored 107 points in 1964, but he had only five touchdowns and made only 12 of 38 field-goal attempts and missed an extra-point try for the first time since 1959. A missed extra point cost Green Bay its first game against Baltimore that year, and five missed field goals spelled the difference in a 24-21 loss to the Colts in their second matchup in 1964. Hornung never kicked for the Packers again after that season.

By 1965, injuries had become a problem and began to cut more and more into his playing time. But he was there for the big games.

Lombardi needed Hornung for a late-season game in 1965 against the Colts. Hornung scored five touchdowns and Green Bay won, 42-27.

On turf that was muddied by a four-inch snowfall at Green Bay's Lambeau Field, the Packers met Cleveland for the NFL championship. Taylor and Hornung combined for 201 yards rushing as the Golden Boy sealed a 23-12 victory with a 13-yard touchdown run.

Hornung scored only five touchdowns in 1966, the season Green Bay beat Kansas City in Super Bowl I. Hornung did not play in that game because of injuries, and Lombardi gambled by not freezing him before the NFL expansion draft. New Orleans selected Hornung, but he never played for the Saints after a physical examination revealed that he had a potentially dangerous neck injury. So, at the age of 31, the immortal No. 5 for the legendary Green Bay Packers decided to retire.

Hornung stayed in New Orleans for 1½ years, working in local radio and television and doing public relations work for the Saints. Then he moved back to Louisville but started to travel about the country as a sports broadcaster. He did Notre Dame games, the NFL, the USFL. Hornung was the face and voice of TV's "Sports Legends," a program on which he talked to great sports stars of the past. And he participated in one of the wildest and wackiest TV sports shows ever, a Saturday night NFL preview show on Atlanta cable station WTBS with Alex Hawkins and Norm Van Brocklin.

In 1982, Hornung filed a $3 million lawsuit against the NCAA, which he charged with interfering with his right to make a living as a sports announcer. The suit followed the NCAA's rejection of Hornung as an announcer for a number of college football games that were to be carried by WTBS. The suit remains in litigation.

The Golden Boy's well-chronicled love life, meanwhile, continued at full tilt over the years even though he finally got married near the end of his Green Bay career. His wife, Patricia Roeder, was a Northwestern graduate and a writer. They were married in Beverly Hills in 1966. "I feel beautiful," Hornung told the world on his wedding day.

But this marriage didn't tie him down for more than about a year and a half. His wife liked Beverly Hills and didn't like Louisville, just the opposite of his preferences. "We just weren't alike," he said.

Was he crushed after waiting all that time to get married, then having it end so soon? "Heck, no," he said. "I just went off on down the highway."

Actually, Hornung and his first wife were married 13 years on paper. Neither bothered to get a divorce, which didn't bother Hornung, who saw himself as a born-again bachelor.

"I'd just tell the girls I dated that I couldn't get serious because I was still married," he said. "That was a good thing for me."

For four years, he dated Deborah Shelton, an actress who is seen in "Dallas" on television. "We hopscotched around—New York, Chicago, Louisville," Hornung said. "She didn't have her feet on the ground. She was career-conscious."

At one time in his life, Hornung would have preferred it that way. But he was looking for a change, a permanent someone in his life.

Hornung found her at a cocktail party in Louisville. Angela Cerelli was passing through town with a friend. At one time, Angela had been a secretary with the Philadelphia Eagles, and she remembered taking Hornung's calls for Boyd Dowler, then an Eagles assistant coach.

Over dinner at the swank Jefferson Club in Louisville, Paul and Angela discussed the development of their relationship.

"I had lived at home with my parents until I was 28," she said. "When Paul asked me out the first time, my dad wasn't too thrilled. 'With the reputation that guy's got?' he told me. My mom said, 'Go for it.'

"I wasn't scared by Paul's reputation. I didn't look on it as taking a chance. The relationship was very good from the start. We laughed a lot. We still do. Humor has a lot to do with it.

"Paul is charming. He knows how to treat a lady. A Southern gentleman. We went together three years before we were married."

Hornung reached over and touched his wife's hand.

"I think I was ready for marriage," he said. "I had been looking for a good lady for a long time. I was tired of the streets. I wanted a home life. I wanted to be in love.

"When I met Angela, I was 40. After three years she said, 'If we're not married by the next Derby, I'm leaving.'"

The old ultimatum trick. This time, Hornung didn't let the lady leave.

"When people ask Angela what it's like to be married to Paul Hornung," he said, "she says, 'Never boring.' I tell her now, 'If you ever leave me, I'll shoot you.'"

He touched her hand again and laughed. She won't ever leave. Neither will he. She married the new Paul Hornung, not the old.

"I'm a firm believer in timing," Angela said. "I know Paul's reputation with the ladies. That doesn't bother me. If he goes on the road, I don't worry about it. I'm kind of happy he's gone. I get a lot of things done I don't have time to do when he's here. If I were younger, maybe I'd worry more when he is away. The way I see it, if you worry all the time, you'll get an ulcer."

"She's been through all the b.s. with the phone calls," Paul said. Old flames of the Golden Boy wishing to rekindle new fires.

"Paul has this thing about being with the boys," Angela said. "He likes to see Max. He leaves next week for his annual golf tournament in Las Vegas. I can't change that."

Paul: "Now, the only thing about getting older is that the guys go to bed around midnight. It used to be 3, 4 in the morning."

Angela: "Paul has educated me to travel. We went to Europe last year with

Max and his new wife. Paul and I took so many suitcases, we looked like Liz and Dick."

Paul: "I decided to do it right: Paris, Nice, Monte Carlo, Venice. That's the most romantic city I've ever seen. We had a limousine every day we were in Europe, except for Venice, of course. We also took the Orient Express."

Angela: "Paul loves art. You can't get him out of the galleries. The owners love to see him coming. It's like he's entering a whole new phase of his life."

Paul, commenting on an earlier phase of his life: "I gave my Heisman Trophy to Notre Dame. What do I need it for? I'm nearly 50 years old. I don't need trophies anymore. Get them out of here!"

Angela: "Giving his Heisman to Notre Dame sure made his mom mad. I'm going to pack his trophies and put them away. I think he should keep them. They're worth something."

Over an after-dinner drink, Hornung told another Max story, this one from Paris.

"Notre Dame cathedral, Montmartre, the Louvre—I could spend three days in the Louvre," he said. "Max wasn't too familiar with all that. We stood before this statue with no arms, and Max wondered why it hadn't been completed."

Driving the white Cadillac through the streets of Louisville on a dark winter's night, Hornung said he was not upset that he had not been voted into the Professional Football Hall of Fame in Canton, O., although Lombardi and eight Packer teammates during the Lombardi years have been inducted. It seems that a lot of voters can't forget about his gambling indiscretions more than two decades ago.

"Herb Adderley was the most talented of all the Packers I played with," he said. "Adderley's in the Hall, and he said, 'Hornung should have gone in ahead of all of us.'

"But not making the Pro Hall of Fame doesn't bother me as much as my just making the National Football Foundation Hall of Fame this year (1985). Did you see the other college players from my era who got in ahead of me? I mean, it's a shame."

Both Halls of Fame should have welcomed Hornung by now. He certainly has the credentials.

"I was Number 1 on three levels," he pointed out. "I was all-state in high school in Kentucky, an All-America and Heisman Trophy winner in college and an All-Pro.

"When I played, there were 33 players to a roster. Lombardi said, 'If I had 33 Hornungs, they'd all make the team.' "

Even if all 33 missed bed check.

"The thing I'm proudest of," Hornung said, his silver hair highlighted by the low beams of a passing car, "is that Lombardi said I was the best player he ever coached."

What more qualifications does a man need?

*Former Notre Dame and Green Bay Packers great Paul Hornung, his golden hair now turned silver, poses with wife Angela at the downtown Louisville office that the Hornungs have renovated.*

# Pete Dawkins

*A soldier, a scholar, an athlete, a singer, a leader of men. He was a "star man," one of the most prolific personalities ever to grace West Point. Pete Dawkins provided the mold for military and athletic excellence. The Heisman Trophy was but one small part of an impressive resume that peaked with his rise to brigadier general and election to the College Football Hall of Fame. Army cadets still stand in awe of the man his peers dubbed St. Peter.*

# Chapter 10

# Born to be a leader

Pete Dawkins was the consummate soldier. If the Army had constructed a master plan to create the ideal officer, he would have been an aide-de-camp to Dawkins. He was too good to be true, a special mold.

At the United States Military Academy, he set a standard of excellence that famous generals who graduated from the academy before him—Pershing, Patton, MacArthur, Bradley, Eisenhower and so on—didn't reach. Dawkins' combined academic and athletic achievements from 1955-59 are unprecedented in West Point history and are regarded with sheer reverence by cadets a generation removed.

Dawkins was first captain of the corps of cadets, putting him in charge of 2,400 aspiring military officers. He was president of the 1959 class, one of the most scholarly classes ever to grace West Point. He was a "star man," meaning he ranked in the top 5 percent academically. He was a member of the cadet choir and the glee club, and he served on the school's special programs committee.

Despite his busy academic schedule, Dawkins still somehow found time to study for the examinations that qualified him as a Rhodes scholar at Oxford University in England.

These accomplishments alone would have sufficed for any gifted student with purpose and vision. Not Dawkins. He thought higher and strived harder than others. He tried out for the West Point hockey team even though he had never played a game of organized hockey before in his life. He not only made the team, he lettered for three seasons, was assistant captain and emerged as the highest-scoring defenseman in the East as a senior.

In 1958, Dawkins was captain of Army's last undefeated football team. He was a unanimous All-America on the field as well as an academic All-America. As a 6-foot-1, 197-pound senior, he received the Heisman Memorial Trophy and the Maxwell Trophy as the outstanding college football player in the country. He concluded his football career by being selected as the outstanding North player in the North-South Shrine Game in Miami.

Then, as Dawkins was graduating seventh in a class of 501 cadets, he received the Army Athletic Association award as the first classman who had rendered the most valuable service to athletics during his career as a cadet, plus the merit medal of the Eastern College Athletic Conference for excellence in athletics and scholarship.

Dawkins' peers at West Point deferentially referred to him as St. Peter. "We have stood in awe of this man," they wrote in the 1959 academy yearbook.

They weren't alone. At Oxford, he introduced the American passing style to rugby while earning three "blues," the equivalent of a varsity letter. He rowed No. 6 on a crew composed of members of the rugby team. He received a master's degree in the grouped study field of philosophy, policy and economics.

From Oxford, he became an Army ranger and paratrooper, serving combat time in Vietnam, where he earned citations for bravery. He was a White House fellow and received his doctorate degree in the Woodrow Wilson School at Princeton. (The degree is in public affairs, although Dawkins said a more accurate description would be international politics.)

In 1975, Dawkins was named to the College Football Hall of Fame. He was 36, the youngest person ever chosen to the Cooperstown of college football.

Dawkins earned the rank of brigadier general in 1981. At 43, he was the Army's youngest brigadier general on active duty. In Dawkins, the Army saw the likeness of another general, even though Dawkins doesn't smoke a corncob pipe. But if he weren't the reincarnation of Douglas A. MacArthur, Army officers told themselves, then such a man can never exist.

MacArthur walks in Dawkins' shadow at West Point. MacArthur was a "star man" and the leading man in his class. He was first captain of the cadets, but he didn't play football. And there is no evidence of his being able to carry a tune.

MacArthur, the only son of a Medal of Honor winner to have won the same medal, did scale the military ladder a bit faster than Dawkins. He became a brigadier general at 38 and a four-star general at 50. That same year, 1930, he was appointed Army Chief of Staff, the youngest in U.S. history.

MacArthur marched at too fast a pace even for one as qualified as Dawkins. Still, Lt. Col. Earl (Red) Blaik prophesied at the time he coached Dawkins in football that the blond first classman would wind up as Army Chief of Staff. The Army knew it, too, and so must have Dawkins.

Then, in a matter of months, it didn't matter anymore.

In 1982, Dawkins was hospitalized for back surgery. A disc was removed. "Too many bad parachute falls," he explained. Flat on his back, his whole life changed. He began to contemplate who he was and what he really wanted for himself.

He decided that it wasn't the Army. Although Army Chief of Staff appealed to him, it wasn't an obsession. He never perceived that title as the ultimate goal.

"Whatever I wanted to do in life," he said introspectively, "I wanted to do it better than anyone else. This was the standard in my mind, I felt, that ought to be set. I wanted to be good, I wanted to excel. But I'm not sure it translated itself in the way that some people assumed, that I wanted to be . . . the . . . chief . . . of . . . staff. I didn't sit around in the evenings musing on what that would take."

From personal observations, Dawkins concluded that chief of staff wasn't the Holy Grail.

"I had watched a number of senior people retire, very successful chiefs of staff and chairmen of the Joint Chiefs of Staff, and it occurred to me that they weren't very happy," he said. "I asked myself why and decided it was their age.

"I would have retired from the Army when I was 56, an age when you're really at the pinnacle of your powers. But at that age, it's a hard time to re-engage. How do you start again at 56? I didn't want to stay in a career that, when I was going to enter my most productive period, was going to doom me to go fishing."

Dawkins decided he would leave the Army, but his decision was only half-complete. He had to figure out next how to tell the Army.

"I spent a great amount of time and effort in trying to retire in a manner that didn't project to people, especially the younger officers, that I was disappointed in the Army," he said. "I wasn't leaving the Army because I was unhappy or unful-filled. I enjoyed the Army and felt it was important.

"I wrote articles to try and moderate any negative influence. I tried to tell people that you can't do everything you want in life, that the tyranny of time makes that impossible. I tried to let people know what I was all about. Universally, senior officers, junior officers and soldiers told me they wished I had come to a different conclusion, but good luck and go for it."

Dawkins snapped off his final salute on July 29, 1983, at high noon in a full-dress parade at Ft. Myer, Va. He was 45 when he left the Army "without a job."

Finding work isn't a problem when you're Pete Dawkins. When he retired, the image-makers gathered about him like ants on an uncovered cake at a picnic. They realized that here was someone born to lead. No one in the country is better equipped to buck the line, charge the hill and sit at the summit table than Dawkins.

To paraphrase MacArthur: "Young soldiers never die, they just fade into poli-tics." Such a future appears likely for Dawkins, although he has resisted all politi-cal offers thus far. "I don't mean to sound cute in my answer," he said, "but the field of public policy is an option I'd like to keep open."

Congressman Dawkins, Senator Dawkins, President Dawkins . . . they all have a nice ring.

"Right now, that's not what I'm focused on," he said. "I have a full-time job on Wall Street, and I enjoy what I'm doing. But my life, by and large, has been involved in world and public service, and that has a great attraction. . . . I'm trying not to foreclose that option."

Dawkins interviewed for six weeks after leaving the Army before accepting a position as senior executive with an investment banking firm, Shearson Lehman Brothers, which is owned by American Express.

"What I'm doing now is learning," he said. "Increasingly, I've become aware that most public policy issues have at their core the issues of finances and econom-ic policies. Budgetary problems, international trade—these are paramount when you're discussing public policy. And what better way to get a sophisticated under-standing of finance than to dive into Wall Street."

Temporarily. Unless everybody's unanimous speculation is off the mark, poli-tics is Dawkins' ambition. The only questions are which election and under whose flag? Dawkins once was a Republican but now considers himself neutral. He is keeping watch for the best opportunities. Why lock himself prematurely into one party affiliation, which most political aspirants do, when the other party might have something more attractive to offer? "I don't operate on carefully prescribed movements," he said.

While Dawkins spent 28 years in the military, counting his time at West Point, he never seemed the military type. Unlike MacArthur, Dawkins had no other generals in the family. His father, Henry E. Dawkins, was a lieutenant colonel in the Air Force Reserve and a practicing dentist who could afford to live in Royal Oak, Mich., a well-to-do suburb of Detroit.

Pete Dawkins was interested in trying everything as a young boy, from sports to music to the Soap Box Derby.

"I was a participator, someone with a lot of energy," he said. "I love being involved, inventing things. I wasn't universally successful, but if you try enough things in large numbers, success is on your side. I also grew up in a neighborhood with older kids. So in playing games with them, even kick the can, I had to keep stretching my limits just to keep up with them."

Dawkins learned to play eight musical instruments—the piano, trumpet, clarinet, trombone, cello, violin, flute and guitar. He played the trumpet "quite seriously" and studied piano for eight years. "I don't play any instruments now, lamentably," he said.

During his boyhood summers, Dawkins lived with his grandparents on their farm in Cadillac, Mich. He had his own horse, a tractor to drive, plus chickens to feed, cows to watch and his own pickle patch.

One summer, when Dawkins became very sick, it was learned that he had a light attack of polio. He had a curvature of the spine, and doctors feared that he would have to wear a brace. The Sister Kenny Foundation was experimenting with a pioneer concept, however, in which polio victims with Dawkins' condition would be rehabilitated through extensive therapy rather than being strapped into a brace. For two years, Dawkins' parents helped him endure rigorous stretching exercises in order to strengthen his back and straighten his spine. He also lifted weights to build up his weakened muscles.

The therapy was successful. Dawkins then sought his doctors' permission to play high school football at the exclusive Cranbrook School in Bloomfield Hills, Mich. Permission initially was denied, but Dawkins pleaded with the doctors, who finally relented. "I was very keen on playing," he said.

Dawkins weighed 110 pounds when he was 15. Through weight training, he built himself up to 170 pounds by his senior year at Cranbrook, where it's acceptable to say "very keen." He was named an all-interstate quarterback two years and an all-interstate first baseman one year.

Dawkins received a well-rounded education at Cranbrook, where he designed furniture, played in the band and sang in operettas. He was part of the chorus in Gilbert and Sullivan's "The Pirates of Penzance."

Dawkins' stubborn determination to excel at anything and everything was evidenced again when it came time to choose a college. His family was composed strictly of University of Michigan graduates, but he didn't want to attend Ann Arbor simply because the rest of his family went there. Dawkins wasn't a follower, even then, and so he narrowed his list of colleges to Yale and West Point. When Blaik, the academy's football coach, expressed little interest in Dawkins based on a high school picture of the skinny 17-year-old, that made Dawkins even more determined to receive an appointment to West Point and make the football team.

There was another aspect of academy life that appealed to Dawkins.

"Coming out of a Midwest high school in the 1950s, if you didn't go to a military academy, you went into ROTC," he said. "The issue of militarism, in my case, wasn't relevant. I saw West Point as a workshop in leadership. Motivating people and mobilizing their energies were things I didn't know about, and this seemed like an excellent opportunity to learn."

Incoming plebes to the Military Academy spend their first summer getting acclimated to military life by suffering through an ordeal unaffectionately referred to as "Beast Barracks." Afterward, the plebes go on a full-pack, five-day hike, followed by a 25-mile high-paced march back to the academy. At the end of the march, if the plebes aren't tired enough already, they get to run up a ski slope.

Dawkins brought along his trumpet from Michigan. He found another trumpet player and a drummer in the company and formed a drum-and-bugle corps, thereby reducing the monotony of the 25-mile march.

"By the time we got back to the academy, everyone was exhausted," Dawkins said. "That's when I decided to run up the ski slope tooting the trumpet. It was somewhat of a 'Charge!' but seldom in the academy's history has a whole company gone running up a slope like ours did. This incident is illustrative in my case because it was spontaneous, not something planned where I said to myself, 'I want to make my mark at West Point.' It just seemed like a good thing to do."

Taking the hill, however, had a carry-over effect on Dawkins. He had given an order, in effect, and others had followed. In motivating others, he, too, was motivated. "These kinds of incidents tended to compound themselves," he said, "so it became a self-fulfilling prophecy. I was propelled by other people's confidence in me. So I tried other things, they worked, and this generated a higher level of competency. Eventually, I found myself pushed out in front.

"The thing I'm most uncomfortable with, though, is this notion or pattern that sometimes gets projected about me that I had set all these goals. It didn't work that way. I was just a kid in college having a good time."

Dawkins played quarterback on the 1955 plebe team, scoring three touchdowns but failing to demonstrate arm strength on his lefthanded passes. In the 1956 West Point media guide, under "Outlook," Dawkins was just another name. To wit:

"Particular attention is being focused once again on the Army quarterback situation. . . . There are now three candidates worthy of the name. Dave Bourland, a second classman, Chuck Darby and Pete Dawkins, a pair of portside yearlings. Bourland, a 20-year-old native of El Paso, surprised all with his performance during spring practice. Coming out of the pack from an obscure third-stringer to boss man . . . Bourland is determined to make it stick. . . . Darby and Dawkins have much in common. . . . both are lefthanded. Both are on the dean's list. Both are products of the state of Michigan, Dawkins from Royal Oak, and Darby from Sturgis. And, both are varsity potential in other sports, Dawkins in hockey and Darby in basketball."

Bourland did become the boss man, and he did make it stick. Darby became the backup quarterback, while Dawkins was shifted to halfback and played little. He carried the football only six times for 30 yards, but he made those carries count by scoring three touchdowns as the Cadets went 5-3-1.

Dawkins went out for the varsity hockey team and scored nine goals and had 16 assists. He had taught himself to play hockey in Royal Oak after he and some friends used garden hoses to turn a vacant lot into a makeshift rink.

Dawkins was elected president of his junior class and was ranked in the top 5 percent academically. The 1957 West Point football media guide was more encouraging about his chances than the previous year's manual. "Newcomers not to be overlooked," it read, "include Pete Dawkins, a second classman who excelled in spring practice, Bob Anderson, Steve Waldrop and George Kaiser, a coterie of erstwhile plebe backs."

Anderson emerged from this coterie to join Dawkins as the halfback starters, presenting Army with its finest 1-2 ground punch since Doc Blanchard and Glenn

Davis. Dawkins and Anderson each would score in Army's first eight games.

Army trampled Nebraska in the 1957 opener, 42-0, at West Point. The Cadets scored touchdowns on their first three possessions and posted a 28-0 halftime lead. Dawkins scored the second touchdown on a one-yard plunge, though he rushed for only 17 yards on five attempts.

A week later, Penn State assumed a 13-6 halftime lead. But in the third quarter, Dawkins scored the tying and go-ahead touchdowns on runs of 10 and three yards as the Cadets went on to win, 27-13.

On Columbus Day, Dawkins scored on a six-yard sweep that gave Army a 14-7 third-quarter lead over Notre Dame. Anderson added a touchdown later in the period to make it 21-7, but the Fighting Irish launched a tremendous comeback that culminated in Monty Stickles' game-winning 29-yard field goal. Stickles, who had failed the eye test that would have made him a cadet, had never attempted a field goal before providing the edge in Notre Dame's 23-21 victory.

Army rebounded against Pittsburgh, 29-13, as Anderson and Dawkins stood out again. Anderson rushed for 96 yards, scored twice on short plunges, intercepted two passes and made a touchdown-saving tackle. Dawkins tallied 88 yards on the ground and caught a 32-yard touchdown pass from Bourland.

Dawkins displayed his pass-catching skills the next week against Virginia. Army was nursing a 13-12 lead in the final period when Bourland hit him on a 35-yard touchdown pass. Army won, 20-12, in Charlottesville.

President Eisenhower, a halfback on the 1912 Army team before his football career at West Point was shortened by injuries, watched from the stands at Michie Stadium as the Cadets drubbed visiting Colgate, 53-7, under leaden skies. And Ike couldn't help but like what he saw as Dawkins turned in his best performance to date. He scored three touchdowns on short runs and threw a 28-yard scoring strike to Anderson.

Army found itself in a dogfight with Utah as Anderson and Redskins quarterback Lee Grosscup were outstanding. Anderson rushed for 214 yards and scored three times. Grosscup passed for 316 yards and two touchdowns, but Army won at home, 39-33. Dawkins scored once, on a 23-yard pass from Bourland.

Anderson was almost as unstoppable against Tulane, pounding for 145 yards. With the Green Wave leading, 14-13, Dawkins, who had scored earlier on a two-yard run, started Army's comeback with a gain of 21 yards on the second play of a fourth-quarter drive. Anderson followed with a 32-yard run and later a 10-yard sweep around left end for the winning touchdown. Dawkins then intercepted a Tulane pass in his end zone to preserve Army's 20-14 victory, pushing the Cadets' record to 7-1.

Dawkins, who had not played in the Army-Navy game as a sophomore, was excited about his first start against the Middies. But his enthusiasm was aborted as Navy triumphed, 14-0, in the rain and mud at Philadelphia's Municipal Stadium. Even though it was a sad finish to an impressive Army season, Dawkins led all rushers with 63 yards, capping a splendid junior campaign. He rushed for 665 yards (5.4 per carry), caught 11 passes for 225 yards, intercepted three passes and returned eight punts for 80 yards and six kickoffs for 140 yards. He scored 11 touchdowns—eight by land, three by air—and threw for a 12th.

Anderson was even more impressive, rushing for 983 yards to break Glenn

Davis' single-season Army record of 944 yards. He also scored 14 touchdowns (second in the nation), passed for No. 15 and was named a consensus All-America.

Army's "Touchdown Twins" would be back together in 1958. However, if either of the two was considered Heisman potential, it was Anderson.

Dawkins improved his hockey production in his second varsity season to 15 goals and 23 assists. Then in his final academic year at West Point, he became the only cadet ever to simultaneously hold the positions of first captain of the cadets, class president and football captain. And that was just for starters.

Prior to becoming a first classman, Dawkins still was the motivated but carefree cadet who wasn't thinking seriously of being a career man. "It didn't work that way," he recalled. "Things just kind of happened in small, incremental ways."

The summer before his last year at West Point, Dawkins and the other cadets toured various Army installations around the country. Dawkins was named the senior cadet on the trip. One of his assignments was to thank the different installations for their hospitality.

Afterward, an Army officer told Dawkins, "You know, if you could learn to march and salute, you might make something of yourself."

It was at this point that cadet Pete Dawkins really decided to pass muster.

"I had this funny way of marching, and my salute was respectful, but it was really a big deal," he said. "I reflected on what the officer said and told myself, 'You *ought* to get serious.' That's when I began to focus my energies a bit more at the academy."

Red Blaik was similarly motivated entering his 25th year of coaching (his 18th at West Point) in 1958. Blaik realized he had good football talent that fall, only not enough of it. He needed an advantage, a psychological ploy, to make up not only for the depth factor, but also Army's lack of size and team speed.

Blaik had top running backs in Anderson and Dawkins. A skinny quarterback named Joe Caldwell had attempted only three passes the year before, but he had a strong arm for a 160-pounder, and Blaik thought he could use him. He had good linemen in center Bill Rowe and guard Bob Novogratz. But the edge Blaik needed was provided by an end who had played little the year before because of injuries and who was about to become a part of West Point and college football lore.

Bill Carpenter. The Lonely End.

No one is quite certain where Blaik got the idea. He already had decided to use Carpenter as a wideout long before fall practice that year, but it wasn't until August 1958 that he developed the one quirk that made this formation memorable. While talking with assistant coach Andy Gustafson about the far-flanker attack he had in mind, Blaik agreed with Gustafson's observation that Carpenter could get worn out quickly by scurrying back and forth from the huddle to his position as well as running his pass routes. This dilemma inspired Blaik's famous solution.

Exclude Carpenter from the huddle. Just leave him standing near the sideline, all by his lonesome, while the other 10 players check signals between plays.

Blaik liked the idea. In addition to letting Carpenter conserve his energy, this device allowed Army to run more plays and forced defenses to spread out and commit their intentions early. And Carpenter was well suited to the role. He had good size and speed, but his best asset was moves. He could outfake a defensive back in a telephone booth.

"Blaik decided that no defensive back in the country could cover Carpenter man on man," Dawkins said. "So if they covered him with a man and a half, with another defensive back dividing his responsibilities, this gave us a half a man advantage. It became geometric football, and it gave Army a definite psychological advantage."

Blaik first used the Lonely End in the 1958 season opener against South Carolina. Amazingly, word hadn't reached Columbia, S.C., about Blaik's shenanigans, and the Gamecocks never saw the punch that coldcocked them. They spent so much time worrying about how to handle Carpenter that they paid less attention to Dawkins, who scored four touchdowns (two rushing, two receiving). Even with Carpenter used mainly as a decoy, Army won in a rout, 45-8.

"Blaik's offense captured everyone's attention," Dawkins said. "It was the new thing in college football and created this mystique, that since Carpenter never came back to the huddle, how did he get the signals? It became a journalist's gold mine."

When journalists discovered that Carpenter was getting his offensive signals from the positioning of quarterback Caldwell's feet, which indicated whether the play was a pass or a run, and from Dawkins, who flashed instructions on the direction the play was heading, they became as interested in Dawkins as in Carpenter. Until that time, reporters were aware of Dawkins as a football player, but not as "the next MacArthur," a designation they were about to bestow on him.

Army stunned Penn State, 26-0, as the Nittany Lions had difficulty deciding whether to cover Carpenter or the other Cadets. In their confusion, they stopped no one. Carpenter caught a 55-yard touchdown pass from Caldwell, while Dawkins scored on a six-yard run and a 72-yard pass from Caldwell.

The Cadets avenged their loss to Notre Dame the year before with a 14-2 victory at South Bend, Ind. Dawkins contributed 75 yards rushing, including a six-yard scamper into the end zone with 7 seconds remaining.

Week by week, the public was learning more about Dawkins. "This boy is a born leader," Blaik said. "He is only 20, yet very mature. He has given us inspiration and direction. I trust him with more responsibilities than probably any captain I have had in the past. When I start listing the assets of this squad, one of the big ones is leadership."

Dawkins pulled a hamstring muscle in the fourth game against Virginia. Caldwell and Anderson led the Rabble (a nickname used at West Point for Army's athletic teams) to a 35-6 victory, but Dawkins was ruled out of the Pitt game. His replacement, Waldrop, scored on a four-yard run as the Cadets bolted ahead, 14-0. With halftime approaching, Pitt's Bill Kaliden then began throwing on almost every down, and Dawkins became concerned.

"I thought the young fellow (Waldrop) taking my place would allow them to throw a long bomb over his head," he said. "I convinced the coach to let me go in, and I would lay back, so they wouldn't get a cheap touchdown."

Kaliden uncorked the ball immediately after Dawkins entered the game, and John Flara caught it behind Dawkins at the 10-yard line and continued into the end zone to complete a 43-yard scoring play. It was Dawkins' last appearance that day as Pitt rallied for a 14-14 tie, the only blemish on Army's nine-game season.

Dawkins was back in the lineup the next week against Colgate, but not for long as Blaik cleared the bench in a 68-6 victory. Dawkins provided one of Army's 10 touchdowns.

The Cadets didn't have it so easy the following Saturday in Texas. Leaving the snow in New York, they squared off against Rice in the heat of Houston. Two thousand-plus cadets watched the game on closed-circuit television back at the academy.

Anderson threw an eight-yard pass to the Lonely End for a touchdown as Army tied the score, 7-7, in the second quarter. That's the way it stood until late in the fourth period, when the Owls mounted a strong drive. Army braced at its 9, and Rice's Bill Bucek lined up for a field goal. Don Bonko, a substitute Cadet fullback, broke through and blocked the kick, giving the Rabble one last shot.

Army moved to its 36 as the clock wound down toward the final minute. Captain Dawkins to the rescue.

"If I had any advantage as an athlete," he said, "it was this detachment I played with. It was like I played outside myself. I always felt I could outfox people by finding the seams, the counterpoints, the weaknesses."

On previous pass patterns that afternoon, Dawkins had noticed the Rice cornerbacks shading him to the outside. With the game on the line, he knew it was time for counterpoint. He told Caldwell, "I'll fake a move outside, then head down the middle, and you throw that sucker as far as you can." Not exactly military deployment jargon, but the proper mission nonetheless.

Caldwell did as he was instructed, and Dawkins caught the football in stride. At the Rice 10, the last Owl defender tripped Dawkins, who stumbled and appeared as if he might fall. Just then, the large television screen went blank at West Point.

There was absolute silence in the room. Was Dawkins down? Would Army have time to score? Would the TV picture come back on? What happened?!

One cadet had a portable radio pressed to his ear. He screamed, "He scored!" The room went bonkers.

Dawkins had regained his balance and completed the 64-yard scoring play with 51 seconds left. Army won, 14-7.

"I was never a strong inside runner," Dawkins said. "Anderson did most of the inside running. I ran mostly outside. I didn't have the blinding speed of the Herschel Walkers, but I had good speed and good balance.

"If I had decided to play professional football instead of staying in the military, I probably would have been a receiver. I was more like a Fred Biletnikoff, who was unimpressive in almost any statistic but success. He wasn't bigger, stronger or faster than the others. He just happened to get free, catch the ball and score touchdowns better than anyone else. I was that sort of garbage player."

Dawkins didn't mean that last remark disparagingly. He was like the Oakland Raiders' All-Pro wide receiver in that he got the job done any way he could, even if it wasn't with panache. Dawkins was that most valuable of athletes—the gamesman.

On a damp, drizzly afternoon in Michie Stadium in 1958, Dawkins beat Villanova three different ways. He returned a punt 80 yards for a touchdown. He caught a 46-yard pass from Caldwell for a second touchdown. He ran six yards for a third touchdown after setting up the score with a 48-yard reception. Army won, 26-0.

Dawkins pulled on jersey No. 24 for his final appearance in a Cadet football game at Philadelphia's Municipal Stadium before 100,000 fans who turned out in freezing weather to watch Army battle Navy for the 60th time. Before the game, Blaik told Dawkins to make sure he didn't fumble the opening kickoff. He fumbled. Navy recovered and scored immediately as sophomore halfback Joe Bellino tallied on a three-yard run. Army hadn't even thawed and it was losing, 6-0.

This Arctic day, however, belonged to Army. Anderson scored twice from short yardage. Used mainly as a decoy, the Lonely End opened up passing routes for other receivers. As for Dawkins, it was not one of his better games, although he did contribute to Army's final tally by completing a two-point conversion pass to Anderson. The Cadets didn't really need him, though, as they won easily, 22-6, to finish an 8-0-1 season.

"Well," Dawkins reflected recently, "so much for the short-term benefits of winning the Heisman."

Dawkins is under the impression that his Heisman victory preceded the Army-Navy game, which was played November 29. The announcement actually was made December 2. His comment that day was that he was "flabbergasted" to have won. He shouldn't have been.

Dawkins was a unanimous All-America and was named Player of the Year by *Sports Illustrated* and *Sport* magazines. He rushed for 428 yards (5.5 average), scored 12 touchdowns (six running, six receiving), completed two of four passes for 12 yards (one pass was intercepted), caught 16 passes for 494 yards and a nation-leading 30.9 yards per reception, intercepted one pass and returned 10 punts for 162 yards and seven kickoffs for 132 yards. Dawkins ended his Army career with 1,123 yards rushing (5.4 average), 719 yards receiving—a glittering 26.6 yards per catch—26 touchdowns and 158 points. Not bad for, basically, two years' work.

"Without the Lonely End (to draw media attention to Army), I wouldn't have been a Heisman candidate," Dawkins said flatly. "The whole thing about the Heisman is to be on a winning team."

Dawkins won the 1958 Heisman comfortably. He received 296 first-place votes and 1,394 overall points, compared with quarterback Randy Duncan of Iowa, who finished second with 194 first-place votes and 1,021 points. Billy Cannon, who led Louisiana State to a perfect 11-0 overall record and the national championship, came in third with 975 points.

"Every one of us who has ever been selected to receive the Heisman Trophy knows deep down in our heart that, in a way, we didn't deserve it," Dawkins said. "College football is a sport with more to it than can be symbolized in one person. We all have the awareness that, somehow, the award is greater than any of us. At the same time, there is the realization that it can only be understood and can only be a symbol if it is made in the person of someone. Flawed, imperfect as we all are, it nevertheless causes me to hold it in a special kind of awe."

Blaik retired from coaching after that '58 season, while Dawkins retired after playing his last game of organized football as the star for the North team in the North-South Shrine Game in Miami's Orange Bowl. He scored on a three-yard run, but the South squad won, 49-20. Dawkins then finished his hockey career with 16 goals and 16 assists as a first classman and was named an All-East defenseman. The Bobby Orr of Heisman heroes.

Dawkins' toughest competition, however, wasn't necessarily found in athletic arenas. As he later found out, the life of a professional soldier with his sterling reputation was far more demanding and competitive. Dawkins was president of a class of perhaps the most talented group of graduates since the 1915 class, known as "the class the stars fell on," which produced several generals, including Dwight D. Eisenhower and Omar Bradley. Dawkins also was one of a record six Rhodes scholars from the class of 1959.

However, Eisenhower, Bradley, MacArthur, Robert E. Lee, Ulysses S. Grant, John J. (Black Jack) Pershing and George S. Patton, all West Point graduates, didn't retire from the Army as early as Dawkins, the man who had surpassed all of their accomplishments at the somber, gray academy overlooking the Hudson River. Of course, none of these distinguished generals was burdened by wearing a "St." in front of his name while a cadet at the academy, either. At that time of their lives, perhaps only MacArthur was projected for the same level of achievement that was forecast for Dawkins. Regardless, St. Peter had a heavy load of expectations to carry, the heaviest, and there was considerable jealousy emanating from fellow Army officers who weren't groomed at West Point. They believed that Dawkins was being protected for promotions and thus received special considerations with these appointments in mind.

"There was this feeling that no one is as good as this guy's notoriety, and certainly this jerk isn't," Dawkins said. "There was the expectation of a number of people that I would fall on my face.

"I had to work to win people over into accepting me factually and not on the basis of any prejudices they might have had toward me. But by and large, people were very supportive, including officers who ought to have had some degree of animus. Overall, people who were substantially skeptical at the outset were willing to accept me on the strength of who I was and what I did."

It's not Dawkins' personality to dwell on the anger and envy of others. He has purposely and conveniently stripped from his mind the displeasure some of his Army peers directed at him, letting the memories scatter and blow away with the past.

But there is the other side. Although the Army was partially jealous of Dawkins, it also paraded him around as its proudest peacock. His military life, at times, swirled in contradiction.

"I had to continually guard against the system drawing me away from the kind of work I needed to develop the skills and experience to be successful as a military officer," he said, "diverting me to things that had more cosmetic character about them. At times, I had to fight and scrap."

Dawkins grew weary of the internal war games. Though he won't admit it publicly, they may have contributed to his retirement. Even as a general, he continued to carry his academy sobriquet, St. Peter, putting more pressure on him.

"I was always uncomfortable with that name because it wasn't in harmony with the kind of person I am or my personality," he said. "But it forced me, in a way, to learn to deal with it, not to diminish positive feelings people had for me, soundly based or not, and by the same token, not to simply accept that inappropriate metaphor as it were."

The legacy of St. Peter lives at West Point long after Dawkins has left. At an evening rally before the 1971 Army-Rutgers game, a skit took place in which a

Scarlet Knight from Rutgers (with a New Joisey accent) and a Black Knight of the Hudson were to joust for the fair Rapunzel. The Scarlet Knight was allowed to win the joust, thus setting the stage for a legendary West Point figure to come to the rescue. And who was this erstwhile Black Knight? Who, indeed.

"ST. PETER DAWKINS!" an Army cheerleader screamed.

A motorcycle appeared from the back of the courtyard with its beam flashing. The rider on the cycle was dressed in a silver lame helmet, large yellow Elton John-like sunglasses, fatigues and boots.

The cadets in the yard parted as if some divine being had just arrived. The cyclist revved his machine and accelerated through the divided sea of gray uniforms to a stage, screeching to a halt.

*Athletic ability is but a small part of Pete Dawkins' vast array of talents.*

With the music of "Jesus Christ Superstar" filling the air, the rider leaped onto the stage and proceeded to rip off his helmet, glasses, fatigue jacket and shirt until he stood bare-chested in the icy night.

The cadets suddenly realized that the individual playing the role of St. Peter Dawkins was none other than Maj. Peter Dawkins. The metaphorical St. Peter had become the satirical St. Peter.

"Take off your shirts!" Dawkins ordered the cadets. A few complied. "Take off your *shirts!*" he ordered again. More cadets obeyed, but not all.

St. Peter went for the gusto. "One way, one corps, together, always!" he bellowed. That did it. Every shirt came off as the cadets climbed wildly on each other's shoulders, waving their shirts and yelling, "Go Rabble!" The man clearly was born to lead. Dawkins assured the goose-pimpled cadets that this demonstration was necessary in order for Army to beat Rutgers, which the Cadets did, handily.

Fourteen years later, Pete Dawkins, retired general, leaned back in his tennis whites at John Gardiner's Tennis Ranch in California's idyllic Carmel Valley, where the rich and the famous come to serve and to volley, but also to hob and to nob.

Memorial Day weekend, 1985, marked Dawkins' first time off from Wall Street in 13 weeks. He had played tennis the day before in a San Francisco tournament sponsored by Ethel Kennedy. Dawkins now had only an hour to talk before having lunch with Paul B. (Red) Fay Jr., who served in the same Navy torpedo boat squadron as John F. Kennedy during World War II and who was under secretary of the Navy under Kennedy and Lyndon B. Johnson from 1961-65. Fay is a wealthy paving contractor who lives in San Francisco and remains friends with the Kennedy family.

Dawkins turned 47 in March 1985 but still is powerfully built, with wide shoulders and a trim, athletic build. His blond hair from West Point days is now brown, with streaks of gray, and the hair nudges over his ears. More growth to his life. "It's different," he said of his new non-GI hair style. Then he flashed a winning smile that politicians would kill for.

Dawkins has looks, intelligence, presence, well-roundedness, articulateness, grace and charm, but mainly an aura of power. Seemingly blessed with everything a politician could need, he is the whole package.

From a political standpoint, Dawkins has two other factors on his side: precedent and time. Two other West Point graduates, Grant and Eisenhower, were generals before becoming President. As for time, Ronald Reagan was elected President when he was almost 70. Dawkins needn't be in a hurry.

Dawkins had been mentioned as a possible baseball commissioner before Peter Ueberroth succeeded Bowie Kuhn, but Dawkins wasn't interested in getting back into sports as a full-time occupation. He was rumored as a congressional candidate in Tennessee, Virginia and Michigan, though he remained noncommittal. He seems content, for now, to study the field, weigh his options, contemplate which hat to toss into which political ring. He is tight-mouthed about all rumors relative to his future and his own aspirations.

"We had some long discussions," Fay would say later of his weekend get-together with Dawkins at the tennis ranch. "Pete was asking for information. I wasn't giving him advice. You don't have to tell Pete Dawkins what to do."

Fay, a Republican who served under two Democratic Presidents, made it clear that he wasn't trying to sway Dawkins toward either political party.

"Pete Dawkins has all the qualities you'd want in a politician," he said. "He's bright, forthright, intelligent, honest. And he won't be pushed around."

Judi Wright Dawkins, a cute, pert woman who married Dawkins in 1961, is equally optimistic about her husband's future, but she offered no more insight on his political ambitions than either Fay or Dawkins himself.

"Pete always knew there was more to his life than just the military," she said. "When he retired, we had a son in college and a daughter in high school. We had two cars and a house, all the things people our age are supposed to have. That was all right because we knew the right thing would come along.

"Most people change careers because something negative has happened—an argument, a philosophical difference. In our case, that wasn't it at all. Pete loved the Army. He had been successful, and the future looked very, very bright. But his decision didn't surprise me. It was the right time and the right decision."

Without question. There was nothing more the Army could give Pete Dawkins but possibly a few more stars and a license, in effect, to go fishing at an age when he wouldn't be ready. So, he decided to cut bait from the military and cast his considerable talents in other directions.

"I would be disappointed if the Army was *happy* that I left," Dawkins said. "On balance, the Army was an enormously supportive institution."

But it seems that the Pentagon didn't have nearly the appeal of, say, the Oval Office. Maybe someday we'll get the whole Dawkins story in his presidential memoirs.

# Ernie Davis

*He was proud, courageous and deeply religious. He was a credit to Black America and a symbol of good things to come. He was a man whose talent transcended football. Nobody expected Ernie Davis to die, at least not at the tender age of 23. But death does not play favorites. He died as he lived — with dignity. Ernie Davis created a long legacy in a short time. A nation still mourns.*

# Chapter 11

# A tribute
# to humanity

The day Ernie Davis died, something inside Marty Harrigan died, too.

"He was the closest person I ever had to me outside my own family," Harrigan said. "The greatest kid I ever knew."

They were quite a sight together—the tall, muscular, exuberant young black and the gimpy-legged, runty white Irishman.

Their relationship began as high school athlete and coach, then developed into something deeper. Davis would come to Harrigan for friendship and advice. Harrigan would counsel him as a father would talk to his son. In time, Harrigan became not only Davis' confidant, but also, some observed, his surrogate father.

"Definitely," said Harrigan's wife, Louise.

"That's what Ernie's mother said," Harrigan admitted.

Then Ernie Davis died of leukemia on May 18, 1963. He was only 23. More than 20 years later, Harrigan still has not fully accepted Davis' premature death. His mourning continues.

"He still doesn't like to talk about it," his wife explained.

Harrigan finds it difficult to speak of Davis as someone who is dead, when everything about this specially blessed young man was so alive and vibrant.

"You have to realize I'm biased," said Harrigan, sitting at Bus Horigan's Tavern in Elmira, N.Y. "But some people got it, some don't. Ernie had it. If he walked in here, his presence would make you look twice."

"Ernie would come over to our house," said Louise, having lunch with her husband, "and get on the floor, play with our kids. Even when Ernie was in college, he was just like a real friendly puppy. Marty and I always said that if we could bring up our boys to be like anybody, it would be Ernie."

Said Harrigan: "We got a kid here in high school right now. They say he's the next Ernie Davis. But there's more to it than athletic ability. Ernie was a very special kid.

"You know they say what might have been if. . . . Well, Ernie would have been somebody even if he wasn't good at sports. He'd have been good for the blacks in America. He'd have been a leader."

Eighteen months before he died, Davis became the 27th college football player—and the first black—to win the Heisman Memorial Trophy. He was already good for blacks, although even this appraisal of Davis seems myopic in scope. He was good for everyone who knew him, or knew about him.

Jim Brown encouraged Davis to attend Syracuse University. They wore the same number (44) for the Orangemen. Davis broke many of Brown's school records, then was signed to play in the same Cleveland Browns backfield as Brown but never got the opportunity. Brown, not one to sprinkle platitudes, except on himself, said Davis was "the greatest, most courageous person" he has ever known.

Art Modell, owner of the Browns, retired Davis' pro number (45) even though he never played for Cleveland. "He is the finest boy I have ever met in my life," Modell said.

Ben Schwartzwalder, Davis' football coach at Syracuse, said at the time of Davis' death: "When you talk about Ernie Davis, you're treading on hallowed ground. We always thought he had a halo around him, and now we know he has."

Davis had an angelic presence. There was nothing conceited or deceitful about him; others were more impressed with his fame than he was. He was friendly to everyone, be they heroes or benchwarmers.

He was a kind person, extremely generous. In college, when a movie ticket cost 50 cents, he once had a dollar to treat himself and a friend to a show. A beggar approached them, and Davis gave away the dollar. When Davis' friend told him that he was crazy, that the beggar was just going to use the money to buy cheap booze, Davis replied: "It doesn't matter. God knew my intention."

Davis was deeply religious; he went to church on Sunday without fail and prayed each night before going to sleep.

Put simply, any character flaws he had were awfully hard to find, if they existed at all.

Ernie Davis' brief but honorable life began on December 14, 1939, in New Salem, Pa. Davis' parents separated after his birth, and he never knew his father, who died when he was young. He lived in Uniontown, Pa., with his grandmother until he was 11.

Young Ernie then rejoined his mother, Marie, when she found work in Elmira, N.Y., a manufacturing center that sits on the Chemung River in Chemung County, a few miles above the Pennsylvania state line.

A stranger set of occurrences led to Harrigan's arrival in Elmira. While serving on the island of Iwo Jima in World War II, Harrigan was wounded when a mortar shell exploded and lodged shrapnel in his left leg and right elbow. Surgery was needed to clean out and fuse the two joints. Harrigan left the hospital with less than full extension of his arm, a permanent limp and a future wife.

Louise Coleman Harrigan had been his nurse. "He was in a cast, so I knew I could handle him," she said.

"No," Harrigan said, "she gave me a shot. When I woke up, I had committed myself."

They were married in June 1947. Harrigan received his master's degree in education from Syracuse in 1951 and began searching for a teaching position that included coaching.

He was passed over on several coaching jobs, ostensibly because of his physical condition. "They didn't say it, but that's what it was," he said.

Finally, a job as a high school history teacher and assistant football coach in Elmira opened up. "I came home and told Louise, 'We're going to Elmira,' " Harrigan said. "She didn't know where it was."

Or care. "I thought it was going to be a stopgap thing," she said.

The Harrigans never left Elmira. The wounded veteran became the head football coach at Elmira Free Academy, and his leg ceased to be a handicap.

"The only time it affects me," he said, "is when I can't get an end seat on the left. I went to the Super Bowl (in 1982) at the (Pontiac) Silverdome, a gift from

Louise. My seat was in the middle of a row, but I couldn't sit there. I explained the problem to a guy at the end of the row, but he wouldn't move. I should have punched him, I was so mad. Finally, he moved. That's why I don't go to the movies often—once every six years. Other than that, I don't know that I have a bad leg."

The two most famous names associated with the town of Elmira are Mark Twain and Ernie Davis. Twain, the author of "The Adventures of Tom Sawyer," married an Elmira girl, Olivia Langdon. Both Twain and Davis are buried in Elmira's Woodlawn Cemetery.

But Ernie shared few characteristics with the protagonist of Twain's most famous novel. He was not known for his foolishness or prankishness. Like Tom Sawyer, though, Davis didn't have a harmful bone in his body.

Playing in Elmira's Small Fry League, Davis once had a 75-pound quarterback in his grasp. Instead of throwing the much-smaller boy to the ground, Davis lifted him up until he heard the whistle, then gently lowered the boy to his feet.

Davis entered high school at Elmira Free Academy, where his reputation had preceded him. "Word got around that there was this kid who was big, who was doing things, who was going to be something," Harrigan said. "You'd think other kids would catch up in terms of ability, but Ernie stayed better. He had the speed and attitude.

"He broke his wrist as a freshman and didn't play a lot, then started out as an end on the varsity. He went out for end, so you don't change things. We had him run some end-arounds. He did a good job. We moved him to running back."

Harrigan put his hand on his wife's shoulder. "Genius," he said, smiling.

Davis, who attracted the attention of pro scouts in baseball, was a high school All-America in football and a scholastic All-America in basketball both his junior and senior years. The basketball team ran off 52 straight victories while Davis was there—a New York state record until Power Memorial and a glandular wonder named Lew Alcindor (Kareem Abdul-Jabbar) broke it.

"Some guys in football, when the score's 6-6, give you the rah-rah," Harrigan said. "Ernie did it by example. He always made the big play when it counted.

"We were losing to Johnson County, 13-6. Ernie just took over. He made two straight tackles to stop them. He got the ball and carried it four times in a row, took it right down the field. It was man against boys, get out of the way, let's get this thing going.

"He could do that. He'd run over you or out-speed you. There was only one thing he couldn't do. The kids in summer camp threw him in the lake. He yelled, 'I can't swim, I can't swim.' They had to go in after him."

It was Harrigan's business as a coach and educator to study young people. He could read them like a book, and Davis was an easy study, a pleasant read.

"He was always concerned about the underdog," Harrigan said. "Mickey George, the son of our athletic director, couldn't get his pads on right. We're getting ready to go on the field for a game, and who spots it but Ernie. And who helps the fifth-stringer but Ernie. It isn't anything, but it's a lot."

Opponents would resort to anything in order to stop Davis, including racial epithets. "We had this game in Binghamton," Harrigan recalled. "Guys were giving Ernie cheap shots, calling him 'nigger.' I told him to keep his eyes open. He said: 'Don't worry, Coach. Nothing's going to happen to me. I'm all right.' He was always in control, no problems."

Davis spent countless hours at the Harrigan home. Marty and Louise have six children of their own (five boys and a girl), and Davis was like a seventh. He'd show up because he felt wanted and because he valued his coach's helpful advice.

"He must have had some respect for me," Harrigan said. "I had the same thing for him. We just hit it off.

"He'd ask me about things. . . . I told him, 'Do your job, be who you are. Don't try to be someone else or somebody others think you should be.' He didn't have many problems."

Davis' high school accomplishments did not go unnoticed, and more than four dozen colleges offered him scholarships, including Notre Dame and Michigan. But Davis opted for Syracuse at the urging of two Syracuse graduates, Harrigan and Tony DeFilippo, an Elmira attorney who later represented Davis in contract negotiations with the Browns. Jim Brown helped, too, but Schwartzwalder said he could not have recruited Davis successfully without the efforts of the two men from Elmira.

One year after he arrived at Syracuse, Davis led the Orangemen to their first and only national football championship. That 1959 Syracuse team won all 10 of its regular-season games, including five shutouts in which the Orangemen amassed a total of 225 points. Overall, the Orangemen outscored their opponents, 390-59, the only close shave coming in a 20-18 victory over Penn State. Syracuse led the nation in total offense (451.5 yards per game), rushing offense (313.6 yards per game), scoring (39 points per game), total defense (96.2 yards per game allowed) and rushing defense (19.3 yards per game allowed).

The Orangemen were invited to play Texas in the Cotton Bowl, but four days before the game, Davis pulled a hamstring muscle. It was feared that the star sophomore halfback, who had led the Orangemen in rushing with 686 yards on 98 carries (a 7.0-yard average) and 10 touchdowns, would not be able to play.

Two hours before kickoff, the team physician gave Davis medical clearance to compete. On the third down from scrimmage, Davis made the biggest play of his collegiate career.

Syracuse ran a reverse pass play on which Davis was assigned to go into the flat. But Davis saw that a Texas cornerback and safety were double-covering a Syracuse end, so instinctively—Davis had natural ability plus good instincts—he broke toward the unoccupied center of the field. Halfback Gerhard Schwedes spotted him and threw the ball, and Davis hauled it in and ran 50 yards to the goal line for an 85-yard touchdown play, the longest on a pass in Cotton Bowl history.

Schwartzwalder ran part of the way with Davis, shouting, "Don't pull it, don't pull it," referring to Davis' hamstring. The coach didn't want to lose his indispensable back. As it turned out, Schwartzwalder could have saved himself the exercise.

Davis scored another touchdown on a one-yard plunge in the second quarter, and he also added a pair of two-point conversions on passes from David Sarette for 16 total points. On defense, he intercepted a pass to set up Syracuse's final touchdown in a 23-14 victory, the Orangemen's first ever in a bowl game. Davis was named the game's most valuable player, and the No.1-ranked Orangemen completed the only undefeated season in their history.

Davis' star was on the rise. He ran 80 yards for a touchdown against Boston

University on his first play as a junior and didn't stop that year until he had collected 877 yards on the ground for an average of 7.8 yards per carry, a school season record for rushing average. He also caught 11 passes for 141 yards and scored 10 touchdowns, giving him his best year statistically. Syracuse lost only two games in nine contests, 10-0 to Pittsburgh and 9-6 to Army, and outscored its opponents, 203-74, but the Orangemen did not receive a bowl bid. Davis was named a consensus All-America that season.

Davis played freshman basketball before deciding to concentrate on football when he joined the varsity. During his junior year, however, the basketball team got off to a 2-12 start, and Coach Marc Guley, in need of help, talked Davis and two of his football teammates, John Mackey and Don King, into joining the team. Though out of condition, Davis led the Orangemen to an upset victory over Penn State and averaged 10.2 points and 9.5 rebounds in nine games. All three of the football players earned basketball letters that year.

Davis also was a good student. He graduated in four years with a degree in economics.

"Ernie got an A in my tax law class, and he earned it, too," said Horace Landry, a longtime Syracuse professor. "He was at most classes, except when the team was on the road, and he was an attentive student. He sat in the front row.

"I was rather close to Ernie. He knew he'd have to deal with taxes one day, and he conferred with me about his future profession.

"He was very dedicated, very religious, very conscientious. Ernie was a lovable guy who always had a smile. But he was more serious than the other great running backs we had here."

Landry was asked to describe each of these backs in a word. "Floyd Little was an extrovert," he said. "Jim Brown was reserved. Larry Csonka was indifferent. Davis was polished. I've had a lot of students come and go in 35 years, but I would have remembered Ernie Davis even if he hadn't won the Heisman Trophy."

Davis' Heisman year, 1961, started off as anything but an award-winning season. He suffered leg injuries and bruised a shoulder in a 19-8, opening-game victory at Oregon State against the Beavers and the 1962 Heisman winner, Terry Baker. Still, Davis scored two touchdowns that day.

Davis was too injured to practice the following week and rushed for only 35 yards against West Virginia, although the Orange prevailed, 29-14. After the game, a television reporter asked Davis if the injuries had hindered his effectiveness. Davis said no, he had just had a bad day. He never offered excuses, even when they were justified.

The "Elmira Express" then popped into gear with two 100-plus-yard rushing days and three 90-plus games to finish the season with 823 yards. He also led the team in receiving with 16 catches for 157 yards, scored 15 touchdowns, threw a 74-yard touchdown pass—on his first pass attempt of the season—to Mackey against Colgate and returned an interception 63 yards for a touchdown against Boston College. Davis, who also returned punts and kickoffs, was a complete football player.

The All-America halfback erased several of Brown's school records, including career rushing; Davis gained 2,386 yards on 360 carries, while Brown, the National Football League's all-time leading rusher until his record was broken in 1984, collected 2,091 yards on 361 carries. Davis ranks third on the school's career scoring list with 220 points (Brown scored 187). He also exceeded the career marks of Brown, Little, Csonka and every other Syracuse player in history by averaging 6.6 yards per rush and 6.8 yards per play in total offense in his three-year Syracuse career.

Davis played his last game with the Orangemen in the Liberty Bowl against Miami of Florida. The Orangemen trailed at halftime, 14-0, as Davis rushed 10 times for only 38 yards. He exploded in the second half with 20 carries for 102 yards, including a one-yard plunge for Syracuse's first touchdown. The Orangemen closed the gap to 14-8 when Sarette connected with halfback Dick Easterly for a two-point conversion. Davis set up his team's only other touchdown by providing 25 yards on four carries in a 51-yard drive. Then he batted away George Mira's long desperation pass near the Orange goal line to preserve Syracuse's 15-14 victory.

The Liberty Bowl triumph made Syracuse 8-3 for the season and 26-5 for the Ernie Davis era, which also included a national championship, two bowl victories and the school's one Heisman Trophy.

Davis won the trophy after the closest race in Heisman history—a 53-point difference. Davis received 824 points to 771 for Ohio State fullback Bob Ferguson. Texas halfback James Saxton was third and Minnesota quarterback Sandy Stephens, from Davis' boyhood home of Uniontown, was fourth.

President John F. Kennedy, who happened to be in New York City at the same time Davis was there for the Heisman presentation, asked to meet Davis. A meeting was arranged at the Hotel Carlyle, and Davis hopped into a taxi for a wild ride. He was delayed by traffic, however, and barely missed the President. Davis then received word at lunch that Kennedy was at the Waldorf-Astoria and still wanted to meet him.

Davis grabbed his trophy, jumped in another cab and rushed over to the Waldorf, where he met and chatted briefly with the President. Davis then got back in a taxi and zipped back to the Heisman luncheon. Grinning broadly, he ordered Schwartzwalder to "put 'er there, put 'er there" with the hand that had just been embraced by the President of the United States. Davis was truly overwhelmed that Kennedy had wanted to meet *him*.

"It was a big thrill for me, the biggest next to winning the Heisman," he said afterward. "I never thought I'd get the honor of shaking hands with him."

During a news conference later that day, Marty Harrigan slipped unnoticed into the back of the room. He drove from Elmira to New York City for the Heisman festivities without telling Davis, who spotted him eventually and ran over to give him a hug.

"What are you doing here, Coach?" a surprised Davis asked with a big smile.

"You're a big man here," Harrigan replied. "What the hell you doing?"

They hugged again, strongly. There were no clues then that leukemia already was ravaging the inside of Davis' powerful 6-foot-2, 210-pound frame. Not even Davis was aware of it.

The people of Elmira staged an "Ernie Davis Day" for their hometown hero in February 1962. They presented him with a new Thunderbird automobile, and the largest sports banquet crowd in Elmira history, 1,500, turned out along with New York Gov. Nelson Rockefeller, Modell, Schwartzwalder and Jim Brown to salute

Davis.

Harrigan, the toastmaster for the affair, told the audience that Davis' only limitation was his inability to swim. Davis responded by saying that he would learn, thanks to the lifetime membership he had just received from the Elmira YMCA.

He never got around to taking a swim lesson.

The NFL draft put Davis in the headlines again as the Washington Redskins, with the first pick in the draft, considered selecting him as the first black ever to play for the franchise. It was a major story at the time, and reporters asked Davis about the possibility of his breaking the Redskins' color line.

"I wish they would quit bringing up this race stuff," he finally told one reporter in frustration. "I don't want to be another Jackie Robinson. I just want to play football, and I'll go where I can get the best offer."

Be yourself, do your job, Harrigan had advised the young athlete.

The government got into the act. Secretary of the Interior Stewart Udall instructed Redskins Owner George Preston Marshall to hire a black player or possibly find himself guilty of discriminatory employment practices. The Redskins eventually drafted Davis in the first round.

Reporters asked Davis if it would bother him to sign with a team that, in effect, practiced segregation. "Not at all," he replied. "I don't worry about racial issues."

Always in control, Harrigan had said.

The Redskins traded the negotiating rights to Davis to Cleveland for running back-receiver Bobby Mitchell, a future Hall of Famer, and the signing rights to rookie halfback Leroy Jackson. Both are black.

Davis signed a three-year, no-cut contract with the Cleveland Browns worth $65,000. He also received a $15,000 bonus, part of which, he said, would pay off the $4,500 mortgage on his mother's home.

"We don't think we are taking any kind of risk," Modell said about Davis' contract, the largest ever paid an NFL rookie at that time. "He'll make the team." The two men then held up Davis' bonus check for the cameras, which clicked and flashed. Modell and Davis smiled confidently.

Davis still had three all-star games in which to participate before he was scheduled to begin his career with the Browns. He was the leading rusher in the East-West Shrine Game in San Francisco with 83 yards on 18 carries, but his East team lost, 21-8. The Syracuse halfback ran for the two-point conversion after the East's only touchdown.

Next was the Coaches All-America game in Buffalo. By that time, Davis' gums had begun to bleed and canker sores had formed in his mouth. He felt tired, but teammates told him it was because of the extreme heat in Buffalo.

Davis suited up for the June 29 game and was booed loudly when introduced. The Buffalo Bills of the American Football League also had drafted Davis and reportedly offered him $135,000 over three years. But Davis chose the NFL, he said, because he wanted to "play with and against the best." The Buffalo fans remembered that comment and booed him loudly whenever he touched the ball, which wasn't often. Davis didn't play well, but the East still won, 13-8.

Davis was asked after the game about the boos. "I've never heard them before," he answered, "but then I didn't play too well, either."

After returning from Buffalo, Davis stopped by his old coach's house. Louise Harrigan always kept an extra supply of hot dogs and soft drinks whenever she knew Davis was in town. He had a sizable appetite, but on this day he politely refused all offers of food. The Harrigans were stunned. Davis then explained about his bleeding gums, which Marty and Louise recommended should be checked immediately. He said that he would see a doctor as soon as he reported to Cleveland's training camp.

The Browns' medical staff diagnosed the problem as trench mouth. Davis had two wisdom teeth extracted, then left for the College All-Star Game in Chicago. But his mouth remained sore, and he continued to have trouble eating.

Davis was the leading rusher in a scrimmage against the Chicago Bears a week before the College All-Star Game against the NFL champion Green Bay Packers. But two days later, he awakened with a swollen neck. Davis, believing that he had the mumps or mononucleosis, was hospitalized for more tests. He was not allowed to play in the August 3 all-star game.

No one was quite sure what was wrong with Ernie Davis. Or if they knew, they weren't prepared to say.

Davis spent the next several weeks in the hospital without knowing the identity of his illness. He said he did not feel sick and that the hardest thing for him was not being able to practice with the Browns. Then on October 4, 1962, the doctors told Davis what was wrong with him: He had acute monocytic leukemia, the most severe form of the blood disease.

The diagnosis shocked Davis initially, but his only reply was "Darn."

Though the doctors did not expect Davis to live more than a year—reporters were sworn to secrecy after being apprised of that prognosis—they said that the disease was in remission, that his physical condition was excellent and that he could start practicing football. For the next 7½ months until he died, Davis stayed active, working out on his own while the Browns practiced nearby and sitting with his teammates on the bench when Cleveland played at home. He spent the winter of 1963 playing basketball with the Browns and working as a salesman for a soft-drink distributor. He also made periodic visits to the hospital for checkups.

Modell, the Browns' owner, became not only Davis' employer, but also his friend. He paid Davis' salary and medical expenses during his illness, and he put Davis to work on a film study for the club. Almost until the day he died, Davis kept apologizing to Modell for all the money he was costing the Browns.

Davis rarely burdened others with the inevitability of his own death, and seldom did he provide friends the opportunity to question him about his disease. He was too busy peppering them with questions about their own lives, always with a genuine interest, that familiar big smile and a veil of optimism.

"Ernie called and asked if he could come by and see me," recalled Michael O. Sawyer, a vice chancellor at Syracuse who then was chairman of the school's Citizenship Program. " 'If?' My God, a Heisman winner, and he had to ask 'if.'

"I knew he was going to die, but he came bounding into my office. What effort that took. He wore a suit with a vest to cover up how emaciated he was. How do you talk to a young man who had his whole life before him but was going to die in a few weeks? Ernie guided the conversation. He wanted to know about my work, how were the students, how was my life going. He didn't give me a chance to ask about him.

"I had always admired Ernie Davis. He was the perfect gentleman and a gentle man. He was such a stylish young man. Now he was a sick young man, sitting in front of me, so positive. I thought to myself that if I were his age and that sick, I couldn't be as strong as he was inside.

"Once he was through asking questions, he jumped up and bounded out of my office." Sawyer never saw Davis again.

Leukemia was stealing a little more of Davis' life every day, but it never robbed him of his inner strength. He never broke down in the presence of others. If he cried, as he must have, he always was alone.

Schwartzwalder and several of his Syracuse assistant coaches went to see Davis in a Cleveland hospital one day. They visited for three hours, then got up to leave.

Davis placed himself in the doorway. "Please don't go," he said. "This will be the last time I'll ever see you."

He said it calmly, without alarm in his voice. They visited some more, talking about football-related topics. Not once did Davis talk about himself or sound depressed.

Finally, it was time to go. Goodbyes were said, and Schwartzwalder and his staff left Davis' room. The coaches walked a few steps down the hall, then began to cry uncontrollably.

Six weeks before Davis' death, the Saturday Evening Post published an article titled "I'm Not Unlucky," which Davis wrote in collaboration with Cleveland sportswriter Bob August.

"Someplace along the line," Davis wrote, "you have to come to an understanding with yourself, and I had reached mine a long time before, when I was still in the hospital. Either you fight or you give up. For a time I was so despondent I would just lie there, not even wanting to move. One day I got hold of myself. I decided I would face up to whatever I had and try to beat it. I still feel that way."

Davis never gave up the fight. Believing in miracles till the end, he visited friends with hello in his heart and goodbye haunting his mind.

Marty Harrigan can't remember specifically the last words he spoke to Davis. "Probably, 'Good luck, you'll beat it,'" he said. "There has to be a crack in the dam to discuss something like that. He never gave you the chance. He was so positive. You wanted to believe it. In your heart you might have questioned it, but you didn't."

Davis came by the Harrigans' house once after that and was turned away. "Susan, our daughter, had chicken pox," Louise Harrigan explained. "Ernie would have been susceptible to picking it up, so I had to tell him at the door, 'Ernie, I can't let you in.'

"I never saw him again, and I'm just sick about that. Susan felt like that, too. She just loved Ernie. We all did."

On May 16, 1963, Davis dropped by the offices of the Cleveland Browns and told club officials that he was checking into the hospital. Apparently unaware that death was imminent, he said that he expected to be released in a couple of days.

Two days later, he died in his sleep.

Newspapers were filled with eulogies describing the multitude of qualities possessed by the young gentleman from Elmira. One of the finest was delivered by his coach at Syracuse.

"Ernie was the perfect boy," Schwartzwalder said. "You hope you find one like him and you never do. He was the friendliest, happiest kid I ever met. In spite of his great skill he was humble, so much a team man that the other boys idolized him as their leader. . . .

"He just radiated pleasantness, and he had the highest ideals. He just couldn't do enough for people, and he did it all with a smile. Gosh, he even thanked folks asking for his autograph. If the fourth-string quarterback wanted to practice forward passing, Ernie would volunteer to stay late with him as his receiver, even though he was the star of the team. No one on the squad resented the publicity he received. They rejoiced in it far more than he did. Perhaps that's the biggest tip-off of all on his character."

About 1,600 people packed the First Baptist Church sanctuary and basement for Davis' funeral, while 3,000 more stood in a park outside the church. President Kennedy paid tribute to Davis in a telegram in which he called the Heisman winner "an outstanding young man of great character who consistently served as an inspiration to the young people of the country." Hundreds more people joined the funeral procession to Woodlawn Cemetery.

★     ★     ★

Seated at Bus Horigan's Tavern in Elmira, Harrigan patted his wife on the shoulder. They got up, waved to other patrons of the tavern and walked outside to their car.

"I'll show you where Ernie lived," Harrigan said.

He drove toward the north side of town and crossed the bridge over the Chemung River. He came to Lake Street and stopped in front of Ernie Davis Park. Davis had lived with his mother on that property, but their house was torn down to build the park. Directly across the street from the park is Ernie Davis Junior High School, which was Elmira Free Academy when Harrigan first laid eyes on the big kid who was going to win the Heisman.

"This part of town is where the poor blacks used to live," Harrigan said, adding that they now live "everywhere." Harrigan studied the scene as one who was lost in a once-familiar place.

"I don't go around here anymore," he said. "The blacks don't know me. I don't know them. And I used to know everyone in town."

Harrigan said it with a touch of melancholy. He looked around once more, then drove off toward the new Elmira Free Academy, which opened its doors in 1963.

Inside a large entrance hall to the gymnasium is an enlarged photograph of Davis. "He could do it all," a plaque reads, "beat every opponent . . . except one." Mementos from Davis' life are found throughout the academy. It makes little difference that he didn't attend the school in its present location; he is the academy's one link to fame.

Harrigan, now retired, still is recognizable at the academy, where he rose in rank from assistant coach to head coach to principal and where he now works as a volunteer coach on the junior varsity football team. He likes to stay active, and he still loves to work with kids.

Marty and Louise Harrigan have lived in the same house in Elmira since 1951. Their home has a warm, lived-in look about it. Upon reaching the house, Harrigan said he would try to reach Davis' mother on the phone. He did.

Marie Fleming works in the cafeteria at Elmira College. She is a big, handsome woman, Harrigan said, and a good Christian. She also is very proud of her dead son.

"He was my only child," she said on the phone. "He was just my child, nothing out of the ordinary. Just like all boys. . . . My son was always very considerate. He wanted to know what he could do to help. He was more concerned about others' welfare than his own. He never neglected his duties.

"I've been asked many times to describe Ernie. How would a mother describe her child? Very loving, caring. . . .

"When I was first told of his illness, they didn't tell me the whole story until quite later. A doctor from the Cleveland Browns told me. I never talked to my son about death. I had a few close friends, a priest. They'd talk to him. Ernie never gave me the opportunity. He was so courageous. He always made you think he could beat it."

Her son's death at 23, when he had just begun to achieve his vast potential, made Mrs. Fleming question her faith—for a while.

"A few days after he passed away, those thoughts were going through my mind," she said. "A priest came to talk to me. He said, 'I guess you're wondering why.' I told him I was. He said, 'If you went into a flower garden, you wouldn't pick the wilted flower. You'd pick the prettiest.'

"That's when my grieving stopped."

But not her dreams—or her curiosity.

"One of the thoughts I have most about Ernie is that I wish I had a grandchild," she said. "I also wonder what kind of man Ernie would have made. With all the corruption you see today, I don't think he'd turn to drugs or alcohol, things like that. My belief is that he would have been what he was in his younger days."

Ernie Davis was a shining example of youth. He could have been the same for adults. "Naturally, I feel that way," his mother said. "That's what they all say."

Marie Fleming, married three times but with no progeny to leave as her legacy, thanked the caller and went back to doing God's work.

Harrigan had a plaque in his hand. "This scroll," Davis had dictated in 1962, "is presented to Marty Harrigan upon my graduation from Syracuse University. In appreciation of your devotion, confidence, understanding and guidance in helping me to achieve this important plateau in my life." Davis had a similar plaque made for Tony DeFilippo.

"Ernie was loyal," said Harrigan, looking at his plaque. "Oh, so loyal. You don't get that today."

Harrigan hung the plaque back on the wall between two photographs. One picture shows Davis and Harrigan together, the coach's hand on the boy's shoulder. The other, which shows Davis in a Syracuse football uniform, is signed: "To the Harrigan boys. Best of luck, Ernie."

"One of our proudest moments," Louise Harrigan said, "was when our son Mickey won the Ernie Davis Award (recognizing the top two-sport athlete who exhibits the best qualities of citizenship and school involvement) at the high school. Tears

*Marty Harrigan, Ernie Davis' high school coach, close personal friend and surrogate father, poses next to Davis' grave in Elmira, N.Y. Note the inscription below the name.*

were in Marty's eyes when he presented the trophy."

Said Harrigan: "Every year I give out the trophy, and I still get a lump in my throat. And it's been more than 20 years."

Harrigan told his wife, "I'll be back in a little while." He got in the car and went out to see Ernie Davis.

Harrigan pulled into Woodlawn Cemetery and parked in front of a large tombstone with the inscription, "Ernie Davis, Heisman Trophy, 1961." Beneath that are the words, "Ernest R., 1939-63."

"I'll say a prayer," said Harrigan, clasping his hands, bowing his head and speaking silently to himself. Then he raised his eyes and fixed them on the tombstone.

"I come here every year on the anniversary of his death," he said. "I pick a basket of flowers to place by his grave. I picked Marie up from the college this year and brought her with me.

"You know, I never talked this way, but if it had ever come to that, I would have adopted Ernie. I'd have done anything for him."

More than two decades later, the same thoughts run through Harrigan's mind when he looks at Ernie Davis' grave.

"I always think to myself, 'Why?' " he said. "Then I think God must have wanted him for something."

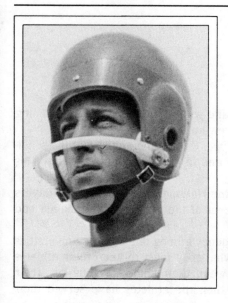

# Terry Baker

*He could do it all. Football, basketball, baseball — nothing, it seemed, was beyond his athletic talent. But there was more to him than met the eye. He was a civic-minded honor student who took as much pride in academics as in sports accomplishments. Whether passing a test or a football, he was a shining example of today's missing link — the scholar-athlete. Where have you gone Terry Baker?*

# Chapter 12

# A gentleman and a scholar

We have lost Terry Baker.

Not Terry Baker, the man. He is alive and well in the Northwest, practicing law in Portland, the Oregon city where he grew up.

Rather, we have lost Terry Baker, the *type*. He was the epitome of the schol-ar-athlete, an All-America both on the field and in the classroom. Somehow, his type is no longer as important.

Figures released several years ago by the National Football League Players Association indicated that less than 50 percent of the players in the league had college degrees.

It's little wonder. There is a general tendency among this nation's universities not to graduate their athletes. Schools do what they must to keep their athletes academically eligible for competition, but when their eligibility runs out, their scholastic standing no longer matters. By then the athletes have served their purpose.

But have the schools served theirs? Is it right that universities admit some students on the strength of their rushing averages, not their grade-point averages? Should athletes be allowed to take a succession of Mickey Mouse courses and to receive doctored grades, thus qualifying them to play football while masquerading as students?

Don't blame the athletes—at least not entirely—for taking advantage of the situation. As football has become a year-round commitment instead of a one-se-mester activity, athletes now are afforded less time to study than the collegiate athletes of yesteryear. Coaches are telling youngsters they have to spend more time on the practice field, in the weight room and in the film room than at the library if they want to keep that starting job.

Nor are the coaches entirely responsible for this controverted system. Many of them are under the gun of the school's alumni, who will pay the coaches' six-figure contracts as long as their teams go 12-0 or 10-2. But don't go 8-4. So, the coaches tamper with transcripts, violate recruiting rules and look the other way as fat-cat alums slip envelopes filled with bills into the hands of poor, appreciative 18-year-old kids.

The deception extends further. College athletic directors and even presidents are aware of the unethical practices, but when the hammer comes down from the NCAA, they act innocent. And it's the coaches who get fired.

Where does it end? Where did it begin?

The student-athlete, in the origin of that coupling, was something totally differ-ent from what exists on college campuses today. It went without saying years ago that young men were, as the name implies, students first and athletes second. The system required that everyone involved work under that assumption.

Terry Baker, the type, was what universities had in mind. Terry Baker, the man, emerged as one of the finest examples of the student-athlete concept.

Baker's list of collegiate honors seems endless. In 1962 alone he was named to every major All-America football team after leading the nation's major colleges in total offensive yardage. The Sporting News, the Associated Press and United Press International, among other publications, selected the Oregon State quarterback as their Player of the Year. Sports Illustrated picked Baker as its Sportsman of the Year in '62, the only time a college football player has received that award, and the Helms Foundation honored him as the top athlete in North America. Oregon State retired his jersey number (11), an honor bestowed on no other male athlete in the school's history.

Baker's gridiron talent did not escape the watchful eye of the Downtown Athletic Club, either. Baker received the Heisman Memorial Trophy in December 1962, making him the first player from a West Coast school ever to win the bronze statue.

Baker excelled in basketball as well as football. The 6-foot-3-inch, 191-pound guard was a three-year letterman in both sports and was a senior captain of the 1962-63 Oregon State basketball team, which reached the Final Four of the NCAA Tournament.

Baker also was a gifted baseball player, although he did not have enough time to compete in three sports in college. In fact, he was a righthanded pitcher. That's nothing remarkable—except for the fact that as a quarterback, he threw with his *left* hand. On top of everything else, the blond-haired youngster was ambidextrous.

"When I started playing baseball," Baker explained, "there weren't any gloves for lefthanders, so I played righthanded."

Baker needed both hands to juggle his many college activities because, amazingly, all the preceding laurels related to just one side of Terry Baker, the athletic side. The other half of Terry Baker—the intelligent, studious, civic-minded half—was just as successful and respected as the athletic half. As a college junior, Baker was elected president of his social fraternity, Phi Delta Theta; the office normally is held by a senior. Then a year later he received the Arthur Priest Award, which is given annually to the top Phi Delt in the nation. He also was a member of the Blue Key, the school's honor society for seniors, and was the state chairman of the Easter Seal drive to help crippled children.

Baker was an honor student in mechanical engineering, one of the most demanding departments in the Oregon State curriculum, and as a senior was named an academic All-America. He graduated in four years with a 3.0 grade-point average and was awarded a $500 scholarship for postgraduate work from the National Football Foundation and Hall of Fame. Only seven other student-athletes received that scholarship.

In short, Baker was almost too much to believe. In a Sports Illustrated cover story, Alfred Wright wrote that 1962 produced "another kind of sportsman, a genus that had seemed on its way to becoming as extinct an American joy as the rumble seat and ukelele: namely, the college football hero. Such was Terry Baker. In an era when the celebrated college athlete is turning into a special kind of mercenary, living and competing in a culture apart from that of the ordinary undergraduate, it is fitting that Baker, a throwback to an epoch in which the likes of Barry

Wood and Byron (Whizzer) White inspired the undergraduates at Harvard and Colorado, should emerge from a bucolic campus deep in the forests of the Northwest, where the simple verities of small-town American life are still held in high esteem."

Like the stereotyped small-town sports legend, Baker was heroic, yet humble. A leader, yet unassuming. Victorious, yet virtuous. And the fact that Baker maintained these qualities while rising from his humble beginnings to the heights of stardom made him all the more appealing. Terry Baker's story is straight from the pages of a Horatio Alger novel.

Baker was born poor, dirt poor, on May 5, 1941, in Pine River, Minn., to a maverick father and a gentle but strong mother. Max Baker was many things— trapper, farmer, machinist, inventor—but not too successful at any of them. "He was always trying to invent something," Terry recalled of his father.

After the Bakers moved to California and then to Oregon, Max Baker abandoned the family, leaving his wife, Laura, to bring up three boys by herself. Terry had two older brothers, Richard and Gary.

Laura Baker worked hard at a variety of jobs for many years. She made sure her sons enjoyed their childhoods, providing for them as best she could, but the responsibility of supporting them with no help from her husband took its toll. "She made $25 a week," Terry Baker said, "and nearly killed herself."

Laura Baker couldn't afford her first automobile until 1962, but she did make sure her boys received college educations. All three sons graduated from Oregon State. Meanwhile, Laura Baker gave her boys a proper moral upbringing.

"I did teach them to be honest," she told the Portland Oregonian newspaper in 1962. "And I always told Terry when he was getting all this glory in high school to just be himself. You just can't beat anybody but your own self."

Fame would bring Terry Baker face to face with a man he never expected to meet as a young adult—his father. The encounter took place in 1960, Baker's sophomore year at Oregon State, when the Beavers were playing Washington State in Pullman, Wash. Baker was leaving the field after the first half when someone grabbed his arm.

"Butch," a man said.

Baker turned and looked into the face of a stranger.

"I'm your dad," the man said.

Terry Wayne Baker was known as "Butch" until he entered high school. He searched for words, then told his father, "I'll see you after the game."

Baker played poorly in the second half. Tommy Prothro, the Beavers' coach, finally removed Baker from the game. Prothro was unaware of what had taken place at halftime, and Baker didn't tell him.

Baker saw his father briefly after the game. "It wasn't strained," he recalled of their meeting. "But it developed into a delicate situation."

Max Baker pressured his youngest son, using him to make contact with the rest of his children. Terry saw through his father's intentions, however, and when Max Baker sent Butch a watch for Christmas, it was mailed back with an unwritten message: It's too late.

"My mom was very hurt by that," Baker said of the watch incident, "so I just cooled it. I've had very little contact with my father since."

Methodically and determinedly, young Terry Baker honed his athletic skills. Every weekend he would work on one phase of his athletic development. Whether it was the sideline pass in football, a jump shot in basketball or a curveball in baseball, he would spend the entire weekend working on that one challenge. By Sunday night he generally had it mastered. Then he would go on to another aspect of one of his favorite sports the next weekend. By the end of the year, Baker had developed 52 new skills.

Baker always had a plan. He was so quietly goal-oriented, however, that others didn't always recognize his fierce dedication. That dedication, plus his natural and developed talent, made it virtually impossible for him not to succeed as an athlete.

His first varsity basketball game at Jefferson High School in Portland was indicative of the success that lay ahead. Baker, a sophomore, was put in the game only because a starting guard had fouled out.

"The game went into sudden-death overtime," said Gary Baker, who played on that same basketball team as a senior. "I came down the court with the ball and was just about set to shoot when I saw Terry and passed over to him. He shot with about three guys hanging on him, and the ball went in the basket. . . . It was his first shot and his first basket, and it won the game."

When Baker was a senior, Jefferson High won three city championships—one each in football, basketball and baseball—and two state championships. Baker was all-city and all-state in all three sports, and schools nationwide recruited him with any of those sports in mind, although most recruiters envisioned him as a future football or basketball player. Pepper Rodgers, then an Air Force Academy assistant football coach, spent so much time at Jefferson in pursuit of Baker that some students thought he was part of the faculty.

As it turned out, Rodgers was wasting his time because Baker wasn't interested in playing college football. For one thing, Baker was rather slim for the violent world of football. He had strong legs, which gave him the appearance of an athlete from the waist down, but from the waist up he looked like a math major. "I wasn't built to take the punishment," Baker said.

Prothro agreed. The Oregon State coach watched Baker in a high school game and got the impression that Baker didn't like contact. Prothro later changed his mind the following summer after scouting Baker in an all-star game of graduated high school seniors, but by that time the 18-year-old youngster had decided to play basketball and baseball in college.

Basketball was the second reason why Baker initially declined to play college football.

"What did the comedian—I think it was Dick Gregory—say?" Baker said. "Something like, 'Success is getting where you want, happiness is getting what you want.' I liked football, and it brought me a lot of success, but I was happy to play basketball."

Baker decided to attend Oregon State, 80 miles south of Portland in Corvallis, because of his family's financial situation—he couldn't afford the cost of transportation to a school too far away—and also because Oregon State had a good engineering department. He also liked the man who gave him a scholarship, Amory T. (Slats) Gill, who coached the Beavers' basketball teams from 1929-64. "He was the most personable high school senior I had ever met," Gill said of Baker a few years later.

Baker was that rare Heisman Trophy winner who did not play freshman football. Instead, he was a ballboy during Beaver varsity games and a general helper in the school's athletic department, a job that brought him a much-needed $15 per month. "The fans really got on me," he said of his ballboy experience.

But when basketball season rolled around, Baker led the freshman team in scoring with 252 points in a 16-game season. He signed up for freshman baseball, but it rained hard that spring—even harder than it normally rains in the damp state—and a number of Beaver games were postponed or canceled. Bored, Baker wandered by the football coach's office one day. Prothro invited him to attend a team meeting, and Baker, who already had given some thought to playing football, agreed.

Prothro, a master psychologist, had something waiting for the youngster. When Baker entered the meeting room, he saw his name on the chalkboard listed right below the starting tailback, Don Kasso. Baker dropped baseball on the spot. From that point on, his two college sports were football and basketball.

In 1960, Baker's sophomore year, he alternated at tailback with Kasso, who was a junior, in Oregon State's single-wing offense. Kasso was injured in the fourth week of that season, allowing Baker to take over the starting job. He compiled 284 yards of total offense against Idaho, 302 yards (87 rushing, 215 passing) against Rose Bowl-bound Washington and 252 yards against California. He ran 83 yards for a touchdown in the California game. Despite the fact that Baker had never played in the single wing before—Jefferson High used the T-formation—his 1,473 yards of total offense for the season was a school record and ranked him sixth nationally.

Delighted with the performance of his new recruit, who was named the team's rookie of the year, Prothro dropped the single wing and switched to the T-formation, making it possible for Kasso and Baker, now his quarterback, both to operate in the backfield at the same time. The transition was rocky; Oregon State fell off from Baker's 6-3-1 sophomore year to 5-5 his junior season. His total offense (1,230 yards) dropped, too.

Prothro, however, was banking on long-term results. Though his junior year was his worst statistically, Baker made several plays that convinced Prothro that better days were on the horizon.

For example, in Oregon State's '61 season opener against Syracuse—a game that matched two future Heisman winners, Ernie Davis and Baker—the junior quarterback turned in the game's most spectacular play. From Syracuse's 36-yard line, he dropped back to pass. Three big linemen descended on him, forcing Baker to retreat farther. At midfield, he made a move that left all three Orangemen lurching for air, and then he weaved through the remaining defenders—in all, nine players had a shot at him—for a touchdown.

"Terry may not look fast," Kasso said after the game, which Oregon State lost, 19-8, "but that long-legged lope of his really eats up ground and fools people. They don't think he's moving as fast as he is."

Baker made another spectacular run against Stanford, galloping 25 yards down one sideline, then 25 yards down the opposite sideline to the 3-yard line. Oregon State failed to score, though, and Stanford won, 34-0.

Despite the disappointing season, Baker made the October 16, 1961, cover of Sports Illustrated as "The Best Athlete in College," a title that took into account his baseball talent and basketball exploits. That article preceded his junior basketball season, when Baker and 7-foot center Mel Counts led the Beavers to the West Regional. They lost the championship game to UCLA, 88-69, but Baker was selected to the All-West Regional team.

Baker was an ideal playmaking guard—smart, decisive, creative and swift on the fast break. "Terry can't work much around the backboards against the tall men," Gill said, "but he is fast and intelligent and competitive and makes wonderful plays."

Adding to Baker's remarkable talents was his amazing adaptability. Most athletes making the conversion from football to basketball require three to four weeks to ease into condition because of the different playing surfaces and the different leg muscles used in the two sports. Baker needed only a week.

Meanwhile, he kept up with his classes—no easy chore in itself considering the tough nature of the engineering curriculum—so that he could graduate on time with his freshman class.

"Because of basketball and playing in the NCAA Tournament, I was forever taking finals late," he said. "I also missed some practices or showed up late because of my class schedule. But my coaches never suggested I change classes in order to make every practice. In fact, they encouraged me not to.

"I don't think the same values are encouraged today. A coach making $100,000 a year doesn't want his career hurt because some 20-year-old kid takes a class and misses practice. The coach is running a big business. We've seen it for years, players who are in school who don't belong there."

No student at Oregon State from 1959-63 carried a heavier academic-athletic-fraternal load than Baker, who somehow still managed to find time for social activities, too. As a junior, Baker began dating Marilyn Davis, an attractive freshman from Newport Beach, Calif. They studied together in the library, then went out later for ice cream sodas. Marilyn kept the social end of his life pretty busy after that even though Baker didn't have much money for dating. He was dubbed the nation's finest all-around college athlete, but that didn't mean that Oregon State gave him special treatment. On the contrary. His scholarship, which was transferred from the basketball budget to the football budget after his sophomore year, took care of his $80 room and board at the Phi Delta Theta house, his $270 tuition and the $40 to $50 he spent annually on books, and that was it. An Oregon State scholarship at that time actually allowed $90 for room and board, but Baker was permitted to pocket the remaining $10, which came in handy for ice cream sodas.

Baker wasn't treated preferentially at the Phi Delt house, either. He and the other members of the fraternity slept in a large room filled with double-decker bunks. Baker was given a small corner room, measuring about 10 feet by 10 feet, in which to study and hang his clothes, but two other Phi Delts shared the room with him.

One night, Prothro and his wife invited Baker to dinner. Baker simply couldn't get over the huge spread of food on the table. "Do you always eat like this?" he gasped. When Prothro said yes, Baker responded, "Gee, I hope some day I'll be rich enough to eat this way."

The experience of coaching Terry Baker had a profound effect on Prothro. "I'd probably have never known him if he hadn't been a football player," the coach said, "but if he hadn't been a football player and I'd known him, I'd still think he was one of the most unusual boys I'd ever known—if not *the* most unusual."

John Eggers, the Oregon State sports information director who played a major role in the growth of the Terry Baker legend, was equally taken aback by Baker.

"Terry had a photographic mind and could memorize pages one at a time when reading books," Eggers recalled. "He was always relaxed, too. One time we were driving to Portland, and all of a sudden he said, 'John, I think I'll take a little nap.' He leaned his head back and was sound asleep in just moments."

Although Baker spread himself thin with all his responsibilities, he was always in control. Adm. Daniel B. Miller, who taught Baker in a general engineering course, said he was "one of the best students I ever had. . . . Terry showed me a clear, decisive mind, and his work is neat and logical. Above all, he knows how to husband his time, and his concentration is remarkable. You could shoot a gun off in the room when he is studying and it wouldn't disturb him."

It can be stated safely that Terry Baker is the most exciting thing ever to happen in Corvallis, a sleepy white-collar town with a current population of about 41,000. But then, not much happens in Corvallis, which is nestled in the Willamette Valley next to the Cascade Mountains. Corvallis' main attraction is good family living with a touch of the peaceful outdoors. If you're looking for nightlife, don't try Corvallis. But if you like good fishing, the Willamette River runs right through town.

Corvallis was mighty proud back when the 1941 Oregon State football team won the only Rose Bowl game not played in Pasadena. The Beavers went all the way to Durham, N.C., to play the game on January 1, 1942, because the United States had just gone to war and the West Coast was petrified by the possibility of a Japanese invasion. No one wanted to risk having 100,000 people inside the Rose Bowl stadium with Japanese submarines lurking in the Pacific. So, Oregon State traveled to Duke and beat the Blue Devils, 20-16. Duke's blocking back in that game was a big, strapping kid named Tommy Prothro.

That victory, however, didn't touch the nation's pulse—or even the state of Oregon's—the way Terry Baker did two decades later. A Heisman in Corvallis? Baker himself, obviously, did the most to build his collegiate legend by excelling in two sports. His image was enhanced, though, by Prothro, who constructed an offense that showcased his talents, and by Eggers, the geographically isolated sports publicity director whose astute approach to his job made Terry Baker well known to sportswriters and fans across the land.

In 1962, Heisman huckstering didn't exist. College flacks sent out the usual weekly press releases, which consisted mainly of dry statistics, hardly the type of thing that would catch a weary sportswriter's eye. Reporters and editors scanned the information if they had the time or the inclination, but as often as not, the releases went straight into the trash can.

Eggers figured correctly that if a shy, polite kid from Corvallis had any chance of winning the Heisman—when no football player west of Norman, Okla., ever had won the trophy before—a selling job was mandatory. So, Eggers obtained a list of Heisman voters and went to work.

Every Sunday morning after a game, Eggers reported to his tiny office, packaged Baker's latest exploits together with quotes from opposing coaches and Prothro and mailed them out.

"You see a lot of this today," Eggers said, "but it was unique back then. I think it helped Terry's chances quite a bit. Terry did, too. After that, other S.I.D.'s who were trying to promote Heisman candidates called and asked me what I did for Terry."

While Eggers carried out his publicity campaign, Baker provided plenty of material for the press releases by turning in an outstanding season.

"My senior year was really phenomenal in the sense that the luck I had was unbelievable," Baker said. "Our first game was against Iowa State. It was a seesaw game. Whoever had the ball would score. We scored on a 50-yard pass (actually 43 yards) to a tight end named Jerry Neil to win the game. It was the only pass he caught the whole day. Prothro moved him to tackle the next week."

Baker threw two other touchdown passes and rushed for three more scores, including one on a 43-yard gallop, thus contributing to every Beaver touchdown that day. After Oregon State's 39-35 victory, Iowa State Coach Clay Stapleton called Baker "one of the truly great quarterbacks in college football history. He can beat you with his passes, and he can beat you with his runs. A great leader and masterful signal caller. He gets my vote for All-America quarterback."

Stapleton's comments, plus Baker's 317 yards of total offense, were duly recorded and sent out in the Sunday mail.

Baker experienced his worst game of the season the second week as Iowa pounded Oregon State, 28-8. Baker tallied only 109 yards of total offense, but Iowa Coach Jerry Burns said he was "one of the great quarterbacks of our time—the finest quarterback we've seen in the past five years."

The Beavers rallied from that defeat and thrashed Stanford, 27-0, behind their quarterback's 217 offensive yards. Stanford Coach Jack Curtice told reporters: "You fellows are really missing the beat if you don't vote Baker All-America. He can just pick an opposing team apart with his passes."

By now, Prothro had joined Eggers' weekly quote parade. "This kid is the greatest college quarterback I've ever seen," Prothro raved. "I can't recall anyone who is a close second to him."

Washington handed Oregon State its second (and last) loss of the season the next week in a 14-13 contest. Baker hasn't forgotten that game. "You could see it on the game film," he lamented, "one of our tackles stepped out of the way and let (Washington fullback) Junior Coffey run 30-some yards (actually 43) for (Washington's first) touchdown."

Baker accounted for 229 yards against the Huskies, whose coach, Jim Owens, said Baker was an "All-America, for sure."

Oregon State won its next seven games. "I don't know what it is," Baker said. "When you're on a roll, you're on a roll. We were on one."

The University of the Pacific fell convincingly, 40-6, as Baker picked up 181 offensive yards and this reaction from Pacific Coach John Rohde: "He's truly an All-America. He can do so many different things with a football."

Baker collected 216 more yards in a 51-22 conquest of West Virginia. "He's the best T quarterback in college I've ever seen," Mountaineers Coach Gene Corum said of Baker. "A great football player. Why, this guy could be a great halfback, just because of his running ability alone."

Although Baker no longer operated out of the single wing, he remained a triple threat. Besides his passing and running, he punted 33 times that year for a 37.4-yard average.

"Prothro believed in squib kicks that we could down close to the opponents' goal line," he said. "They were effective, but they invariably hurt your average.

"I guess my biggest strength as a football player was my versatility. I was a unique threat in that I could throw the ball or pull it down and run with it. I could hurt someone with the pass or run.

"We had no drop-back passing. It was all sprint-out. Everything started out the same way, where I'd go four or five steps and either pass, pitch out or run. The defenses needed a second to tell what I was going to do, which gave me an advantage."

Baker ran and threw for 182 yards as Oregon State edged Washington State, 18-12. Eggers slipped a fresh piece of paper into the typewriter and quoted Cougars Coach Jim Sutherland thusly: "That Baker is phenomenal, the best quarterback I've seen in a long, long time. I'm sure all my kids would agree with that. We set our game plan around Baker. We figured we would have to stop him, and I think we did a better job than most teams would do. But it still wasn't good enough. We thought we had to keep the ball—keep it away from Baker. That's the only way you can really stop him."

A week later, Oregon State overpowered Idaho, 32-0, as Baker totaled 320 more yards. "He's one of the best quarterbacks I've ever seen in college football," Vandals Coach Dee Andros said. "He gets my vote for All-America. I coached Joe Kapp at Cal (as an assistant) and felt he was great, but Baker is better."

Against Colorado State, Baker rushed for an incredible 163 yards and passed for 226 more. His favorite target, as usual, was All-America end Vern Burke, who led the nation in 1962 with 69 catches and 1,007 receiving yards. Baker's 389 yards in total offense—still a school record—in that 25-14 victory prompted Rams Coach Mike Lude to anoint Baker as "the greatest one-man football team in the nation."

Eggers ran to the mailbox with that quote.

In the regular-season finale, rival Oregon had Oregon State down, 17-6, in the fourth quarter. But Baker, despite collecting only 117 offensive yards, brought the Beavers back for a thrilling 20-17 victory. The Oregon State players hoisted Baker to their shoulders and carried him off the field in triumph after the game.

"In all my years in football," Prothro said, "I have never seen the players do that to one of their teammates."

Baker never let his success go to his head. He was a humble hero, as Oregon State President James Jensen pointed out while watching students hurry from class to class a few days after the Oregon game. "They were all so proud of Terry (in that game)," he said. "He's one of them in every way. That's because Terry is always the first to realize he is just one of a group."

He was an ordinary guy on campus, but on the football field he was head and shoulders above the competition. Baker led the nation in total offense with 2,276 yards, nearly double his yardage from the year before. That total remains an Oregon State record. He threw 15 touchdown passes (10 to Burke) and scored nine on the ground. Baker's career total of 4,979 yards placed him second in NCAA history behind Johnny Bright of Drake (5,903) until the pass-happy offenses of the last two decades and the rescission of the freshmen-ineligible rule allowed several quarterbacks to surpass their marks. In those days of single-platoon football, Baker also played defense, making five interceptions for 64 yards in his career.

Before 1962, the highest finish by a West Coast player in Heisman balloting was third, that feat being accomplished by Stanford quarterback Frank Albert in 1941 and UCLA halfback Paul Cameron in 1953. Twenty-seven years after the Heisman was created, Baker finally brought the trophy west.

He won narrowly. Baker received 707 points, followed by halfback Jerry Stovall of Louisiana State with 618 and tackle Bobby Bell of Minnesota with 429.

Oregon State's combined effort—Prothro's offense, Baker's accomplishments and Eggers' mail campaign—had paid off.

"I'm a very lucky boy," Baker told the world from Corvallis when he was brought out of class to be informed of the honor. Then he added, "I've got to get back to class."

One week later, the poor kid from Portland was in New York City for a six-day visit. In addition to receiving the Heisman Trophy, Baker appeared on Ed Sullivan's and Johnny Carson's television shows, toured Manhattan and enjoyed the city's nightlife.

The thrill of winning the Heisman was as great for Laura Baker as it was for her son. Terry's mother had worked in relative obscurity all her life, but when Baker won the Heisman, Laura Baker found herself featured in the company magazine of Sears, Roebuck and Co., her employer. She also accompanied Terry to New York for the Heisman ceremony. It was the biggest trip of her life.

"Those New Yorkers have a lot of money, and my mother's the kind of person you like to do things for," Baker said. "She was given a chauffeur-driven limousine. She was asked where she wanted to go, and she said Harlem. Can you imagine going there in a Cadillac?"

U.S. Atty. Gen. Robert F. Kennedy was the keynote speaker at the Downtown Athletic Club's dinner and award ceremony on December 5, 1962. Kennedy and Baker enjoyed a long conversation that evening, and the President's brother was impressed with the young collegian's intelligence. He suggested that Baker consider enrolling in law school or business school, a piece of advice that influenced the course of Baker's life.

Baker, meanwhile, handled the media blitz admirably, refusing to dwell on his individual accomplishments. "No player does everything by himself," he told reporters. "I have no great speed. I just follow my blockers."

After the festivities were over, Baker hustled back to Corvallis to take final examinations and to prepare for the Beavers' December 15 Liberty Bowl matchup against Villanova. Before Baker knew it he was headed back across the country for the bowl game in Philadelphia.

At game time, the temperature was 25 degrees and getting colder. There was snow on the ground, too, but 17,048 brave souls still came out to see the Heisman winner. "The field was like concrete," Baker said. "We all wore tennis shoes."

Five minutes into the game, Villanova downed a punt at Oregon State's 1-foot line. The Beavers were in trouble, but not for long.

"It was a fluke, you know," Baker said, reflecting on what happened next. "Prothro and I disagreed on this 20 years later. He said he called the play. I said I called it. I took responsibility for calling stupid plays, and this was a stupid play. You don't call a play like that unless you want to get tackled in the end zone."

Baker took the center snap and rolled to his left. He was a perfect target for a safety, and two Villanova tacklers almost had him, but he shook free. Thanks to some key blocks, Baker escaped the end zone, shook off another tackler and turned the corner. He looked up the sideline and saw the other goal line 99 yards away—and almost no one in between.

"Some guys ice-skated by me, but that was it," he said. "After the 15-yard line, there was no one there."

Baker galloped the length of the field for a 6-0 lead and the only score of the day. It remains the longest run from scrimmage in bowl-game history.

"I got a telegram from Sports Illustrated afterward," he recalled. "They said that run iced it (the Sportsman of the Year award)."

After the Liberty Bowl, Baker crossed the continent for the fourth time in less than two weeks, arriving in Corvallis on a Sunday morning in time for basketball practice. "I was so sore, I could hardly walk," he said.

Three days later, Baker was back on a plane bound for Lexington, Ky., where the Beavers were playing in the University of Kentucky Invitational Tournament. Oregon State lost its opening game, 70-65, to West Virginia, but Baker, with his "basketball legs" already in shape, led his team with 15 points. The next night, Oregon State defeated Iowa, 61-55, as Baker scored 14 points and made the all-tournament team.

Oregon State's basketball record was 46-14 in Baker's last two years. He sank 87 percent of his free-throw attempts as a sophomore, a mark that still stands as a school record. He averaged 10.7 points per game as a junior and 13.4 points (No. 2 on the team) as a senior, when he and Counts led the Beavers to an 83-65 victory over Arizona State in the West Regional championship game. Baker was named to the all-regional team for a second straight year, but that glory soon was shattered as the Beavers were embarrassed by Cincinnati, 80-46, in the NCAA semifinals and then lost to Duke, 85-63, in the Final Four consolation game.

Baker loved basketball, but his future was in football. The Los Angeles Rams made him the first overall selection in the 1962 National Football League draft even though they already had Roman Gabriel at quarterback with two backups.

"Baker is so outstanding, we couldn't afford not to take him," said Elroy Hirsch, the Rams' general manager.

Rams scouts had given Baker the highest rating a college senior could receive. Strangely, the San Diego Chargers of the young American Football League selected Baker in the 12th round before trading his signing rights to Oakland.

Baker signed with the Rams and reported to training camp with a sore arm. The Rams, who had signed Baker for three years at roughly $25,000 per year, were noticeably upset and put him through several physical examinations.

Nothing wrong could be found with the arm. As a last resort, Rams Coach Harland Svare brought in a psychiatrist to talk with Baker.

"The shrink sat me on a chair in the center of a room," Baker said, "then he turned out the lights. He told me to think about one person. We had just been talking about Svare, so I thought of him. The shrink then asked me who it was I was thinking about. I said, 'Svare.'

" 'That's it!' he said, turning on the lights. 'Your arm *hates* Harland Svare!' "

Baker and his hateful arm started the 1963 season opener against Detroit. The Rams couldn't wait to rush their prized rookie into the NFL arena, but it was a mistake. In fact, a disaster. Baker threw three interceptions, one of which was returned 70 yards for a touchdown. Gabriel replaced Baker early in the second half as the Lions coasted to a 23-2 victory.

After the Rams had gone 0-5 in their first five games, Gabriel was reinstated as the starting quarterback and finished out the rest of the season without relief. Baker quickly became an afterthought with the Rams from that point on over the next three years. His NFL passing career amounted to 12 completions in 21 attempts for 154 yards, no touchdowns and four interceptions. The Rams, realizing that Baker wasn't a pro-type quarterback, moved him to running back at about midseason of his second year. He rushed 58 times for 210 yards (3.6 average) and one touchdown in his NFL career, but that didn't work out, either. As a last resort, Los Angeles tried him as a receiver. He caught 30 passes for 302 yards and two touchdowns in his career, but he made most of those receptions as a running back, and the Rams finally released him during the 1966 preseason. Baker played one more professional season, in 1967 with Edmonton of the Canadian Football League, before finally calling it quits.

Baker blames his disappointing pro career on injuries that wouldn't go away.

"I developed a lot of nagging injuries in the pros that I never had in my life," he said. "I never bounced back. I did fine at running back until I got more nagging injuries. I just never had this problem in college."

Baker's failure at the pro game was as much philosophical as physical. He excelled in college because of his versatility. He could pass, run and punt, making him a tremendous threat and a terror to defend. The pros, however, don't demand versatility; they require strength in one area. The NFL is a specialized game, and Baker wasn't a specialist. Consequently, the pro-type passing offense wasn't made for him. Had Baker played for a team that used a sprint-out offense, his pro career might have turned out much differently.

"The biggest problem with Baker," said Don Heinrich, the Rams' quarterback coach when Baker was drafted, "is that he didn't have a very strong arm and couldn't put any velocity on the ball. He was more of a timing kind of guy. His arm strength was the poorest I've ever seen among front-line choices. It wasn't an accuracy factor, because he was accurate. But the ball would stay in his hand too long, and people would come and get it.

"Quite frankly, in today's wide-open game he would have been more effective. Very possibly, he wouldn't be a bust."

"Terry was able to do anything," said Merlin Olsen, the Rams' great lineman and a teammate of Baker's. "There wasn't anything you asked him to do that he couldn't do *adequately*. That was the problem. He was adequate at every position they tried him at."

Baker married Marilyn Davis, his college sweetheart, in 1964 before his second year in the pros. Also while a member of the Rams he heeded Robert Kennedy's advice and attended law school at Southern California in the off-season. He graduated in 1968.

That same year, Baker's and Kennedy's paths crossed again. Kennedy was seeking the Democratic presidential nomination, and he asked Baker to campaign for him. Baker agreed and introduced Kennedy at several campaign stops throughout Oregon. He admired and respected Bobby Kennedy, especially for his willingness to speak frankly. "Some people characterized it as bluntness," Baker said, "but I characterized it as forthrightness."

Baker was supposed to be at the Hotel Ambassador in Los Angeles that fatal night in June 1968 when Sirhan Sirhan shot Kennedy in the hotel kitchen, bringing even more tragedy to the star-crossed Kennedy family. But Baker was unable to attend the scheduled celebration of Kennedy's recent primary victories because he was having dinner with his in-laws before moving his wife and two children—a son named Brian and a daughter named Wendy—to Portland the next day.

"We got back from dinner and I turned on the TV," Baker recalled. "That's when I found out. Here I had known him, had just been with him. . . . We had just gone through the thing with his brother. . . . It was a pretty disgusting experience."

Kennedy had urged Baker himself to enter politics, advising him "not to start at the bottom" and to consider running for a high office such as the U.S. Senate as soon as possible. Baker pondered the idea. He would have been a good politician; he was intelligent, honest, compassionate and dedicated, not to mention idolized in the state of Oregon. And for a while it appeared that he was headed in that direction.

"That's why I came back to Oregon after law school, to get into politics," he said. "But I couldn't do it. It's not the (political) offers I would find distasteful. It's the running. Speech after speech. I don't like giving speeches."

That would mean talking about himself, and there isn't an ounce of braggart in Baker. So, Baker pursued his law career while maintaining an active interest in the political scene.

In 1970, Baker was appointed to the staff of the President's Commission on Campus Unrest and the Kent State Task Force. Baker visited different universities and found "a division in this country between generations as big and as deep as any that has existed since the Civil War," he said.

Baker worked through the summer and early fall of '70 with other lawyers and college professors who constituted the commission's staff. Their investigations led to the preparation of a detailed report that the commission submitted to President Nixon.

"He thanked us for our work and dismissed us," Baker said. "No implementation was done. Nixon's attitude was that the problem had solved itself because it had been a quiet summer. The reason it was a quiet summer is that most of the kids weren't in school. Art Buchwald wrote a cute column after that, about how there is an area set aside in Arlington Cemetery for these kinds of reports."

Baker eschewed showy, large-scale politics for smaller, back-page politics such as being vice president of the school board in Lake Oswego, the Portland suburb where he lives, and county chairman for something called the Limit Tax Levy Elections/Safety Net for Schools Committee. Baker was happy. He didn't have to talk about himself.

Baker's blond hair, which already was thinning in his college days, has

*Terry Baker traded in his football uniforms for business suits and now operates as a lawyer in Portland, Ore.*

thinned into baldness. He has added 20 pounds to his elongated physique, but it's all muscle, thanks to the Rams' experiment with converting him to running back. His stomach is flat, and Baker still looks very much like an athlete.

Baker has lived by himself in his Lake Oswego condominium since he and his wife were divorced a couple of years ago. The Heisman Trophy is nowhere to be found in the condo.

"I kept it in a spare bedroom for years—I've never been one to display trophies—until Oregon State asked me if they could have it," Baker explained.

"They're building a trophy case in Gill Coliseum. I wasn't doing anything with the trophy, so I said sure."

Baker tugged at the heartstrings of America back when, a couple of years before the seeds of campus unrest sprouted in Berkeley, Calif., the campus hero still was the quarterback. Baker's quiet, strong, bright, good-guy demeanor made him all the more heroic. He was an ideal role model for kids and a natural for the Heisman.

"Everything had to fall into place for me to win," he said. "If we had had a 5-5 season, there was no way. I doubt that you could win an Oscar in a crummy movie.

"I do think people like the idea of a college athlete who would be in college if he weren't an athlete. There were also the factors of my mother raising three boys by herself, our not having much."

Baker understands the significance of being a Heisman laureate, but he isn't carried away by it. "I won a lot of awards, and it was all a wonderful experience," he said, "but I don't dwell on these kinds of things. Other than questions I'm asked in an interview, I don't think I've spent one second thinking about what it meant to me."

There are continual reminders, however, and not always in the form of an interview. Sometimes in the wee hours of the morning, the phone rings.

"It will be two drunks from some place like Cincinnati wanting to know if I won the Heisman in 1962 or '63," he said. "I tell them. It's not my nature to be rude."

Winning the Heisman opened many doors for Baker. In 1968, when he was interviewing with law firms in Portland, another attorney told him, "Terry, you're like a hog running up and down the trough trying to figure out where to start eating first."

Baker now is a respected attorney in a corporate business firm. His cases involve commercial litigation, and as a trial lawyer he presents his cases before juries. How much does being a Heisman winner help him with a jury?

"In that close situation, where a case can go either way, you can flip a coin," he said. "But if the jurors have heard of you—I came out of college with a good press, so the jury may say, 'He's a clean-cut guy'—they may transfer that to your client."

He wouldn't be upset, he said, if the verdict swung in his direction because he was Terry Baker the Heisman winner as well as Terry Baker the lawyer. "These subtle things are a part of life," he said. "I'd rather have a judge like me than not like me."

The wonderful thing about Terry Baker is knowing that the judge—or anyone else for that matter—would like him regardless of his football exploits or his public stature. He is an affable guy who ignores his own honors and cares about others. Moreover, he was blessed with the intelligence to build a distinguished career for himself outside the world of pro football. He didn't need the Heisman Trophy to become successful.

But isn't it nice that Terry Baker did win the Heisman? Since 1962, when a true scholar-athlete received the most prestigious award presented to a collegian, there just haven't been many like him.

And that's a pity.

# Roger Staubach

*Like it or not, he'll always be remembered as America's Quarterback. The image fits the man. First at the United States Naval Academy and then with the Dallas Cowboys of the National Football League, Roger Staubach combined brains, strong personal beliefs and superior athletic talent. He was a winner, both morally and physically. He passed life's tests with the same high grades that he passed a football.*

# Chapter 13

# The man and the image

This is his image: Roger Staubach, mild-mannered Dallas businessman, sprints toward a phone booth, hastily shedding his coat and ripping open his shirt, then emerges moments later as—ta-da!—Captain America, defender of virtuousness and goodness, attacker of communism and other ideologies that threaten democracy, a man who can leap all vices and evil temptations in a single bound, a man for all Americans.

Not all of the image fits the man. That is, Staubach doesn't wear a red, white and blue uniform decorated with a Texas-sized lone star on the chest under his three-piece suit. "Captain America is an exaggeration," he said, "a stereotype."

A natural extension, too. When the Dallas Cowboys dubbed themselves "America's Team," thereby confirming how hard it has been for that franchise to remain humble, it was only normal to label Staubach, team leader and offensive captain, Captain America.

But the rest of the image is true. Staubach is a flag-waving spokesman for America. He is among its most loyal patriots, a staunch supporter of liberty and justice for all, a self-appointed crusader. He *is* Captain America.

Need someone to fight smut on television? Call on Captain America, as Morality in Media did in 1981. The New York-based organization, which monitors what it considers obscenity in the media, recruited Staubach as part of its mission and mailed out 200,000 letters with his picture on the letterhead.

The Rev. Morton Hill, a Catholic priest and leader of Morality in Media, explained that Staubach was chosen to add credibility to the group's cause because of his wholesome image and the public's respect for him.

And Captain America was more than willing to do his part. "We wanted to let people know about the dangers of pornography in cable television," Staubach said. "We're talking about brutal, hard-core pornography, like soliciting young people for prostitution. The long-term dangers of hard-core pornography on TV make the magazines and skin flicks look like nothing."

Captain America has spoken out for other causes, including the sensitive issue of abortion. "I'm anti-abortion, the killing of a fetus, or life," he said. "I'm anti-pro-choice."

He is anti-drugs, too. "I have never taken any (hallucinatory) drugs, nor do I feel the need to," he said. "Even if I were a kid today, with drugs being so prevalent, if I went to a party and kids were smoking marijuana, I'd just walk away. It's a matter of a strong Christian commitment."

Captain America is deeply religious and moral to the core. Aside from his religion and family, he thinks of his country first. With that in mind, when it was time to choose a college, he selected a military academy—the United States Naval Academy at Annapolis, Md. In contrast, John Wayne, perceived by many as the true Captain America, attended Southern California, a training ground for professional football players, not Green Berets.

Staubach would make the Duke proud, however, as he hammers willingly and endlessly on the evils of communism. "Communism isn't the answer," he said. "It only makes things worse. Communism is a cancer, but the cancer is curable. Revolutions have taken place in countries to drive communism out. But once it's locked in, it's definitely a godless mentality, and the people are not better off than before, and probably worse off in most cases."

Captain America speaks! But not as a Bible-waving, imperialism-trumpeting fanatic. He isn't made that way. His orations, spoken in soft tones, are based on a genuine concern about the direction this country is heading in terms of its moral principles and global intentions.

"We think of every situation as a crisis," Staubach said. "We get that Armageddon philosophy that we're going to destroy ourselves. I'm a cautious optimist. We're now confronted internationally with a tremendous threat, the communism in the world. I'm not an alarmist, just a realist. Between the two ideologies, you have nuclear capabilities that change the parameters of potential destruction. We've got to try to seek control in that area. From a position of strength, that will be important to us.

"Obviously, we've got internal and economic problems that will be cyclical, that we can handle. External problems are the biggest threat that we have. How we handle those will determine our future."

Staubach is a Republican, but he believes the conservative can live with the liberal, the hawk can co-exist with the dove. Image-makers can see that he tries hard to see both sides of issues, then make the most intelligent decision. Naturally, his name has come up in political circles.

"Politics?" he said. "I don't think I'd be a good politician right now. I'm pretty strong-willed and I may not want to change my mind on some issue just to get votes. And the timing isn't right. At this stage of my life, I'm trying to be known as a businessman and not an athlete. And I'd like to see my kids grow. So there is nothing in my life at this point that would make me pursue politics."

Staubach has made the transition from athlete to businessman more smoothly than most. In 1970, his second year with the Dallas Cowboys, he obtained a real-estate license. He formed a real-estate partnership in 1977 and, five years later, launched The Staubach Co., a full-service commercial real-estate company in Dallas that employs around 110 people and is involved with development on a "modest scale," according to Staubach. By modest, he meant his company had invested $45 million in construction in April 1985. And the construction division is just one of five divisions (and not the biggest) in The Staubach Co. The company also offers such real-estate services as brokerage and leasing. Staubach said his company would lease well over 1 million square feet of office and industrial space in 1985.

"Things are going fine," Staubach said of his business career. "We have a pretty successful company. I'm fortunate to be where I am financially."

From Captain America to Captain Industry.

In one other way, 1985 always will be considered a very good year by Staubach. He was elected to the Professional Football Hall of Fame in his first year of eligibility (the minimum wait is five years after a player's retirement). Also inducted in the class of 1985 at Canton, O., was O.J. Simpson. Staubach and Simpson are the first Heisman Memorial Trophy winners to make the professional hall, although Simpson contends good-naturedly that he really is the first, because his name begins with "Si" while Staubach's begins with "St."

Staubach would dispute Simpson's alphabetical edge, once again in good fun, by pointing out that he won the Heisman in 1963, five years before Simpson. Staubach also received the Heisman as a junior, while Simpson earned it as a senior. And Staubach had more rank as a college student. So there, O.J.!

"In winning the Heisman," Staubach recalled at his office desk, "I was really uncomfortable with the significance of it at the time. A big deal was made of it. I always get uneasy when I've been singled out. When it was announced in Dallas that I had made the pro football hall, I just wanted to get through that, too. Those kinds of things are nicer to look at when they're behind you."

Captain America is genuinely nice, adding to his many other attributes. For all his heroic acts in football, he can match them, deed by deed, with humility. And humor. He isn't just another boring masked man with a shield. Captain America enjoys laughing and making others laugh. He has, in his own words, a "strange sense of humor."

In 1962, Navy played Southern Cal in Los Angeles. The Middies visited Disneyland and Staubach bought a dozen yo-yos that glowed in the dark. After returning to the academy, he passed them out. At night, he and other pranksters would spin the yo-yos up and down outside their windows, causing some anxiety among unsuspecting midshipmen on watch.

A Navy teammate of Staubach's, 1963 team captain Tom Lynch, dated a girl who was named Navy Queen for the Cotton Bowl. Staubach obtained a publicity photograph of her and signed it: "To Roger. I miss you very much. Love, Kathleen." At the dinner table that night, Staubach passed the photo around to everyone but Lynch. The other Middies busted out laughing before Lynch finally saw the picture. Staubach explained, with all his blue-eyed innocence: "Gee, Tom, I only met her once. I didn't know she was so taken by me."

His most outrageous prank, marking probably the only time in his life that Captain America has been a wild and crazy guy, happened when he was playing for the Cowboys. He had an appointment to see Tex Schramm, the team's president and general manager. Staubach was on time, but Schramm kept him waiting. When 30 minutes had passed, Staubach decided to inform Schramm of his impatience.

With no one looking, Staubach climbed out the window of the 11th-floor office onto a four-foot ledge that surrounded the building. Latticework on the ledge protected Staubach as he maneuvered carefully toward Schramm's office. Only problem was, there wasn't any latticework directly in front of Schramm's windows. Undaunted, Staubach positioned himself for the final move.

"Tex kind of had his feet propped up, looking out the window," Staubach said. "I leaped in front of his window, and I scared him to the point where his eyes rolled back in his head. I thought, 'Geez, I hope he isn't having a heart attack.' Tex told me later, 'I saw my quarterback's life flash before my eyes.' "

Staubach's ultimate caper could have gotten him killed, but what's Captain America without a sense of daring? "I wasn't in any danger . . . unless I had slipped off the ledge," he said. "But the ledge was wide enough. There's a chance of getting hurt in doing anything, but I wouldn't have done it if it was dangerous. At the time, the temptation to do it was greater than my 1-in-20 chance of falling off."

The incident eventually found its way into the Dallas newspapers and was picked up nationally. The Cowboys have had their share of unusual personalities— Don Meredith, Pete Gent, Lance Rentzel, Duane Thomas and Hollywood Henderson, just to name a few. That's why, when the public read about the team's new aerial acrobat, it gasped: Roger Staubach! What's a man on a pedestal doing on a ledge?

Staubach's answer might be: What's life without challenges? He faced them repeatedly as a National Football League quarterback. Invariably, he won. Staubach brought Dallas from behind 23 times in the fourth quarter, 14 times in the last two minutes or in overtime. Few quarterbacks in the history of football have beaten down as many challenges. Therefore, an 11th-story walk around the outside of a building might be in keeping with his unflinching personality.

"Those who know me knew it was something I would do," he said. "The others who didn't know me, but had heard of me, probably thought I was on drugs."

Drugs? Not Captain America. Drugs represent to him another ledge of more treacherous footing. "I do like a beer every now and then," he said, confessing his nearest approximation of a vice.

Staubach is every bit what he appears—God-fearing, hard-working, clean-living, faithful to his wife, devoted to his five children, unfailingly true to an unimpeachable value system. He is a wonderful role model for children, and, even more, a perfect example for everyone of how to conduct his or her life properly.

Yet, there always will be skeptics of goody-goodies.

"What amazes me," Staubach said, "is that I consider what I do normal, but it has been perceived by some that my values and the way I live are abnormal. I'm not a prude or a religious zealot, though people have tried to stereotype me as such. I'm really a three-dimensional creature."

Staubach's values were taught to him at an early age by parents who provided the moral foundation that is the root of everything he represents.

"My parents preached high values to me that they tried their best to practice," he said. "I had great examples in my parents. I loved them so much, I didn't ever want to fail them."

Staubach grew up in Cincinnati as Bob and Betty Staubach's only child. Early in Roger's life, he did fail them. Once, he couldn't control the urge to place his hands in wet cement, and he was spanked for his curiosity. Another time, he stole a little statue of the Blessed Virgin and a medal from a religious store, not long after he took a few coins off a table in a neighbor's house.

A few days later, the guilt overcame him. "I'll never forget it," Staubach said. "I was lying on the couch and it just came over me. I started crying. My mother came into the room to see what was wrong. I told her what I had done. I felt so terrible that I had let my parents down. My mother made me take the money back to the neighbors and apologize. To this day, it was the most embarrassing thing I've ever done."

At that point, Staubach exorcised all evil from his body. "I wasn't false behind my parents' backs again," he said. Though his parents died in the early 1970s,

Staubach's value system remains intact. "If I was investigated for a Cabinet post," he said, "they wouldn't find any skeletons."

Bob Staubach was a manufacturer's representative in the shoe, leather and thread business. Betty Staubach went back to work as a secretary for General Motors when Roger was about 9. "My mother was more ambitious than my father, who didn't make very much money but was a hard worker," Staubach said. "The two of them pinched and saved to give me what I needed in school. They just wanted me to be happy and a good person. I was lucky to have them as parents."

As a child, Roger Thomas Staubach played all sports and showed an ability even then to perform well under pressure. "I wanted the ball hit to me so I could make the last out, or I wanted to be up at the key time to make the big hit," he said. "I wanted to take the last shot in a basketball game. It didn't always work, but I wasn't bashful about trying."

He starred in football, basketball and baseball at Purcell High School, a parochial school in Cincinnati. He leveled off in basketball as a senior but was a talented prospect in football and baseball. He pictured himself playing quarterback for Notre Dame. The Fighting Irish didn't recruit him, though, and he signed a tender to enroll at Purdue.

What happened next "is one of those ironic things that happen in your life," Staubach said. Rick Forzano, an assistant football coach at Navy, visited Purcell to recruit the team's center, Jerry Momper. While looking at films of Momper, Forzano became interested in the quarterback. Staubach had absolutely no interest in attending an academy, but Forzano convinced him at least to take a look at life at Annapolis.

"I went for a visit and liked it," Staubach said. "The atmosphere was solid, and I could see a moral environment there. I had already been recruited by other colleges. The first thing the players I met at those schools wanted to do was go to a bar and get drunk. I said to myself, 'Hey, I don't want to go through four years of this.'

"I remember Forzano saying toward the end of Navy's recruiting me: 'Roger, we can't promise you anything, except that when you graduate you get your own battleship.' We both laughed over that one. But I really believe praying had a lot to do with my decision. I prayed every night for guidance to help me make the right choice."

Staubach almost said no to Navy because of the academy's stringent academic requirements. On the college entrance examinations he had scored high in mathematics but low in English. But he agreed to attend New Mexico Military Institute in Roswell, N.M., to prepare for academy academics.

The football coach at the military institute, Bob Shaw, was a veteran of the National Football League. Shaw taught Staubach, who had been basically a running quarterback in high school, the rudiments of the passing game, and Staubach led the institute to a 9-1 record. Staubach's academic work improved, and he entered Navy as a freshman, or plebe, in 1961.

"My first year at the academy was miserable," he recalled. "I was homesick and having a difficult time conforming to academy life. I had a lot of demerits as a plebe from not having my shoes spit-shined every moment and from failing to have my reef points memorized at all times."

"Reef points" are innocuous questions contained in a book that upperclassmen use to quiz plebes. For example, an upperclassman might ask a plebe how long he has been a seaman. He would have to answer correctly: "All my blooming life, sir. My mother was a mermaid, my father was born on the crest of a wave. . . ." Plebes who fail to respond correctly receive demerits. Staubach, the non-conformist, had trouble remembering the answers and already had 150 demerits by Christmas of his first year. Another 150 demerits in his first year would mean dismissal from the academy. He changed his attitude the following spring, learned to deal with the harassment and picked up only 20 additional demerits the rest of the year, and just 15 to 20 more over his remaining three years at the Naval Academy.

Staubach was not an immediate sensation in football, either. He was the No. 6 quarterback in spring practice before his sophomore year. He played only six minutes over the first three games of the 1962 season, two of which Navy lost. But in game No. 4, the college football world finally learned about Roger Staubach.

The Navy-Cornell game was scoreless in the first quarter when Middies Coach Wayne Hardin sent him in. Seizing the opportunity, Staubach passed for one touchdown and ran for two more, including a one-yarder that he personally set up with a 68-yard burst, and Navy won, 41-0. The Staubach era at Navy had set sail.

Navy's record was only 5-5 that season as Staubach scored seven touchdowns, passed for seven more and led the nation in passing accuracy at 67.3 percent. Southern Cal won the national championship in 1962, but the Trojans beat Navy by just a seven-point margin, 13-6, as Staubach had a great afternoon, running 18 yards for the Middies' only score and compiling 219 yards of total offense (113 rushing, 106 passing). He was named the Pacific Coast Back of the Week even though he attended college on the opposite coast.

Staubach was involved in a controversial play as a sophomore, a sleeper play against Pittsburgh. The Panthers kicked off to the Middies, one of whom faked a block and rolled off the field. Navy huddled with 10 men, but Jimmy Stewart, a receiver, left the huddle and limped toward the bench. Dick Ernst replaced him in the huddle, then lined up at tackle. Stewart stopped just short of the sideline and was wide open when Staubach hit him with a 66-yard touchdown pass. Hardin believed in gimmickry, but that play brought him under much criticism from Pitt and the media, even though it had little bearing on the outcome. Behind Staubach's eight-of-eight passing for 192 yards, Navy won, 32-9.

Staubach's two greatest thrills in football were his first Army-Navy game in 1962 and Dallas' first Super Bowl victory after the 1971 season.

"I can still remember sitting in the stands as a plebe," he said, "and realizing what the Army-Navy game means to both academies. To the guys who play in the game, it's the ultimate situation because of the pressure you're under. You've got 4,100 midshipmen in school, and all they're talking about is the Army-Navy game. The plebes get special considerations if you win. Meanwhile, the fleet is sending you letters and admirals are sending you telegrams. Plus you've got 102,000 in the stadium (in Philadelphia).

"Coaches have lost their jobs because they lost the Army-Navy game. I've never felt more pressure in one game, even the Super Bowl. There has been only one game where I couldn't sleep the night before, and that was the '62 Army-Navy game."

Army was favored to win, but Hardin wasn't concerned. "We're gonna run up the score on Army," he promised a pep rally. To further inspire his players, he had skull-and-crossbones patches put on the fronts of their helmets, symbolizing "Jolly Roger," a ship that never lost a battle. Navy did run up the score, 34-14, as Staubach ran for two touchdowns and passed for two more. Staubach soon became known as "Jolly Roger" as well as "Roger the Dodger" (because of his elusive running style).

As a junior in 1963, Staubach led Navy to a 9-1 season. He accounted for 15 touchdowns (eight running, seven passing) and 1,892 yards of total offense and again led the nation by completing 66.5 percent of his 161 passing attempts. He appeared on the cover of Time and Sports Illustrated magazines and played his finest game for Navy—14 completions in 16 attempts, two touchdown passes, a five-yard TD run and a single-game school record (since broken) of 307 offensive yards—as the Middies beat Michigan in Ann Arbor, 26-13.

Navy's only regular-season setback was a 32-28 defeat to Southern Methodist, a game filled with unsportsmanlike incidents such as eye-gouging, late hits and piling on. Staubach injured the same shoulder twice that day but still finished the game.

Eight days before the scheduled 1963 Army-Navy game, President Kennedy was assassinated. Staubach was crushed. "I remember thinking, 'What's this life all about?'" he said. Kennedy served in the Navy during World War II, was a Navy football fan and had attended the Army-Navy game the year before.

"We met him at our training facility, then his life was washed out," Staubach recalled. "We showed up for practice the day he was shot, but all we did was kneel and pray. Practice was canceled. The game itself was almost canceled but was played a week later (on December 7). We were told that Kennedy's family requested the game be played."

Staubach's picture was scheduled for the cover of Life magazine in the issue published after Kennedy's death. Staubach made the cover, but only for a brief press run, at which time his picture was removed and replaced by an assassination photograph.

"That Army-Navy game was played in Kennedy's honor," Staubach said, "plus it was really an electrifying game between two strong teams. The winner was to go to the Cotton Bowl. It was one of those unique moments where there was excitement in the air and also a sadness. That day probably crossed all downs when it came to emotions."

Among all the Army-Navy games, the 1963 contest might finish in the top 10, not only for compelling reasons, but for the game's conclusion as well. Navy fullback Pat Donnelly's three touchdowns had put the Middies ahead, 21-7, but Army, fighting back behind quarterback Rollie Stichweh, narrowed Navy's lead to 21-15 and had the football on the Navy 2-yard line when the gun went off.

Thus it would be No. 1 Texas against No. 2 Navy in the Cotton Bowl. Navy's invitation and the news that Staubach had won the Heisman Trophy—an announcement that actually was made just four days after Kennedy's assassination—brought joy to the Navy campus, but the celebrations were subdued. The nation still was mourning its slain president. "I was really uncomfortable at the time," Staubach said of his mixed feelings about that long-ago, tragic autumn.

The 6-foot-2, 190-pound Staubach was the fourth junior and, as it turned out, the last academy football player to win the Heisman prior to the 1985 season. His 1,860 points easily outdistanced runner-up Billy Lothridge of Georgia Tech (504 points) and Sherman Lewis of Michigan State (369).

"My mom and dad were at the Heisman dinner, and they asked my dad to get up and say a few words," Staubach said. "I'll never forget what he said: 'God gave us only one child, but he gave us a good one.'

"In my speech, I said something about cutting up the trophy into 44 pieces, or whatever the size of our traveling squad was. I still get letters today from guys I played with at Navy who want to know, 'When am I going to get my piece?' "

"When Roger won the Heisman, he didn't want to keep it in his room because he thought it would be showing off," recalled L. Budd Thalman, Navy's sports information director at the time. "So he gave it to me. I was a bachelor at the time. I kept it for a week in my car trunk, right next to the groceries, then shipped it to Cincinnati.

"Roger was Mr. Straight Arrow. He always had a sense of humor just below the surface, but if you didn't know him, you'd think he was colorless. He appeared one night on Ed Sullivan's TV show. When the camera moved to him, Roger put his hand under his chin and wiggled his fingers. He looked like some fool, but he had promised the guys at the academy that he would wave to them.

"Roger is just a nice person. If you'd like to reconstruct someone into your son, he would be the prototype."

Hardin said of Staubach in 1963: "Rog's one asset is that he can do everything better on a football field than any man I've ever seen. Other people can run better, throw better and lead better, but Staubach does it all better."

Hardin called the dodger in Roger "a sixth sense. A feeling. ESP. I don't know what it is, except that it's something other people don't have. It's like when you build a ship. At first, it's just another ship. But put radar in and the ship becomes pretty good."

Navy ran aground in the Cotton Bowl. Texas toyed with the Middies in a 28-6 victory behind a tremendous defense led by Scott Appleton, Tommy Nobis, Jim Hudson and George Brucks. Nevertheless, Staubach set Cotton Bowl records of 21 completions (in 31 attempts) and 228 yards passing.

Even though Navy lost its opportunity to finish No. 1, Staubach maintained his sense of humor. At a football dinner, a speaker paid tribute to the Navy quarterback by saying, "Only God and Roger Staubach know what he's doing out there." When it was Staubach's turn to speak, he quipped, "I want to amend that to God, Roger Staubach and Scott Appleton."

Staubach left 'em laughing, but he would need all the wit he could muster just to get through his final football season at Navy. He injured an Achilles tendon in the opening game against Penn State, a 21-8 Navy victory. "I didn't tear it," he said, "but I popped it pretty good." He participated in only four plays in the next game, although he did find time to throw one touchdown pass as the Middies beat William & Mary, 35-6. But the ankle wasn't getting any better. Two weeks into the season, Staubach's chances for a Heisman encore already were scuttled.

"It really wasn't until half the season was gone that I could get going again," he said, "and I really didn't get back to my old self until the last three games."

Staubach was partly to blame for that season. He wanted to play against

Michigan in the Middies' third game, but Hardin initially wouldn't let him because of the ankle. Staubach pleaded with his coach, and Hardin relented. But in order for him to play, he agreed to have his ankle injected with a pain-killing drug. The ankle was injured even worse against the Wolverines, who blanked the Middies, 21-0, and Staubach spent the next several days in a hospital. He did not play against Georgia Tech, which registered a 17-0 victory.

So Captain America did take drugs after all, a conscious act that was diametrical to the image he tries to project. Is this another instance of a children's role model being rolled off as a sham? Please, say it isn't so, Captain.

"I was a player who wanted to play," he explained. "I was so competitive, I *had* to play. The doctors wouldn't inject me unless I begged them to. I was refused at times even then. I took a shot in the hip so I could play against the New York Giants. Once again, I pushed the doctors.

"I don't advocate taking drugs. I don't even like aspirin. I can't take pain drugs orally because I get a sick stomach. So I would take injections of Novocain or cortisone. Football is a very physical game. Sometimes you have to play hurt."

Staubach certainly wasn't the only college or professional football player who received injections so that he could play when injured. There is an unwritten code in the game: If you can walk on it or it isn't broken, you can play. Those who won't may lose their jobs.

But Staubach has been such an outspoken critic of drugs that just the thought of him taking them suggests a contradiction.

"Definitely," Staubach agreed. "I would advise high school and college athletes not to take drugs to play. I don't tell others to play when they are hurt. But they still have to make their own decisions. I can advise them, but I can't tell them. The same is true of my own son, Jeff. I'd advise him not to take drugs to play sports, even if I did, but I'd also tell him that it's his decision.

"There is a contradiction here, but you've got to be careful with this. I am conservative, but I had a different personality on the field than I did away from the game. But I'm not contradictory in other aspects of my life."

Perfection minus one equals humanness. In a way it's nice to know that Captain America has a flaw; that makes it easier for the rest of us to identify with him.

Nevertheless, Staubach's damaged ankle turned his senior football season into his worst at Navy. The dodger could no longer dodge, rushing 104 times for minus one yard. This statistic is somewhat misleading, however, because when a college quarterback is tackled while attempting to pass, the minus yardage comes off his rushing total. At the professional level, the same yardage is subtracted from the team's gross passing yardage.

Staubach actually threw more passes in 1964 (204) than in any other season at Annapolis. But with his mobility restricted, he couldn't throw as much on the run and his passing accuracy fell to 58.3 percent, which isn't bad, but it was his lowest mark in college. He threw only four touchdown passes, compared with 10 interceptions, as a first classman. His total offense amounted to 1,130 yards and he rushed for only two touchdowns.

It was a season to forget. Staubach received no consideration for the Heisman, and Navy finished with a 3-6-1 record. After two season-opening victories, Navy dropped six of its remaining eight games, managing to tie Pitt, 14-14, and beat

Duke, 27-14. The Duke game is the only one in which Staubach really looked like his old self as he passed for 217 yards and ran for another 91.

In addition, the Middies' five-game winning streak against Army came to an end by an 11-8 score, and Hardin was fired. The academies *really* don't like losing to each other. Staubach said Hardin's ouster wasn't directly attributable to that last Army game, however. "Wayne was very outspoken," Staubach said, "and he upset a lot of people."

Because Staubach had attended junior college before arriving at Navy, he was eligible for the NFL and American Football League drafts after his junior year. Dallas selected him in the 10th round, while Kansas City of the AFL chose Staubach as its third pick of a separate draft of college players with athletic eligibility remaining after the Chiefs had completed the regular phase of the draft. Kansas City took two Notre Dame linemen, Paul Costa and Jim Snowden, as "futures" ahead of Staubach.

Gil Brandt, Dallas' player personnel director, admitted after the draft that the Cowboys had selected Staubach 10th on the basis of his athletic talent and the possibility that he might not be able to serve four years of active duty following graduation because of color blindness.

Staubach is partially color blind. From a distance, light green and white appear the same to him, and dark colors come out as . . . dark colors. He can't distinguish between some of them. Although Staubach never faced teams dressed in black and white, his color blindness didn't affect his performance on a football field.

But the question remains: How did Staubach get into the Naval Academy, which doesn't allow color-blind midshipmen? Staubach took his pre-entry physical for the academy at an Army hospital in Denver. Fortunately, the seaman administering the eye test was lazy. Staubach took the dot test, in which different colors are flipped over each other to form dotted patterns of numbers. Staubach had to identify the numbers. He missed quite a few, but the seaman passed him anyway.

Once Staubach was enrolled at Navy, the eye problem was discovered. By that time the Navy could not dismiss him, but he was restricted from becoming a flier or line officer on a ship. He couldn't fly because of carrier landings, especially at night when the signals are transmitted through red, green and white lights, colors Staubach can't distinguish. A line officer must be able to distinguish port and starboard lights, making color identification important in this occupation, too.

The Naval Academy was criticized for admitting a future Heisman hero who was color blind. The criticism was unjust. The eye problem simply was a foul-up in the physical. Navy had no way of knowing that it was getting a future unanimous All-America quarterback and Heisman Trophy winner when it recruited Staubach, or even at the time the test was given. The situation worked out well for Navy in the end, of course, and in retrospect, the Secretary of the Navy probably should have found that lazy seaman in Denver and decorated him.

When Staubach received his engineering degree from Navy in 1965, he didn't give much thought to playing professional football. He had a four-year military obligation to fulfill first.

"When I graduated, another four years seemed like an eternity," he said. "I was thinking seriously about making the Navy my career."

But he still was not quite through as a collegiate football player. He played in the Coaches All-America Game in Buffalo in June 1965, although mostly on defense and specialty teams. John Huarte, who had won the Heisman that year at Notre Dame, was the starting quarterback, and Staubach played his normal position only briefly in relief. Staubach did start the College All-Star Game in August, but he injured a shoulder in the first half while making a leaping pass and was forced to leave the game, which the Cleveland Browns won, 24-16.

A month later he married Marianne Hoobler, a girl he had known since his schoolboy days in Cincinnati. Theirs had been an off-and-on romance for years, but when Staubach proposed after his senior year at Navy, Marianne accepted. They first lived in Annapolis, where Staubach helped coach Navy's plebe football team before moving on to Athens, Ga., for more Navy training.

The Chiefs knocked on Staubach's door before the Cowboys. While he was in Annapolis, Kansas City offered him a $5,000 signing bonus and $250 to $300 per month while he was on active duty. If Staubach remained in the Navy after his four-year commitment, he did not have to return the money. But if he joined Kansas City, he would receive a $50,000 bonus plus $25,000 annually for three years.

Dallas' offer was even more lucrative: a $10,000 signing bonus plus $500 per month during active duty, again with no strings attached. Afterward, if he signed with Dallas, he would have a three-year contract at $25,000 per year, plus a bonus option of $55,000 to $60,000 up front or $100,000 deferred over 10 years.

The Navy cleared both contract offers, and Staubach accepted Dallas' for three reasons: The Cowboys offered more money than the Chiefs, they had drafted him higher and, in Staubach's opinion, the caliber of football in the NFL was superior to the AFL. (Ironically, Kansas City won a Super Bowl two years before Dallas.)

At that point, Staubach disappeared from the spotlight for three years, serving one year in Vietnam as a non-combat supply officer, a job classification not hindered by color blindness. In Vietnam, however, Staubach had no difficulty seeing Red.

"In theory," he said, "trying to stop the spread of communism in Southeast Asia was the important thing to do. Where I have a problem is with the vulnerability of our country's leadership. We had horrible leadership directing our involvement in Vietnam, and I don't mean the military. Secretary of Defense Robert McNamara, who directed our escalation policy over there, didn't take into serious consideration that we had a lot of young men over there risking their lives.

"And we didn't intend to win the war, which is a horrible approach. I'm sure, if we had to do it all over again, we wouldn't have gone over there. I think there were similarities in Vietnam to our involvement in Korea, except for one thing: The American men in Southeast Asia came home and found that they had been fighting an unpopular war. That whole mess got us nowhere and set us back as a country."

More than a decade later, the communist menace continues to spread, even here in Captain America's own country. "Marx's philosophy is a lunch-box philosophy," he said. "It doesn't allow for the soul, it doesn't allow for Christianity. What is communism anyway but the state as God? The whole spiritual side of man's existence is taken away. I'm a Christian and I have to be against it."

Captain America was getting worked up.

"It's amazing what they get away with in Russia," he said, "a government controlled, really, by a few men. And it's a government strictly of force. We have sit-ins in our country about South Africa, which are justified. But people in Russia don't have a right to protest.

"Communism is a much more serious problem to Americans than is South Africa because communism is right here in our country. If someone wants to be a communist, that's his prerogative, but understand what it means. Go talk to Yugoslavia, Hungary, Poland and the Solzhenitsyns of the world. And look at the race riots in our country. Communism is behind that."

Captain America was now at a feverish pitch.

"Obviously, there are sinister elements in this country, to what degree, I don't know," he said. "There's a McCarthy mentality, that if you believe in Medicare, you're a communist because you believe in socialism. There are others who get off their rockers, too, the John Birchers."

Captain America paused.

"I'm not a John Bircher," he said, laughing. "I'm a conservative thinker, but not that conservative. But there are people looking out for their own self-interests. Conservatives can be as wrong as ultra-liberals. Even though I'm not a liberal, I believe a man's initiative and creativity should never be compromised."

Four years of active duty convinced Staubach that the military would not be his life. He was honored to serve his country as a naval officer, but he simply could not get the urge to play football out of his system. While in Vietnam, he practiced throwing passes to anyone who would catch them. Upon returning to the United States, Staubach sharpened his dulled quarterbacking skills in two seasons at Pensacola Naval Air Station, which had a service football team that played small colleges. Then he used two weeks of military leave from the Florida air base in 1968 to work out with the Cowboys at their summer training camp.

Dallas' quarterback at the time was Don Meredith, a strong-armed, witty Texan who helped build the Cowboys into a playoff team. His backup was Craig Morton, who was a senior at California in 1964, when Staubach also was in his final season at Navy. Morton was an All-America his last year, then was drafted No. 1 by Dallas in 1965 and became the heir apparent to Meredith's job. In the summer of 1968, Meredith and Morton watched a Navy officer practice twice a day with other Cowboy prospects.

"I tried to make it a joke," Meredith recalled. "I said to Craig: 'I'm sure glad that it's you instead of me against this guy, because anybody who takes a two-week vacation and comes to two-a-days has got to be a little weird. He's gonna get your job, Curly.'"

Meredith retired after the 1968 season, the same day Staubach retired from the Navy, and Roger the Dodger immediately became the No. 2 quarterback behind Morton when he joined Dallas in 1969.

Two years later, Dallas Coach Tom Landry said the quarterback job was open and that Morton and Staubach would have an equal shot at No. 1. Whomever had the hot hand would play. After six weeks, the battle remained so even that Landry shuttled plays with his *quarterbacks* the seventh week, a 23-19 defeat to Chicago that left the Cowboys' record dragging at 4-3.

Going on impulse, Landry named Staubach as his permanent quarterback, and Dallas snapped off 10 straight victories, including a 24-3 drubbing of Miami in Super Bowl VI. Staubach completed 12 of 19 passes for 119 yards, two touchdowns and no interceptions against the Dolphins and was named the game's Most Valuable Player by Sport magazine. With that honor came a new sports car, but Captain America made the country chuckle when he instead requested, and was given, a station wagon.

Well, a station wagon is square, like its driver, the pundits jested.

The Staubachs had three children by that time, so the man of the house was merely being practical. Nevertheless, Staubach's squeaky-clean image was, by comparison, making Mr. Rogers look like a hard-metal rocker.

"My most satisfying moment as a professional was in that locker room in New Orleans," Staubach said of Super Bowl VI. "Dallas had been a winning team, but until that moment had the reputation of not being able to win the big one. No team wants to hear that it chokes. I looked around that locker room at Bob Lilly, Chuck Howley, Lee Roy Jordan, Cornell Green, Mel Renfro, George Andrie and other veterans. I could see the pride on their faces. It was a great feeling."

Staubach had only two differences with Landry, the great Lone Star stoic. Staubach wanted to call his own plays, but Landry wouldn't allow it. And Landry doesn't like running quarterbacks, but Staubach wouldn't compromise on that point, either.

Rog should have dodged, however, the next summer when he chose not to step out of bounds and collided with Los Angeles Rams linebacker Marlin McKeever at the end of a nine-yard run, three yards away from a touchdown. Staubach separated his right shoulder in the preseason game and missed most of the season. But in the playoffs, Staubach staged one of his greatest comebacks after replacing Morton late in the third quarter in San Francisco with the 49ers leading, 28-13.

San Francisco was still ahead, 28-16, when Staubach got the football back at his 45-yard line with 1:53 left in the game. Twenty-three seconds later, he threw a 20-yard touchdown pass to Billy Parks. On Toni Fritsch's onside kick, the 49ers' Preston Riley draped his body over the ball, but somehow it popped loose into Mel Renfro's waiting arms. Staubach's 10-yard touchdown pass to Ron Sellers on a crossing pattern with 52 seconds on the clock finished off the stunned 49ers, 30-28, marking the third consecutive year Dallas had eliminated San Francisco from the playoffs.

Staubach was the Cowboys' No. 1 quarterback again in 1973, and he didn't budge from that position until his retirement after the 1979 season. The Cowboys traded Morton to the New York Giants midway through the 1974 season. Rookie Clint Longley then became the No. 2 quarterback in Dallas. After Staubach was knocked dizzy against Washington on Thanksgiving Day, 1974, Longley led three touchdown drives, the last of which culminated in a 50-yard touchdown pass to Drew Pearson in the game's fading moments to give the Cowboys a 24-23 triumph. The youngster's future looked bright.

Staubach was fairly close to Longley, although he noticed the younger quarterback was "disturbed," in Staubach's non-professional opinion. Staubach reached that conclusion after watching Longley shoot and kill squirrels after Cowboy practices, then walk over and kick the dead animals in the head. By training camp before the 1976 season, a number of other Cowboys had come to the same conclusion that Longley had emotional problems.

That same year, quarterback Danny White joined Dallas from the defunct World Football League. Longley immediately felt threatened by White and the possibility of losing his No. 2 role. He stopped throwing passes with Staubach and White in practice, then he stopped running laps with them, and finally he stopped talking to them. Staubach tried to draw Longley out, to find out what was bothering him, but Longley retreated even more.

One day, Longley threw a long pass to Pearson, who dropped the ball. Longley cursed at Pearson, half-serious, half in jest. But anyone who swore at Pearson, Staubach's other half when it came to football heroics, was, in effect, insulting Staubach.

"Clint, I'm getting tired of your talking behind people's backs," Staubach told Longley. "Someone is going to knock those Bugs Bunny teeth of yours in."

Longley asked him if he'd like to try, Staubach said he would, and after practice the two walked over to the baseball diamond next to the football field at California Lutheran College in Thousand Oaks, Calif., where the Cowboys train each summer.

On the way over, Staubach thought to himself: "What am I doing, a 34-year-old man, about to get into a schoolyard fight? What if I break my hand?"

Staubach decided he would only wrestle. Longley said, "Let's take off our shoulder pads." Staubach refused. "Just our helmets," he replied.

Almost before the helmets hit the ground, Longley swung. "He tried to sucker-punch me," Staubach said. "The blow grazed my head and made me furious. I went for him and knocked him to the ground. I got on top of him and could have done anything I wanted, but I just held him there."

Dan Reeves, an assistant coach, broke up the skirmish. On the way back to the locker room, Reeves said to Staubach: "Roger, I'll tell you one thing. Don't ever turn your back on him again." Sage advice, which Staubach failed to heed.

A few days later, Staubach slipped on his shoulder pads in the locker room. He never saw the punch that knocked him into a floor scale. Longley jumped on Staubach, whose head was fuzzy. The two combatants were separated, but Staubach, his head now clear, lunged for Longley. He was restrained.

Dallas trainer Don Cochren drove Staubach to a nearby hospital to have stitches placed above his left eye. Upon his return to the training camp, Staubach jumped out of the car and headed for the dormitories to find Longley. The troubled quarterback was gone. His bags were packed before he sucker-punched Staubach again, and his paycheck already had been cashed. The whole premeditated incident was Longley's way of saying goodbye to Dallas and Staubach. He officially was traded shortly thereafter.

Nine years later, Staubach, the mild-mannered Dallas businessman, was given a "just suppose." Just suppose he and Longley happened to be alone in the same truck stop, just the two of them, a long way from Dallas. Would Staubach suggest that they step out back to settle old business?

Captain America blinked. "You mean in a fistfight?" he said. "No. That was a long time ago, and I've forgotten about it. I might talk to Clint about it, but I wouldn't suggest violence. That's not the Christian way."

Staubach has turned the other cheek a number of times in his life, but how would he do if he were forced to use his fists? "Very well," he said. "I've handled myself in boxing classes. I've always been able to defend myself. Even now I stay in shape. The other day, I bench-pressed 300 pounds, which is pretty good for my size."

It's almost expected that a tall, strong, silent type like Captain America would keep a muzzle on his macho. But he stepped out of character when he told the nation that he was every bit the he-man, in a romantic sense, as the NFL's leading sex symbol.

Phyllis George, in a television interview before a game, was able to draw out Staubach. "She was comparing my lifestyle with Joe Namath's, which was free-wheeling and having a good time, while I had a family and was restricted," he said. "I told Phyllis I enjoyed the same things that Namath did, like sex, but it was with the same woman. It kind of surprised Phyllis a bit. I know my wife, Marianne, was surprised. She almost fell off the couch."

Staubach's comeback lines may have registered surprise, but never his come-backs. Something stirred inside him in the late stages of football games when a touchdown or two was needed to save the Cowboys. A change came over him. One would swear that Staubach's teeth turned to fangs and hair grew on his fingers, so great was the transformation.

"It seemed that I had total control," Staubach said of those crucial instances when he milked drama until it was udderly dry. "I enjoyed performing at those times more than any other moment. The bottom line was preparation, the intangibles and the confidence I had in myself and was able to instill in 10 other men. It also helped knowing that the Drew Pearsons of the world can make the big play. I don't know of any one person who has made more than Drew. As for me, I seemed to be more alert when we had to score in a hurry. I wanted it more badly. And if you want something badly enough, usually you can get it."

Staubach was never harder to beat than in the 1979 season, his last. With 1:16 left, he set up a 27-yard field goal by Rafael Septien that beat St. Louis, 22-21. He threw a 22-yard touchdown pass to Tony Hill with 1:53 remaining to stun Chicago, 24-20. With 2:24 showing on the clock against the New York Giants, Staubach threw a 32-yard touchdown pass to Pearson and then positioned Septien for a 22-yard field goal with 3 seconds left for a 16-14 Dallas victory.

Staubach's crowning moment, perhaps more kingly than his miraculous come-back against the 49ers in 1972 and even his incredible 50-yard "Hail Mary" pass to Pearson that beat Minnesota, 17-14, with 24 seconds remaining in the 1975 playoffs, might have been his final regular-season game for the Cowboys in 1979. Washington was leading Dallas, 34-21, with 3:41 left. Staubach promptly directed the Cowboys 59 yards on a three-play drive that was capped by his 26-yard scoring strike to fullback Ron Springs. Staubach came right back, marching Dallas 75 yards in seven plays. He connected with Hill on an eight-yard touchdown pass with 39 seconds remaining, and the Cowboys won, 35-34, in a game that not only defied the odds, but logic.

Staubach accomplished these last theatrics with a flourish even though he was 37 and had taken a severe beating that autumn. He received five concussions in 1979, temporarily losing his memory on four of those occasions.

In his final football game for Dallas, a first-round playoff contest against the

Rams, Staubach was in his accustomed position of attempting to rally the Cowboys from defeat. However, in an effort to ground the football, he inadvertently threw a pass that was caught by Herb Scott, a Dallas guard. A 10-yard illegal receiver penalty was walked off against the Cowboys, sealing a 21-19 defeat.

"What a way to end your career, completing a pass to Herb Scott," Staubach said afterward.

He wasn't joking. Although the Cowboys tried hard to convince him otherwise, Staubach retired the following spring.

"I was 38 years old at the time," he said. "Dr. Fred Plum, a neurologist in New York, told me the concussions possibly were accumulative. He noticed reflex changes in my body. His advice was for me to retire. Plus my kids were growing up, and I wanted to spend more time with them. So it just all came together."

The Cowboys may never again have a quarterback as effective and

*Roger Staubach brings the same kind of class to the real-estate business that he displayed for years on football fields.*

dramatic as Staubach. He led the NFL in passing in 1971, 1973, 1978 and 1979, and he won the National Football Conference passing title in 1977. He started in four Super Bowls, and the Cowboys won two of them. Staubach was named to five Pro Bowls, but he never was picked on the major All-Pro teams.

It was a glaring omission because, at the time of his retirement, Staubach was rated the NFL's all-time No. 1 quarterback on a system that took into account his 2,958 passing attempts, 1,685 completions (57 percent), 22,700 yards passing, 153 touchdown passes and 109 interceptions. Though Landry hated it when Staubach ran, his career rushing average was an impressive 5.5 yards per carry, plus another 20 touchdowns. And there's no telling how much greater Staubach's pro career would have been had he not spent four years of anchors away after college.

"I was The Sporting News Player of the Year one season (at Navy, in 1963, and was The Sporting News NFC Player of the Year in 1971), and I won some other awards like the Heisman, so I always felt I had more honors than I deserved," Staubach said. "Some players received bonuses for making All-Pro teams. I never wanted an incentive bonus because I felt it would influence the decisions I would be making as far as touchdown passes."

Though slighted in some ways, Pro Football Monthly did select Staubach as the quarterback on its NFL "Team of the Decade" for the 1970s. On the league's own all-star team for that decade, however, Pittsburgh's Terry Bradshaw was selected ahead of Jolly Roger.

After retiring, Staubach devoted his time to his family, his real-estate business and, for a while, broadcasting. He worked as a color commentator on football games for CBS from 1980-82. He was well received by football fans, although a comment he made regarding his youngest daughter, Amy, then a preschooler, developed into a political controversy.

Precipitating the comment was the televised debate between President Carter and Ronald Reagan. In the debate, Carter said he asked his daughter, Amy, what was the most important issue in the 1980 presidential campaign, and Amy said it was nuclear proliferation.

Staubach, amused by what he interpreted as a "facetious remark" by Carter, decided to have some fun with it the following Sunday in a game he was covering. He prepared the play-by-play man, Frank Glieber, to ask him the proper straight line: How will Dallas stop St. Louis?

When the time came, Glieber asked the question and Staubach answered: "I checked with my daughter Amy before the game, and she said they (the Cowboys) had to stop the bomb to Mel Gray (the Cardinals' speedy wide receiver)."

When Staubach returned home that night, the newspapers already were calling. What had he meant on TV? "I told them that the remark wasn't meant to be political, that I was just having fun," he recalled. "I also said: 'I can't believe people are making a big thing of this. If we don't have a sense of humor after the last four years, we're really in trouble.' So I dug an even deeper hole for myself. CBS didn't censor me, but I haven't heard the end of it yet."

The network did object to Staubach's comment, which prompted a hasty phone call from a CBS official who told Staubach to refrain from further political references. Staubach eventually left CBS, but he wasn't forced out. He simply wanted to spend more time with his family and his business.

Though Staubach stopped playing football in 1979, he is not forgotten. He continues to inspire others.

Steve Young, who in 1984 signed a contract worth an estimated $40 million to play quarterback for the Los Angeles Express of the United States Football League, said Staubach was his boyhood hero. "He always won in the final seconds," Young explained, "and there was no change in his values when he became rich and famous."

In the spring of 1985, a Dallas business group visiting Mexico City presented Mexican Finance Minister Jesus Silva Herzog with a special gift—a Dallas Cowboys jersey with his name across the back and the number 12. Captain America's number. Staubach's image crosses not only generations, but borders.

It was Landry, of all the great quote-makers, who best captured the essence of Roger Staubach. "He is the best we have in football," the Dallas coach said in 1976.

Staubach, the player, has left us. Gratefully, Staubach, the image, hasn't. He may be the closest thing to human perfection that can be found among modern American sports heroes. He has been a winner in all phases of his life, an example in most. He has won fairly and squarely, without stepping on people, without making concessions in his own values, without walking a crooked path.

Staubach remains, as he has often been described, the straightest arrow in the quiver. Captain America lives!

# John Huarte

*When opportunity knocked, he was there to answer. He was the most unlikely of football heroes, a sidearming backup quarterback without illusions of grandeur. But football found John Huarte and John Huarte found Camelot. For one brief shining moment he stood a nation on its ear and collected college football's highest honor. He was a one-year phenomenon, a twist of fate. John Huarte was God's gift to Notre Dame.*

# Chapter 14

# The biggest Heisman upset

John Huarte is surrounded by tiles.

Big tiles. Small tiles. Square tiles. Round tiles.

Tiles for your bathroom, tiles for your entrance hall, tiles for your counter top, tiles for your jacuzzi.

Tiles decorated with flowers, seashells, fruit baskets and sunbursts.

Tiles with women's names (Sharon, Grace), tiles that paint images of European nights (Perugia, Siena), tiles with worldly tones (Arctic, Yukon), tiles that work up an appetite (Toasted Almond, Raisin) and tiles that make one drowsy (Wicker, Silenzio).

Tiles for the budget-minded, tiles with class. "Irresistible . . . y resiste!" reads the tag line below Gres Catalan, one of the more stylish tiles in the showroom of the Arizona Tile Co. in Tempe, Ariz.

Tiles attractively displayed. Tiles stacked in boxes in the warehouse behind the showroom. Tiles everywhere—in Phoenix, Tucson, Denver, Albuquerque, San Diego and Anaheim, the six branches of the Arizona Tile Co., which Huarte owns.

Tiles in the family. Huarte has two brothers, Greg and Jim, each of whom owns his own tile business in California. Fourteen branches among three brothers.

"If it's good tile, it sounds like a bell," John Huarte said, knuckling a piece of Perugia and hearing a resonant ring. "You can tell good tile by strength and hardness and the density of weight. If the tile absorbs moisture, it's porous like a sponge. That's not good tile. If the moisture holds on the surface, that means it's dense. That's good tile."

The harder the tile, Huarte explained, the better it wears, the longer it lasts. A tile's hardness is determined scientifically in laboratories through measurements. Knuckling for a bell sound is the final test.

Huarte buys tile from top-of-the-line factories in Italy, Spain, Germany, Japan, Korea and Brazil. He travels to these countries to personally inspect the product. The best ceramic tiles in the United States, he said, come from Florida and Georgia because of the availability of clay in the South.

"It's fun to sell something that's beautiful and lasting," Huarte said with genuine pleasure in his voice. "We've got some knockout material."

Tiles change as tastes change every two or three years. Earth tones (browns) are not as popular these days as monochromatic tones (grays). Tiles also change from region to region. What's fashionable in Albuquerque (rustics) may not be what's in vogue in Tucson (off-whites).

Huarte tiled his own home in Tempe in off-white. "Suitable for the desert," he said.

Huarte is a tile tycoon, but he becomes as impenetrable as his best tile when asked to disclose the extent of his wealth. "It's not my policy to gloat on those things," he said. "We have all the things we need to send our children to private schools."

John and Eileen Huarte have five children—three girls and two boys. The middle child, Bridget, plays the piano. When practicing at home, she needs something on top of the piano to prop up her sheet music.

The Heisman Memorial Trophy does the trick perfectly.

"Got to use it for something," her father said, laughing.

John Huarte won the Heisman as a quarterback at Notre Dame in 1964. It was, without a doubt, the greatest of Heisman upsets.

The Heisman field that year was among the most talented ever. The candidates included Roger Staubach (who had won the Heisman the year before), Joe Namath, Gale Sayers, Dick Butkus, Craig Morton, Jerry Rhome, Tucker Frederickson, Ken Willard, Bob Berry, Brian Piccolo and Jack Snow, the other half of Huarte's success at Notre Dame.

All would go on to professional football. Some became All-Pro players and Super Bowl heroes, and some were voted into the Pro Football Hall of Fame.

Huarte had a pro career, too, but it wasn't much to speak of. In eight seasons in the American Football League and the National Football League, Huarte was on the rosters of six different teams. In all that time he threw 48 passes.

"That's not even eight a year," he said. "That's nothing. I was a nonentity."

But in 1964, Huarte was everything, including a consensus All-America quarterback and the Heisman Trophy winner. From the wire services to football coaches, Huarte was on almost everybody's national honor lists.

Oh yes, he earned another award that year, a varsity football letter. That might not seem like much, but he had not earned one before. No athlete before or since Huarte has won the Heisman as a returning non-letterman.

Huarte missed most of his sophomore year because of injuries. He completed four of eight passes for 38 yards and carried the ball three times for minus 14 yards. Huarte saw little more action as a junior, completing 20 passes in 42 attempts for 243 yards while rushing for minus 53 yards on 11 carries. He played 42 minutes that year, not enough for a letter.

Notre Dame, which was not blessed with a multitude of strong quarterbacks entering Huarte's senior year, hardly looked to the Anaheim native as the savior of what in 1964 was a flagging football program.

The Notre Dame media guide for that season had this to say about its senior signal caller: "Quarterback probably is the biggest question mark, as it has been for several years. . . . There has not been a quarterback of All-America rating since 1956, Paul Hornung's last season.

"However, in spring practice, (Coach Ara) Parseghian said he was 'pleasantly surprised' with the work of John Huarte, senior, a pretty good passer who, although not earning a monogram last year, did have 42 minutes of playing time.

"However, near the end of spring drills, Huarte suffered a shoulder injury. It is expected that he'll be ready for the start of fall practice. But at this time, quarterback still has to be considered a question mark."

Doctors recommended surgery on Huarte's separated shoulder. But Huarte, with his big chance ahead of him, opted to rebuild the shoulder instead. As it turned out, he made a wise decision. His shoulder never bothered him that year, and his unorthodox throwing motion propelled him to the summit of collegiate achievement.

"It was an incredible series of events," he said of winning the Heisman. "It wasn't like I was fated to win it. The whole thing was an oddity."

To say the least. From 1961, when Huarte left Mater Dei High School in Santa Ana, Calif., for Notre Dame, until 1975, when he retired from pro football (a generous description of the World Football League), Huarte enjoyed but one brief, shining moment in Camelot: The 1964 season.

"The year before, I was a scrub, burning up time," he said. "I'd stay at the end of the practice field, just scrimmaging. I wasn't even on the first three or four teams."

And Notre Dame's record was 2-7, the fifth straight year the Fighting Irish had failed to post a winning season. The cry in South Bend no longer was "Win one for the Gipper," but instead simply, "Win one."

Parseghian was hired away from Northwestern in 1964 to change the chaotic situation. He had barely moved into his coaching office at Notre Dame when there was a knock on the door. It was Huarte and Snow.

"We told him we were the best pass-catching team on campus," Snow said from his real estate development office in Long Beach, Calif., his hometown. "It wasn't a braggart's statement; it was a last-gasp thing."

Snow was more California laid-back and outwardly confident than Huarte. He did most of the talking while Huarte, typically quiet, shifted his eyes nervously from the floor to Snow to Parseghian and back to the floor. But even for the extroverted Snow, facing Parseghian never was easy.

"Ara was a little aloof," Snow said. "You could joke and kid with his assistants, but there was a little fear of God when you went to see him."

Parseghian told the two seniors that they would have the opportunity in spring practice to prove their worth. That's all they needed to hear.

Snow had been a scrub like Huarte, although he had earned a letter at wingback in 1963. Parseghian moved Snow to split end with the stipulation that he get his weight down from 230 pounds to 205. Snow complied.

As for Huarte, Parseghian had little reason for being optimistic.

"The general feedback we got from the previous coaching regime was negative toward John's ability," Parseghian said from his business office in South Bend, Ind. "They didn't think he had either the physical or mental ability, or leadership qualities, to be the regular quarterback."

Other than that, nice kid.

"We took credit for only one thing that year as far as John Huarte," Parseghian said, "and that was restoring his confidence."

Before hurting his shoulder that spring, Huarte had demonstrated quickness in setting up to pass and in getting rid of the ball. He said he also had a mental grasp of the job.

"I had scrimmaged for three years," he pointed out. "I was not a great runner or long-ball thrower. I was very effective at medium-deep play-action passes."

Even with his funny throwing style. Snow said it was three-quarters (midway between overhand and sidearm), while Parseghian remembered it as sidearm. "But I learned long ago," the coach said, "not to fool with what Mother Nature gives you."

But Huarte apparently was the only person aware of his aptitude. He began "at the bottom rung" on Parseghian's depth chart before moving quickly up the ladder.

Parseghian didn't inherit the South Bend chapter of The Little Sisters of the Poor when he came to town. Notre Dame was teeming with pro talent, including Alan Page, later an All-Pro defensive tackle for the Minnesota Vikings, and Jim Lynch, a 10-year linebacker for the Kansas City Chiefs. But the Irish, frustrated with losing, had another essential ingredient.

"We were a very hungry team," Huarte said.

Huarte and Snow played catch all summer on the beach in Southern California, perfecting their timing and strengthening the quarterback's shoulder. When the season opened at Wisconsin, their act was synchronized. The Badgers were a heavy favorite but never had a chance. Notre Dame won, 31-7, as Huarte threw touchdown passes of 61 and 42 yards to Snow. The California connection accounted for 217 of Huarte's 270 yards passing in his first collegiate start.

"After that game," Parseghian said, "Huarte and Snow became known as a dangerous passing combination." Every bit as dangerous, in retrospect, as other famous Notre Dame aerial acts: Gus Dorais to Knute Rockne, Bob Williams to Leon Hart, Terry Hanratty to Jim Seymour, Tom Clements to Dave Casper and Joe Montana to Kris Haines. In game after game, key Huarte-to-Snow completions kept Irish drives going and put points on the scoreboard.

Notre Dame thrashed Purdue the second week, 34-15. Huarte connected on nine passes for 127 yards and two touchdowns, including a two-yarder to Snow. Huarte accounted for four touchdowns the next week in a 34-7 triumph over Air Force. He threw for two scores, one to Snow, and ran short yardage for two more.

By now the country was conscious of Notre Dame, which was becoming college football's surprise team, and of Parseghian.

"Ara was a tremendous teacher . . . the best coach I was ever exposed to, vastly superior to the others," Huarte said. "He was a great manager of people. That was his strength."

Huarte and Snow teamed up on their fifth touchdown play in four games as Notre Dame pushed around UCLA, 24-0. Huarte had a 10-of-15 passing day for 209 yards and two touchdowns. One week later, Huarte completed 21 of 37 passes for 300 yards and a touchdown as Notre Dame manhandled a spirited Stanford team, 28-6.

The Fighting Irish were 5-0 at the halfway mark of the season. Heisman voters, wondering how to decide among Butkus, Namath, Sayers and the rest, had a new name to consider, one they weren't sure how to pronounce: Huarte. Was it Wart? War-tay? Hart?

The voters found out that it was Huarte as in Stewart and that he was of German-Basque ancestry, not Spanish. They couldn't believe that a player with his talent had been hiding in virtual oblivion for two years.

Huarte's next game was against Navy, which would have been a Heisman confrontation except that Staubach was injured much of his last year at Annapolis. But Staubach played that Halloween Saturday against the Irish, and it turned out that the trick was on him as Notre Dame and Huarte buried the Midshipmen, 40-0.

Huarte treated Irish fans to three more touchdown passes, including a 74-yarder to Nick Eddy and a seven-yarder and a 55-yarder to Snow, and he set a school record that still stands by averaging 27.4 yards per completion (10 for 274 yards.)

It wasn't until the seventh game, when the Fighting Irish faced Pittsburgh, that Notre Dame was tested. Pitt entered the game with a 2-3-2 record, and when the Panthers fell behind early, 14-0—the second score coming on a 91-yard Huarte-to-Eddy completion that ranks as the second-longest pass play in Irish history—it looked as if they were headed for another inglorious defeat. But Pitt made a strong upset bid, and only a 30-yard field goal at the end of the first half provided Notre Dame with a narrow victory, 17-15.

Huarte then made his first appearance on national television and promptly wrapped up the Heisman for himself with a 34-7 triumph over Michigan State, which had won the last eight matchups between the two teams. In his finest all-around game that autumn, Huarte completed 11 of 17 passes for 193 yards and a touchdown. He also had his longest college run, a 21-yard bootleg in which he leaped over one tackler and outran another for a touchdown.

"Huarte played a perfect game," Spartans Coach Duffy Daugherty said afterward.

All that, and right before the Heisman ballots were due.

It snowed the day before Notre Dame's ninth game, against Iowa, and the stadium floor in South Bend was covered with a white blanket at kickoff. Huarte attempted only 10 passes, completing four. One of them was a 66-yard touchdown bomb to—who else?—Snow. It was a cold day indeed for the Hawkeyes, 28-0 losers.

Then, in Huarte's words, "the roof fell in." One game from possibly an undisputed national championship, the Fighting Irish flew to Los Angeles to face archrival Southern California, which had struggled the first nine weeks to a 6-3 record while Notre Dame was sitting pretty at 9-0.

"USC had material as good as ours," Huarte said. "They had just had a so-so year."

Notre Dame jumped ahead quickly, 17-0, on a field goal, a 21-yard pass from Huarte to Snow and a short run by halfback Bill Wolski. Huarte was astounding, Southern Cal was floundering, and it looked as though the Trojans would walk away whimpering.

Parseghian would allow none of that kind of thinking from his players, however, and he gave them a halftime pep talk to keep them from letting up.

"Let's have your attention up here," the coach said. "Thirty minutes stand between us and the greatest sports comeback in history. Thirty minutes! You have to go out there and play this second half, boys—a 60-minute football team. This is the way we started this football season, and this is the way we're going to finish, you understand? I want that defense down there knocking them on their butts. You go after it, understand? I mean, really gang tackle 'em. You did a damn good job in there, and I'm real proud of you. I want to be prouder of you when you come back here after the second half, boys. Let's really go out there and give them 30 more minutes of Notre Dame football!"

But as it turned out, 30 minutes was too much to ask from a team beset by injuries to several key players, including Lynch and Page, as the season wound down. Page left that final game in the second quarter with a shoulder injury, and after that the Trojans found ways to needle through the Notre Dame defense.

"USC found some things that worked," Huarte recalled. "They were relaxed, got some luck (such as an Irish fumble deep in Trojan territory) and beat us."

Trojan quarterback Craig Fertig's desperation pass to Rod Sherman with 1:33 left in the game was the crushing blow as the Irish fell, 20-17. Huarte had another big day—18 completions for 272 yards and one touchdown—but statistics offered little consolation as Notre Dame's storybook season came to a sad ending.

The Irish won the MacArthur Bowl, presented by the National Football Foundation and Hall of Fame to the national champion. But the Associated Press and United Press International recognized Alabama (10-0 before an Orange Bowl loss to Texas) as No. 1, while the Football Writers Association of America crowned Arkansas (11-0) as the national champion.

Huarte's incredible season resulted in a bundle of school records for both himself and Snow, who earned All-America honors while hauling in 60 of Huarte's 114 completions, nine for touchdowns (still a Notre Dame record). Huarte ranked third in the nation in total offense (2,069 yards) while passing for 2,062 yards and 16 TDs.

His biggest accomplishment that season, of course, was winning the Heisman, which was announced before the Southern Cal game. Huarte was followed in the voting by Rhome, the Tulsa quarterback who threw a phenomenal 32 TD passes and led the nation in passing and total offense, and Butkus, the great center-linebacker at Illinois. Snow finished fifth.

To this day, Huarte is amazed that it's his Heisman Trophy holding up his daughter's sheet music.

"How can you get a guy who hadn't won a letter to win the Heisman? It was crazy," he said. "Those were great athletes I was competing against. I didn't see myself as a great athlete. I was a good athlete who was a student of the game.

"You know how Pete Rose is in baseball? I had the same attitude. I was never motivated to play football; I was *happy* to play football.

"But to win the Heisman, it takes a combination of things: getting a chance to play, playing your heart out and p.r., although I was a guy who was *unknown*."

Huarte had no idea he was even attracting Heisman consideration until late in the season. "One day I picked up a newspaper and read I was a candidate," he said. "Some writers threw my hat into it."

But was it the media who built the Huarte bandwagon and got it rolling faster than Rhome's, Butkus' and the others? Or was it the Notre Dame public relations office?

Neither, really.

"It was the dramatic aspect of Notre Dame having been down a lot of years," Parseghian said. "And now with Notre Dame back, people wanted to know who was making it happen."

But not everyone voted the Irish ticket.

"I'm reasonably positive I voted for Frederickson, who was a helluva athlete for Auburn," said Furman Bisher, sports columnist for the Atlanta Journal and Constitution and The Sporting News. "He was a two-way player—a safety, I believe, on defense—which was something even at that time.

"There weren't any preseason or even midseason Heisman promotions back then. I doubt that Notre Dame got anything out (on Huarte) but the weekly releases.

"Notre Dame won the thing (the Heisman) more than Huarte. He could have been the quarterback at any other school in the country and not won the Heisman."

Maury White, a Des Moines Register columnist and the Midwest sectional representative for the Heisman, didn't vote for Huarte.

"I believe I voted for Butkus or Morton," he said. "I saw Butkus a lot, being around the Big Ten. But I saw Morton . . . and was very impressed. But for any Heisman candidate, it helps to have Notre Dame as a mailing address."

History has shown that to be true. Notre Dame has produced six Heisman winners, more than any other school. But Huarte couldn't get a Heisman vote in South Bend. Joe Doyle, then sports editor of the South Bend Tribune, voted for Snow.

"I felt Snow was a better athlete than Huarte, which Snow proved in the pros (with the Los Angeles Rams)," Doyle explained. "But I do think Notre Dame athletes during an undefeated year—the school hadn't lost a game when the Heisman vote was taken in '64—do have an advantage. Rhome was an outstanding quarterback, but he was at Tulsa, which doesn't have national appeal."

But if the sports editor of the South Bend paper didn't vote for Huarte, who did? Some believe it was the Eastern voters, who were regarded suspiciously at the time by other sections of the country.

"My impression is that I voted for Morton or Sayers; I may have been home-townish enough to vote for Morton (who played for California)," said Art Rosenbaum, sports columnist for the San Francisco Chronicle. "But there was a certain resentment that the Heisman was an Eastern thing. I don't know who our West Coast representative was, but what representing did he do? We were just a voice in the West."

Doyle said he knew of a number of sportswriters in the 1960s "who hadn't worked in years, but who still had a Heisman vote. Most of them were in the East."

Pat Livingston, a Heisman voter in 1964 but now retired as sports editor of the Pittsburgh Press, didn't help Huarte win the Heisman. Livingston succumbed to sectionalism and went with Alabama's Namath, from nearby Beaver Falls, Pa.

"Being from Pittsburgh, you almost had to vote for Namath," Livingston said, shrugging. "If you didn't, it would be like voting against Tony Dorsett, who's from Aliquippa, Pennsylvania. It's a good thing there are secret ballots. But every section votes sectionally."

Murray Olderman, who was based in New York as sports editor and cartoonist for the Newspaper Enterprise Association when Parseghian resurrected Notre Dame football in '64, said he is reasonably certain that he voted for Huarte.

There's one!

"Huarte was a sidearm quarterback, so he wasn't a good pro prospect," Olderman said. "But he had a great senior year. It was a unique year. A lot of players played their way out of it (Heisman competition)."

Staubach, the obvious Heisman favorite entering the '64 season, eliminated himself through injuries. Namath did the same. Morton had a strong senior year, but Cal was 3-7. Sayers, despite earning consensus All-America honors at Kansas, had his least impressive collegiate season, gaining only 688 yards in total offense. Butkus was a phenomenal collegian, but center-linebackers don't win Heismans. And the other candidates simply couldn't compete with the Notre Dame mystique. By all rights, Rhome had a "Heisman year." Had he played for Oklahoma, not Tulsa, Rhome might have won the award. But as it turned out, he lost in a close vote to Huarte, who received 1,026 votes to Rhome's 952.

Huarte also benefited from the Fighting Irish schedule, which exposed him to sportswriters from coast to coast. The Irish won in Madison, Wis., Philadelphia (against Navy), Pittsburgh and Colorado Springs, Colo. (against Air Force), while adding home victories over two West Coast teams, UCLA and Stanford.

"What might have happened," Doyle said of the Heisman balloting, "is that you voted for Morton first, then voted Huarte third without knowing it."

And all those thirds, plus a plurality of firsts and scattered seconds in a balanced field, may have given Huarte the Heisman. The Californian received 216 first-place votes, only 30 more than Rhome.

But has there ever been a more deserving Heisman winner than John Huarte, not only for what he achieved, but for what he overcame? Has there ever been a better Heisman example?

Certainly, Huarte played for Notre Dame, which, with its national appeal, was a built-in advantage. But Huarte didn't fail his opportunity. Perhaps other athletes of similar or even greater ability, if given the same chance, would not have responded as dramatically or successfully. Even at Notre Dame.

The key word is opportunity.

"You have to have undaunting faith," Huarte said. "You keep plugging. If things fail, make sure they fail because of you and not because of what management thinks of you. Sometimes *opportunities* fail."

Huarte could have quit football after his junior year. Hundreds of football players with All-America or Heisman potential have quit the game. Maybe they didn't like to practice or go to class. Maybe they weren't treated like superstars from the first day of workouts. Maybe they wanted to get married, find a job. So they walk away, while friends tell them they're crazy to waste all that talent.

It takes a lot more character to persevere than to quit, especially when no one wants you. Huarte had that character; he just needed an opportunity. He got it, in the nick of time.

"Without trying to put a feather in our cap," said Parseghian, sounding for all the world like Yankee Doodle Dandy, "one wonders what would have happened to John Huarte without a change in management at Notre Dame."

Huarte shares that speculation.

"Talk about not giving up on yourself," he said. "You can take all kinds of athletes, not just at Notre Dame. Everyone gets disappointed. They say, 'The coach doesn't like me.' Kids quit.

"You can still work your butt off and *not* win the Heisman. It all comes down to management. Sometimes you get poor results, sometimes fair, sometimes really good. It depends on management.

"I happened to be a kid who worked his butt off and was hurt by bad management. Fortunately for me, management changed."

Huarte and Snow staged their last exciting pass-and-catch show in the North-

South Shrine Game in Miami. They combined on several passes in the final min-utes of the game—the last one for a touchdown with 5 seconds left—to spark the North team to a 37-30 victory.

Huarte also was selected for the College All-Star Game, but he didn't play until the third quarter. He ignited a defused All-Star offense by directing two 80-yard touchdown drives and cut the winning margin of the Cleveland Browns to 24-16. Huarte was an overwhelming choice as the game's most valuable player.

Huarte entered the professional ranks with momentum—and money. The New York Jets of the American Football League drafted him in the second round and reportedly paid him $200,000 for his rookie year. "That's close," Huarte said.

Huarte, at the time, was one of the highest-paid rookies in pro football history. Unfortunately for Huarte, the highest-paid rookie at that time also was a Jet quarterback: Joe Willie Namath. Benevolent Sonny Werblin, the Jets' owner, paid Namath, the club's No. 1 pick, $400,000. There was little doubt who would be the team's quarterback, though it wasn't a question of money as much as talent.

Namath had the purest throwing motion pro scouts had seen in years. Huarte had that awkward sidearm delivery. And if ever an athlete was meant to play in one city, Namath was meant for New York. He had the talent, the smile, the flamboyance. New York's nightlife was his life. Broadway Joe.

Huarte, on the other hand, was more withdrawn, not really one of the guys. "You've got to get to know John," Snow said.

Huarte began his pro career as the No. 3 quarterback behind Namath and Mike Taliaferro. One month later, Huarte was waived by the Jets, who recalled him and assigned him to the taxi (reserve) squad for the 1965 season.

"Namath was the big star; I was just there," he said. "I had dreams of being an All-Pro, but I didn't even come close. I had a heckuva time staying on the team. I failed to get game experience my first two years in the pros, and that hurt me."

After his rookie year, Huarte caught the pro football shuttle service and never stopped moving, making a number of transfers. The Jets traded him to Boston for end Jim Colclough and a No. 4 draft pick. In 1½ years with the Patriots, Huarte completed eight of 20 passes and rushed nine times for 45 yards. Boston released him in 1967, and he next was signed by Philadelphia, where he spent the remain-der of the '67 season on the Eagles' taxi squad.

That brought chuckles in South Bend. The Eagles' coach was Joe Kuharich, who had kept Huarte on the bench while coaching at Notre Dame during Huarte's sophomore and junior seasons. Their relationship in Philadelphia was even more brief. Huarte threw 15 passes for the Eagles in 1968.

He surfaced next in Minnesota but within days was on his way to Kansas City, where he enjoyed his longest tenure with any pro team. He was assigned to the taxi squad in 1969, then played in one game for the Chiefs in 1970, one in '71 and two in '72 before being sold on waivers to the Chicago Bears.

In Chicago, Huarte couldn't beat out Bobby Douglass, and the Bears waived him during the 1973 exhibition season. He had come to the end of the road.

But only in the NFL. A new league was forming, the World Football League, and Huarte signed with the Memphis Southmen in 1974. After 10 years, he was a starting quarterback again.

"I finally had the satisfaction I was looking for (in the pros)," he said. "I was at

*John Huarte, once surrounded by cheers during his unlikely rise to the top of the college football world, now is surrounded by the tiles that he sells at his Tempe, Ariz., business.*

my finest as a quarterback those two years. I even kept Danny White on the bench my first year. But in the second year, his ability came through."

So, with the WFL folding after the 1975 season, Huarte completed his professional career as he had begun it, watching someone else play his position.

His pro experience did offer a couple of lasting rewards, however. While with the Jets, Huarte met his wife, Eileen, on an elevator at Shea Stadium. Eileen had been working as an elevator operator while taking classes at St. John's University.

And while in Memphis, Huarte met Glenn Whitt, a tile distributor and a Southmen fan who first interested the quarterback in the tile business. After helping his brother Greg with his tile company in San Diego for 1½ years, Huarte moved his family to Tempe, just outside of Phoenix, and started selling tile himself in 1978.

Huarte went to Arizona not only for the state's "clarity of air and lack of population," he said, but also to prosper, unlike many who come to Arizona to retire. He faced the same obstacle in business, however, that he had encountered in athletics: Skepticism.

"A competitor informed me I couldn't sell tile here," he said. "He even described how I couldn't outsell him. I said, 'We'll see.' But I knew he was full of crap. I knew it would sell."

It has. So much so, in fact, that Huarte's competitor, for all practical purposes, no longer competes. "We're outselling him by a lot, I'm sure," Huarte said.

It was another example of John Huarte beating the odds, proving his detractors wrong. Even though his pro career didn't work out as he had hoped, he rose to the top in 1964 and was judged the best in the college ranks. Now he has done the same in the tile ranks.

Huarte mentioned another athlete—a skinny, blond skier from the United States—who had been a dark horse before schussing faster than his peers.

"It's like the Olympics," Huarte said of his Heisman season. "You've got one chance to ski down the mountain and be a Bill Johnson."

But the analogy is not precise. The world had advance warning of Johnson. He had won some pre-Olympic events in the downhill and had boasted that he would win the gold in Sarajevo, Yugoslavia.

There was no advance notice of Huarte in 1964. He was just another name on the roster, an unnoticed quarterback who became a starter because of attrition, not reputation. Boast? There was nothing to brag about.

But Huarte knew he had the talent to become a champion. It's like the difference between good tile and bad tile. Were Huarte porous to the criticisms and snubs of others, he would have remained average. Instead, he had a strong character and a firm belief in himself, and he graded out at the top of the line.

Knuckle Huarte's Heisman and you hear a bell sound.

# O.J. Simpson

*He was a state-of-the-art half-back. He is a show business personality in much demand. But when all is said and done, Orenthal James Simpson remains in private as he comes across in public — a genuinely nice person. He brought grace to the football field, charm to the screen and broadcast booth and enthusiasm to life. He is a multidimensional superstar. O.J. Simpson avoided defenses, but he tackles life with style and sincerity.*

# Chapter 15

# A nice guy finished first

It has always been O.J. Simpson's main objective, more than the Heisman Memorial Trophy, the National Football League records, the movie contracts, the endorsements, the financial security and the impression that he can humanly fly.

He just wants to be the nice guy.

"My big motivation in life is to be known and liked," he said.

He has achieved his dual ambition. Simpson is known, certainly. He is the most visible of Heisman winners. Open almost any magazine and there is Simpson pushing some product. Turn on the television and Simpson appears again, chatting with the Giffer on "Monday Night Football," playing golf with Arnold Palmer on a Hertz commercial, acting with Richard Burton or Paul Newman in a late-night movie.

Simpson's visibility is an extension of his fame, but it is more directly related to his winning personality. Numerous other football stars retired with the same opportunities as Simpson, but they didn't capitalize on them as he has done. Instead of his stardom dissipating into stardust, Simpson, remarkably, is as popular as ever.

The reason, obviously, is that Simpson is so well liked. His clean-cut good looks can tug at a mother's heart or make a young girl's eyes light up. His friendly, unaffected manner also comes across well to grown men and makes little boys look up to him with adulation.

O.J. appeals to everyone.

"I like people, and that evidently comes across," he said. "It goes back to that original motivation, to be recognized and liked. I haven't gotten enough of it, although I don't crave it like I used to. But I still like the idea of mothers coming up and wanting to shake my hand, or kids asking for my autograph."

How nice is O.J. Simpson?

The nicest.

"I was eating in a restaurant," he said, recalling the ultimate test of niceness. "This lady walked over and casually took the fork out of my hand and said, 'You've got to sign this for my son.' "

Took the fork right out of his hand! The woman couldn't have been more rude or disrespectful. Simpson had every right to stand up and pour his escargot butter over her head. So what did he do?

"I signed it," he said, "because that's the way it is. I'm not going to get pushed out of shape. I'm the most gracious guy there is."

One can't be positive that other sugar-and-spice sports heroes—Steve Garvey, Julius Erving, Roger Staubach and Palmer—would have reacted as sweetly as O.J.

Simpson prefers to be a public figure, and if that means public disturbances, he is willing to make the sacrifice. But that's his nature anyway. He finds it extremely difficult to be critical. "I don't like to look at the bad sides of people," he said.

Though Simpson was reared in a San Francisco ghetto, living in government housing, he shows no traces of animosity or reverse bigotry. "I'm not prejudiced," he said. "That's someone else's problem."

When Simpson was, in effect, demoted by ABC in its television coverage of Super Bowl XIX in 1985, he wasn't angry. He was replaced in the main booth by the Washington Redskins' windup talking toy, Joe Theismann, and assigned the pregame show. Still, Simpson viewed the incident as something positive.

"(ABC President) Roone Arledge called me before the change was made and explained ABC's policy of switching around announcers when it came to major events," Simpson said. "They had already set that precedent in baseball. I knew I'd be visible in the pregame show. And, quite frankly, as a game announcer, I need work. Working in the booth on Monday nights, it also got jumbled in there at times. I knew I could be pretty effective in the Super Bowl pregame format, and as it turned out, I was."

Numerous radio-television analysts who previously had chided Simpson for his poor grammar usage, such as dropping the "ly" ending off adverbs, praised his expert analysis before that Super Bowl game between San Francisco and Miami, and, in fact, said Simpson was the highlight of the network's coverage.

If Simpson felt any anguish over his demotion, he gave no public indication of it. He has a resiliency, an ability to bounce back without stepping on toes, either his own or someone else's. Part of this resilience is a reluctance to say something he might regret later, such as a verbal attack on ABC. Why make waves, Simpson seems to be saying, if it will only create troubled waters? Instead, he keeps the sailing smooth.

"Every time in my life there has been a negative, I've been able to turn it into a positive," he said. "I grew up in what people would look at and think wasn't a good situation—the Potrero Hill district of San Francisco. I lived in the projects, in a building with eight other families. But we were like one big family. I thought Potrero Hill was the greatest place in the world. There was always a park to play in, always someone's house to go to if you needed something. I grew up in a lot of love."

Orenthal James Simpson has a brother and two sisters. Their parents separated when O.J. was 4 or 5, he said. Jim Simpson, the father, was a custodian at the Federal Reserve Bank before developing culinary skills and becoming a chef at the bank. Eunice Simpson, the mother, worked for 27 years as an orderly on the graveyard shift in the psychiatric ward at San Francisco General Hospital. She was known as the "Flying Nun" for escorting patients back to their homes in the western part of the United States. It was hellish work, too. Eunice sometimes returned home from the hospital scarred and bruised from encounters with violent patients.

Although divorced, the Simpsons spent holidays together with their children. And both parents participated actively in the rearing of their children. If O.J. needed disciplining, his mother called his father, who came right over. So, O.J. Simpson had the best of broken homes.

He wasn't always the best of kids, however. He was in a club, the Superiors, and they roamed the neighborhoods, breaking into parties, getting into fights.

Consequently, he spent a few nights at the local juvenile hall.

"I got into some trouble," he said, "but it was always for fighting. I was a good kid, basically, just aggressive."

Drugs started to become popular with young people in the 1960s, when Simpson was attending Galileo High School in San Francisco. But neither he nor his friends were interested.

"All the friends I had were athletes or wanted to be," he said. "The code among the group was that you had to get your sleep, you had to work out. I always considered myself the best-conditioned athlete around."

On Sundays in the fall, Simpson would sneak into games with his buddies at Kezar Stadium, where the 49ers played through 1970. One such day, after the 49ers opposed Cleveland, Simpson was hanging around inside an ice-cream store, when in walked the Browns' great fullback, Jim Brown.

"I'm going to break all your records, suckah," Simpson said to Brown, who paid little attention to the jive-talking kid and walked away with an amused smile.

"Years later, I asked Jim if he remembered that day," Simpson said. "He didn't. Of course, I didn't break all his records, either."

Simpson laughed in his office on the sixth floor of a bank building in the fashionable Brentwood section of Los Angeles. He has traveled a long way from the projects, in miles and material gains. He has a home worth seven figures in exclusive Brentwood Park, an area whose history numbered Shirley Temple, Joan Crawford, Cole Porter and Judy Garland as residents. Simpson's neighbors now include Linda Ronstadt, Tony Orlando, John Ritter, Helen Reddy and Hal Linden.

Simpson has a second home, also worth seven figures, in Laguna Beach, just south of Los Angeles. He calls it his "beach house."

"Aw, come on," he pleaded when asked if he is a multimillionaire, then admitted, "Obviously. I give my mother money. I bought her a nice home. I give other members of my family money. Everyone in my family is doing well. Well, my parents both had surgery, but they're doing OK now. They're both retired. Seeing my family happy gives me a bigger kick than being a millionaire.

"I'm financially secure, and the way things are going, I'm going to be more financially secure. The security gives me the luxury of putting on jeans and tennis shoes, playing basketball and tennis with my buddies, lying back on the beach, enjoying the simple things. What security has given me is time. And my idea of a good time is being at Laguna Beach, kicked back with a beer. I'll always be like that."

Considering the fast-paced life he lives, Simpson would appear to have little time to relax. He is everywhere and, seemingly, everything, all at once. He became a football superstar, but he has branched out in many other directions as well. He has acted in movies and on television and has produced five TV movies. He has endorsed orange juice, boots, tennis shoes, legal printing material and—the greatest constant as far as his visibility—rental cars. Instead of flying through airports, though, Simpson may have the resources someday to buy one of his own. He also has ownership in franchises that sell fried chicken and freshly baked and sealed hams. He has numerous other investments in hotels and apartment complexes that have paid off handsomely. Then there is ABC, which was sufficiently impressed by his work on "Monday Night Football," plus a Sunday at the Super

Bowl, to pick up the first of two options on his two-year contract, which expired in 1984.

Other financial opportunities have come Simpson's way, but he has turned them down because he either doesn't believe in the product or doesn't need the money.

"I'm busier now than I've ever been," Simpson said, "but all the business comes to me. I don't speak anymore unless it's for the company I work for. It used to be that I'd fly to some town to tell sports stories at some dinner for $5,000. I just felt I had to be there. Today, I turn those kinds of speeches down for a lot more money.

"I could make $50 million this year, afford anything in the world," Simpson said with a dreamy look on his face, "but nothing can compare to the feeling of being in a stadium of 80,000 people, and they're all yelling, 'Juice, Juice, Juice!' My God, it's such a high!"

In college, O.J. Simpson became known as Orange Juice Simpson, which then was shortened to Juice. By any name, he was The Best.

There has never been a better pure halfback than Simpson. There have been others who were more versatile, but none was a better runner. And that's a halfback's primary responsibility, to run with the football.

Fullbacks are a separate category, distinguishable from halfbacks, even though they are lumped together as running backs in today's modernized but boring terminology. The best of the pure fullbacks was Jim Brown. Bronko Nagurski and Ernie Nevers were awesome in their day, and Doc Blanchard and Jim Taylor were equally devastating runners, but none of these gentlemen hit any harder than Brown, and none was as fast. Joe Perry was a halfback masquerading as a fullback. Franco Harris was a fluid, big-play runner, but he didn't inflict the punishment of Brown and couldn't match his records even with added time. The fullback who comes closest to Brown in speed and brute strength is Earl Campbell.

There is an even wider selection of great halfbacks than great fullbacks. Red Grange dominated college football in the 1920s in the same way Babe Ruth dominated baseball. Had Jay Berwanger played at Michigan instead of the University of Chicago, he would be remembered in the same manner as Tom Harmon. Glenn Davis and Doak Walker were the last of the spectacular all-around halfbacks. Hugh McElhenny was poetry in motion, Gale Sayers pure electricity. Walter Payton runs with sheer force, like a fullback. Eric Dickerson runs like a long, sleek automobile with cruise control, only he's a crossbreed—part fullback, part halfback. A running back.

Simpson was as fluid as Dickerson, as poetic as McElhenny, as electrifying as Sayers, as durable às Berwanger and Harmon, as dominant as Grange. Davis, Walker and Payton (a placekicker in college) symbolize versatility, which Simpson didn't. He was an average receiver and blocker, although he was effective on the halfback pass. However, he was a notch above the other great halfbacks as a runner, in a class by himself.

No other halfback has ever matched his combination of speed (9.4 seconds in the 100-yard dash), power, grace, moves, stamina, durability, game-breaking qualities and ability to excel against the strongest opponents.

No other halfback since Grange has had two better touchdown runs in one game than Simpson's incredible efforts against top-ranked UCLA in 1967.

No other National Football League halfback—or fullback—has rushed for 2,000 yards in a 14-game schedule.

No other halfback or fullback has won the Heisman Trophy and been inducted into the Professional Football Hall of Fame.

Another example of Simpson's greatness was the day he was "contained" after compiling 256 yards running and receiving against a Woody Hayes-coached Ohio State team in the Rose Bowl. With other great backs, being held to under 100 yards is the normal barometer for defensive success. But with Simpson, an entirely different scale was utilized. In his last game at Southern California, Simpson rushed for 171 yards, including an 80-yard touchdown run, and caught eight passes for 85 yards. Nevertheless, Hayes said his Buckeyes did a good job of containing Simpson.

Ohio State certainly contained Southern Cal—the Buckeyes won, 27-16, and the Trojans' other touchdown (a pass to Sam Dickerson, who did not appear to have possession of the ball in the end zone) was highly questionable—but by containing Simpson, Hayes' game plan must have been to keep him under 300 yards of offense.

"When you look at a great runner," The Juice said, "it's like looking at a puzzle. They're all getting to the same point (a touchdown), but some do it more logically than others. You watch Dickerson and Marcus Allen, and they make logical, conscious moves. But some of the logic is so shocking, and so unexpected when you think about it, that you find yourself coming out of your seat, cheering. There's a big difference in watching this kind of run and seeing a bad runner break a tackle and get away for a big gain. On those kinds of runs, you stay in your seat.

"Herschel Walker is a great football player, but as a former runner, it isn't fun for me to watch Herschel run. He's just not exciting. I wouldn't pay to watch him run with the football. I would pay to watch Curt Warner, Billy Sims, Dickerson and Allen, because you're watching those who are educated about running."

Simpson, more than any other halfback or fullback, made running an art form. Only Sayers was in his class when it came to creative, ad-libbed excitement. In the field of educated runners there were many masters, but only Simpson, among halfbacks, was a Ph.D.

The question was put to Simpson: If he were a novelist, how would he describe his running style?

He leaned back in his chair against the rolltop desk and looked out his office window at the smog-shrouded hills. Ten seconds passed.

"Fluidity," he said, finally. "And a certain gracefulness . . . and a spontaneity that, at times, was shocking."

A second question: Does Simpson believe he was the greatest natural runner ever to play the halfback position?

This time, the answer was instantaneous.

"I feel that if I were in an equal situation with anybody, I would have done better," he replied. "That's just my feeling, but in a five-year period, every rushing record that could be broken, I broke.

"My favorite runner from the past was Sayers. The runner I appreciate most now is Dickerson. But placed in any situation you can name with all the great running backs, I would come out ahead.

"Some of my records have been broken, like my single-game rushing record of

273 yards, but Walter Payton had more carries. Or my single-season rushing record, but Dickerson (2,105 yards in 1984) had two more games. So my records were broken, but not my performances."

If Jack McBride, the junior varsity football coach at Galileo High School, had had any indication that Simpson was capable of such performances, he wouldn't have pegged the kid as a tackle, which is exactly what McBride did the first time Simpson showed up for practice. Simpson was about 5-foot-10 and 160 pounds at the time, and since Galileo's student body was approximately 70 percent Oriental, the lanky kid who towered over his teammates looked like a tackle to McBride. That all changed, of course, as soon as McBride saw Simpson run one day. O.J. promptly was moved to the backfield.

Galileo was outmatched physically by most of the San Francisco high schools, but Simpson's extraordinary performance in a varsity game as a senior led to one of the biggest prep upsets in the city's history.

St. Ignatius High School had won 19 straight games when it faced Galileo, which had lost 19 of its previous 23 games. St. Ignatius was in control of the game, leading 25-10 in the third quarter and driving for another touchdown, when Simpson, playing cornerback, stole the football from an opposing halfback and raced 90 yards for a touchdown. He followed that play by catching a screen pass and sprinting 80 yards for a touchdown. He then took a swing pass and bolted 60 yards for another touchdown that gave little Galileo a 31-25 victory.

Simpson was named to the all-city team with two other running backs, one of whom, Nate Kirtman, received a scholarship to Stanford. Simpson felt he was better than Kirtman and the other all-city back, but he received no scholarship offers out of high school, partly because of his low grades and partly because of Galileo's weak football program, which rarely attracted college recruiters.

So, Simpson went to City College of San Francisco, a two-year school, to build up his grades and football reputation. City College's top halfback, Chris Ransom, was returning as a sophomore, which meant Simpson played his first game at the school as a defensive back. Ransom was injured, however, and Simpson replaced him the next week. What happened after that is difficult for Simpson to fathom 20 years later.

"It was incredible," he said. "I was a nobody, and three games after my first start at halfback it seemed like I had every college in the country after me."

He was a junior college All-America in each of his two years at City College, which went 17-2-1 (including two Prune Bowl games) with O.J. in its backfield. He set national junior college career records with 2,445 yards rushing (9.8 yards per carry) and 50 touchdowns. Suddenly, a teen-ager's dream looked like it would come true: Simpson would play football for Southern Cal.

"When I was a kid, I really didn't know about college football," he explained. "I was a 49er fan. Then on New Year's Day, 1963, I noticed that a California team would be playing in a bowl game. It was the Rose Bowl, but I didn't know anything about it, either. Then I heard the announcer say that the California team was named USC, and it was undefeated and going for the national championship. I noticed that USC had a black star in (halfback) Willie Brown. That impressed me.

"First, USC beat the hell out of the other team, Wisconsin. And every time USC scored, this guy in a Trojan helmet would ride a horse around the field. At halftime, people were doing card tricks and cheerleaders were doing flips. I wasn't used to anything like this because there were only marching bands at halftime of 49er games. Then Wisconsin came back in the second half and beat the hell out of USC. USC finally won, 42-37. I was 15 at the time, and I thought USC was the only team to play for."

Simpson didn't have the grades to enter Southern Cal after his freshman year of college, when Utah, Utah State and Arizona State also recruited him. At Arizona State, he met two football players, Ben Hawkins, who would later play with the Philadelphia Eagles, and Reggie Jackson, who had just signed a lucrative baseball contract with the Kansas City Athletics. At Utah State, Simpson was escorted around by several players, including Roy Shivers, who was about to join the St. Louis Cardinals.

"All these guys were driving big cars," he recalled. "Everywhere I went on a recruiting trip, everyone tried to impress me with how big they were. At USC, it was different. Everyone was so regular. Mike Garrett, who had just won the Heisman Trophy, was driving a Chevrolet and wearing jeans and tennis shoes."

Simpson nearly committed to Utah and Arizona State before Marv Goux, the Southern Cal assistant coach who recruited Simpson, told him that if he stayed in junior college through the fall semester of his sophomore year and worked on his grades, he could be a Trojan.

Simpson was sold on Southern Cal all over again. Then the University of California entered the picture. He didn't have the grades to enter Cal, a prestigious academic school located across the bay from San Francisco in Berkeley, until the university installed the Economic Opportunity Program, which allowed a certain percentage of minorities to enroll at Cal even though they failed to meet the entrance requirements. The EOP plan went into effect at Berkeley during Simpson's time in junior college, and Cal launched a strong last-minute recruiting drive in an effort to get Simpson, whom Cal Coach Ray Willsey called "a young Ollie Matson."

Forced to make a decision in the wee hours after a hectic night of phone calls, Simpson went with his original choice: Southern Cal. This time, the decision was final. He enrolled in Los Angeles in the spring of 1967 and ran a leg on the Trojans' 440-yard relay team, which set a world record.

That June, he married his high school sweetheart, Marguerite Whitley. They had met while she was dating Al Cowlings, later a teammate of Simpson's at City College of San Francisco, Southern Cal and with the Buffalo Bills. Simpson was attempting to patch up an argument between Whitley and Cowlings and found himself playing the part of John Alden. Their romance took off from there.

The first time Simpson touched the football for Southern Cal, he went 15 yards with a swing pass against Washington State. He finished the game with 94 yards rushing as the Trojans won, 49-0.

Simpson and the Trojans took off at that point. He rushed for 158 yards and a touchdown in a 17-13 triumph over Texas. He was even more effective against Michigan State, flashing for 190 yards and two touchdowns in a 21-17 victory. Simpson kept up the assault with 160 yards against Stanford as the Trojans coasted to a 30-0 win. Then came the football game that made the nation aware of The Juice.

Since 1926, Southern Cal and Notre Dame have had an intense rivalry that has been interrupted only by World War II (1943-45). Before Simpson's arrival in Los Angeles, the Trojans hadn't won in South Bend since 1939. In the 1967 game, which was played on the Fighting Irish's home turf, Notre Dame drew first blood, taking a 7-0 lead. The Trojans then recovered a fumble at the Irish 18-yard line on the second-half kickoff. Simpson carried the ball six times in the seven-play drive, which ended with O.J. catapulting into the end zone from a yard out. The extra point made it 7-7.

In the third quarter, Southern Cal moved to the Notre Dame 36, where the Trojans faced a third and four. Simpson took off to his left, received a clearing block from fullback Dan Scott on the Notre Dame end and sprinted into the end zone. The Irish were through. Simpson scored again in the fourth quarter and wound up with 150 yards rushing on 38 carries as the Trojans prevailed, 24-7.

"That was O.J.'s first great media exposure," said Don Andersen, who was Southern Cal's sports information director at the time, "but he was cooperative with the media right off the bat. His willingness to make himself available for the media was something I'll always remember about him. He never felt it was an obligation. He just liked to talk to them."

Simpson's most productive game as a junior followed the Notre Dame victory. He carried 30 times for 235 yards and two touchdowns, including an 86-yard burst, as the Trojans ran roughshod over Washington, 23-6. He sprained an instep against Oregon and left the game after rushing 23 times for only 63 yards, although Southern Cal had no trouble winning, 28-6. Simpson sat out the next game, a 31-12 victory at Cal.

The Trojans then were defeated for the only time that season, 3-0, in the rain and mud at Oregon State. But the soggy field didn't slow down Simpson, who rushed 33 times for 188 yards. The loss dropped Southern Cal from it's No. 1 ranking nationally, a spot assumed by crosstown rival UCLA, which had only one blemish on its record, a 16-16 tie against Oregon State.

Never has there been a USC-UCLA game of greater magnitude. Not only was a Rose Bowl berth riding on the game's outcome, but possibly the national championship, too. Both schools also had the two leading Heisman candidates, UCLA quarterback Gary Beban, a senior, and Simpson, both of whom were poised for a classic individual confrontation in a classic football game.

Simpson had developed the habit that year of getting up slowly after a tackle and taking his time walking back to the huddle, allowing him to get some well-deserved rest during a game. He averaged 29.6 carries in nine regular-season games that season, but the Bruins weren't about to let Simpson recharge his batteries between plays.

"I had a horrible first half against UCLA," he recalled, "because every time I hit the ground, they'd pick me up right away. Their coaches told them not to let me rest. It took me a while until I could develop a rhythm."

In the second quarter, Simpson found the rhythm. With the score tied, 7-7, he slashed into the teeth of the Bruin defense from the UCLA 13-yard line. One tackler hit him but fell off. A second and third tackler grabbed Simpson. He shrugged them loose. Two more defenders lunged for him. He powered past them toward three fresh Bruins who were waiting for him near the goal line. He blasted right through the trio for the touchdown. In 13 yards, Simpson had broken eight tackles without veering his course of direction. UCLA Coach Tommy Prothro called it the greatest run he had ever seen. So did Bobby Dodd, a former Georgia Tech coach.

Whether it was Simpson's greatest run of the day, however, was questionable. There still was another half to play as Southern Cal took its 14-7 lead into the intermission. Beban, who wound up completing 16 of 24 passes for 301 yards and two touchdowns that afternoon, came on strong in the second half and brought the Bruins back to lead, 20-14, with 3:19 elapsed in the fourth quarter.

Simpson returned the ensuing kickoff to the Trojan 34 after nearly breaking it for a touchdown. On first down, O.J. plowed ahead for three yards. Quarterback Toby Page, who had replaced starter Steve Sogge in the third quarter, then was dropped for a one-yard loss. UCLA had the momentum, and the game, unless something happened fast for Southern Cal. It did. Super fast.

Page asked Simpson how he felt. The fatigued back said, "Give me one more play (of rest)." So, Page called a passing play. But at the line of scrimmage he yelled, "Red Alert," meaning the next number would be an audible. Then Page yelled "23," which signaled a run by Simpson to the left side. "I was shocked," Simpson said.

Page was gambling that UCLA would be thinking pass and that the Bruins' standout linebacker, Don Manning, would drop back into the passing lanes. That's exactly what happened as Simpson faked to the right, then ran around left end. Taking advantage of blocks by tackle Mike Taylor and guard Steve Lehmer, Simpson hopped over a fallen Bruin and cut for the sideline. With Earl McCullouch leading the interference, Simpson then cut back across the middle of the field, into the flow of the pursuit. Where he had scored on muscle and will in the second quarter, this time it was sheer speed as he avoided all contact and made it into the end zone at the opposite corner. He dropped the football after he crossed the goal line but couldn't stop running for 15 to 20 yards. He was too tired to stop. Rikki Aldridge's conversion kick gave the Trojans a 21-20 victory, the Rose Bowl invitation and the national championship.

"Those were my two favorite runs," Simpson said in retrospect, "because of the game. So much was at stake. I had some great runs against nobodies, but the ones I think about were against UCLA and the Steelers (a 94-yarder and an 88-yarder in separate games against Pittsburgh's famed Steel Curtain defense), because you know you went against the best."

Simpson finished the UCLA game with 30 rushes for 177 yards, upping his season totals to 266 carries, 1,415 yards rushing and 5.3 yards per carry, all figures that led the nation. He threw five passes, completing three, all for touchdowns. He caught 10 passes for 109 yards, returned seven kickoffs for 176 yards and scored 11 touchdowns.

United Press International named him the Player of the Year. The Heisman, however, went to Beban, who totaled 1,968 points to runner-up Simpson's 1,722. Don Andersen hasn't forgotten "the grace that O.J. showed after not winning the Heisman," he said years later. "He said all the right things. It was fabulous."

"I don't begrudge Gary," Simpson said, recalling that close finish. "He had better years his previous two years at UCLA. In those days, a player's college career had a bigger influence on his winning the Heisman than it does today. But in my heart, I believe that Gary was just as valuable to his team in 1967 as I was to mine."

Nice touch, but so like Simpson.

Dwight Chapin, now a general news columnist for the San Francisco Examiner, covered Southern Cal for the Los Angeles Times while Simpson was in college. Chapin, too, was caught up by his graciousness.

"He's a most special person," Chapin said. "I was struck, really struck, by how good he was on his feet. At a Rose Bowl press luncheon, the Midwest writers came to hate O.J., and he absolutely charmed them. I've seen him talk to businessmen where he had them in the palm of his hand, mesmerized.

"After O.J. retired from professional football, I wrote a column for the Examiner saying goodbye to him. Now I hadn't written about him in a decade, but I got a note from O.J. thanking me for all I had done for him. How many athletes thank writers for a body of work? How many celebrities? It's unheard of. I've never received one letter from an athlete other than from O.J."

The Trojans beat Indiana in the Rose Bowl, 14-3, as Simpson rushed for 128 workmanlike yards on 25 attempts and scored both touchdowns. After the game, Mike Garrett, Southern Cal's first Heisman winner in 1965, hosted a party at his home. Simpson came with his wife.

"Mike's Heisman was sitting there, and I spent the whole night looking at it," Simpson said. "That's when it dawned on me how close I had come to winning it. The Heisman didn't really matter my junior year. My senior year, I expected to win it."

The 6-2, 205-pound Simpson was even more devastating as a senior, even though Southern Cal suffered a talent drop-off from the previous year. "We were a young team in 1968," Simpson said, "and we really didn't have a great defense." It didn't matter, though, because the Trojans' opponents couldn't outscore The Juice.

He pounded at Minnesota 39 times for 236 yards, caught six passes for 57 yards and tallied four touchdowns in a 29-20 victory to open the '68 season. He scored three more times and rushed for 189 yards on 34 carries as Northwestern fell, 24-7.

Trojans Coach John McKay was asked if Simpson might wear out from carrying the ball so often. "It doesn't weigh that much," McKay deadpanned. "O.J. doesn't belong to a union, so we can work him as long as we want to."

Southern Cal played Miami (Florida) the next week, and McKay devised a game plan in which Simpson would run at, not away from, the Hurricanes' great defensive end, Ted Hendricks. The concept worked as Simpson rushed 38 times for 163 yards and two touchdowns in a 28-3 Trojan rout.

Before the Stanford game, Simpson was helped off the field after warmups. He had injured a thigh earlier in the season, and the fluid in the thigh had circulated down to the knee, causing him to limp. The knee was drained just prior to the opening kickoff, and Simpson came back to run an amazing 47 times for 220 yards and three touchdowns, including a sweep around the right end for 46 yards. McKay called the play "Student Body Right."

Simpson's most important play of that game wasn't a run, however, but a pass. On fourth down and short yardage with the ball on the Stanford 22-yard line, Simpson took off on another Student Body Right. Stanford's defense, meanwhile, had shifted into Student Body Left, and Simpson was stymied. He reversed direction to his left, where his path was blocked again. Hemmed in and about to be tackled, Simpson spotted Scott, his backfield mate, 15 yards downfield and threw to him for a first down at the 7. It was Simpson's only completion of the season (in three attempts), but it couldn't have come at a more strategic time, setting up Ron Ayala's 34-yard field goal that turned back Stanford and sophomore quarterback Jim Plunkett, 27-24.

Simpson scored the Trojans' only two touchdowns in a 14-7 win over Washington, a game in which he rushed 33 times for 172 yards. Oregon, which gave Simpson his roughest afternoons in college, shut him down with 67 yards on 25 carries, plus a touchdown, as Southern Cal was lucky to escape with a 20-13 squeaker.

The Juice rebounded for 164 yards rushing and two touchdowns as California, whose "Bear minimum" defense was considered the best in the country entering that game, was blown out in Los Angeles, 35-17. The Trojans had problems with Oregon State for the second straight season but managed to outlast the Beavers, 17-13. Simpson again carried 47 times, matching his career high (college or pro) for attempts, in rushing for a college-high 238 yards and another touchdown.

By now, Simpson's name was all but etched on the Heisman Trophy. He worked over UCLA again—40 carries, 205 yards, three touchdowns—in a much easier Trojan win this time, 28-16. Southern Cal was 9-0 and back in the Rose Bowl.

"We were undefeated going into the Rose Bowl," Simpson said, "but we were the worst undefeated team in history."

The Trojans had, atypically for them, a soft schedule. They were short on horses, long on colts, except for the big horse, Simpson. Southern Cal's last opponent, Notre Dame, devised a "triangle" defense—designed not for penetration, but for enclosure—to stop Simpson. It worked perfectly as Simpson was checked with 55 yards on 21 carries and one touchdown. Sogge brought the Trojans back from a 21-7 halftime deficit, and the game ended in a 21-21 tie.

Simpson finished his two years at Southern Cal by equaling or bettering 19 school, conference and NCAA records. He established an NCAA single-season rushing mark (since broken) of 1,709 yards and led the nation with 22 touchdowns. He averaged 4.8 yards on 355 rushes, caught 18 passes for 126 yards and brought back six kickoffs for 131 yards, giving him 1,966 all-purpose yards, also tops in the country. He shattered Southern Cal's career rushing record in two years with 3,423 yards (including bowl games). No running back in NCAA annals has ever had a more impressive first two years of college.

And in the first 50 years of Heisman voting, no one has won the Heisman more decisively than did Simpson in 1968. He accumulated 2,853 points, a margin of 1,750 points over Purdue's Leroy Keyes, who finished second. The second-widest margin in the Heisman's first half-century was 1,477 points in 1955, when Ohio State's Howard Cassady defeated Texas Christian's Jim Swink.

"There was no surprise or false modesty when I won it," said Simpson, who had achieved what he set out to do that season. "I was in a daze the whole time I was in New York. The day I got the trophy, Marguerite was in labor with our first child. Then they handed me a note at the dinner telling me I had a baby girl. I remember telling everyone that even though I had won the Heisman, that I had gotten something dearer, a daughter."

Then Simpson brought home his Heisman. His name had been etched correctly on the trophy, but the Downtown Athletic Club's name hadn't. "Athletic" came out "Atletic."

"Every time I hear that Archie Griffin won two Heismans," Simpson mused, "I say to myself that it would have been nice to win two. Archie was a great college player, but I felt I was just as important to my team as he was to his."

The "worst undefeated team in history" was unmasked in the Rose Bowl by Woody and his Buckeyes, closing out Simpson's short but phenomenal Trojan career. Football was only part of his education in Los Angeles, though.

"When I came to SC, I wanted to learn where the forks go," he said. "I was looking for all the things that would help me climb the social ladder, not just the financial ladder. I grew a lot at SC."

So much so that when he visited the state capital in Sacramento in April 1969, Gov. Ronald Reagan asked for O.J.'s autograph, adding, "My son, Skipper, wants you to know that if it were a contest between us for governor, he'd vote for you instead of me."

Simpson didn't complete his degree in public administration at Southern Cal—he is one semester shy—but his relationship with the school has never really ended. He recruits football players for Southern Cal and attends Trojan games when his busy schedule permits. Among his closest friends is Marcus Allen, a Trojan who won the Heisman in 1981. "Marcus is like a little brother," Simpson said.

Even before he signed with the Buffalo Bills, who selected him as the first player in the 1969 pro football draft, Simpson signed three other contracts—with Chevrolet, Royal Crown Cola and ABC-TV, for an acting role in the debut episode of the television series "Medical Center." No college football player—Doug Flutie included—has experienced so much exposure so quickly. O.J. remained in the incredible spotlight even without his shoulder pads, as an actor and sports broadcaster, during his pro football career.

Buffalo's coach when Simpson joined the Bills, John Rauch, toyed with the incredible idea of making Simpson a wide receiver. Rauch wasn't about to let Simpson carry the football as often as he did at Southern Cal.

"That's not my style," Rauch explained at the time. "I couldn't build my offense around one back, no matter how good he is. It's too easy for the pros to set up defensive keys. O.J. can be a terrific pass receiver, and we expect him to block, too."

It's a wonder Rauch didn't ask Simpson to punt and play defense. Rauch wouldn't, or couldn't, recognize the great talent he had and chose to use him sparingly and often as a decoy on passing routes. Simpson packed the ball only 181 times for 697 yards (3.9 yards per carry) and two touchdowns as a rookie. He scored three times on pass receptions.

His statistics slipped the following year to 488 yards rushing (4.1 average) for five touchdowns, although he tore some tissue in his left knee and missed the last six games. Rauch resigned during training camp the next summer and was replaced by Harvey Johnson, the Bills' kindly director of player personnel whom Simpson called "Uncle Harvey." Simpson rushed for 742 yards (4.1 average) and five touchdowns in 1971.

Three years had passed and Simpson hadn't come close to emulating his glittering college statistics. The NFL no longer whispered. It wondered out loud: Was Simpson a bust? The Bills had won fewer games in three years (eight) than Southern Cal had won in each of Simpson's two seasons. Johnson was replaced after 1971 by Lou Saban, a peripatetic type who would be an ideal spokesman for a moving company, but who, at least, believed in the running game and had enjoyed success in Buffalo in the club's early years. Encouraged, Simpson signed a new four-year contract with Buffalo.

"The press was making excuses for me: 'Poor O.J. He is playing for a bad team. He has had two coaches,'" Simpson recalled. "But the truth was that for three years, I hadn't done a thing. Nothing.

"What turned it around for me was a chapel meeting early in my fourth season. My mother always told me that when in doubt, turn back to the Lord. Well, I'm sitting there listening to some guy who was invited in to speak, someone whose name I can't remember. He was talking about businessmen, the kind who come to work before others and stay later. But even though they're putting in all that time, they have no idea where they're going. No goals. They're just spinning their wheels.

"It hit me like a ton of bricks. I said to myself, 'This guy is talking about me!' All my life, I wanted fame and money, but I never stopped to think, 'What do I want now?' I've always been a positive guy, but it was that chapel meeting that put a focus on it. From that day, I began thinking what I wanted to be in football, and what I wanted to be when I left football, and really defining both."

Simpson rushed for a league-leading 1,251 yards in 1972, carrying 109 more times than in any previous season in Buffalo and improving his per-carry average to 4.3. Saban realized, as McKay had realized before him, that Simpson gets stronger the more he is worked. His 94-yard run against Pittsburgh in 1972 was vintage Simpson and set a Bills record.

By 1973, Saban had rebuilt the Buffalo offensive line. Donnie Green, a holdover Buffalo lineman from 1971, was the right tackle. Joe DeLamielleure, a rookie from Michigan State, was the right guard. Paul Seymour, a rookie from Michigan, was placed at tight end for his blocking, not his receiving (he was a tackle in college). New England castoff Mike Montler became an ideal center after the Patriots found him too slow to play tackle, his college position. Reggie McKenzie, a second-year man from Michigan, was the left guard. Dave Foley took over at left tackle after being picked up from the New York Jets in 1972.

Introducing the Electric Company, which turned on The Juice.

Simpson opened the 1973 season by ripping for 250 yards on 29 carries against New England to break the NFL's single-game rushing record. He scored two touchdowns, one on an 80-yard run, as the Bills won their season opener, 31-13, for the first time in Simpson's pro career.

In only three of 14 games in '73 did Simpson fail to rush for at least 100 yards, and in one of those games, against Cincinnati, he missed by only a yard. After 11 games, Simpson had 1,447 yards rushing. The Bills then traveled to Atlanta to meet a Falcon team that was enjoying a seven-game winning streak. Buffalo crunched Atlanta, 17-6, as Simpson danced his way for 137 yards.

After the game, reporters surrounded Simpson for about an hour. After they were gone, Simpson said: "I'm dying of thirst. Does anyone have a cold drink?"

Someone handed him a chilled bottle about the same time that a locker room attendant walked up to him. The attendant said that his little boy had been holding a cold drink, waiting to give it to him, the whole time reporters were talking to Simpson. Without hesitating, Simpson threw his cold drink in a garbage can, went over to the little boy, took the bottle—which by then was warm—and drank the beverage.

Larry Felser, sports editor-columnist of the Buffalo News, witnessed similar class acts by Simpson during the latter's nine years in Buffalo.

"When things were at their worst, when the team couldn't win and Simpson was thought to be just one more Heisman flop," Felser said, "he always found time to answer reporters' questions, even to the point of being suicidal about his own career.

"When the other players wouldn't talk to the press, O.J. always did. He never lost his temper. I'll always remember his being very decent, cooperative and nice under the most trying of circumstances. When a man can maintain his decency under intense adversity, that says a lot about him."

The Professional Football Writers Association of America several times voted Simpson the most cooperative player in the NFL. He was special any way you looked at him.

Simpson proved harder to tackle than a man in a revolving door the last two weeks of that memorable 1973 season. The Electric Company blocked furiously as it turned on The Juice to heights never before scaled in pro football. Together, they once again trampled the New England defense, with Simpson carrying 22 times for 219 yards, and the Bills won, 37-13.

On the final day of the season, in the snow, mud and chill of Shea Stadium, Simpson passed Jim Brown's pro football season rushing record of 1,863 yards and then became the first runner to gain 2,000 yards in one season. Simpson blasted into the New York Jets' defense 34 times for an even 200 yards to bring his season total to 2,003 yards. The 34-14 victory gave Buffalo its first winning record (9-5) in the O.J. Simpson era.

At the postgame press conference, Simpson brought along the Electric Company. Simpson's attitude was that he hadn't gotten 2,003 yards by himself, so why should he acknowledge his record alone? It was typical Simpson, unselfish as always.

The Juice and his electrifying friends continued to shock defenses over the next three years. Simpson rushed for 1,125 yards in 1974 as Buffalo finished its second consecutive 9-5 season and made the playoffs for the only time in Simpson's career. Pittsburgh eliminated the Bills, 32-14, holding Buffalo's running game to 100 yards. Simpson scored one touchdown on a three-yard pass from Joe Ferguson.

Buffalo turned things around against the Steelers, 30-21, the second game of the following season behind Simpson's 227 yards rushing, including an 88-yard gallop. The Steeler defenders became so frustrated in trying to stop Simpson that Montler, the center, put his hands on the football to snap it before one play and found the ball wouldn't budge. That's because Mean Joe Greene's foot was on it.

"You can't have it," Greene snarled at Montler. "I'm not gonna let you play with it anymore. That cat has done enough to us all day."

That cat, Simpson, completed 1975 with 1,817 yards rushing, tops in the league, and set an NFL single-season record of 23 touchdowns. That year also marked the third consecutive season in which the durable running back had led the league in rushing attempts, this time with 329. Simpson came back in 1976 with 1,503 yards rushing, 273 coming on Thanksgiving Day at Detroit to break his own single-game NFL mark.

The Bills' record, however, plummeted from 8-6 in 1975 to 2-12 in 1976 as frustration shuffled into Buffalo. A number of Bills players—Ahmad Rashad, Pat Toomay, Earl Edwards and J.D. Hill—had been let go, and Simpson felt that management had given up its commitment to winning. He became despondent in '76 when Saban left as coach. Saban was replaced by Jim Ringo.

In 1977, Buffalo went back to a passing attack, upsetting Simpson even more. On October 30, he reinjured his left knee in Seattle as the Seahawks blew out the Bills, 56-17. At 30, O.J. now faced the possibility of surgery. Simpson's future in Buffalo seemed as bleak as his early years, especially since the Bills were in the midst of another dismal season.

Into this gloom came an old familiar face with a new request. Don Andersen, the public relations man at Southern Cal, now held a similar position with the Seahawks. Andersen found Simpson after the game and told him about a teen-ager with terminal cancer who was in attendance that day. The youth was waiting on the field, specifically to see The Juice, his idol.

Andersen didn't have to say anything more. Simpson limped back on the field, played catch with the youth and then chatted with him for 20 minutes.

"When you think of O.J., you have to put 'considerate' high on the list," Andersen said.

Simpson's '77 season read almost like '70: 557 yards rushing. He had averaged 4.4 yards per run, but it was his first and only season without a touchdown. He had surgery for torn knee cartilage in November, and he did not play after the Seattle game.

More than ever, he wanted to get back to the West Coast. His wife and family, which now numbered three children, remained in Los Angeles during the football season because Marguerite didn't want to take the children out of school.

Even during the off-season, Simpson found himself away from home much of the time, filming such movies as "The Klansman" with Richard Burton, "The Towering Inferno" with Paul Newman, "The Cassandra Crossing" with Sophia Loren and "Capricorn One" with James Brolin. Simpson also left to film commercials.

"Earlier in my life," he reflected, "I was on the road all the time, trying to do . . . I don't know what I was trying to do."

Pressure was building on the marriage. "We have practically lost our private life," Marguerite was quoted. "I have been shoved out of the way, pushed and stepped on by more than one beautiful woman. I admit I'm jealous."

O.J. Simpson found himself talking to gossip types as well as sportswriters. "I guess any healthy, good-looking guy who's self-confident—and I'm certainly that— could conceivably get girls," he said a few weeks before the injury in Seattle. "Groupies would have been a problem in my youth, when I was more insecure and needed to prove something. Now that I'm older, let's say I'm more selective. My wife knows I'm under control. . . .

"I guess the price of fame was our (he and his wife's) biggest problem. I hope those things are behind us now. Every time you get over a hump, the marriage gets stronger. A few years ago, we got over a hump."

In spending time away from his family year-round, chasing financial security, Simpson also was "trying to find out who I was," he said. He realized, finally, that he had married too young and that he and Marquerite were two different people.

"As you grow older, you understand things better," he said. "You can be in love with a person and not like her. There was no doubt about Marquerite and our love. But she's an introverted person and I'm an extrovert. My wife was very private. I like being around the guys, and she didn't like them coming over all the time.

"If Marquerite and I were to meet for the first time as older people, we would find that we like each other but that we're too different."

Simpson was granted his wish in 1978 and traded to a West Coast team. Buffalo dealt him to the San Francisco 49ers for five draft choices—a No. 2 and No. 3 in 1978, a No. 1 and No. 4 in 1979 and a No. 2 in 1980. The 49ers also inherited the NFL's highest salary—$733,358 in 1978 and $806,668 in 1979—for a part-time player. Simpson's legs were giving out.

"Home at last!" Simpson exclaimed at his first news conference as a 49er. "Thank God Almighty, I'm home at last."

Forty-Niners General Manager Joe Thomas explained the costly trade: "O.J.'s charisma cuts across generations. He's the most visible person in the United States outside of the President and perhaps (Muhammad) Ali."

Thomas was looking for gate appeal to salvage the franchise he had decimated. Simpson had more knee problems, plus a shoulder separation, and missed the final six games in 1978. He finished with 593 yards rushing, the 49ers wound up 2-14 and O.J. underwent more knee surgery in the off-season.

While Simpson was at training camp in 1979, he received the tragic news that his 23-month-old daughter, Aaren, the youngest of his three children, had fallen into the swimming pool of her mother's home (O.J. and Marquerite were separated at this point). Eight days later, Aaren died.

"It was God's will," Simpson said.

His 11th, and final, pro football season was beset with continued physical problems and Simpson rushed for only 460 yards and three touchdowns. He was honored in his final home game as a 49er, against Tampa Bay, which, ironically, was coached by John McKay. In his speech to the 44,506 fans who showed up at Candlestick Park, Simpson thanked, among others, McKay, Marv Goux (who had recruited him for Southern Cal) and Don Andersen.

If athletes never thank writers for all the nice words, they also forget the public relations men for all the same reasons. Simpson's display of gratitude toward Andersen in a stadium, of all places, is equally rare. "I still have the tape of O.J.'s speech in my desk," Andersen said proudly.

Simpson's career ended with 11,236 yards rushing, 1,076 yards behind Brown. They ranked 1-2 on the all-time rushing list at the time.

In 1979, Pro Football Monthly selected a Team of the Decade for the 1970s. Roger Staubach, Franco Harris, Charley Taylor, Merlin Olsen, Jack Ham, Ken Houston and Mean Joe Greene were among the stars chosen. Pro Football Monthly's Player of the Decade? O.J. Simpson.

Even greater honors were forthcoming. In 1985, Simpson was voted into the Professional Football Hall of Fame the first time he was eligible. True to form, he spread flowers in the path of his fellow inductees.

"I'm especially glad to go in with the class I'm in," he said in May 1985. "Joe Namath finally got the recognition he deserved. I don't think the general public realizes what Joe did for us as players. He showed that athletes aren't just apple pie, that they can speak frankly about things, and that—hey!—some athletes like their women blonde and their Johnny Walker Red. And how can you not like Roger Staubach? And look at Pete Rozelle's contributions to the game."

If Simpson hadn't forgotten Frank Gatski, he would have had something nice to say about the old center, too.

O.J. and Marquerite were divorced. His two surviving children from that marriage are teen-agers. His son, Jason, lives with him full-time, while his daughter, Arnelle, lives with him much of the time. Marquerite lives close by.

Simpson remarried in February 1985. His new wife, the former Nicole Brown, is blonde, 12 years younger than O.J. and has interesting ancestry lines: half-German, half-Kansan.

"If someone were to ask me about Nicole," Simpson said, "I would say that I like her first before I would say that I love her. She's a wonderful person who doesn't mind if the guys come over. She even enjoys cooking for them."

O.J. Simpson is starting a new family. He was an expectant father in 1985. "I'm excited and my kids (from the first marriage) are excited," he said. "After Nicole and I have our first kid, we're going to have another right away. I may have missed my other kids growing up, but I won't miss these two, I guarantee you."

The 1980s are thought of as more enlightened times, certainly more than the 1950s when it comes to interracial marriages. Society is more receptive to such relationships, though it hasn't come full circle. Did Simpson worry at all that his new marriage might cost him possible endorsements?

"You say to yourself that it's a blink of the eye you're here on Earth," he said. "A blink of the eye. I mean, who cares? I've got one person in this world I have to please, and that's me.

"How can anyone who loves his brother, who treats everyone the way he wants to be treated, not be allowed to fall in love with someone who makes him happy? We're just people."

Simpson spoke in a philosophical sense, yet it was clear that he was talking about himself. He doesn't tell others whom they should marry or how they should live. This is a man whose world is technicolor, not black and white. Why should others make his marriage an issue?

Unfortunately, they have tried—and not advertisers, both those who work with Simpson in a management relationship. They discussed his new marriage with him, though he wouldn't say whether they actually advised him not to go through with it.

"This same faction," he said, "advised me not to go on 'Saturday Night Live' because they felt it would be bad for my image. I balked at that so-called good-guy image. Before these people came into my life, I was popular, in demand. My popularity was established. Therefore, my image was a by-product of me, the

# Johnny Rodgers

*He knew hell and he found heaven. But in between, he had to scratch and claw for every step up life's ladder. As a product of Omaha's ghettos, Johnny Rodgers learned to dodge knives and bullets as nimbly as he later would dodge opposing tacklers. Football was his ticket out. Rodgers parlayed that ticket into a Heisman Trophy and a successful career. He cashed in on fame and found fortune. His dream had a happy ending.*

# Chapter 16

# College football's anti-hero

On a serene, cloudy summer afternoon at a dockside restaurant in San Diego, Johnny Rodgers lunched on champagne chicken, which he washed down with a blended mixture of Creme de Cassis and champagne. Relaxing on the restaurant's deck, he watched the boats bobbing in the harbor while his doll-like, toothy lady friend purred in his ear. Rodgers smiled at the scene before him and at his own good fortune.

"Heaven and hell is on Earth," he said. "I left hell to come to heaven."

Rodgers' hell was Omaha, and, to some degree, Lincoln, both located in the Plains state of Nebraska. It would be an understatement—not to mention a bad pun—to say that Rodgers led a scarred, troubled life in the Cornhusker state.

"Here, let me show you," Rodgers said, standing up and lifting his polo shirt to reveal an ugly two-inch scar on the right side of his back.

The stabbing occurred at a teen-age hangout in Omaha when Johnny was about 15. Someone walked up to Rodgers from behind, as casually as if he were going to pat Rodgers on the back, and plunged a knife into him.

"Omaha is like Chicago," Rodgers said. "Omaha is like war. Half the guys I knew there are dead or in prison."

Rodgers' family life was at least partly responsible for his wild, violent teen-age years. He did not meet his father until he was 17. By that time, however, he already had moved out on his mother and stepfather. He was uncontrollable as a youth, and so much happened to him—most of it bad—during those years that it's best to examine his life chronologically to fully understand the scope of his personal inferno on the north side of Omaha.

At 13, he already had shot another boy in the stomach.

"When I was in junior high school, a partner took his auntie's gun and brought it to my house," Rodgers recalled. "We both skipped school that day. We emptied the gun and cleaned it. And while I was calling some girls who had skipped, too, to come over and join us, my partner kept pointing the gun at me and clicking it, like Russian roulette.

"I told him to stop, but he wouldn't. So I grabbed the gun, pointed it at him and pulled the trigger. It went off. There was one bullet in the chamber, and I didn't know it.

"My partner lived. . . . He called me a couple of years ago to be the best man in his wedding. I told him I would. But right before the wedding, he committed suicide."

At 14, Rodgers became the father of his first illegitimate child. At 16, he had a second son. Fast times at Omaha Technical High School.

"They wanted me to get married," he said. "I didn't know the rules, but I wasn't about to get married."

He ran away from home when he was 14, taking $14, his cousin and his uncle's 1951 Chevy and driving to Detroit. Johnny was behind the wheel part of the time, despite the fact that legally he was too young to drive.

The authorities eventually caught up with the youngsters and brought them back to Omaha. But Rodgers wouldn't go home, instead choosing to live with his grandmother.

"My mother used to make me come home from junior high to report to her before I could go to basketball practice," he said. "That would make me late for practice, and the coach would whip me with this big ol' strap in front of the other guys. Hoooooooo! I hated that.

"My mother was a nurse's aide, my stepdad a construction worker. They didn't want me to play sports. They didn't want me to go to college. They wanted me and the other (three) children in the family to work like they did. I was afraid if I stayed in that environment, I would turn out the same way as everyone else in the house. So I got out."

At 16, Rodgers had his own apartment. He lived there for a year, earning rent money by selling newspapers and classified advertising space in the newspapers. And by gambling.

"I'd go to the craps houses in Omaha," Rodgers said. "Shoot craps, play poker, blackjack. Some nights, I'd make enough money to pay my rent for four, five months.

"I can't tell you half the things I did," he added, grinning.

Wherever there was trouble, Rodgers almost always was part of it. The scuffles weren't always his fault, though. He became a four-sport letterman at Omaha Tech, and while that type of notoriety often has brought success and respectability to others, it simply made Rodgers a more visible target.

"Guys wanted to fight me because I was so popular," he recalled. "Where I'm from, it's not best to be knowledgeable in an unknowledgeable environment. It's not smart to be around thieves and not steal. That's one reason I got into trouble—I wouldn't join the gangs. My gang was the football team. And so I had to fight the other gangs. If I went to parties Friday, Saturday and Sunday, I'd have to fight Friday, Saturday and Sunday."

One such night, Rodgers got into a fight and quickly discovered it wasn't one against one. "There were 20, 30 guys around us (Rodgers and his opponent) in a circle, all his partners," he said. "I'm pretty good with my dukes as long as it's just one guy. But I can't fight everybody.

"I'd hit this guy and cover up because his buddies would hit me. But I couldn't protect myself because I didn't know where the punches were coming from. I was getting woozy, but I had to stay on my feet because if I went down, I really thought they would kill me.

"Then a partner of mine showed up. This guy is really strong and tough. He got me out of it. He probably saved my life."

Rodgers' health was in jeopardy daily. He would leave his apartment for school before the sun was up and would return after dark "because guys were looking for me," he said.

Rodgers found success in athletics, especially as a football player. He was a high school All-America and a prized college recruit. His sports accomplishments appeared in the newspapers and were talked about on the streets. Johnny Rodgers was becoming well known in Omaha.

But what price glory? On the north side of Omaha, success is looked upon negatively. Instead of becoming a hero, Rodgers was, among his peers, an anti-hero.

"If I got something, people there figured it was something they didn't get," he said. "They thought someone had given me a break. It was like I was a traitor to the drug pushers, hustlers and pimps. They couldn't wait for me to fail."

Rodgers had to get out of Omaha, and he knew of only one way to do it: By playing college football. "Sports was going to be my break, my jump," he said.

Rodgers was befriended by one of the Omaha Tech coaches, Dick Christie, who helped the troubled youth make that jump.

"He knew I had problems," Rodgers said. "He told me my junior year to get my grades up for college. So I did. I finished in the top third of my class, and I was a senior class president, king of the prom, the whole nine yards.

"Christie loved me then. He loves me now. I owe him a lot."

Omaha Tech has since closed. Christie moved over to South High School in Omaha, where he is an assistant principal and the athletic director.

"John was a handful, but he wasn't the only kid in school in trouble," Christie recalled. "We put more work into other boys.

"We took knives from John all the time. And he'd say, 'How am I going to get home?' He didn't sleep well at nights. It wasn't unusual to get a call from him at 3 a.m.

"John was at odds most of that time with his mother. But she's a super woman who cares a great deal about John. They made up his senior year, and now they have a love affair. I told his mom his sophomore year at Tech that he'd be an All-America in college. He was the strongest kid in school and the smallest. And he's an intelligent kid. He could have been Number 1 in the class if he had worked harder. He was such a great all-around athlete. He could do anything. And he was such a hyper kid. Even in the halls he was doing back flips.

"Let me tell you this about John: I've never heard him tell a lie. I can describe him in two words: Jack Armstrong. The all-American boy from the ghetto."

Growing up in the ghetto makes a person conscious of money, which always is in short supply. Rodgers was no exception. He wanted gratification and glory to come with his success, but he especially wanted gold.

"I kept thinking that all I needed to make it in this world was $100,000," Rodgers said. "I knew that when I was 14. The Los Angeles Dodgers drafted me (in 1969) as an outfielder out of high school. I went to L.A. to try out, the whole thing. They offered me $50,000 to sign, but it wasn't enough. I still wanted $100,000, but I didn't know how to get it. I didn't know the rules of the game."

He matriculated at the University of Nebraska. The Cornhuskers, year in and year out, are among college football's greatest powerhouses. Scores of professional players learned their trade in Lincoln, the home of one of the most enthusiastically supported football programs in the country. For many Nebraska players, the jump from the collegiate to the professional ranks is a natural progression.

For Rodgers, playing football at Nebraska meant getting a shot at big, big dollars—maybe even $100,000—as well as an escape from Omaha.

But Lincoln was not Rodgers' Shangri-La. Trouble followed him from Omaha to Lincoln and roomed with him for the next four years.

"Lincoln is worse than Omaha," Rodgers said. "Lincoln's police department is like the gestapo." In time, Rodgers became well acquainted with the Lincoln police.

It all started in 1970 as Rodgers and some friends were celebrating the end of their freshman year by drinking vodka and orange juice. The amount of liquor consumed brought about the inevitable result, and the group began to feel prankish. Go on a panty raid? Cover trees across campus with toilet paper? No, those stunts were too tame for these students. They wanted to do something more original, more risky, more illegal.

Like rob a gas station.

"We decided we could pull it off," Rodgers said. "Well, I was the one who actually masterminded it. I convinced the guys that we wouldn't get caught. I laid out a perfect plan. We showed up at the station. I had a hand in my pocket, like it was a gun. So did another partner. Another partner, standing across the street, was holding a board. I told the guy in the station that it was a shotgun."

The Rodgers gang made off with $91.

"I didn't need the money," Rodgers said. "I had money in my pocket. It was just a challenge to see if we could do it."

Bonnie and Clyde couldn't have done it better. No suspects, no clues, no leads, no sweat. Clean getaway.

For a year, that is.

"All that time, I thought about sending the money back," Rodgers said. "There was this white guy with us in the holdup. He went home and bragged to his friends how he did this and that with Johnny Rodgers. You know how word gets around. They came and got me a year later."

In May 1971, Rodgers was placed on two years' probation because of the gas station incident. But that was just the beginning of his legal problems in Lincoln. It wasn't long before his driver's license was suspended because too many points had been charged against it for various traffic violations, and that led to another problem.

"My best friend was going with this girl who was a narc (narcotics agent)," Rodgers said, "only he didn't know it at the time. She was just one of several girlfriends. None of us knew it, either.

"One night, she called and said she was in trouble and could I come help her? It was my best friend's girl. So I get pulled over for running a red light. The light wasn't red. They (the Lincoln police) made it red."

Rodgers was found to be driving with a suspended driver's license, and a trial date was set. Shortly thereafter, Rodgers, still delegated to the role of passenger, was riding with a friend one day when a Nebraska highway patrolman pulled them over. In a July 1, 1972, New York Times article, Nebraska football Coach Bob Devaney is quoted as saying that the driver of the car was traveling at 90 mph. "We weren't speeding," Rodgers said. "They stopped us because they thought we had marijuana.

"They told us, 'Get out of the car because we're busting you for transporting marijuana. They didn't ask me for an ID. One cop said, 'Put your hands on the fender, Johnny."

There are conflicting reports on whether marijuana was found in the automobile. The driver of the car ultimately was fined for marijuana possession, while similar charges against Rodgers were dropped for lack of evidence, according to an Associated Press report. Rodgers maintains that there was no marijuana in the car. "They (the state patrol) tore the car apart," he said, "took the seats out and checked with dogs, but they didn't find anything." Rodgers is convinced that this arrest, like the red-light incident, was set up by his friend's ex-girlfriend.

"After that, the police were after me every day until I left school," he said. " 'Magazine salesmen' would come into my house, and they'd start talking about women and drugs. There was this one guy (a policeman) who I had to *tell* to follow me when I would leave the house to go somewhere. The whole thing got to be funny, once I got over the paranoia."

In June 1972, Rodgers was sentenced to serve 30 days in jail because of his suspended license conviction. His sentence remained on appeal until after he had completed his football eligibility at Nebraska.

Rodgers was liked by his Nebraska teammates, who saw him not as a criminal, but as a concerned friend.

"He's a good guy," said Jeff Hughes, a former college roommate. "He really cares about people, and once a guy talks to him, he knows that, too."

Rodgers also defended his teammates. A Nebraska player once was worked over with the butt of a shotgun by a gang of hoodlums. "His face was so beaten up, you couldn't even recognize him," Rodgers said. "We couldn't let that happen."

Rodgers recruited some teammates as well as "protection" from back in Omaha and got the word to the hoodlums that a meeting was in order. A conversation was held, but there wasn't a rumble. As Rodgers returned to campus, however, he heard gunshots. He discovered that they were being aimed at him, and he took off running for his dormitory.

"I dove inside the dorm just as a bullet grazed me on the knee," he said. "Another quarter of an inch and my kneecap would have been shot off."

Rodgers got to his feet on the restaurant deck in San Diego and lifted a leg of his pants. Across the knee was a thin scratch about three inches long. Another scar for life.

Somehow, with adversity clinging to him like a second layer of skin, Rodgers managed to become one of the all-time greats in Nebraska football history. Rodgers' rise to the top was even more remarkable considering his diminutive size: 5-foot-10 and 173 pounds.

Rodgers was a flashy runner, as elusive as he was creative. He might have invented breakdancing with his electrifying moves, which seemed to feature every conceivable body gyration. Tackling Rodgers was as simple as trapping a hummingbird or bagging a jackrabbit. He was, in short, an escape artist.

"If I had a style," he said, "it was to react at a moment's notice. I never waited."

Rodgers certainly didn't wait to make his presence known on the football field. In his first collegiate contest against Wake Forest in 1970, the sophomore wingback snared a pass from quarterback Jerry Tagge and raced to the end zone, completing a 61-yard pass play. Seven weeks would elapse before Rodgers would fail to score at least one touchdown in a game for the Cornhuskers.

Tagge connected with Rodgers on a 15-yard touchdown pass the next week against Southern California, but the game ended in a 21-21 tie. No other team came close to beating the Cornhuskers that year, however, until the season finale against Oklahoma. With the Sooners nursing a 7-0 second-quarter lead, Tagge completed a 53-yard pass to Rodgers, who crossed the goal line for the 11th time that year (seven times on pass receptions, twice on running plays and twice on punt runbacks). A fingertip catch by fullback Dan Schneiss that went for 24 yards set up a short fourth-quarter TD run by Tagge, whose score broke a 21-21 deadlock and clinched the Big Eight Conference championship for Nebraska. With a 10-0-1 record, the Cornhuskers proceeded to the Orange Bowl, where they overcame Louisiana State, 17-12, to win their first national championship ever. (United Press International, which at that time selected its national champion before the bowl games, had Nebraska No. 3 in the rankings, but the Associated Press, which took bowl-game results into account in its final poll, voted Nebraska No. 1 following January 1 upsets of Texas and Ohio State.)

In 1971, Devaney produced what is considered by many to be the best team ever to grace a college football field. Numerous players were cited for postseason honors, including quarterback Tagge, noseguard Rich Glover and halfback Jeff Kinney. In addition, two defensive players—end Willie Harper and tackle Larry Jacobson—were named consensus All-Americas, while that honor went to one offensive player: Johnny Rodgers.

The elusive wingback's uncanny ability to score and to make big plays was one major key to Nebraska's incredible '71 season. Whether he was rushing, receiving or running back kicks, Rodgers had a fierce desire to put the ball in the end zone.

"We had such a good team that every time I got a punt, I was desperate," Rodgers said. "I didn't want to carry it to the 5 or 10 so that someone else could take it in. Every time I got the ball, I wanted to score."

And score he did. After being barred from the end zone in the Huskers' season-opening victory over Oregon—one of only six games in his collegiate career in which he did not score—Rodgers took three passes from Tagge in for touchdowns a week later as Nebraska rolled to a 35-7 victory over Minnesota.

The following Saturday against Texas A&M, Rodgers opened the second half with a 98-yard kickoff return for a touchdown. He again scored on a 32-yard pass from Tagge later in the third quarter, and the Huskers beat the Aggies, 34-7, the same score by which they had defeated Oregon. The Tagge-Rodgers connection accounted for a touchdown in each of the next two games, a 42-6 win over Utah State and a 36-0 shutout of conference foe Missouri.

Rodgers amazed observers with his strength as well as his speed and moves. Bob Broeg of the St. Louis Post-Dispatch wrote this about the little wingback's scoring play in the Missouri game: "On the touchdown—a 28-yard pass play from Tagge to Rodgers—the shifty flanker carried (defensive back Lorenzo) Brinkley piggyback fashion the last six yards into the end zone."

Rodgers tallied two TDs in each of the next two games—a 55-0 trouncing of Kansas and a 41-13 win over Oklahoma State—including a 92-yard punt runback in the latter contest. He was held scoreless in a 31-7 conquest of Colorado but came back in the next two weeks to score four times while leading the Huskers to victories over Iowa State (37-0) and Kansas State (44-17).

That last win gave Nebraska a 10-0 record entering a crucial Thanksgiving Day matchup. That game, which pitted the No. 1-ranked Cornhuskers against No. 2-ranked Oklahoma (also unbeaten), was promoted as "The Game of the Century." For once, the hype did not exceed its reasonable bounds; that November 25, 1971, game in Norman, Okla., truly was a magnificent spectacle to behold.

Rodgers wasted no time making the game exciting. After Oklahoma stalled on its first possession of the game, the little speedster grabbed the Sooners' ensuing punt, avoided the horde of tacklers that hemmed him in and raced 72 yards for a touchdown.

"I started to the right, cut back left and must have gone 70 yards before I started for the sideline," he recalled. "I remember thinking, 'They're closing in and I'm out of gas.' But Joe Blahak threw a block to cut me loose. Blahak was always doing stuff like that."

Oklahoma narrowed Nebraska's lead on a 30-yard John Carroll field goal, but the Huskers made the score 14-3 when Kinney barrelled across the goal line and Rich Sanger kicked the extra point. The Sooners struck back later in the second quarter, however, and a keeper by quarterback Jack Mildren and a Mildren-to-Jon Harrison pass gave Oklahoma a 17-14 lead at the half.

Then it was time for a Nebraska surge. Two Kinney TDs put Nebraska back on top, 28-17, but another keeper by Mildren brought the Sooners back within four points after three quarters. Mildren then connected with Harrison again on a 16-yard scoring pass to give Oklahoma a 31-28 lead with 7:10 left in the game.

Rodgers, who caught five passes for 61 yards that day, was yet to make what turned out to be the biggest play of "The Game of the Century." That play came with the Huskers facing a third-and-eight situation at the Oklahoma 46-yard line with 4:50 left in the game. A first down was crucial.

Devaney ordered a pass to Rodgers up the middle. Tagge, under intense pressure, threw a low, sinking spiral 11 yards downfield, and Rodgers dived to catch the ball with his fingertips.

Seven plays later, Kinney scored his fourth touchdown of the game, and Nebraska won, 35-31.

"I don't remember the pass, but I remember my orders," Rodgers said. "They told me not to try to run but just catch the ball and go down. That's all I was thinking of."

All Huskers fans were thinking of was a second consecutive national championship as Nebraska sailed by Hawaii, 45-3, en route to an Orange Bowl date with unbeaten Alabama. It was supposed to be another "Game of the Century," but this time the media hubbub was unwarranted. Rodgers contributed a 77-yard punt return for a touchdown as the Huskers thrashed the Crimson Tide, 38-6, and were voted the No. 1 team in the country by both major wire services.

"They just toyed with us," Alabama Coach Paul (Bear) Bryant said afterward. "They were one of the greatest (teams), if not the greatest, I have ever seen. . . . They just flat whipped our butts in every way known to man."

The Cornhuskers were in for a bit of a rude awakening in 1972, Rodgers' senior season. After going 32 games without a loss—the tie with Southern Cal in '70 was the only blemish in that stretch—Nebraska lost its season opener against UCLA, a team that had won only twice the year before, on an Efren Herrera field goal with 22 seconds left. The Huskers bounced back, however, and won their next seven games (including four consecutive shutouts) before escaping with a 23-23 tie against Iowa State. The Cyclones squandered a probable victory by missing an extra-point attempt with 23 seconds remaining. Nebraska then blasted Kansas State, 59-7, but lost to Oklahoma, 17-14, to finish 1972 at 8-2-1.

Though the season was a bit of a letdown for Nebraska fans as well as Devaney, who had hoped to become the first coach ever to win three consecutive national championships, it still was a showcase for the talents of Johnny Rodgers.

The speedy wingback matched his junior season scoring production by crossing the goal line 17 times (seven rushing, eight receiving and two returning punts), giving him 45 touchdowns for his career. Rodgers set numerous Nebraska records as a senior, including most catches in a season (55) and a career (143) and most yards receiving in a season (942) and a career (2,479).

"And . . . he is half-blind," said Christie, the Omaha Tech coach who befriended Rodgers. "He has terrible vision. I asked him once how he caught the ball, and he told me, 'I just look for a fuzzy brown thing and grab it.' "

Rodgers also was devastating as a runner, especially as a kick returner. He shares NCAA career records for most touchdowns on punt returns (seven) and on punt and kickoff returns combined (eight). He also became Nebraska's career leader in all-purpose running with 5,586 yards as well as the school's record holder in numerous other categories.

Rodgers complemented his obvious talent with a flair for the theatrical. In a 49-0 defeat of Minnesota in 1972, Rodgers scored twice, on a two-yard run and a punt runback. That play was described in the New York Times: "Rodgers returned a punt 64 yards for a third-period touchdown in a twisting, turning run that brought a Memorial Stadium record crowd of 76,217 to its feet roaring when he spun and trotted backward the last five yards into the end zone."

Rodgers' dazzling runs even caught him by surprise while watching game films. "I couldn't remember doing those things," he said. "It made me nervous to know that the Creator would let me do them. I didn't have the rules to his game." Nor did Rodgers—or anyone else—have the rules to the Heisman game. So, when Rodgers picked up a newspaper one day as a senior and read that he was a candidate for the Heisman Memorial Trophy and, at the same time, that he should not be a candidate, he didn't know what to think.

"I didn't even know what the Heisman was until they told me I couldn't win it," he said.

For the first time in the history of the Heisman, the prestigious trophy caused a moral dilemma: Does it matter if a Heisman winner is an All-America on the football field but has a well-publicized criminal record?

The purist would say it does matter, that there is a whole generation of young boys, including future Heisman aspirants, who would be badly influenced if "the wrong kind" won the trophy.

Others, however, agreed with Devaney, who defended his player. "The Heisman is not a Sunday school or Fellowship of Christian Athletes trophy," Devaney said. "It goes to the best football player on the field."

Rodgers won the Heisman in 1972, easily as it turned out. He received 1,310 points, compared with 966 for the runner-up, Oklahoma running back Greg Pruitt. Nebraska's Glover, despite playing an interior line position that generally is overlooked by Heisman voters, was third with 652.

Rodgers' victory received mixed reviews. Many people, obviously, were happy for him, but he also was the subject of nasty editorials and columns. Scorn and contempt became new adjuncts of the Heisman.

Rodgers was confused.

"You don't know what to feel when you don't know what they're talking about," he said. "In some ways, I thought they (his critics) were right. I had made some mistakes. But I never thought I was a bad person."

Rodgers said he believes a Heisman winner should represent "what the rules are. If they say you should be an all-American boy and a great football player, then that's how it should be. But the rules don't say you can't come up and make mistakes."

Because there are no rules and guidelines for Heisman voters, Rodgers has proposed his own. "The Heisman should be given to the best person who inspires his team to winning and getting the most attention," he said. "That doesn't mean you can't party on weekends or make illegitimate babies because girls trip out on you. You can't be all the best of everything to win one prize.

"Besides, there are no pure people anyway. Everybody's got something in their background they don't want someone to know about."

Rodgers is convinced that Nebraska was embarrassed, not thrilled, when he became the school's first Heisman winner.

"They didn't want me to get out of there with the Heisman," he said. "There were only two men who stood up for me the whole time: Bob Devaney and Tom Osborne, my receivers coach. Devaney treated me like a son. He still does. He'd talk to me like a father, and I didn't have one.

"And he stood up for me not knowing if I'd help him win the national championship. He did it because he cared about me. He took an unpopular stance by letting me come back on the team (after being sentenced to jail)."

Devaney, who retired as coach after the '72 season and became Nebraska's athletic director, said the decision was easier than it appeared.

"Johnny had one serious problem (the gas station holdup), and he was put on probation for it," he said. "We more or less felt we'd put him on probation, too. In the eyes of the law, he hadn't done anything wrong, and that's how we looked at it.

"And anytime you can save a person, you've got to try. If we had dropped him from the team, we'd have ruined his life. He hadn't any way of making real money at the time other than what he did on the football field."

And Devaney certainly admired Rodgers for his skills on the gridiron. "He was the greatest football player I ever coached," he said. "He had so much ability. . . . (He was) maybe the greatest punt returner of all time. He had an intense desire to be the best."

Rodgers is among a select few Heisman winners whose primary function was catching passes. He lined up in the backfield and was given handoffs on occasion— his season high for rushing was just 267 yards as a senior—but he made his greatest impact on the game as a receiver and kick returner. Larry Kelley of Yale and

Leon Hart of Notre Dame, who played both offensive and defensive end, are considered the only pure receivers to win the Heisman, but Rodgers was most effective—and most feared—when he caught the ball on the run with only one or two potential tacklers in his vicinity.

Few football players have followed their Heisman selection with a better postseason performance than that of Johnny Rodgers in the Orange Bowl against Notre Dame on January 1, 1973.

Despite being moved to I-back from his normal wingback position for the first time in his three years at Nebraska, Rodgers was incredible against the Fighting Irish. He carried the ball 15 times for 81 yards and three touchdowns. He also performed his usual receiving role, catching three passes for 71 yards, including a short pass from quarterback David Humm that he carried most of the 50 yards from the line of scrimmage to the goal line for his fourth touchdown of the night. As if that wasn't enough, Rodgers also attempted his first pass of the season that night, a perfect spiral that was good for a 52-yard touchdown to Frosty Anderson.

"He hurt us at each one (running, receiving and passing)," former Notre Dame Coach Ara Parseghian said. "He is a truly outstanding athlete."

Nebraska won, 40-6, and became the first team ever to win three consecutive Orange Bowl games—all with Rodgers in the backfield.

"If there's any guy in the country who doesn't think Johnny Rodgers deserves the Heisman Trophy," Devaney said after the game, "he should quit writing sports or broadcasting or whatever he does."

But Heisman or no Heisman, Rodgers still was faced with a conviction for driving with a suspended license. He had appealed his sentence, but that appeal was dropped, and Rodgers had 30 days to serve in jail.

At first it appeared that Rodgers would not be put behind bars. A work-release program at Boys Town, Neb., was considered, but Msgr. Nicholas H. Wegner, director of Boys Town, said, "We don't want him."

Rodgers later was approved for a work program at Nebraska, where he would attend classes in the morning and work in the athletic weight room in the afternoon. Rodgers ended that program himself after four days out of concern that such a cushioned arrangement would embarrass Devaney and his coaching successor, Osborne.

"So many people in the public wanted me to serve out these 30 days," Rodgers said on May 9, 1973, the day he was released from the Lincoln-Lancaster County Jail. "The people who thought I should go to jail thought it would make a better person of me if I did, but they're wrong. It hasn't made me a better person at all. All it's done is give me an experience I hadn't had before."

Then Rodgers walked away carrying the fur coat and cap and the zebra-striped silk sheets that the jailers wouldn't let him use in his cell.

Rodgers was drafted in the first round by the San Diego Chargers of the National Football League in 1973, but he signed as a free agent with the Montreal Alouettes of the Canadian Football League because of the money—the richest CFL contract ever at that time. Rodgers' agent, Mike Trope, said the agreement was worth "in excess of six figures per year for three years."

Rodgers finally had what he had always wanted: $100,000.

"But it wasn't enough," he said. "One hundred thousand dollars is nothing."

One hundred grand might be enough for the rest of us, especially those of us who don't sleep between zebra-striped silk sheets. Of course, most of us don't live like Johnny Rodgers, or Johnny R. Superstar, as he was known in Canada.

"I like class," he explained.

Class was one Rolls-Royce for himself, plus another for his agent, Mike Trope, all part of the contract package. Class was six or seven fur coats for himself, plus another line he wore while representing a fur company. "You might not have seen me in the same fur for a month," he said.

Class, to Rodgers, is "creating the highest possible positive image." Class presented well, he added, brings "controversy and attention. All blacks like Cadillacs; that's the stereotype anyway. But if I drive a Cadillac, it's the pimp days. If I drive a Rolls, it expands the consciousness."

Rodgers played and lived in the fast lane, and he enjoyed having a good time. But he said the drug scene was neither prominent nor important in his life.

"I've been associated with people who used drugs," he said. "I've been associated with drugs, although I'm not a serious drug user. I could have sold drugs, but what good would it do me? I could make money, but if I lead others astray, the Creator is going to kick my butt."

Rodgers was named the CFL Rookie of the Year in 1973, and he played three more years in Montreal after that. He twice led the Alouettes to the Grey Cup (the CFL Super Bowl), one of which Montreal won.

"The first couple of years he played magnificently," said Marv Levy, Rodgers' coach in Montreal. "He has that Muhammad Ali sense of the public. He loved it. He was very popular in Canada.

"Then he became involved in too many activities outside of football, and his concentration waned. He tested team discipline all the time. He drifted more and more away from making football the Number 1 thing in his life. He'd sleep through team meetings, come up with strange maladies on the day of a game that would keep him out. He could still play at the same ability level, but not with any consistency."

The night before the Alouettes lost to Hamilton, 23-0, in a 1976 conference playoff game, Rodgers missed a team meeting. Levy said it was "the most unprofessional, bush-league thing I've seen as a coach, and I told him so."

Asked about those final two years, Rodgers said: "I missed some team practices, I don't deny that. I may have some different values in life, but I don't have an attitude problem. But do you think a $500 fine is high enough for the biggest bush-league thing you ever saw?"

Levy always found Rodgers personable. "He liked to be talked to," Levy said. "He was very big-hearted, generous. He had 14 people (eight, by Rodgers' count) living with him." The coach believed that Rodgers had one team at the stadium, another at home, and that it was tough to carry both.

The Alouettes were partly to blame for disturbing his concentration, Rodgers said, because of their treatment of quarterback Jimmy Jones.

"They dogged him, then got rid of him (in 1976), and the two of us were the whole offense," he said. "I was angry about that—I'm still angry—and I wouldn't stay quiet about it."

A contract settlement was worked out so that Rodgers could leave Montreal

*Johnny Rodgers has risen from the Omaha ghettos to a San Diego office where issues of his magazine, Tuned In San Diego, bear testimony to his success as a publisher.*

after the '76 season.

"Bob Devaney told me when we signed Johnny originally, 'You're getting a great player, but he's going to take up 80 percent of your time,'" Levy said. "I saw Bob five years later and said: 'You were wrong. He took up 95 percent.'"

Rodgers joined the Chargers for the 1977 season. "I came to San Diego to kick butt," he said.

Rodgers returned a punt 68 yards for a touchdown in his first preseason game with the Chargers. Then he pulled a hamstring muscle and damaged a knee, and his NFL career was over after two years in San Diego. He did not score a touchdown for the Chargers.

"I didn't know what the Creator had in mind for me," Rodgers said of the future.

So, Rodgers went into the publishing business. It nearly broke him at first, but he rebounded, and his Tuned In San Diego, a popular TV-entertainment magazine, is highly successful. Tuned In outsells every magazine in the San Diego area except one, TV Guide, which is Rodgers' main competitor as well as the top-selling magazine in the nation. Rodgers said he was determined—and financially prepared—to overtake TV Guide in sales. "I'm self-sufficient," he said.

Rodgers now has six children. Five were born out of wedlock by three different mothers. A sixth child was adopted. Rodgers married once, in the late 1970s, but is divorced.

"The children live with me, basically," he said, "although they go back and forth between me and their mothers. I'm financially responsible for the children. I began taking care of my children when I went to Montreal."

He speaks proudly of his children and of the responsibility he feels for them. Though five of the six were conceived without the convention of marriage, they are no less Rodgers' children than the sixth who was conceived by another couple. Rodgers lives a fast life, but he believes in accountability.

Of his four sons, two already are football stars. Terry and Kevin Rodgers were teammates at Sweetwater High School in National City, near San Diego, in 1983. In one game, Terry ran 72 yards from scrimmage for one touchdown and Kevin returned a kickoff 98 yards for another, with Dad grinning in the stands.

Recalling his own goal in life, making $100,000, Rodgers advised his sons about what they would need to get ahead in the world.

"A billion dollars," he told them. "Think of power."

Rodgers elaborated: "The only reason I said a billion is that it comes to you as you believe. If you reach for a star and miss, grab the moon when you come down."

Johnny R. Superstar reached for a star and got it when he won the Heisman. The award obviously meant that he could become wealthy, but what did it mean to him in non-monetary terms?

"Pressure . . . in living up to it," he said. "I can't afford to go backward. If I can beat TV Guide, from where I came from. . . ."

"Fire!"

Rodgers' purring lady friend saw it first. A boat in the harbor was on fire. Smoke and flames billowed from the hull. She ran off to find out what had happened and who was hurt.

Rodgers didn't move. He studied the fire with the interested but unconcerned look of one who had lived through enough personal fires, in the Omaha and Lincoln infernos, that one more blaze wasn't about to faze him.

The fire lasted 20 minutes. The woman returned with the news that some children had been burned, none seriously. They had escaped from the boat in time.

Rodgers nodded. "There have been so many times that I've gotten in and out of jams," he said. "The Creator must have been keeping me around for something later."

Rodgers spoke often of the Creator that afternoon. "I'm spiritual," he said. "I'm a corporal in the Creator's army. I have a responsibility for the people around me. I'm not on my back. I'm not crippled. I'm not broke. I've got no reason not to trust him."

No reason at all. Rodgers hears only distant gunshots in his mind now. He has long forgotten what a flesh wound feels like. Danger no longer lurks for him around every ghetto street corner. Rodgers has come out of the violent, troubled darkness of his youth and into a peaceful light. It had to be the Creator.

"Yes indeed," Rodgers said, studying the quaint harbor setting, his heaven on Earth. "He's promoted me."

# Archie Griffin

*He was twice blessed. And that's a fitting tribute to his amazing talent. The Archie Griffin legend began at Ohio State, spread through the Big Ten Conference and eventually captured the imagination of a nation. See Archie run! And that he did, for more than 5,000 yards. He became living testimony that big things do come in small packages. And that hard work and determination can pay big dividends. They did for Archie Griffin. Twice.*

# Chapter 17

# Ohio State's little big man

Archie Griffin was too small.

Obviously, he was too small. If he were only six feet tall and 200 pounds, Griffin would have found it so much easier to lug around his two Heismans.

Poor Archie. When he topped out physically, it was at exactly 5-foot-7¾ and 182 pounds, even though press guides listed him anywhere from 5-9 to 5-11. My word, at those heights, he might have taken home the Heisman as a sophomore, too.

"This is all I have to live with," Griffin lamented, checking himself out, up and down.

Cruel fate. With a little more meat on his small bones, Griffin could have rushed for 8,000 yards at Ohio State instead of a measly 5,177. That was an NCAA record at the time he said goodbye to Columbus, and it still ranks him fifth of all time, but with a bigger pair of shoulders, he might be first right now.

Don't misunderstand, he is proud of his accomplishments, winning two Heismans and all, especially when he thinks of the other six Heisman winners as juniors who didn't repeat as seniors—Doc Blanchard, Doak Walker, Vic Janowicz, Roger Staubach, Billy Sims and Herschel Walker. It takes a pretty big man, regardless of size, to go that kind of select company one better.

But Arch, as Buckeyes Coach Woody Hayes used to call him, sure must be envious of those other six because of the way they filled out their uniforms. Arch filled his out, too, but it was such a small uniform.

Herschel Walker, who looked like Mr. America in shoulder pads compared to Arch, signed a contract with the New Jersey Generals of the United States Football League and therefore was unable to challenge Griffin's Heisman double. The other junior winners, almost to a man, were hampered by injuries as seniors.

Griffin was injured, too, as a senior. He injured his shoulder the fourth week of the season against UCLA, but he didn't come out of the game. And he broke his hand on the third play of the Rose Bowl, but again he continued to play. In college, Arch was virtually indestructible.

Yet imagine what Griffin might have accomplished if the good Lord, in whom he places great trust, had molded him in the physical image of Bronko Nagurski or Marcus Allen. Stunned Big Ten Conference opponents probably would have thought that Superman, disguised by a Terry Thomas gap between his two front teeth and a 45 on his scarlet-and-gray jersey, was playing halfback at Ohio State.

Even though Griffin looked like a ballboy among behemoths, there was no denying him a second Heisman. He had the heart of a lion, a quality without which he never could have earned a special niche in football history. That courage was necessary to absorb the abuse that was inflicted on his little body week after week.

"Arch gets hit almost every play, and when he has the ball, he gets hit about four times," Hayes said during Griffin's senior year. "But he got piled on a couple of times, too—every game. Those things don't need to happen. There's no place for cheap shots in football."

Hayes equipped Griffin with linemen's thigh pads to protect his short legs, but that did little good. Arch seldom practiced before Wednesday or Thursday of each week, though he was always ready to play on Saturday.

Bruised and battered, Griffin still managed to set an NCAA record by rushing for 100 or more yards in 31 consecutive games. Griffin also was the first college running back to break the 5,000-yard mark.

"I've never had a fella I enjoyed coaching more," Hayes said in his best John Wayne imitation, "never a fella I liked more."

Griffin was someone you circled the wagons around.

"I've never seen a greater football player than Arch," Hayes said in Griffin's second Heisman season, "yet he's even a greater leader. In three years, I've never seen that young man do one thing to be criticized for. He's the most popular player we've ever had, by far."

Griffin's gridiron exploits certainly made him popular with Heisman voters. As a junior, he beat Anthony Davis of Southern California by 1,101 points. The next year was slightly closer, but he still collected 1,070 more points than the runner-up, California's Chuck Muncie. What makes his accomplishments even more remarkable is the fact that 1975 was the year of the running back. Trailing Griffin and Muncie in the Heisman voting were Ricky Bell of Southern Cal (third), Tony Dorsett of Pittsburgh (fourth) and Joe Washington of Oklahoma (fifth).

"I owe a lot of it," Griffin said of his unparalleled Heisman experience, "to being at the right place, with the right coaches and the right teammates and the right support system—the fans and the Ohio State band."

Griffin credits everyone for his success, right down to the student who dotted the "i" when the Ohio State marching band spelled out the school's name, in cursive yet, before every home game. Even that student towered over the little running back.

Indeed, Griffin lacked the size that, combined with his natural talent, would have guaranteed him success at any school in the country. He had to be in the right situation with a strong supporting cast. Had he followed his earlier inclinations and enrolled at Northwestern, which boasts a strong curriculum but a weak football program, he almost certainly would not have won a single Heisman, much less two.

But the right situation has existed at Ohio State for years. That program has produced a long, gray line of great running backs, all taller than Griffin, and among them, Les Horvath, Howard Cassady and Janowicz have won the Heisman once apiece. John Brockington, Ollie Cline, Bob White, Bob Ferguson, Jim Otis and Matt Snell didn't win it at all.

Maybe the best presents do come in smaller packages.

"Winning the Heisman is a dream I first had when I was 9," Griffin said. "To have it happen once was great. Then to go back again . . . it's a great feeling. It amazes me. I say to myself, 'I did that?' "

Seated in his office on the Ohio State campus, Griffin revealed a golden smile and silver teeth. He wore braces. "I've had them for a year and a half," he said on

Columbus Day, 1984. "I always wanted my teeth to be closer together. We all pretty much have gaps in my family."

Griffin, sporting a three-piece suit, perfectly aligned teeth and a closer-cropped haircut than the larger Afro he wore as a Buckeye, traced his roots. He didn't have far to trace. "I was born on the Ohio State campus, in University Hospital," he said.

A baby Buckeye. What chance did Northwestern really have?

"I was always considered a fat kid," he continued. "In Little League football, they called me Tank. I played in a 135-pound league, and I was close to 135 pounds at 11. At 12, I was above it."

Griffin was the fourth of eight children born to James and Margaret Griffin. To support a large family, the Griffins at one time ran a small mom-and-pop grocery store called Griffin's Grocery. The only problem with their store was Archie, who literally ate up his parents' business—Almond Joys, Hostess chocolate cupcakes, ice-cream bars, anything he could sneak. Griffin's Grocery eventually closed down.

Archie's parents took one look at his protruding belly and called him Butter-ball. With that build, he certainly wasn't mistaken for a running back as a child. He looked more like a future Ohio State tackle, and, in fact, he was a lineman in those days back in the neighborhood. Some of the backs he blocked for were nifty runners, even if they were girls.

"We had this game called 'smear the queer,'" Archie recalled. "You'd throw the ball up and everyone would go for it. We had some girls who played who could really hit. I still have a scar on my back from where a girl tackled me and I fell on some glass."

It was about this time that Griffin grew tired of looking like Fat Albert. He filled two cases of beer bottles with dirt, attached them to the ends of a mop handle and began lifting "weights." On hot summer days, Griffin would put on extra layers of clothing, climb into the family's disabled station wagon, roll up all the windows and do push-ups and sit-ups until his head spun and his muscles ached. "I could lose five to six pounds doing that," he said.

Griffin melted away the flab and hardened it to the point that when he entered college, he looked like Arnold Schwarzenegger in Mickey Rooney's body.

One day the 13-year-old Archie Griffin showed up for Little League football practice and there was no fullback. The coach asked if anyone could play the position. Griffin's hand shot up. "I thought I'd do it for a day," he recalled.

He never played in the line again. In his first game for that junior high team, he ran 50 yards for a touchdown, but the play was nullified by a penalty. Griffin ran 55 yards on the next play, but it, too, was called back. He then ran 60 yards to score on the next play, and this one held up. "Man, we got something here," James Griffin Sr., sitting in the stands, said to one of his older sons.

Griffin also was emerging as a bright student. James Retter, his junior-high school English teacher, once said that Griffin was "the most motivated, single-minded youngster I've ever seen. He got the best grades . . . was the most spontane-ous . . . a model student."

That keen mind made him a good student of the game of football. When it came to game plans, strategies, fundamentals and techniques, he learned quickly.

Griffin was first-string varsity as a sophomore, first-string all-district as a junior and first-string all-state as a senior at Eastmoor High School.

By his last year of high school, Griffin was, in Coach Bob Stuart's words, "just scary. I can never remember one man tackling him. . . . Heck, Archie played the last three games with a broken bone in his foot, and they still couldn't catch him."

That bit of information didn't escape Hayes, who also was aware that Griffin wrestled at 167 pounds his last two years in high school. Hayes preferred his running back recruits 20 pounds heavier, but he looked mainly at the size of Griffin's will and realized he had to have this pint-sized phenom.

Griffin was a student of local history, and he knew of Hayes' penchant for big fullbacks carrying the ball 20 to 30 times per game. Griffin balked at being a Buckeye. "People told me: 'Why go to Ohio State? You're too small to play there,' " he said.

That's one reason why he first looked at Northwestern. The Griffin family's perception of the treatment of blacks in the Ohio State football program was another.

"When we first came to Columbus," said Griffin Sr., who, like his wife, was reared in a West Virginia coal-mining camp, "people told us that Coach Hayes didn't like colored."

Rudy Hubbard, a black assistant coach under Hayes, was aware of the Griffins' feelings and arranged for the parents to have dinner with six black businessmen who had played football for Hayes. According to Hubbard, the Griffins found out that "most white coaches are prejudiced," that the trend was changing and that "Woody is more than fair in most cases." The Griffins were happy to learn that Hayes, for all his gruffness, had a genuine interest in his players and continued to look after their welfare long after they had left Ohio State.

The recruiting of Archie Griffin continued with Hayes' wife, Anne, taking Mrs. Griffin to lunch. Woody then visited the Griffin home, making his grand entrance and immediately setting the family at ease. For his final act, Hayes showed up one day at Eastmoor High, locked himself and Archie in a room for two hours and showed the youngster on the blackboard how halfbacks, regardless of size, also carry the ball for Ohio State.

At that point, it became Ohio State's gain, Northwestern's loss.

Griffin's performance in his first game for the Buckeyes, the 1972 opener against Iowa his freshman year, consisted of his bobbling a pitchout that turned into a five-yard loss. Officially, he did not carry the ball in 1½ minutes of action.

Griffin's second game . . . ah, the second game. What Griffin did on September 30, 1972, at Ohio Stadium now is a part of Ohio State lore. In all likelihood, no other Heisman winner ever has made such an impact on college football so early.

"The night before the game," Griffin said, "Coach Hayes took the varsity to stay in a hotel. I was a freshman and I stayed in the dorms. That night, I prayed to get into the game. I always prayed at night, but I never prayed that the coach would let me play. But it was a miracle that I even played the next day."

North Carolina, the Buckeyes' opponent that memorable day along the Olentangy River, blocked a punt early in the game and recovered it in the end zone to lead, 7-0. As the Ohio State offense sputtered, Hubbard, sitting in the press box, pleaded with Hayes over the coaching phones to send Griffin into the game. The discussion grew heated before Hayes, who was not yet sold on the new rule allowing freshmen to play on the varsity, relented midway in the first quarter.

"They kept calling my name," Griffin said. "I hesitated because I thought it was a mistake. Finally, I went in."

At first he forgot his helmet. But once he found the helmet, got everything snapped into place and said a prayer, Griffin was off and running. Six yards on his first carry, six more on his second, another six on his third. Then 32. Later, 22. Finally, 55. He also caught one pass for a 17-yard gain and scored the Buckeyes' last touchdown on a nine-yard run.

"I don't remember much about that game," Griffin said. "It happened so fast."

When it was over, more than 86,000 delighted Buckeye fans stood and cheered Griffin's name. He had rushed for 239 yards in roughly three quarters to break Cline's 1945 single-game Buckeye rushing record by exactly 10 yards.

North Carolina was not only beaten, 29-14, but mesmerized. "We came here not even knowing Archie Griffin existed," Tar Heels Coach Bill Dooley said, "and now you tell me he's a freshman!"

Griffin was astonished by what he had done. "I didn't know how to take it just out of high school," he recalled. "I had done that in my high school championship game—260 yards rushing. I thought I should do it all the time."

The rest of Griffin's freshman year wasn't nearly as sensational. He rushed for 40 yards the following week against California, then amassed 192 yards on the ground a week later against Illinois. Griffin did not hit the 100 mark again the rest of the season.

When Archie began his Ohio State career, it complicated an already-difficult logistical problem for his parents. But for the Griffins, it was a pleasant problem.

James and Margaret Griffin attended as many of their sons' football games as was humanly possible. But with seven sons born within 14 years of each other—and with all seven playing college football—the Griffins were constantly racing against time. James would drive and Margaret would keep an eye out for the state police, hoping to make kickoff but not wanting to chance a speeding ticket even if it meant hearing part of the game on the car radio.

If Archie played a day game in Columbus, his parents would jump in their car immediately afterward and speed off, say, to watch Daryle play that night for Kent State. They'd visit with Daryle afterward before facing the long drive back to Columbus in the middle of the night.

The Griffins were a devoted family. If there were Heismans given annually to the outstanding father in the country, James Griffin, like his fourth son, would have been a multiple Heisman winner.

To provide the best living environment for his wife and children, he worked two and often three jobs. Those jobs often required him to be away from the house for 20 hours a day. He drove a sanitation truck in the daytime, worked at a steel foundry at night and labored as a high school custodian in between. He kept up this remarkable pace for more than 20 years.

"My father is the hardest-working man who ever lived," Archie said proudly.

Because James Griffin was home mainly to sleep—and only four hours a night at that—he assigned his oldest son, James Jr., as "second daddy" in the home. There was no drinking, smoking, bragging or swearing inside that middle-class home, which Griffin Sr. bought for his family in a nice residential district in Columbus after carefully saving and investing his hard-earned money. White families lived on either side of the Griffins.

The Griffin patriarch believed "in the Ralph Bunche dream, that if you do your best, you will succeed regardless of color or class," James Griffin Jr. said.

The Griffin children never got into trouble. They wouldn't dare, so great was their respect for their father. "It was very easy to get into trouble with your father not around," Griffin Jr. added. "But the fact that none of us ever did shows the respect we had for him."

The father of eight once said: "People used to laugh, but I always said I was going to send all my kids to college. I didn't know how, but I knew I'd get them through some way. You've got to reach out and do things for yourself. Sometimes I'm so tired I can't see. But it's worth it. Now we are free of all the troubles. Now we don't have to run anymore."

As James Griffin had predicted, all seven of his sons graduated from college: James Jr. from Muskingum, Larry from Louisville, Daryle from Kent State, Archie, Ray and Duncan from Ohio State, and Keith from Miami of Florida. The baby of the family, daughter Krystal, attends Drake and is a member of the university's women's track team.

James Jr., Larry, Archie and Keith were running backs; Daryle, Ray and Duncan played defensive back. Three Griffins played in the National Football League—Archie with the Cincinnati Bengals, Ray with the Bengals and Seattle Seahawks, Keith with the Washington Redskins. Ray and Keith are still active.

The Griffin boys were almost all like their father—solid, determined, hard-working, even-tempered men of few words. Only Ray broke the mold; he was more emotional than his brothers. Yet it took a lot to set the Griffins off, and Archie might have been the hardest to rile.

In college, especially as a senior, Archie was the victim of aggressive tackling, to say the least. But he seldom complained. "Nice hit," he would say, then bounce up and rejoin the huddle.

Once in the middle of an NFL game between intrastate rivals Cincinnati and Cleveland, a Browns player spit on Griffin. It was more than he could stand. Tackle him hard, yes. Twist a leg, maybe. Spit on him, never.

"I lost it! I lost it!" he said. "I wanted to grab him. But I had my senses. I didn't want our team to be penalized."

But in "losing it," Griffin didn't, really. He turned the other cheek. "It was the Lord taking over," he believes. "I trust in God completely. He must have restrained me."

James and Margaret Griffin made sure that theirs was a devout Christian home. They kept the New Testament miniatures in the living room, and they made their unquivering faith in God plain for all to see. "Every time I made one dollar," Griffin Sr. once said, "God fixed it so I'd make the next one."

That parental example spread to their children, all of whom are religious. Daryle was named the 1975 Ohio Christian Athlete of the Year. Woody Hayes tried to leave the Ohio State dressing room at halftime any number of times, only to stumble over Archie, who was down on his knees, praying. "Oh, my God, he's so honorable!" Woody said of Arch.

Griffin finished his freshman year with three touchdowns and 772 yards rushing, plus 95 more in the Rose Bowl as Ohio State lost to Southern Cal, 42-17. With a new zeal, Hayes began recruiting high school seniors who could play college ball right away.

In his first game as a sophomore, Griffin ran for 129 yards as Ohio State crunched Minnesota, 56-7. It was the first of Griffin's 31 straight 100-yard rushing performances. Later that same year, he broke his own Ohio State record with 246 yards rushing against Iowa in a 55-13 Buckeye victory. Superman *was* at Ohio State, and he really didn't need a cape. Griffin already could fly, or so it seemed.

A quick examination of the final scores and the wire-service rankings shows that Griffin was at Ohio State at the right time. The presence of Griffin on the Ohio State roster, along with such All-Americas and future professionals as Randy Gradishar, Tim Fox, Doug Plank, Brian Baschnagel, Pete Johnson, Neal Colzie, John Hicks, Ted Smith, Kurt Schumacher, Steve Myers, Morris Bradshaw, Bob Brudzinski, Doug France and Ray Griffin, made the Buckeyes the scourge of the Big Ten in the first half of the '70s. Griffin led the Buckeyes to a 40-5-1 overall record, four Big Ten titles (three shared with Michigan), four Rose Bowl appearances and four Top 10 ratings in his four years. In addition, the Buckeyes scored 30 or more points 25 times, 40 or more 15 times, 50 or more seven times and 60 or more once.

The one honor that eluded the Buckeyes during Arch's years, however, was a national championship. The closest they came was runner-up to Notre Dame in the 1973 Associated Press poll. And in the four Rose Bowls, the Buckeyes won but once. Hayes had the horses, but they were mainly plow horses. Southern Cal and UCLA understood the passing game, which was largely an enigma to the Big Ten at that time, and the Pacific-10 Conference representatives dominated the ground-conscious Buckeyes in Pasadena.

The one exception was Griffin's sophomore year, when he rushed for 1,428 yards, scored eight touchdowns and finished fifth in the Heisman balloting. Hicks, the Ohio State offensive tackle, finished second that year to Penn State's John Cappelletti.

"I got a friend I grew up with," Griffin said. "He told me after my freshman year that I would win three Heismans. I told him, 'Bobby, you are crazy.'

"Well, it turns out that he made a bet I would win three. He must have made a lot of money because after I won my second, he bought me a new suede coat. I don't think that's illegal."

Ohio State finished that 1973 regular season with a 10-10 tie against Michigan, leaving both schools deadlocked for the Big Ten championship with identical 7-0-1 league records and throwing the conference into a quandary. The Big Ten had just decided two years earlier to repeal its no-repeat rule, which previously had made it impossible for the league champion to go to the Rose Bowl in successive years.

Now the Big Ten had a dead-heat finish. How to break the tie? A vote of the conference's athletic directors was decided upon.

But wait! There were 10 athletic directors, so suppose the vote came out 5-5. What then? It finally was determined that in such a case, Michigan would go to the Rose Bowl because it hadn't gone the previous season. The whole dilemma was getting more confusing by the moment.

A day after the Buckeye-Wolverine tie, the athletic directors voted to send

Ohio State to Pasadena. Although the final vote never has been documented, a rumor surfaced that it was 6-4, with Michigan State casting the deciding vote for the Buckeyes.

When Michigan Coach Bo Schembechler heard that, he exploded. It was bad enough that the vote had gone against Michigan, he believed, but the idea of one intrastate university voting against another was more than Schembechler could stand, if it were true. And in Bo's mind, it was. Case closed. But his complaints fell on deaf ears.

"There was something about that year," Griffin reflected. "I guess it had to do with the makeup of the team and beating USC in the Rose Bowl after people said we shouldn't be going."

Ohio State made the athletic directors appear as prophets by stomping Southern Cal, 42-21, in Pasadena. It was Griffin's finest bowl game. He rushed 22 times for 149 yards and his only postseason touchdown.

By this time, all of Ohio was in love with Griffin. And Griffin was falling in love, too, with Ohio State student Loretta Laffitte. They met in calculus class as sophomores. The entire class had done poorly on an examination, so the professor decided to give it again. Archie and Loretta studied together for the makeup test, and his off-field romance was on.

Griffin's on-field romance with Buckeye faithful, meanwhile, intensified in 1974. Arch compiled his best statistics as a junior, when he tallied 12 touchdowns and a nation-leading 1,620 yards rushing. Ohio State's only regular-season defeat was a 16-13 setback against Michigan State, which supposedly had sided with the Buckeyes in the previous year's Rose Bowl controversy. Two weeks later, Michigan prepared to seek its revenge on Ohio State.

"Playing Michigan," Griffin said, "I was always glad it was the last game of the year. My sophomore year, I was hit so hard, there was no way I could have played the next week if we had had a game. They never played dirty against us, we never played dirty ball against them. It was just good, hard football."

The rivalry was intensified by the lack of mutual admiration between the schools' respective head coaches, Schembechler and Hayes. Bo had been an assistant under Woody. Their relationship threw off sparks then, and later, as opposing coaches, they were like two boiling teapots on the same stove.

Hayes loved to gloat that without one Michigan player on his roster, his Buckeyes could beat Schembechler's Wolverines, many of whom had been recruited from the Ohio prep ranks. Woody crawled inside Bo's skin like a 250-pound tick.

Before the 1974 game, a Michigan player announced, "If Archie Griffin gains 100 yards against us, it will be over my dead body."

Ohio State called a mortuary in Columbus to discuss funeral arrangements.

"That player's comment didn't bother me," Griffin said, "but our offensive line really got angry. They said, *'We're* going to get 100 yards.' "

One hundred and eleven yards, to be exact. Griffin and his line convoy pounded Michigan, 12-10, keeping the Wolverines out of postseason bowl consideration for the third straight year. At that time, the Big Ten sent one team to the Rose Bowl and everyone else stayed home. Though Michigan was 30-2-1 during Griffin's first three years, its two defeats and a tie all were against Ohio State, and that's all it took to keep the Wolverines out of Pasadena. Dead bodies, indeed!

Ten days later, Griffin won his first Heisman in a landslide vote. Arch received 1,920 points, more than double the total for runner-up Anthony Davis of Southern Cal (819 points). Oklahoma's Joe Washington finished third with 661 points.

It was a time of celebration in Columbus, where the most popular bumper sticker in town was "Thank You Mrs. Griffin." And James Griffin Sr. said that Woody Hayes' wife "kisses me whenever she sees me. I don't care how many people are around."

Griffin might have trouble deciding which Heisman was harder to win, but there is no question as to which of his Heisman speeches was harder to give. The first, hands down.

"I got caught up in the emotion and started crying," he said. "I got a few words out and I was boo-hooing like a baby. I didn't know how I would make it to the end."

Somehow, between sobs, he did, and by the time he was through, he had won the audience's admiration with one of the most inspirational speeches in Heisman history.

"First of all, I'd like to thank my mother and father," he said. "They taught me all that's right and the ways to excellence. . . . And I look at my older brothers and I love them. . . . And there are my younger brothers . . . I really want to set an example for them and my little sister, Krystal. . . .

"To me, football represents the good things in life. I'll do everything in my power to set the greatest example. If today's young people look up to the Heisman winners and other stars the way I did, they'll do as I did."

Tears of heartbreak, not tears of joy, awaited Ohio State in the Rose Bowl. The Buckeyes had the lead, 17-10, and apparently the victory until Southern Cal's Pat Haden threw a touchdown pass to John McKay Jr. late in the game to bring the Trojans within one point. John McKay Sr., the Southern Cal coach, eschewed the tie and decided to go for the win. Haden rolled to his right and threw to Shelton Diggs in the end zone for an 18-17 triumph. Griffin, despite suffering a rib separation in the first half, had 20 carries for 75 yards.

The Buckeyes finished the season with a 10-2 record and broken hearts. After being ranked No. 3 in the final United Press International poll and No. 4 by the Associated Press, the Buckeyes steeled themselves for one final run at the national championship during the Archie Griffin era.

Ohio State rolled over its first 10 opponents in 1975 with little trouble. In those games, Griffin produced anywhere from 107 yards (vs. Wisconsin) to 160 yards rushing against UCLA, his most productive game of the fall. Too bad the fans back in Columbus couldn't all travel to Los Angeles to watch that 41-20 victory in person; they would have loved it.

"Playing football for Ohio State was a special feeling," Griffin said nostalgically, "especially the spirit in the stadium. The team felt a closeness with the students and band. They always played 'Sloopy' when we were going in for a touchdown. I remember 'Sloopy.' They still play it."

When Ohio State took its 10-0 record to Ann Arbor for the regular-season finale, Griffin hit more than one "dead body" as Michigan ended his streak of 31 consecutive 100-yard rushing games. The Wolverines shut him down with 46 yards rushing in 19 attempts, just over two yards a pop. But Ohio State won the game,

21-14, thereby keeping Michigan winless (3-0-1) in four cracks at Griffin-led Buck-eye teams.

Griffin's statistics fell as a senior. He rushed for 1,357 yards, sixth best in the nation, and only four touchdowns, despite the fact that he had nine more carries that year than in any of his three other collegiate seasons. But injuries slowed him down, as did defenses that, more than ever before, keyed on him. His career statistics were 5,177 career rushing yards on 845 carries, or an average of 6.1 yards per carry, which still stands as an NCAA record (minimum 785 rushes).

Despite Griffin's many records and his feat of becoming the first player ever to rush for 5,000 yards in a career, it was quarterback Cornelius Greene, not Griffin, who was voted the most valuable player for both Ohio State and the Big Ten in 1975. For Griffin, those weren't exactly Heisman credentials. And on the West Coast, Chuck Muncie had led a long-dormant Cal football program almost to the Rose Bowl. Muncie had outrushed Griffin by 103 yards and had averaged 6.4 yards per carry to Griffin's 5.5. There was sentiment not only in the West, but also around the nation, that Muncie deserved the 1975 Heisman Trophy.

"I had heard about him," Griffin said of Muncie. "But my senior year, I really wanted to win the Heisman. I figured that all I could do was the best I could do and then see what happens."

Muncie was handicapped from a publicity standpoint in that he didn't have a drumbeater in his corner to match Wayne Woodrow Hayes.

Make no mistake, Hayes doted on Griffin as a father does a son. The coach thought not only that the sun rose and set on Arch, but also that his little halfback might have caused an eclipse or two. He could get that carried away by Arch, and that's why Hayes did something totally out of character: He hyped Griffin for the Heisman.

Normally, Hayes declined to publicize his players. For instance, he didn't openly promote Howard Cassady for the Heisman before Hopalong won it in 1955. Hayes never let Ohio State's selections on Playboy's preseason All-America team get within two states of Hugh Hefner's mansion. But, because it was Arch, Hayes became a one-man campaign director.

"I always like to quote Duke Ellington," Hayes said of the pianist-composer. " 'If you want your music to come out just right, you've got to use both your black keys and your white keys.' It's the same thing in football. What kind of guy is Arch? He blocks. That should tell you. He's no prima donna.

"You see all this publicity about how many yards some other back has or how many points they've scored, but no mention of how many times they carried the ball. Well, it's no secret that at our goal line, our fullback is going to carry or else our quarterback. But nobody has two better blockers at our goal line than our two halfbacks. No sir, some backs feel imposed upon to block, but not so for Archie and Brian Baschnagel."

Hayes was rolling, and when he gets rolling, he's unstoppable.

"Your greatest football player willing to do more than his share of blocking—boy, that epitomizes leadership," he added. "He blocks—boy, does Arch block. No fancy Dan. He does anything that needs to be done. He'll catch the big pass that bails you out. He'll block. He'll run. That's why he's so enormously effective and valuable to our team, why our morale is so high, and that's probably why our opponents try so hard to stop him.

"Arch only averages about 20 carries a game," Hayes said, getting back to his original point. "Shucks, if we'd let him run like other teams run their backs, we'd get him 200 yards a game easy."

Hayes repeated that speech almost verbatim for anyone who asked about Griffin. Arch was deserving of the praise, of course, but skeptics believed that Hayes was pushing that second Heisman as much for Ohio State recruiting as for Griffin.

Griffin, for his part, had the utmost respect for his coach. "It's great to play for Coach Hayes," he once said, "because he stresses discipline. You've got to have discipline in anything you do in life."

That admiration for Hayes has stuck with Arch over the years, even after a shocking incident when Woody punched a Clemson player during the 1978 Gator Bowl. That emotional outburst cost Hayes his job after 28 years at the Buckeyes' helm.

"He's an intense man," Griffin said of his college coach. "When he's coaching, it's like he is playing. He's just like the players. It (hitting the Clemson player) was just an instance where he lost his cool. . . . I knew something would be done (about replacing Hayes at Ohio State). For me, it's forgivable, knowing the man."

Griffin, of course, did win the second Heisman, and again the vote was not even close. Arch tallied 1,800 points, compared with 730 for Muncie. The Heisman announcement was followed by some criticism, but, in retrospect, not nearly as severe as that directed at Hayes for his ill-timed Gator Bowl jab.

"That (the Heisman criticism) did bother me a bit," Griffin said, "but if it meant giving the trophy back, I wasn't going to give it back. If Muncie had gotten it, people would have said, 'Well, Dorsett deserved it.' There will always be comment and criticism. You can't satisfy everyone."

Griffin's eyes were dry during his second Heisman acceptance speech. "It was pretty much giving everyone the praise they deserved," he reflected. The next day, Griffin was back in Columbus, studying for final exams and beginning practice for the Rose Bowl.

Ohio State was 11-0 and ranked No. 1. A Rose Bowl victory would give the Buckeyes the national championship. However, UCLA Coach Dick Vermeil had done his homework after the Bruins' earlier 21-point defeat to the Buckeyes and was much better prepared the second time around.

Griffin played valiantly with a broken hand, carrying 17 times for 93 yards, but UCLA broke the game open in the second half to win going away, 23-10. Ohio State's national championship flew out of the Rose Bowl Stadium and disappeared over the San Gabriel Mountains. "That game was the biggest disappointment of my career," Griffin recalled sadly. The incredible phase of Archie Griffin's life had ended on a real downer.

He graduated from Ohio State one quarter ahead of his class—now *that's* a switch for an athlete—with a 2.6 grade-point average on a 4.0 scale. Griffin took his degree in industrial relations manpower early for a reason: To talk to youngsters about how to pull themselves up by their sneakers and get their lives headed in the right direction, just as Griffin had done nearly a decade before as a blubbery child. Griffin's motto was Desire, Dedication and Determination, and he spread the "three Ds" to school kids throughout Ohio. The main thrust of his speeches was to encourage children to learn how to read, an appropriate message coming from an athlete who had graduated early.

It was a perfect job for him. "Kids look up to him," Bob Stuart, Griffin's high school coach, once told a reporter, "because Archie lives the kind of life he talks. He's normally not very talkative, but he's great talking to kids."

Griffin, who had been active in the university's Fellowship of Christian Athletes chapter, coupled his motivational talks with warnings about drugs. "What I want most . . . the one contribution I'd most want to make, is to influence young people to stay away from drugs," he said back when he was making regular visits to elementary and junior high classrooms.

Griffin married Loretta Laffitte on June 26, 1976, and moved onto the next phase of his life—the National Football League. Cincinnati selected Griffin with its second pick of the first round (24th pick overall) in the 1976 draft. Oklahoma wide receiver Billy Brooks was the Bengals' first choice.

"When you first look at him," Bengals Coach Bill Johnson said of Griffin, "you say, 'My God, look how little he is.' "

Arch did not feel slighted by those teams that passed him over in the draft, ostensibly because of his size. "I have decided there are two things in my favor," he said philosophically at the time. "First, going high in the draft usually means you are being taken by a losing team. And second, the oversight by the top 23 meant that I could go with a club in the state in which I was raised."

He also pointed out the mistake many people make by connecting the Heisman with professional potential. "A lot of people are confused over what the Heisman is all about," he said. "It doesn't mean you are the best prospect in pro football. It simply means that you were an effective player in college."

In Griffin's first pro game, the '76 preseason opener against Green Bay, he rushed for 49 yards on 12 carries and scored one touchdown. The next week he scooted 49 yards on one carry to score a touchdown against Buffalo. He carried that momentum into the regular season and had his greatest game as a Bengal late in the year against Kansas City—139 yards rushing, including a 77-yard touchdown run.

He finished his rookie year with 625 yards rushing on 138 carries (4.5 average), 16 pass receptions for 138 yards and three touchdowns. The only season in which Griffin came close to matching or surpassing those statistics was in 1979, when he rushed 140 times for 688 yards (4.9 average), caught 43 passes for 417 yards and scored two touchdowns. Though he was a steady player for the Bengals, Arch never achieved the dominance he enjoyed as a college player.

"When I came into pro ball, I had high expectations," Griffin said. "I wanted to gain 1,000 yards in a season, but then I realized that I wouldn't carry the ball enough. I never had 20 carries a game; the most I had was 18."

At first, Boobie Clark had the majority of carries and led the team in rushing. Next came Pete Johnson, Griffin's teammate at Ohio State. Cincinnati then drafted Louisiana State's 6-1, 226-pound Charles Alexander in order to have a larger back to pair with Johnson. Thus, Griffin went from a regular starter to a backup runner and a pass receiver.

"When I got to Cincinnati," he said, "I was used in the running game. When I left, I was used in the passing game."

The Bengals maintained their confidence in and support of Griffin as long as he was healthy enough to play, even though he was not stinging NFL opponents the way he had at Ohio State. "We're not disappointed one bit in him," Bengals General Manager Paul Brown said early in the '79 season. "He's just what we thought he'd be. He's responsible, solid, and makes very few errors. He plays if it's snowing, raining, hailing. And the most impressive thing is the way he's taken to the pass offense. This man has learned all about catching a football, and he never saw a pass in college (a slight exaggeration since he caught 30 passes as a Buckeye)."

As a pro, Griffin continued to give inspirational talks to youngsters and remained involved in Campus Crusade for Christ and the FCA. "I try to get it across to them that if they apply these things . . . there is no reason to fail," he once said. "Then I end it up giving a little testimony, tell them the effect of Jesus Christ on my life."

Arch once tried to change his Bengals jersey number from 45 to 1 as a symbol of his religious beliefs. "I wanted the number because Christ is first in my life, and I wanted Number 1 to be symbolic," he explained. "The NFL told me all running backs are 20 to 49."

When the Bengals made it to Super Bowl XVI after the 1981 season, Griffin was used sparingly. He rushed one time for four yards. But his only Super Bowl experience will be remembered for another play, a kickoff return just before halftime. Griffin fumbled a squib kick and the 49ers recovered, setting up a 26-yard Ray Wersching field goal to extend their lead to 20-0. San Francisco eventually won, 26-21.

That same season, Griffin watched Southern Cal's Marcus Allen receive the Heisman on television, and he cried. Griffin hadn't forgotten what it was like. That happened a year after he had asked the Bengals to trade him in what might be his last chance to prove that he could play with the big boys. "I really don't know what pro football has against small backs," he wondered. "I've been popped good, but that doesn't mean I can't compete with the others."

Griffin isn't certain the Bengals tried seriously to trade him, but he didn't show public outrage when he wasn't. He remained a model team player until the end, which was, for all intents and purposes, the summer of 1983. In the Bengals' preseason finale, he pulled muscles in his stomach and groin. He tried to come back midway through the season but pulled the same muscles again.

The Bengals did not offer Griffin a new contract when his old one expired after the '83 season. It obviously was not an easy decision for the club's general manager to make.

"Archie Griffin is a class person," Brown said. "We haven't had anybody with better character on our team. . . . He did a lot of good things for us. He made important plays for us over his career. . . . I don't think he has to apologize for his pro football career."

Neither does Griffin. In his mind, he stood tall in his eight seasons with the Bengals. He left Cincinnati as the club's fourth-leading rusher (2,808 yards) and fifth-leading receiver (192 receptions) of all time.

"People don't think I'm happy with my NFL career," he said. "But I averaged four yards a carry and I caught a lot of passes. I had a good Super Bowl year when

*Archie Griffin found reason to flash a big smile during a break in his 1985 fling with the United States Football League's Jacksonville Bulls.*

Charles was hurt. I really do feel satisfied."

Alexander, in spite of his size advantage over Griffin, had a career rushing average through 1984 of 3.5 yards. That's a little more than a half-yard below Griffin's. Computers, stopwatches and yardsticks can measure almost everything there is to know about a running back—except what's in his heart. Griffin's heart was filled with desire, dedication and determination—the three Ds.

Griffin began a business venture, while still with the Bengals, that ended disastrously. Three Griffin brothers—Archie, Ray and James Jr.—owned an athletic footwear business, Griffin Shoe Corp., which piled up more than $200,000 in debts by November 1981. Most of that total was sought by the Ohio Department of Taxation for sales tax and by manufacturers who had made loans to the Griffins.

"We expanded too fast," Archie said. "We had six or seven stores, and times weren't good for retail business.

"It caused us some problems in the family. It was a strain. I lost a lot of money myself. It was just something that happened, but we had to declare bankruptcy. It's over now. Things are better in the family. But I still don't joke about it."

On the suggestion of Woody Hayes, Griffin went to work for his alma mater in March 1984. "He felt I would be a good asset," Griffin said. "I feel the same way. College, in general, was the greatest time of my life—the people I know, the people who helped me, the education I received. Those things will be with me forever. The Heisman is a part of all this."

Within five months, Griffin had become Ohio State's acting assistant director of staff employment. "My job is to place displaced persons into civil service jobs," he explained, sitting in his office on the south side of campus in the fall of 1984. "They're trade jobs—like electricians and dispatchers—and clerk jobs. . . . I'm in charge of civil service testing on campus, screening the applicants, plus the problems that come across this desk, like layoffs and dissolving of jobs. I have a lot of paperwork and phone work, too."

Griffin was happy with his new job, and he appeared settled in this post-football career with the university. He and his family, which now included Loretta and their son, Anthony, and daughter, Andrea, were comfortable in Columbus. Many people speculated that he eventually would wind up in the Ohio State athletic department. But such advancement was postponed, at least temporarily, when he signed a contract with the Jacksonville Bulls of the USFL on January 22, 1985.

Griffin negotiated his own contract. "I wanted the experience," he explained.

Bulls Coach Lindy Infante planned to use the same offense he had installed in Cincinnati as the Bengals' offensive coordinator—a single-back system, predominantly. Griffin had played in Infante's offense in Cincinnati, and so the coach planned to use him as the single back, an opportunity that prompted Griffin to come out of retirement.

Then Jacksonville signed Mike Rozier, the 1983 Heisman winner from Nebraska, who was a free agent after playing for the USFL's Pittsburgh Maulers in 1984. Rozier became the single back, while Griffin became a halfback who carried the ball little, caught it less frequently and split out as a receiver much of the time. The role had a familiar ring to it.

"I didn't want to end my career doing the same things I did in Cincinnati," he said.

Jacksonville's fourth game of the 1985 season was in Oakland on March 17. Rozier carried 17 times for 70 yards, Griffin three times for three yards. After the game, which the Bulls lost, 42-36, Griffin appeared before the press. He smiled, an orthodontist-created smile of perfect teeth and no braces, and told the reporters, "You can't judge a person on three carries."

Said Infante: "I told Archie I wish he could have more yards. Archie understands. He is very professional in his approach.

"Archie's a credit to every place he has been. The greatest compliment you can pay a person is that you hope your kids will grow up to be like him. I've got two kids, and I hope they grow up to be like Archie."

Two days later, Griffin announced his retirement. This time, he affirmed, it would be permanent.

"I felt I should hang it up," he said. "I had thought about it (retirement) during the season, so it wasn't a big decision. I had to get football out of my system, and now it's gone. It's time to get on with life's work."

On the morning of March 26, Griffin arrived back in Columbus from Jacksonville. His leave of absence from Ohio State ran five more days, and then he returned to his desk at the staff employment office. But lo and behold, two months later he was named to a post in the athletic department. As special assistant to Athletic Director Rick Bay, Griffin now does public relations and fund-raising work for the Ohio State athletic program.

"There are a lot of opportunities to have at the university," he said about the future. "Right now, I'm thinking of working here for the rest of my life. The university has been good for me. I'd like to feel I've been good for it.

"I'd like to nurture that relationship."

# Other Winners

*They are as different as night and day. Yet all have a common bond — the superior athletic ability that resulted in a Heisman Trophy. Following are short profiles of the other 32 men who captured America's football fancy and were rewarded with the sport's highest honor. To some it has meant fame and fortune. To others it has meant little in terms of material rewards. But all have that special satisfaction of having carved their own little spot in sports history.*

# Chapter 18

# The rest of the best

## CLINT FRANK
### Yale—1937

Clint Frank looked like a walking—or limping—advertisement for an adhesive tape company his senior football season at Yale in 1937. "My ankles were taped, and so were my shoulders, my wrists and, I'm sure, a few other places," he said. "I didn't have my knees taped, but maybe I should have from the way they feel today."

Frank's 5-foot-10, 175-pound body took a severe pounding that long-ago autumn in New Haven, Conn., when he was called "the most taped player of our time." But he didn't miss one game for Yale, for he had something else holding him together besides adhesive.

"Desire," he said. "That's what made great players then, and that's what makes them today. That part of football never changes."

Without desire, Frank wouldn't have played football at Yale. As a high school senior in Evanston, Ill., he injured his shoulder seriously enough that doctors told him to give up football. He didn't play the sport in prep school or during his freshman year at Yale. But he turned out as a sophomore with a special pad to protect the shoulder.

As a junior in 1936, Frank and Larry Kelley were considered the greatest two-man team in the country on the basis of Frank's marvelous passes and Kelley's miraculous catches.

In 1937, the Bulldogs were rated average in ability. That assessment would have been true except for Frank. His passing, running and gritty overall play kept Yale undefeated until the final, traditional game of the year against Harvard. Frank, who was labeled by Yale assistant coach Earle (Greasy) Neale as "the best back Yale ever had and a miracle on defense," scored four touchdowns against Princeton, one on a 77-yard run. Only a tie against Dartmouth marred the season up until the Harvard game, when Yale was beaten, 13-6. "It was a sad day," Frank said. Spoken like a true Yalie.

Frank, a consensus All-America and the team captain, won the third Heisman Memorial Trophy with 524 points. Byron (Whizzer) White of Colorado, now a U.S. Supreme Court justice, was runner-up with 264.

Frank entered the advertising field after college. In 1941, he was drafted into the Army and served as an aide to Gen. James Doolittle. After the war, he and two other men formed their own advertising company in Chicago. In 1953, Frank bought out his partners, then expanded the agency to New York, Los Angeles, Dallas, Houston, San Francisco and Richmond, Va. When he sold his company to Interpublic in 1976, Clinton E. Frank Inc. was the 23rd-largest advertising agency in the United States.

Frank had detached retinas in both eyes, and at different times he was legally blind in each eye. Two operations, in 1962 and 1972, restored his vision. A knee injury dating to his football-playing days required surgery in 1985.

Frank lives in Northbrook, Ill., and heads the Bridlewood Corp., a private holding company created in 1977 from the non-advertising assets of Clinton E. Frank Inc.

# DAVEY O'BRIEN
## Texas Christian — 1938

There never was any argument about how good Davey O'Brien was. Just how tall. Some football historians contend he was 5-foot-7, others 5-5. Reportedly, a physical examination required when O'Brien joined the Federal Bureau of Investigation measured him at 5-5.

"He was bigger than that," said Mason Mayne, a Texas Christian guard who played with quarterbacks Sammy Baugh and O'Brien. "I was in the FBI with Davey for a time, and he was about the same size as my wife. She's 5-7.

"Davey was a little guy, but he was as tough as scrap iron. He was very strong for someone 150 pounds, but the greatest thing he had was tenacity. You knew he could take you down the field."

O'Brien was the fourth Heisman winner and the first to bring the trophy west of the Mississippi. In 1938, he completed 55.7 percent of his passes, 19 for touchdowns, and threw only four interceptions. He led the Horned Frogs to an 11-0 season, including a 15-7 Sugar Bowl victory over Carnegie Tech as O'Brien threw a 44-yard touchdown pass and kicked a field goal. Texas Christian won the national championship.

"Davey was the first quarterback to really step up in the pocket," Mayne said. "I don't remember Sammy, who was two years ahead of Davey, doing it that much. Davey would duck under those big linemen, step up and throw, even though the natural reaction in those days was to run from trouble. Davey's attitude was, 'I don't go anywhere without my friends.' "

O'Brien was honored at a parade in New York prior to his Heisman presentation. His mother was quoted thusly after her son received the trophy: "At first I was afraid that Davey might be hurt (playing football) because he is so small compared to the other players. But gradually I came to realize that defeat hurt my boy more than physical injury. After that, I concentrated on the score."

The Philadelphia Eagles reportedly gave O'Brien a $12,000 bonus and $10,000 per year plus a percentage of the gate to entice him away from a career in geology. In his rookie season, 1939, he passed for an NFL-record 1,324 yards. The next year he set more league marks with 60 passes in one game, completing 33 against Washington and Baugh.

After winning just two games in two years, O'Brien joined the FBI and became a crack shot with a pistol and a rifle.

"I used to bury a hatchet in a tree," Mayne said, "and nail an object on either side. With one shot, Davey could split a bullet on the hatchet, and half of the bullet would hit each of the objects."

In the 1950s, O'Brien retired from the FBI and became a business executive. He died on November 18, 1977, after a long battle with cancer. A Fort Worth club now presents a trophy annually in his name to the club's choice as the best quarterback in the country.

"Davey got so sick, his weight dropped to 125 pounds," Mayne said. "He thought by some miracle that he'd beat cancer. He didn't know what the word 'surrender' meant.

"I never saw anyone as tough as he was. He was double tough."

# BRUCE SMITH
## Minnesota—1941

Lucius Smith doesn't practice law eight hours a day anymore. But he does put in 7½ hours, which is a good day's work for someone who celebrated his 94th birthday in 1985 and has been an attorney since 1912.

At precisely 4:30 every afternoon, a taxi shows up at his law office and drives him back to the rest home in Faribault, Minn. There, with supper waiting on the table one evening, he broke away to talk about his late son Bruce.

"I say this advisedly because of my being his father, but he was a most modest young man," he said. "Yet he was thought of as the toughest opponent. Ohio State voted him the toughest player they had played against.

"And Bruce was a handsome young man. When he went to Hollywood to make a play ("Smith of Minnesota," a movie), someone wrote on his scrapbook, 'The Clark Gable of the movies.'

"One of the starlets followed him back to Faribault. A nice girl, very beautiful. But she went home. Bruce cared a lot for her, but he didn't want to marry her."

Bruce Smith didn't have glittering statistics, but he was superb in the clutch, hence his nickname, "The Game Breaker." His most famous touchdown was an 80-yard run on a muddy field that beat Michigan and Tom Harmon, 7-6, in 1940.

Smith had a number of great days, but he saved his finest effort for his final game as a Gopher. Playing on a gimpy knee against Wisconsin, Smith ignited Minnesota with a 45-yard pass to Bill Garnaas, then followed with an 18-yard touchdown run for the first score of the game. Smith later faked a pass and ran 42 yards to the Badger 5-yard line, where he lateraled the ball to Bob Fitch, who carried it into the end zone. Smith set up the Gophers' third score by returning an interception 43 yards to the Badger 11. And for his finale, he threw a 20-yard scoring pass to Bill Daley before being helped off the field. Minnesota won, 41-6, to wrap up its second consecutive unbeaten, national championship season.

The 6-foot, 193-pound Smith wasn't fast, but he was a strong runner with cutback ability. He was the first Minnesota player to have his number (54) retired.

He received the Heisman two days after the Japanese attacked Pearl Harbor. "Those Far Eastern fellows," he said in his acceptance speech, "may think that American boys are soft, but I have had, and even now have, plenty of evidence in 'black and blue' to show that they are making a big mistake. I think America will owe a great debt to the game of football when we finish this thing off. . . . It teaches team play and cooperation and eggs us on to go out and fight hard for the honor of our school. And likewise, that same spirit can be depended on when we have to fight like blazes to defend our country."

Smith passed the physical examination to enter the U.S. Naval Reserves even though he had badly torn cartilage in one knee. In essence, he made it into the Navy on one leg. He was the most valuable player in the 1942 College All-Star Game, was a standout in service football and then played four NFL seasons with Green Bay and Los Angeles.

He married a Philadelphia model, returned to Faribault and became the father of four children. He sold sporting goods and lawn mowers for a while, then men's formal clothing. "He was a terrific salesman," his father said, "but he didn't have a real specialty. Football was his life."

Bruce Smith died of cancer in 1967.

# FRANK SINKWICH
## Georgia—1942

Take it from Frank Sinkwich, having flat feet is no way to run for the Heisman Trophy.

"They didn't help at all," he said. "Flat feet make the muscles tighten up in your legs. My feet bothered me all the time when I played football. They still do."

Flat-Foot Frankie, one of several sobriquets he picked up at Georgia, flip-flopped his way to a national career total offense record of 4,602 yards while becoming the first Heisman winner in the Deep South.

"What got me the national publicity was when I broke my jaw my junior year and continued to play," he said.

Sinkwich wore an aluminum mask that season and led Georgia to the Orange Bowl as he finished fourth in the Heisman voting. His fantastic performance in the Orange Bowl gained him even more publicity and made Sinkwich the leading Heisman candidate the next fall.

Against Texas Christian in Miami, Sinkwich left the Horned Frogs flat-footed as he threw for 243 yards and three touchdowns and ran for 139 yards and another touchdown. Sinkwich's 382 yards of offense was an Orange Bowl record, and the Bulldogs won, 40-26.

Though playing with sprained ankles most of his senior year, Fireball Frankie, another of his bynames, amassed 2,187 yards of offense, becoming the first collegian to break the 2,000-yard barrier in a single season, and accounted for 26 touchdowns to lead the nation. He scored Georgia's only touchdown in a 9-0 Rose Bowl victory over UCLA.

Sinkwich was an overwhelming choice as the 1942 Heisman winner. He received 1,059 points, compared with 218 for Columbia's Paul Governali, the runner-up. Sinkwich was the first Heisman recipient to lead all five voting districts. Instead of receiving the actual Heisman Trophy in 1942, he was presented a scroll designating him as the winner. Because of a shortage of war materials, the Heisman committee decided that a trophy should not be cast at that time. Sinkwich received his trophy several years later.

Sinkwich enlisted in the Marines after the 1942 season but received a medical discharge because of his flat feet. He played for the Detroit Lions in 1943-44, being named the NFL's Most Valuable Player in the latter season. He then was accepted into the Army Air Corps and tore up his knee in a service football game. He later spent two years in the All-America Football Conference with New York and Baltimore, but the knee had reduced his effectiveness, and he retired in 1947.

Sinkwich coached at the University of Tampa from 1950-51 and then opened a furniture store in Athens, Ga., near the Georgia campus. He now is partners with a son and daughter in a wholesale beer distributorship in Athens.

# ANGELO BERTELLI
## Notre Dame—1943

Angelo Bertelli is the only football player to have won the Heisman Trophy on a half-season's work.

"The combination of war, a national championship team and my previous two years accounted for that," he explained. "It was an odd time."

Bertelli finished second in the Heisman balloting as a sophomore, sixth as a junior. As a senior in 1943, he played in only six of Notre Dame's 10 games, but the Irish averaged 43.5 points per game with Bertelli at quarterback.

That average dropped to 19.8 points when he joined the Marines and was sent to Parris Island, S.C. Boot camp lasted 10 weeks, and the Marines denied Bertelli permission to travel to New York for the December 8 Heisman ceremony. The presentation was rescheduled for January, when Bertelli was on furlough.

Even with the delay, Bertelli hadn't forgotten how he had earned the trophy. He thanked his mother, who had been widowed in 1938, for rearing him properly. And he thanked his coach, Frank Leahy, for rescuing his college career.

"I was a fourth-string tailback on the freshman team and a terrible runner," he said. "And there were three varsity tailbacks coming back the next year. Then Leahy became our coach. He remembered what he had had at Boston College, a passing quarterback in Charlie O'Rourke, and I went from seventh string to first string overnight."

Bertelli had a strong passing arm. Leahy, however, did not change to the T-formation, the system under which "Angelo the Arm" truly flourished, until 1942. So, Bertelli was a passing single-wing tailback in 1941, completing 70 of 123 attempts for 1,027 yards and eight touchdowns while leading Notre Dame to an 8-0-1 season.

A year later, the 6-foot-1, 173-pound quarterback connected on 72 of 159 passes for 1,039 yards and 10 touchdowns. In so doing, he impressed the nation's most famous sportswriter with his deception.

"The T-formation was all faking back then," said Bertelli, who also excelled as a defensive back and kicker. "Grantland Rice called me the 'T-formation magician.' He was very good to me."

Angelo the Arm threw for 10 touchdowns (on only 36 pass attempts) and scored a career-high four TDs in six games as a senior before hurrying off to war. Notre Dame went on to complete a 9-1 season, losing only to Great Lakes Naval

Training Station, 19-14, in its final game. The Fighting Irish still won the national title.

Bertelli distinguished himself as a Marine on Iwo Jima and Guam. He spent three seasons in the All-America Football Conference, with the Los Angeles Dons and the Chicago Rockets, but a knee injury that sidelined him much of the last two seasons and required three operations eventually forced him to retire.

Bertelli now owns five liquor stores in Clifton, N.J., plus holdings in a plastics company and real estate.

"Life has been good," he said.

# LES HORVATH
## Ohio State—1944

After Les Horvath, the football-playing dentist, retired from pro football, he married. His wife, Shirley, wanted to know about the trophy on the shelf. Horvath explained that the trophy is given only to a select group of men. Shirley was impressed.

It just so happened that the Horvaths were practically neighbors with Tom and Elyse Harmon and Glenn and Harriet Davis. The three couples were often guests at one another's Los Angeles homes. Shirley noticed that the same trophy was in the Harmon and Davis homes.

In 1955, Notre Dame was playing in Los Angeles, and the Horvaths were invited to a party at which Terry Brennan, the Irish coach, was present. Shirley said she wanted to meet Brennan, and Horvath brought him over.

"Why do you want to meet me? I'm just a coach," Brennan told Shirley. "Your husband is a really big star. He won the Heisman Trophy."

"Oh, that's not such a big deal," Shirley told Brennan. "Everyone in Los Angeles seems to have one."

Horvath had defeated Davis for the Heisman in 1944, when they finished 1-2 in the voting. "It was a pure accident that I won," Horvath said. "I didn't even play football the year before. I was in the Army Specialized Training Corps as a dental student. Although I was still taking classes at Ohio State, those in the ASTC couldn't play college sports."

In 1944, the Army determined it had enough dentists, and Horvath received his discharge. The NFL's Cleveland Rams offered him $5,000 to turn professional, but Horvath wanted to complete his dental education. He turned out for football at Ohio State even though the Buckeye coaches were dubious that the little 5-foot-10, 167-pounder could get in good-enough shape to make the team after the year's layoff. He not only made the team, he *made* the team.

The Buckeyes were predominantly freshmen that fall, but Horvath led them to Ohio State's first undefeated, untied season (9-0) in 28 years. Though he had dental labs to attend before practice, and occasionally on Saturday mornings before games, Horvath rushed for 905 yards (5.6 average) and scored 12 touchdowns. The Buckeyes used the single wing about 75 percent of the time, and Horvath was the tailback. "I probably excelled as a runner," he said. "I had good balance and well-developed legs. I was just sort of an average passer." He threw only 31 passes as a senior but completed 14 for 345 yards and four touchdowns.

In his final game for Ohio State, the man known as the "Playing Coach" was hobbled by injuries but still scored two of the Buckeyes' three touchdowns in an 18-14 victory over Michigan that locked up the conference championship.

"When I was called into the dean's office to learn that I had won the Heisman, I was stunned," he said. "I had no idea I was even in the running."

Horvath played for two years with the Los Angeles Rams and one season with the Cleveland Browns before starting his dental practice in Los Angeles. At one time, he was the Rams' team dentist.

# JOHNNY LUJACK
## Notre Dame—1947

Johnny Lujack's fame is sealed for decades to come as one of the finest T-formation college football quarterbacks ever, but he is remembered mainly for his defense—and one play in particular.

In the battle of the titans, Notre Dame vs. Army in 1946, Doc Blanchard, the Cadets' great fullback, was barreling freely down the sideline toward a certain touchdown. Only one player, Lujack, the Fighting Irish's 6-foot, 180-pound junior defensive back, had a chance to stop him.

"We were both going at full speed, and he tried to give me a little juke," Lujack said, recalling the play from his automobile dealership in Davenport, Ia. "I just happened to corner the bear. I got both arms around his ankles, and he went down solid."

Lujack's tackle is one of the most famous in modern football, not only because it preserved a scoreless tie, but also because one future Heisman Trophy winner had dropped the reigning winner.

For all his offensive greatness in college, it was Lujack's defense that first brought him attention after arriving at Notre Dame. Lujack's fierce tackling in a freshman drill against the Notre Dame varsity made him an instant favorite with the Irish coaches. His career ascended from there.

Lujack became Notre Dame's quarterback in the seventh game of the 1943 season after Angelo Bertelli, the Heisman hero of that fall, joined the Marines. In Lujack's first start, against Army, he threw two touchdown passes, ran for another score and intercepted a pass in a 26-0 victory.

He went into the Navy after that season and returned to South Bend, Ind., in 1946. In two-plus seasons as a college starter, Lujack's record was 20-1-1, and Notre Dame won three national championships.

"I wasn't real fast, but I was quick and I had good instincts," he said. "I could plan in my mind what the other team was trying to do, which enabled me to anticipate the next play.

"I'm not in a position to judge what made me the Heisman winner. That's for others to do. But I could run, pass, kick, play defense. And playing for Notre Dame, losing one game in three years, being the quarterback . . . it probably was a combination of all that."

Lujack played for four years in the National Football League with the Chicago

Bears after becoming an instant sensation—on defense. He intercepted eight passes as a rookie in 1948 to tie a club record. He set a Bears mark the next year by passing for 468 yards in one game (against the Chicago Cardinals). Lujack was named an All-Pro quarterback in 1950 and played in the NFL's Pro Bowl after the 1950 and '51 seasons. He retired from pro football before the '52 season to become Notre Dame's backfield coach for two years. He then entered the sports broadcasting business, a career that kept him busy for several years, and now runs his auto agency.

# DOAK WALKER
## Southern Methodist—1948

Shortly after Doak Walker was born, his father told friends, "I've got an All-America." Doak's daddy wasn't wasting words because his son would become a three-time consensus All-America, the 14th Heisman Trophy winner and one of the greatest football players to originate from the Southwest.

"My dad taught me to drop-kick a football over a clothesline when I was 8," Walker recalled. When he enrolled at Southern Methodist, Walker already was a complete football player—runner, passer, kicker, blocker, receiver, return man, defender. "I could do about anything, and excel at it," he said, finally, after considerable prodding to get him to talk about himself. Walker is terribly modest.

He had such a fabulous four-year career at Southern Methodist that it's difficult to decide where to begin in recalling his many accomplishments. His greatest game probably was in a non-winning effort against Texas Christian in 1947, his sophomore year. Walker passed and ran for 223 yards and brought the Mustangs back from a 19-13 deficit with less than 2 minutes left by returning a kickoff 55 yards, then making a fantastic catch and powering his way inside the Horned Frog 10-yard line. Southern Methodist tied the score, but Walker missed the conversion kick.

"I remember that play more than anything I did in college," he said. "I was tired and should have called a timeout. But a lot of good it does now talking about it."

That 19-19 tie ruined an unbeaten, untied season for the Mustangs, but Walker was even more fantastic as a junior in 1948. The 5-foot-11, 168-pound halfback averaged 4.9 yards per rush, passed for six touchdowns, caught three touchdown passes, intercepted three passes, punted for a 42.1-yard average and scored 88 points in becoming the second junior to win the Heisman.

In 1949, Walker had a "bad charley horse" that reduced his playing time. Although he had his finest year offensively with 1,054 total yards, he wrote Collier's, asking the magazine not to consider him on its All-America team. "They considered me anyway," he said, "naming me as a fifth All-America back."

Walker finished third in the '49 Heisman race (he also was third in 1947) after amassing 3,582 yards of total offense and 288 points for his career, making him the finest all-around football player in Southern Methodist history.

He married the campus queen and went on to a productive career in the National Football League with the Detroit Lions (1950-55). Walker led the league in scoring twice (including his rookie season) and played in five Pro Bowls and on two NFL championship teams.

His first marriage, which produced four children, ended in divorce. After that, he became "the guinea pig" in a newspaper promotion on how to learn to ski in six lessons. His instructor was Skeeter Werner from the famous Werner skiing family. Doak and Skeeter later were married. "She asked me," Walker said. "She'll be the first to tell you."

Walker is vice president for a mechanical and electrical contracting company in Denver, and he also has a home in Steamboat Springs, Colo.

# VIC JANOWICZ
## Ohio State—1950

Vic Janowicz might have been the first two-time Heisman Trophy winner not only at Ohio State, but also in the United States, if he hadn't had the misfortune to run into Woody Hayes.

In 1950, Janowicz became the third junior to receive the Heisman, following Doc Blanchard in 1945 and Doak Walker in 1948. While Blanchard and Walker had injuries that drastically reduced their chances of repeating as Heisman recipients as seniors, Janowicz was perfectly healthy. But he didn't even finish among the top 10 Heisman vote-getters in 1951. "Woody used me as a decoy," he explained.

Janowicz's last year at Ohio State was Hayes' first. Hayes immediately dropped the single-wing offense of his predecessor, Wes Fesler, and installed the split-T, which Bud Wilkinson was having success with at Oklahoma. The single wing was made for Janowicz's versatile skills; the split-T was not. He and Hayes had a philosophical difference.

"Absolutely," Janowicz said emphatically. "You know what Woody's offense is like. Well, I still haven't figured it out. The only time he used me as a senior was when the going got tough. That's when I got the ball.

"I think the world of Woody Hayes. But he has said at some banquets that the only thing that stopped me as a senior was Woody Hayes."

Janowicz, from Elyria, O., was the most heavily recruited high school football player in Ohio history up to that time. His immense potential was reached as an Ohio State junior when he amassed 875 yards of total offense and was responsible for 16 touchdowns (11 passing, five running). Against Pittsburgh, he completed all six of his passing attempts, four for touchdowns. In the Buckeyes' 83-21 embarrassment of Iowa, he accounted for 46 points, including a 61-yard punt return.

He ran, passed, punted (36.5-yard average), tackled and handled the place-kicking. Janowicz wasn't big (5-foot-9, 189 pounds), but he was elusive. "I was more finesse," he said. "It was like playing tag as a kid. I didn't want to get tagged then, and I didn't want to get tackled in football."

His rushing yardage improved slightly as a senior, although his carries decreased (114 to 106). As a split-T halfback, he also threw 52 fewer passes than he did as a junior, causing his total offense to drop to 450 yards.

Janowicz is the only Heisman winner to play professional football and baseball. He spent two years with the Pittsburgh Pirates, 1953-54, as a catcher and third baseman. He then played the 1954-55 seasons with the Washington Redskins, leading the team in rushing and scoring in '55.

Tragedy struck twice in 1956. Janowicz learned that his daughter, Diana (one of his three children), had contracted cerebral palsy, a disease that took her life eight years later. Also that year, Janowicz was involved in an automobile accident that nearly took his life, ended his athletic career and, eventually, paralyzed the left side of his body.

Through physical therapy, Janowicz was able to overcome the paralysis. But in 1979, the car he was driving was rear-ended by a van in Columbus, O. He has had severe headaches ever since. Numerous doctors have examined him, but the headaches persist. "I just have to live with them," he said dejectedly.

Even after two car accidents, Janowicz drives 35,000 miles per year as a traveling salesman for an Ohio company that makes steel strappings.

By his count, Janowicz has attended the last 15 Heisman alumni dinners in New York. "They lift my life," he said.

# BILLY VESSELS
## Oklahoma — 1952

Billy Vessels is the friend of Presidents. He fished with Richard Nixon. Gerald Ford singled out Vessels for a private conversation in a room filled with football greats on the night in 1974 when Vessels was inducted into the College Football Hall of Fame.

"Billy is a first-class gentleman," Ford said recently.

Vessels campaigned for John F. Kennedy and served on his Physical Fitness Council. Vessels knew Lyndon Johnson, although Texans, whether they held the nation's highest office or not, were very much aware of Vessels, the Heisman Trophy-winning halfback from rival Oklahoma.

Vessels never thought as a boy that he would mingle with Presidents. When his parents moved from Cleveland, Okla., to Oklahoma City so his father could take a civilian mechanic's job at an Air Force base, Vessels, then 15, stayed behind. He lived, at times, by himself in the home his parents still owned, and, at other times, with another family. He worked in a drugstore, feed store and bank to help support himself. "You learn maturity," he said of that period of his life.

At Oklahoma, he needed maturity to get through several small crises. He had scholastic problems as a freshman, but he remained eligible for football by buckling down with the books and attending summer school. He rushed for 870 yards and scored 15 touchdowns as a Sooner sophomore, then missed six games as a junior with a broken leg.

He rebounded as a senior with 1,072 yards rushing and a nation-leading 18 touchdowns. The 6-foot, 185-pounder turned in one of the best individual efforts ever against a Frank Leahy-coached team when he rushed for 195 yards on 17 carries (11.5 average) and three touchdowns, including two long runs and a 28-yard reception, at South Bend, Ind. But Oklahoma lost, 27-21, in its first game ever against Notre Dame, and Vessels was crushed.

"It was not a good game for me because we lost," he said. "It ruined my entire season. It took me 10 years, no 14, to get over that defeat."

Nevertheless, he added, that game earned him the Heisman Trophy, even though Vessels thought his teammate, quarterback Eddie Crowder, was more deserving of the award.

"Billy was a remarkable athlete," said Bud Wilkinson, his coach at Oklahoma. "He was the first player that I had ever been around who was the fastest player on the field and also the toughest. Those two things don't normally go together."

Vessels played in the Canadian Football League in 1953, at Edmonton, and won the Schenley Award as the league's most outstanding player. He starred in service football while serving in the Army from 1954-56, then played for the Baltimore Colts in 1956 before injuring his knee and retiring from the gridiron.

He has lived in Coral Gables, Fla., since that time, working in real estate. "I guess you could say I'm retired now, although I'm still looking," he said, laughing.

A very likable, modest man, Vessels works tirelessly at numerous civic projects, wanting no credit—just like his football days at Oklahoma.

# JOHNNY LATTNER
## Notre Dame—1953

"I don't think I was that good," Johnny Lattner said. "If it was the two-platoon system, I never would have won."

Lattner was a narrow winner of the Heisman Trophy in 1953. The 6-foot-1, 190-pound halfback received 1,850 points, while Paul Giel of Minnesota was second with 1,794. The 56-point difference is the second-closest margin of victory in Heisman history behind Ernie Davis' 53-point edge over Bob Ferguson of Ohio State in 1961.

"Giel was a better offensive back than I was—no ifs, ands or buts about it," Lattner said. "He could run and cut better than I could, and he was a better passer. But in the one platoon, they look at you as an offensive and defensive back."

And the year before as a junior, Lattner was unanimously selected as a consensus All-America while playing both offense *and* defense, even though it was the last year of the two-platoon experiment before college football reverted to the single platoon in 1953. But even then, Lattner didn't think he was any great shakes as a football player.

"The best back I saw was Billy Vessels," Lattner said of the 1952 Heisman winner. "He could run, pass, play defense, and he had speed."

That same '52 season, Lattner fumbled five times against Purdue, which recovered two of those bobbles. "That's the only record I have at Notre Dame," he quipped.

In 1953, Lattner didn't lead the Irish in rushing, passing, scoring or receiving. So how did he win the Heisman?

"I was there at the right time," he replied.

Notre Dame went 9-0-1 in 1953 and was ranked No. 1 in the country by every major rating service except the Associated Press and United Press International. Lattner may not have been the Fighting Irish's best player in any one area, but he was the team's most well-rounded athlete. He played 421 of 600 minutes, scored nine touchdowns, accounted for 855 yards in rushing and receptions, intercepted four passes, had 424 yards on kickoff and punt returns and punted for a 35-yard average. And he did, in fact, set a few school records in the process.

Lattner was best in the big games, especially in front of Heisman voters on the East and West coasts and in Texas. "I came to play," he said, "but the timing was right."

There can't be too many Heisman winners who are more modest than Lattner. It was left up to others to describe what made him an outstanding collegian.

"He is the Eddie Stanky of football," Charlie Callahan, Notre Dame's sports information director, said in 1953. "He can't run, he can't pass, he can't dodge. But he'll beat you every time."

Lattner can't even take a compliment well. "I'd fumble the ball or make some mistakes on defense," he said, "but the ball used to bounce my way a lot. I'd screw up, but (Coach Frank) Leahy would keep me in the game and I'd eventually do something well."

Enough, Johnny, enough!

Lattner had a solid rookie season with the Pittsburgh Steelers in 1954 before entering the military. He injured a knee so severely in a service game that he never played football again.

Lattner opened two restaurants in Chicago. One burned down, the other he sold. He now is an executive with a business forms company.

# ALAN AMECHE
## Wisconsin — 1954

Alan Ameche became a sports agent in 1984, 30 years after winning the Heisman Trophy. But values in sports had changed drastically, he was shocked to learn, and he dropped his new career after only six months, a disillusioned man.

"It was a rude awakening," Ameche said. "I was trying to play by the rules, which I've done all my life. But I was working against guys who break all the rules."

He said he was left with the impression that sports agents, in general, "are totally unscrupulous. I won't tell you all the things they do, but it's awful, absolutely something I can't live with. So I got out. I really didn't need it anyway."

Ameche is a wealthy man. He owned, together with former Baltimore Colts teammate Gino Marchetti, a chain of 550 East Coast restaurants called Gino's. The Marriott Corp. bought the chain in 1982, two years after Ameche had sold his interest in the company. Ameche, an avid tennis player, now operates three indoor tennis clubs he had built in the Philadelphia area.

A tycoon? "I've stayed busy," Ameche replied.

His football career is most closely linked with one play—his touchdown plunge for Baltimore that defeated the New York Giants, 23-17, for the 1958 National Football League championship in the league's first overtime game.

Nicknamed "The Horse" for his durability and punishing running style between the tackles, the 6-foot, 215-pound Ameche played for the Colts from 1955-60 before retiring because of injuries.

"I was always known as a workhorse, starting with my sophomore year in college when I rushed for 946 yards," he said. "From workhorse, the name was changed to Horse. But it had nothing to do with my speed. I was not a stallion."

He was more like a plow horse in college, pounding for 3,212 career yards rushing in 673 attempts (4.8 average) and scoring 25 touchdowns. "I never had outstanding games like O.J. Simpson and Gale Sayers," he said, "but I had a lot of 100-yard games and I played hurt."

Ameche's worst rushing season was his senior year, when he tallied 641 yards on a college-low 146 carries. But he won the Heisman that autumn for a number of reasons: He hadn't missed a game in four years; he played fullback and linebacker his last two seasons after single-platoon football returned, temporarily, to the college scene; he was an academic All-America as well as an All-America in football his last two years, and Ameche came from a famous bloodline. He is a second cousin to actor Don Ameche, a fact that was played up heavily during The Horse's final Heisman run.

Ameche said his running style was similar to Larry Csonka's, "except that I might have been a little faster than Csonka," he said. The Horse earned an entry in "Ripley's Believe It or Not" by galloping 79 yards for a touchdown the first time he carried the ball for Baltimore. "Everybody made their blocks," he explained.

# HOWARD CASSADY
## Ohio State—1955

Hoppy and Hop. They were quite a pair in the 1950s, the nation's most popular cowboy and the country's best college halfback. And both were Buckeyes.

Hopalong Cassidy, the kindly white-haired cowboy affectionately known as Hoppy, was portrayed on television and in the movies by actor William Boyd, who was born in Cambridge, O.

Howard (Hopalong) Cassady, the big-play, versatile star from Woody Hayes' first successful team at Ohio State, was Hop to his friends and grew up in the heart of Buckeye country, Columbus.

The two Hopalongs appeared together at state fairs and parades. When Ohio State played in the Rose Bowl after the 1954 season, Hoppy came to several Buckeye practices.

"I had some pictures taken with him," Hop the halfback said of his experience in Pasadena, Calif. "I'm wearing his guns and he is carrying the football. He later sent me a picture of him, which he signed, 'From one Hopalong to another.'"

Ohio State beat Southern Cal, 20-7, in that Rose Bowl game to complete Hayes' first undefeated season. Cassady rushed for 92 yards on 21 carries and made two open-field tackles of the Trojans' standout breakaway back, Jon Arnett.

As a single-wing tailback at Central High School in Columbus, Cassady was known as Red because of his hair. "But I was always jumping over the line when I ran," he said, "so a number of sportswriters stuck the name Hopalong on me." The cowboy connection would have been made regardless.

"I'm sure the name Hopalong didn't hurt him in winning all those awards,"

Hayes said of Cassady, "but he won them on his own ability. He was a very inspirational player because he was able to turn the game around at any time. Time and time again, he'd make the big play. He was a climax player."

In 1954, Cassady returned an interception 88 yards for a touchdown to break open a close game with a strong Wisconsin team led by Alan Ameche. The Buckeyes won that day, 31-14.

The next year, the 5-foot-10, 172-pound senior rushed for 958 yards (6.0 average) and scored 15 touchdowns. Ohio State finished with a 7-2 record, and Cassady won the Heisman Trophy by nearly a three-to-one margin over runner-up Jim Swink of Texas Christian. Cassady also was named the Associated Press Male Athlete of the Year for 1955.

He spent eight years playing in the National Football League, mainly with the Detroit Lions, and now is a minor league baseball scout for the New York Yankees. He resides in Tampa.

# JOHN DAVID CROW
## Texas A&M—1957

Preparing to play for Coach Paul Bryant was not as difficult for John David Crow as for other youngsters because Crow had a taskmaster at home who was every bit as irascible as the legendary Bear.

"My father was a tough disciplinarian, a very rough person," Crow said of his boyhood in Springhill, La. "He didn't miss many words."

Not that Bryant was easy to play for, because he wasn't. Back in the mid-1950s, when Crow attended Texas A&M, Bryant was the demanding drill sergeant who was as physical as most of his players. Bryant wouldn't become the father figure, the guy who read philosophical sayings to his players, until after he had left Texas A&M to return to his alma mater, Alabama.

"I felt like I was going to die every day in practice," Crow recalled. "I had to get out of school before I ever thought I could like Coach Bryant."

Bryant didn't hit any harder or scream any louder than Crow's father, so the Bear wasn't able to make young John David quit or cower like so many other Aggies.

"I was fortunate to get into a system that matched my personality and upbringing," Crow said. "It was, 'By God, I'll show you I can do it.' "

Crow showed not only Bryant, but also Texas A&M opponents and the nation. As a college senior in 1957, when he won both academic and athletic All-America acclaim, he rushed for 562 yards (4.4 average), completed five of nine passes for 68 yards, scored six touchdowns, kicked one extra point, intercepted five passes and returned punts and kickoffs. It would have been an even more impressive year had Crow not been injured early in the season, but it still was good enough to capture the Heisman Trophy.

"I didn't know what the Heisman was until I won it," Crow said, "but like good wine, it gets better with age."

Bryant, who never coached another Heisman winner, said of Crow: "Watching him play was like watching a grown man play with boys."

Crow did grow to like Bryant. In fact, after Crow spent 11 productive years as a running back and tight end with the Chicago-St. Louis Cardinals and San Francisco 49ers, he rejoined Bryant as an assistant coach at Alabama, where they became close friends. He also was an assistant with the Cleveland Browns and San Diego Chargers.

Before the 1976 season, Crow was named head coach and athletic director at Northeast Louisiana University, making him the first Heisman winner to coach a major-college team. (Frank Sinkwich had coached at the University of Tampa in 1950-51.) He resigned after the 1980 season and now is associate athletic director at Texas A&M, the school that Bryant built into a football power.

"I'm proud of the fact that I helped bring this school from the cellar, or from down pretty low, to national prominence," Crow said.

# BILLY CANNON
## Louisiana State—1959

"Never," Johnny Robinson, Billy Cannon's friend and former teammate, was saying. "No one can figure it out. It's just out of the realm of thinking. As smart as Billy is, why that?"

Dr. Billy Cannon, successful Baton Rouge, La., orthodontist, disgraced himself in 1983 when he was arrested and sent to prison as the mastermind of a counterfeiting scheme that printed and distributed $6 million in $100 bills.

On August 19, 1983, Cannon was sentenced to five years in prison and fined $10,000, the maximum punishment. He entered a federal penitentiary in Texarkana, Tex., three weeks later. He became eligible for parole in May 1985.

Cannon reportedly was earning $300,000 in his dental practice, so why the need to print bogus money? The speculation is bad investments. Court records in Baton Rouge show that Cannon had been involved in 38 civil lawsuits over the years, and that from December 1982 until his arrest on July 9, 1983, five suits totaling more than $500,000 had been filed against him.

U.S. Atty. Stan Bardwell, whose office investigated the counterfeiting operation, said Cannon was a heavy gambler. Cannon also was an easy touch for friends. However, he owned property worth $2.5 million, plus a $500,000 shopping center that housed his dental office, and he had invested $200,000 in a Houston office complex. Adding up all the debts Cannon had to pay upon entering prison, his net worth still was estimated between $2 and $3 million, although he may have been experiencing a cash-flow problem at that time.

If these numbers are correct, or if Cannon is even solvent, why would he resort to something as criminal as counterfeiting? Many of his friends, such as Robinson, don't know because Cannon is living inside a mental prison as well.

"I've asked to come see him, but he hasn't responded," said Robinson, who played with Cannon at Louisiana State and later with the Kansas City Chiefs. "My name is on a list. I sense he doesn't want to see anybody.

"I know a hundred people who are friends of Billy's who want to see him, but they don't know how. People don't know how to do things when someone is in prison or very sick in a hospital. It must be a lonely thing to go through when you're by yourself."

Robinson stays in touch with Cannon's wife, Dorothy, known as Dot to friends. "I talked to her by phone last week," Robinson said in May 1985, "and she is holding up well. Billy's still her hero. He has a successful family life (five children). They're a close family."

Dot Cannon told Robinson, who runs a boys' home in Monroe, La., that Cannon is jogging 12 to 15 miles a day and has cut his weight from 280 pounds to 200, about 20 pounds below what he weighed while leading Louisiana State to the national championship in 1958 and winning the Heisman Trophy in 1959.

Statistically, Cannon had a more impressive season as a junior, but one play as a senior—probably the most famous play in Louisiana football history—guaranteed him the Heisman.

On Halloween night, 1959, Cannon returned a Mississippi punt 89 yards through the rain to give the top-ranked Tigers a 7-3 victory over the third-ranked Rebels. Although Ole Miss turned things around, 21-0, in the Sugar Bowl, Cannon's famous run still is discussed reverently in the Bayou State and is replayed every year on Louisiana television stations the week before the Ole Miss game.

Cannon was a strong back with sprinter's speed who rushed for 1,867 yards, caught 31 passes for 522 yards, scored 24 touchdowns, intercepted seven passes, averaged 36.7 yards per punt and led the Tigers to a 25-7 record (including two bowl games) in three varsity seasons. He then played 11 seasons of professional football for the Houston Oilers, Oakland Raiders and Kansas City. He shifted from running back to tight end and started for the Raiders in Super Bowl II.

Billy Cannon thinks about the past—and the future—in the privacy of his own shame. But will the state that regards Cannon as a living legend be willing to forgive and forget once he comes home from prison?

"The legend thing will help him and hurt him," Robinson said. "The critics will take advantage of that, and the people in Louisiana will still want to keep him a hero, so there will be a conflict. I've already seen comic characters and jokes about Billy. It will probably never pass.

"The biggest question is what Billy will do. My feeling is that he won't go back into the dental profession, although that's what I'd like to see him do. I think he should get out (on parole). He has a talent to use. He wouldn't be harmful to society. But there's a question: Can a felon hold a (dental) license?"

A more important question: Can Billy Cannon, a tarnished legend, survive the inevitable publicity that will swirl about him when he is a free man?

"I would have absolute confidence in him myself," Robinson said. "I don't understand it, but Billy can make it in whatever he wants to do. Only this time it will be harder. If there's another Heisman Trophy in his life, it will be more difficult to win."

# JOE BELLINO
## Navy—1960

As a high school senior, Joe Bellino narrowed his college choices to Army and Navy. When he visited West Point, it was winter, snow was falling, the temperature was freezing and cadets were marching against a backdrop of gray buildings.

"It looked like Siberia on the Hudson," Bellino said.

When he visited Annapolis, it was spring, the sun was shining, flowers were in bloom, midshipmen were sailing on Chesapeake Bay and pretty girls were everywhere. "This is the place for me," Bellino told himself.

Bellino since has learned that West Point also has a picturesque location, but having grown up in Winchester, Mass., where six retired admirals lived at the time and a number of Bellino's high school classmates were Navy offspring, he practically had sailor's blood. It had to be Navy.

Bellino's father had even sailed to this country as an Italian immigrant. Working as a foreman at a tannery, Bellino's father raised six children, although the oldest boys helped support the family. Joe was one of the youngest children, and the first to receive an opportunity to attend college. Bellino did the most with that opportunity, becoming the first midshipman to win the Heisman Trophy.

"Wayne Hardin, my coach, believed that if he had a runner, he'd build the offense around a running game," Bellino said. "If he had a passer, he'd build a passing game. I shudder to think what would have happened if Roger Staubach and I had been in the same backfield."

Staubach won the Heisman under Hardin at Navy in 1963, three years after Bellino received college football's most glorious honor.

"I was a scatterback," Bellino said. "My first step was at top speed. I could hit the hole as fast as anyone, then get outside. I could move laterally without losing speed."

Bellino was 5-foot-9 and 181 pounds, and most of that weight was packed in his legs. "Anyone who hit me there," he said, "was out of luck."

Bellino, who also was a talented catcher on the Navy baseball team, rushed for 834 yards (5.0 average), caught 17 passes for 280 yards and returned punts and kickoffs for another 383 yards in his final season at Annapolis. He scored 18 touchdowns and two conversions for 110 points as Navy finished with a 9-1 record before losing to Missouri in the Orange Bowl.

He served for four years as a naval officer following graduation and then played for three seasons with the Boston Patriots of the American Football League. He now is the marketing director of an automobile leasing financial plan in New England.

Bellino's son, John, was a first-year midshipman at Annapolis in 1985. "He might play lacrosse, but not football," his father said.

# MIKE GARRETT
## Southern California—1965

Mike Garrett had many great games for Southern California, but he said his most memorable performance occurred in a workout.

"It was double-days in fall practice before my sophomore year," he said. "Coach John McKay put the ball on the field, then said to me, 'Now we're going to see how good you are and how tough.' "

Garrett carried the ball anywhere from 12 to 15 consecutive times and scored a touchdown. On the next series, he rushed seven straight times for another touchdown.

The modern perception of the Southern Cal tailback was born that day.

Southern Cal has had great tailbacks for 60 years, from Mort Kaer to Marcus Allen. But Garrett was the first to pack the football 20 to 30 times per game, every game.

His preparation for this heavy-duty role began at Roosevelt High School in Los Angeles, where Garrett was a quarterback in the shotgun formation. "I carried the ball all the time," he said, "and the more I ran, the better I got."

As a Southern Cal sophomore, he averaged 12.8 carries per game. As a junior he averaged 21.7, and as a senior, 26.7. His productivity increased each year until he led the nation in 1965 in carries (267) and rushing yardage (1,440) while averaging 5.4 yards per carry.

At 5-foot-9 and 185 pounds, Garrett wasn't very big, but he made up for it with excellent field vision, balance and body control. He scored 16 touchdowns in an explosive senior year, including 87- and 74-yard punt returns in one game against California. He ran 77 yards from scrimmage against Stanford for another touchdown. And Garrett became the first of all the great Southern Cal football players to win the Heisman Trophy.

"I'm proud that I set the mold for other USC backs," he said, referring to numbers of carries, not the Heisman. "Not to sound conceited, there's a tradition at USC that you never give up. Every game is special and you play with tenacity. We're Trojans. The more you give me the ball, the better I'll perform."

Garrett was an all-league outfielder in baseball, a sport he calls "my first love." The Pittsburgh Pirates drafted him, but he chose professional football instead.

He rushed for 1,087 yards for Kansas City in 1967 and for 1,031 yards with San Diego in 1972, making Garrett the first professional to run for 1,000 yards with two different franchises. He scored a touchdown in Kansas City's 23-7 victory over Minnesota in Super Bowl IV, but his fondest memories are of Southern Cal.

"When you're a Trojan, you're a Trojan for life," said Garrett, a department store executive trainee in San Diego. "USC took a chance on a short guy from East Los Angeles. I'm proud of the university. It's a great marriage."

# STEVE SPURRIER
### Florida—1966

Steve Spurrier definitely had a penchant for the dramatic. When the going got tough, Spurrier got going. Eight times in the fourth quarter during his fantastic Florida career, he brought the Gators back from defeat.

"We didn't play a wide-open offense, normally," Spurrier recalled. "That was the nature of football then. You didn't throw the football much unless you were tied or behind."

The Gators, with Spurrier, were at their most dangerous when behind. One thrilling comeback was as much the result of his foot as his arm. As a senior, he kicked a 40-yard field goal with 2:12 left to beat Auburn, 30-27. But his greatest comeback, in the 1966 Sugar Bowl, fell just short. Florida trailed Missouri, 20-0, in the fourth quarter. The 6-foot-2, 203-pound junior quarterback then led the Gators to three touchdowns, scoring one and passing for two, but three missed two-point conversions left a stunned Mizzou team with a 20-18 victory. Spurrier completed 27 passes for 352 yards, both Sugar Bowl records, as he became the first player from a losing team to be named that game's Most Valuable Player.

"I scrambled around a lot in college and got the job done," he said. "What made me the Heisman winner was that we jumped out to 7-0 that year, the South hadn't had a Heisman winner in seven years and the press down here got behind the Southern boy."

Spurrier's statistics helped build his case, too. He completed 61.5 percent of his passes as a senior for 2,012 yards and 16 touchdowns. In the Heisman Trophy balloting, he more than doubled the point total of runner-up Bob Griese of Purdue.

As great as Spurrier was in college, he was equally disappointing in the National Football League. He blames only himself.

"I wasn't the most ambitious or dedicated player," he said of his 10-year NFL career. "I was more suited for the college game because I didn't have a strong arm, but I didn't try to strengthen it. Physically, I didn't improve much from my college years. I just didn't work that hard."

Spurrier spent nine years with the San Francisco 49ers, largely as a backup to John Brodie, before playing his last season for the winless Tampa Bay Buccaneers.

Spurrier worked as an assistant coach at Florida, Georgia Tech and Duke before being hired to guide the Tampa Bay Bandits of the United States Football League in 1983, making him the only former Heisman winner to become a head coach on the professional level. Through 1985, he was yet to suffer a losing season as a head coach.

"If I'm a good coach," he said, "it's because of my mistakes. We all learn from mistakes."

In his second time around in the pros, Spurrier has found a work ethic, and it is paying dividends.

# GARY BEBAN
## UCLA—1967

In a town of theater, Gary Beban commanded national attention with his football theatrics. He passed, he ran, he innovated, he won. And he resurrected.

UCLA's football program was suffering through a down cycle when Beban joined the varsity in 1965. Over the next three years, the Beban-led Bruins posted a 24-5-2 record, including a 14-12 major upset of top-ranked Michigan State in the Rose Bowl after the 1965 season. Beban, a 6-foot, 191-pound sophomore, scored both UCLA touchdowns against Bubba Smith and friends.

Beban was a single-wing tailback in high school, although no triple threat. "Punting wasn't my game," he said, "and I didn't want to get close to making a tackle." His passing and running skills were perfect, however, for the imaginative coaching of Tommy Prothro, who installed the same quarterback rollout system for Beban that he had used at Oregon State for Terry Baker. One system, two Heisman Trophy winners.

"Tommy's intelligence, strategy and preparation made us better than we were," Beban said. "We had trick plays, sleeper plays. After our first touchdown in the Rose Bowl, we came back with an onside kick, recovered and scored again. That's how confident we were."

Beban accumulated 5,197 yards of total offense, scored 33 touchdowns and passed for 23 more during his regular-season collegiate career. His best performance came in a losing cause against crosstown rival Southern California in 1967.

At the time, UCLA was ranked No. 1 in the country, Southern Cal No. 2. The outcome of that game was for the city, state and, possibly, national championship. Playing with badly bruised ribs, Beban was remarkable as he completed 16 of 24 passes for 301 yards and two touchdowns. O.J. Simpson was equally remarkable for Southern Cal, scoring twice on scintillating runs, and the Trojans won a squeaker, 21-20.

"It was the greatest game I've played in," Beban said, "because all the chips were on the table."

Beban, who was called "The Great One" in Los Angeles, and Simpson staged another battle in 1967—for the Heisman. Beban won narrowly, 1,968 points to 1,722, even though his senior year had been his least productive offensively.

"I was honored for my career," he said, "although my senior year was a good year. O.J. had a phenomenal year."

During his Heisman trip to New York, Beban was interviewed by Howard Cosell, who wanted to know about campus protests, which were taking place at UCLA and universities around the country. "This isn't the proper forum," Beban said. Cosell didn't pursue the matter.

After a brief, unsuccessful pro career with the Washington Redskins, Beban went to work for Coldwell Banker. He now is a senior vice president in the Chicago office of the nation's largest full-service real-estate company.

# STEVE OWENS
## Oklahoma—1969

Steve Owens grew up in Miami, Okla., a small town in the northeast corner of the state. His father was a trucker who drove the big semis. But there were no "semis" in the Owens' household, which included 11 children.

"My father raised us with the idea that if you want something in life, you have to work for it," Owens said.

Nothing halfway. Do it right or don't do it at all. With a strong work ethic implanted in his mind from his childhood, it seemed only natural that Steve Owens should win the Heisman Trophy.

"I'm a firm believer that if you work hard, you'll have your rewards," he said. "I had a certain amount of talent. I didn't have great speed, for instance. So I worked harder to develop my strength and quickness and my blocking. I refined the talents I had."

The 6-foot-2, 215-pound Owens had little time to block because he averaged 35.8 carries per game his last two years at Oklahoma, including 55 carries against Oklahoma State as a senior. Despite the heavy workload, he didn't miss one game in college or high school.

"The best compliment I received as an athlete," he said, "was from a Cincinnati Bengals scout who said, 'Owens may run a 4.8-second 40-yard dash, but he runs a 4.5 in his mind.'

"He was right. I had to think faster, not make mental errors, be able to read defenses. I also had a high pain threshold, which allowed me to carry the ball a lot game after game."

He also carried the ball as many as 150 times in one Oklahoma practice, sprinting 20 to 30 yards each carry. It's no wonder that Owens led the nation in carries as a junior and senior, and in rushing yards (1,523) and touchdowns (23) his last year, 1969, when he won the Heisman. He wound up his three-year Sooner career as college football's all-time leading rusher (3,867 yards) and scorer (336 points).

Though injuries hampered Owens' National Football League career, he spent seven seasons with Detroit and, in 1971, became the first Lion to rush for 1,000 yards (1,035).

Owens now has his own banking and investment business in Norman, Okla., where he continues to practice what his father preached.

"We do work with 400 financial institutions," Owens said. "In sports, you have your ups and downs. We've had our ups and downs in starting this business. It's a lot of hard work, but my philosophy is that we'll outwork you."

# JIM PLUNKETT
## Stanford—1970

Jim Plunkett's life was positioned squarely behind the eight ball from the very beginning. But his ability to beat the odds has made him an inspiration to people everywhere.

He was the youngest of three children born to blind parents—his mother is totally blind and his father, who died while Plunkett was in college, was legally blind.

Plunkett was reared in poverty. His father operated a newsstand in a San Jose, Calif., post office, a job frequently given to the blind. It wasn't enough money to support the family, which lived mainly on state aid.

Plunkett grew up tall, strong, proud. Not only was he proud of his parents, but also of his Mexican heritage. He wasn't embarrassed to be poor, but, instead, was driven to be great.

More obstacles awaited him as a Stanford freshman. One month before Plunkett enrolled at Stanford, a tumor appeared on his neck. He thought he had cancer and underwent surgery, but the tumor was benign.

He then was asked to switch from quarterback to defensive end. He refused and, three years later, became Stanford's only Heisman winner before leading his school to a stunning 27-17 upset of Ohio State in the Rose Bowl. The 6-foot-2, 210-pound quarterback had passed for 2,715 yards and 18 touchdowns that year.

In August 1978, Plunkett was released by the San Francisco 49ers after failing, up to that point, to realize his tremendous potential coming out of college, although he had been named the National Football League's Rookie of the Year with New

England in 1971. The Oakland Raiders invited him to try out for a roster spot, and the No. 1 player taken in the 1971 NFL draft became the Raiders' No. 3 quarterback. But key injuries made Plunkett a starter, and he went on to direct the Raiders to Super Bowl championships following the 1980 and 1983 seasons.

"I've had a lot of setbacks (including 11 operations)," he said, "but I'm the kind of guy who doesn't let them upset me. And I'm not sure why. The setbacks have taught me not to get discouraged, even though it's hard not to at times. I keep plugging away."

Plunkett is the perfect longshot. There never has been a dark horse quite like him. Even after others give up on him, he always wins.

His greatest accomplishments, he said, are his young children, a son and a daughter. "Being a father is the greatest experience I've ever had, bar none," he said, beaming. "I've never had so much fun in my life."

# PAT SULLIVAN
## Auburn—1971

Pat Sullivan is reminded of his winning the Heisman Trophy every Thursday night when he watches "Hill Street Blues." One of the cops on the popular television program was his main competition.

"Ed Marinaro's now making all the money," Sullivan said, "and I'm working for a living."

The 1971 Heisman race is remembered largely because an Ivy Leaguer was a candidate. Marinaro, the durable, record-setting Cornell running back who now portrays Sgt. Joe Coffey on TV, was bidding to become the first Heisman winner from an Ivy institution since Dick Kazmaier of Princeton in 1951.

Marinaro was quite candid about why he felt he deserved the Heisman, and a national debate ensued: Should a school that doesn't play a major-college schedule produce a Heisman hero? When Kazmaier was at Princeton, Ivy League football was on a par with other major conferences around the country. That was before de-emphasis changed the Ivy format in the mid-1950s.

"Marinaro was very outspoken about his situation, and I wasn't," Sullivan said. "I couldn't have spoken out. That wouldn't have been me."

Sullivan had the statistics worthy of a Heisman recipient even if he didn't have the nation's total support. The 6-foot, 192-pound baby-faced quarterback tied an NCAA career record by being responsible for 71 touchdowns (53 passing, 18 running). As a junior, while leading the country in total offense, Sullivan established another major-college mark by averaging 8.6 yards per play. Auburn won 25 of 30 regular-season games during Sullivan's three years at quarterback, including two victories over Alabama for state bragging rights, and appeared in three bowl games.

"That was the most exciting period of Auburn football for throwing the ball," Sullivan said. "That helped create an image."

So did the 45-rpm record "The Legend of Pat Sullivan."

"It was very flattering," Sullivan said of the attention showered on him. "I felt I was in the groove throwing the football, but the best thing I had was rapport with my teammates. Whatever I said, went."

The final Heisman point count that year was Sullivan 1,597, Marinaro 1,445, making him the only Heisman winner from a school once coached by John W. Heisman, for whom the trophy was named. Sullivan doesn't think of that narrow margin of victory when he watches "Hill Street Blues." Instead, he considers the total Heisman experience. He regularly attends the Heisman alumni dinner, "where the older you get, the stories and times get better," he said.

Sullivan spent four undistinguished years with the Atlanta Falcons. He now owns a tire dealership in Birmingham and is the color commentator on Auburn football broadcasts.

# JOHN CAPPELLETTI
## Penn State—1973

It was the night the Heisman cried.

"The youngest member of my family, Joseph, is very ill," John Cappelletti told those in the audience on December 13, 1973, the night he received the Heisman Trophy. "He has leukemia. If I can dedicate this trophy to him tonight and give him a couple days of happiness, this is worth everything.

"A lot of people think that I go through a lot during the week and on Saturdays, as most athletes do. You get your bumps and bruises, and it is a terrific battle out there on the field. Only for me it is on Saturdays, and it's only in the fall. For Joseph, it is all year round, and it is a battle that is unending with him. And he puts up with much more than I'll ever put up with, and I think that this trophy is more his than mine because he has been a great inspiration to me."

Of all the Heisman acceptance speeches in 50 years, Cappelletti's touched the most hearts. Archbishop Fulton J. Sheen was to give the closing prayer that night. "There is no need for a benediction tonight," he said, "for God has already blessed you with John Cappelletti."

Joey Cappelletti, 13, died of leukemia in April 1976 with John at his bedside. Later, a television movie, "Something for Joey," was based on the loving relationship between the two brothers.

John Cappelletti said that half of his Heisman speech was written before he left his hotel room for the ceremony. "The last part, about Joey, was thought of at the last moment," he said. "If I had tried to write it, I would have cried all the way through.

"There's still a reaction inside me now about Joey when people who meet me for the first time tell me that they remember my speech or saw the movie. But I don't let people know what I'm feeling. I can always picture Joey in my mind. He's kind of standing there with a grin on his face, looking back at me."

At 10 pounds, 3 ounces, John Cappelletti was a large baby. He walked at the age of nine months, which left him bowlegged. From ages 2 to 6, he wore corrective shoes and outgrew his condition.

At Penn State, he was moved to defensive back as a sophomore because Lydell Mitchell and Franco Harris were the running backs. Cappelletti returned to offense the next year and responded with 1,117 yards rushing in 1972. As a senior, he ran for 1,522 yards (5.3 average) and 17 touchdowns. Penn State had a perfect 12-0 season, including a 16-9 win over Louisiana State in the Orange Bowl.

"I didn't have exceptional speed," Cappelletti said, "but I was strong, durable and consistent."

Cappelletti, Penn State's only Heisman winner, played for the Los Angeles Rams for five years and the San Diego Chargers for four. He now builds swimming pools in Southern California.

# TONY DORSETT
## Pittsburgh — 1976

It would be the ultimate testimony to Tony Dorsett's greatness. It is possible that Dorsett could become the all-time leading rusher at the college and professional levels.

Through 1984, nearly a decade after he finished playing at the University of Pittsburgh, Dorsett continued to hold the NCAA career rushing record with 6,082 yards. Entering the 1985 National Football League season, the 5-foot-11, 189-pound running back had amassed 9,525 yards rushing as a pro, sixth on the all-time list. Walter Payton of the Chicago Bears is the career leader with 13,309 yards, but he has played for two more seasons than Dorsett, giving the Dallas Cowboys' star a chance to overtake Payton.

"Tony is our catalyst," Dallas Coach Tom Landry said. "He is the one who makes us go on offense."

Jim Brown, whom Payton surpassed in rushing yardage in 1984, said of Dorsett: "Tony is the epitome of an artist. There is no small back in football who can touch him."

And there are few running backs in history who can touch Dorsett when it comes to football accomplishments. He was the first college back to rush for 1,000 yards or more in four different seasons and for 1,500 yards in three seasons. No other collegian has ever rushed for 6,000 yards.

"I wanted to push that record up so far that no one would ever dream of beating it," Dorsett recalled. "Maybe they could hope for Number 2, but I wanted that record to be mine as long as I'm on this Earth."

Herschel Walker's decision to sign a professional contract after his junior year at Georgia likely preserved Dorsett's record. But not even Walker can touch Dorsett's unprecedented "hat trick" of winning the Heisman Trophy, playing on a national college champion (1976) and earning a Super Bowl ring (1977 season with Dallas) in roughly a year's time. "That was unbelievable," he said.

It was, but no more incredible than Dorsett's accomplishment during the 1982 strike-shortened season. Dorsett set an NFL record with a 99-yard touchdown run against Minnesota—a play on which there were only 10 Cowboys on the field and Dorsett wasn't even supposed to get the ball. Fullback Ron Springs was the intended ballcarrier, but he mistakenly left the field. There was nothing else for Dorsett to do but take it all the way.

Despite his consistency in college, Dorsett didn't win the Heisman until he was a senior. He thought he deserved it as a freshman but gave up any hope of winning it as a junior.

"I really wanted to win the Heisman," he said. "It meant the same to me as a doctor or lawyer wanting to win a Rhodes scholarship. Now that I have it, it's a good feeling for me. Years from now, I can show people that I was up there with the best."

# EARL CAMPBELL
## Texas—1977

It was a curious trade. The Houston Oilers sent the once-untouchable Earl Campbell to the New Orleans Saints for a first-round draft pick. This meant that two Heisman Trophy winners, George Rogers and Campbell, would share the same halfback position. The Saints' I-back became a We-back.

In 1984, Campbell had his worst NFL season, rushing for only 468 total yards for both Houston and New Orleans. He used to get that in less than three games! Word has circulated through the National Football League that Campbell has slipped, that the end is in sight.

"I'm not a dummy," Campbell said. "I hear what people are saying. But it doesn't bother me. I heard it before, that I wasn't supposed to make it in college. People didn't even think I would make my grades. You can take it sweet or you can take it bitter. I don't hang around with the bitter."

Campbell understands himself better than others. Although he already had been named to the All-Southwest Conference team in his first two seasons, Campbell rushed for only 653 yards as a junior at Texas, and word spread through Longhorn country that the "Tyler Rose" had lost his bloom. Campbell's weight had been too high that 1976 season, but he had been injured, too, missing four games and most of two others. He chose not to hang around with the bitter back then, either.

Campbell cut his weight from 240 to 223 pounds and turned the 1977 collegiate football season into "The Earl Campbell Show." The 5-foot-11 running back exploded for 1,744 yards rushing and 19 touchdowns. Against Texas A&M, he ran for 222 yards and scored four touchdowns.

Campbell nearly doubled the Heisman vote of runner-up Terry Miller of Oklahoma State. He then flew to New York for the Heisman ceremony, which became an extravaganza for the first time. CBS televised the presentation, which starred entertainers Elliott Gould, Leslie Uggams, Connie Stevens and Robert Klein.

Campbell was the No. 1 pick of the 1978 NFL draft and became the first rookie to lead the league in rushing since 1957, when Jim Brown did it. He topped all rushers in 1979 and 1980, too, setting an NFL record with four 200-yard games in one season ('80). Entering the 1985 season he was eighth on the all-time rushing list.

After his disappointing 1984 season, Campbell remained optimistic. "I had problems last year," he said. "It's a year I'm not proud of. But whatever a year is, get over it and make next year a better one."

The trade to the Saints may prove to be a good move for Campbell, especially after New Orleans sent Rogers to Washington in a trade with the Redskins the following April. That leaves Campbell as the Saints' No. 1 running back.

In the off-season, Campbell worked out every day. His physical condition reportedly is the best it has been in several years.

"My wife tells me, 'All you do is practice football,' " he said. "I tell her why: 'I just want to be the best someday.' "

Earl already was the best once, and it's not too late for a comeback.

# BILLY SIMS
## Oklahoma—1978

At one point in his Oklahoma football career, Billy Sims almost said so long to the Sooners and headed back home to Hooks, Tex. He had played little as a freshman behind Joe Washington. He fractured a shoulder the next year and was redshirted. The following year, he severely sprained an ankle and sat out about half of the season.

"I felt like going home because it wasn't working out at all," he recalled. "But I never was a quitter. I never shied away from hard work. I knew that sooner or later, I'd stay healthy and have a good season.

"There was another reason I stayed—Barry Switzer, one of the classiest coaches in the business. He never gave up on me. He told me I could be a great player if I stayed healthy."

In 1978, the 6-foot, 205-pound Sims was the picture of health. He rushed for 1,762 yards—including three consecutive 200-yard games—and scored 20 touchdowns. He averaged 160.2 yards per game, and despite fumbling away Oklahoma's No. 1 ranking at the Nebraska 3-yard line, Sims won the Heisman Trophy by a narrow 77-point margin over Penn State quarterback Chuck Fusina. Oklahoma then beat Nebraska, 31-24, in a rematch at the Orange Bowl to finish with an 11-1 record.

Sims was a junior in athletic eligibility when he earned the Heisman, so he had an opportunity to match Archie Griffin's Heisman "double" at Ohio State in 1974-75. Although Sims wasn't quite as spectacular as a senior, he still gained 1,506 yards rushing and increased his number of touchdowns to 22. Sims set an NCAA career record by becoming the first runner with more than 500 carries to average seven yards per attempt (7.09). However, Charles White of Southern California won the Heisman in 1979.

"I felt White deserved it because he had a good year," Sims reflected. "I wasn't disappointed. I had a good year myself, and I was the Number 1 player taken in the National Football League draft."

With the Detroit Lions, Sims has rushed for 1,000 yards three times, but he missed in two other years because of injuries (and the 1982 strike). It seems as though he has passed this way before. "Without a question of a doubt," he said, "what happened to me in my first few years at Oklahoma has helped me with what I have gone through at Detroit."

Sims nearly jumped to the United States Football League after signing a contract with the Houston Gamblers. But a 1984 court decision ruled that he had been represented improperly by his agent, and he was allowed to remain with Detroit.

Sims hasn't broken his ties with Oklahoma. He talks with Switzer at least once a month and continues to help with recruiting.

As for being a Heisman winner, Sims said, "it's special being among the elite." He keeps his bronzed statue in his Detroit condominium as a reminder of what can happen to those who don't throw in the towel.

# CHARLES WHITE
## Southern California — 1979

It was unheard of, a college freshman announcing that he wanted to win not one Heisman Trophy, but two.

"I was boasting at the mouth," Charles White said in retrospect. "But I wanted to get one Heisman. It was my goal to be the best football player in America."

As it turned out, White had as much dash as brash. It took him four years to achieve half of his initial Heisman goal, receiving the coveted trophy in 1979.

"I knew something special was going to happen to me," White said. "All I had to do was stay healthy and do well on national television."

White wasn't even concerned that Oklahoma's Billy Sims was trying to win his second consecutive Heisman that fall. "Our team was stronger than his team," White pointed out.

Southern California was undefeated (10-0-1 in the regular season) White's senior year as he rushed for 1,803 yards to lead the nation. Over his productive college career, White averaged 127.2 yards per game on the ground and finished with 5,598 yards, placing him second on the all-time rushing list behind Pittsburgh's Tony Dorsett.

White sparkled on television, exploding for 261 yards and four touchdowns against Notre Dame in 1979. That performance, more than any other, earned White his Heisman.

He then closed out his playing days at Southern Cal by rushing for 247 yards on 39 carries as the Trojans rallied to defeat Ohio State, 17-16. White ignited the winning drive by blasting for 60 yards on the first two plays, then tied the score on a one-yard dive. "I tell all the Ohio State fans around Cleveland that Ohio State was good to me," he said.

White was the Cleveland Browns' first draft pick in 1980, but he hasn't come close to matching his college accomplishments, partly because of his size (5-foot-10, 187 pounds). Injuries also have been a factor. He missed the 1983 season with a broken ankle and a good share of the 1984 schedule with back spasms. He was cut by the Browns on June 4, 1985, after totaling a mere 942 yards in four seasons.

He has had other troubles. In the summer of 1982, White admitted himself to a Southern California hospital for treatment of a cocaine problem that, he said, affected his play. "I feel good about myself now," he said in the spring of 1985. "I've been off the stuff for four years."

White was signed by the Los Angeles Rams in July 1985. "I'm happy because I've made it this far," he said. "Hopefully, I can go on and be a better player. Or if it doesn't work out, maybe I can relate my (drug) experiences to some of the young people, so they won't have to go through what I did."

# GEORGE ROGERS
## South Carolina—1980

"If you only knew what it took me to get there," George Rogers recalled of his winning the Heisman Trophy in 1980.

Rogers' parents separated when he was a child in an Atlanta ghetto. His father then fatally shot his girlfriend and spent eight years in prison. Rogers, his mother, two brothers and two teen-age sisters—each with a baby—moved from town to town until an aunt took them into her home in Duluth, Ga., just north of Atlanta.

"It was the best thing I ever did," Rogers said. "It was a chance to come up there and go to school."

At Duluth High School, Rogers turned out for football but found that he was afraid of contact.

"I was chickening through the hole," he said. "My coach reached down and picked me up from the bottom of the pile. I wasn't but 180 pounds and he was 6-5, 220. He started shaking me and said, 'You're gonna run the ball or I'm gonna kick your rear end.' I was, like, crying, but that helped motivate me."

Three years later, more than 100 colleges recruited Rogers, who told his mother as a high school senior that he was going to win the Heisman for her. He then selected that non-Heisman football factory, South Carolina, because he believed he could trust its coach, Jim Carlen.

"George is, without a doubt, the finest football player in the nation," Carlen once said. "First day, first practice, first time he tucked the ball under his arm, I knew George Rogers was something special."

Rogers gave South Carolina, the Rodney Dangerfield of football in the South, some long-needed respect. The Gamecocks hadn't won eight games in one season since 1903 until Rogers led them to an 8-3 record and a Hall of Fame Bowl berth in 1979. A year later, South Carolina duplicated that record and went to the Gator Bowl.

As a senior, Rogers led the nation in rushing with 1,781 yards (6.0 average). But it was his consistency over a longer period—22 consecutive games (including bowls) of rushing for 100 or more yards—that moved Mr. Rogers into that select neighborhood of Heisman winners.

The New York Daily News then reported that it had a recorded interview with Rogers in which he said Carlen had asked to represent him in negotiations with the National Football League team that drafted him. Then Carlen found out it was against NCAA rules for a coach to represent a player, and he relinquished his role as an agent, adding that he intended to do it for free.

After being made the first pick in the NFL draft by the New Orleans Saints, Rogers led the league with 1,674 yards rushing and was named Rookie of the Year in 1981. He told federal investigators the following June that he had spent more than $10,000 on cocaine during his first year in the league. He underwent testing and treatment for drug abuse at a Florida clinic in July 1982.

Rogers averaged 1,244 yards rushing over his three full seasons in New Orleans (excluding the 1982 strike season) before the Saints traded him to Washington in 1985.

# MARCUS ALLEN
## Southern California—1981

Run, Marcus, run.

And Marcus Allen did run in 1981, 403 times, or a staggering 36.6 carries per game, in becoming the first NCAA player to rush for 2,000 yards in one season. He finished with 2,342 yards and a 5.8-yard average, which is amazing considering how often he had the football. He was a Trojan workhorse.

"Marcus Allen is the greatest football player I have ever seen," said John Robinson, his coach at Southern Cal.

Allen had the additional support of his buddy O.J. Simpson, who once said: "I think he can win the Heisman. He'd better, because I'm not about to lend him mine."

Allen did win the Heisman Trophy in 1981, which came as no great surprise after he had rushed for 200 or more yards in eight games that fall and had established or tied 16 NCAA records. Certainly, Allen wasn't surprised.

"This may sound self-centered or conceited," he said, looking back, "but if I had had a Heisman vote, I would have voted for myself."

Allen wasn't born to play tailback at Southern Cal. At Lincoln High School in San Diego, he was a quarterback. But in the city championship game, Allen ran for four touchdowns and returned an interception for a fifth.

Robinson had no trouble recruiting Allen. "It was always USC for me, even when I was a kid," he said. After backing up 1979 Heisman winner Charles White as a freshman, Allen was moved to fullback to block for White.

Switched back to tailback as a junior, the 6-foot-2, 202-pound Allen responded with 1,563 yards rushing and 14 touchdowns. He had his mind set on 2,000 yards as a senior, and he was successful, scoring 23 touchdowns besides. Entering 1985, his 1981 rushing totals for yardage and carries still ranked as NCAA records.

"I found my place in history as the best player in the country at that particular time," Allen said.

The National Football League, however, viewed him as the 10th-best player in the 1982 draft. Two other running backs, Darrin Nelson of Stanford and Gerald Riggs of Arizona State, were chosen by Minnesota and Atlanta, respectively, before the Los Angeles Raiders selected Allen.

He led the NFL in scoring with 84 points as a rookie during the nine-game, strike-shortened 1982 season. A year later, he led the Raiders to a 38-9 victory over the Washington Redskins in Super Bowl XVIII. He was named the Most Valuable Player in that game after rushing 20 times for a Super Bowl-record 191 yards, including a 74-yard touchdown run for another Super Bowl mark.

During that season, Allen complained to Al Davis, the Raiders' managing general partner, that he wasn't doing enough running. Davis told him to jog after practice. Allen complained again to Davis at the tail end of the 1984 season that he wasn't being used enough and that it had cost him some contract incentives. In the off-season between the '84 and '85 seasons, Allen voiced his displeasure with the Raiders' offensive line, too.

Allen lost none of his outstanding football talent in the transition from college to professional football, only his innocence.

# HERSCHEL WALKER
## Georgia—1982

But for the flip of a coin or names in a paper bag, Herschel Walker might have won the Heisman Trophy for Alabama . . . or Clemson . . . or Southern California. Georgia? That was the last school on Walker's mind.

Walker had rushed for 6,137 yards and 86 touchdowns at Johnson County High School in Wrightsville, Ga. The recruiting of Walker became so intense that college coaches virtually camped out at the bottom of the long dirt driveway leading to the Walkers' home on a highway just outside of Wrightsville. Confused by it all and unable to make up his mind, Walker resorted to games of chance.

"Georgia wasn't even high on my list," he recalled. "But every time I mentioned Alabama to my parents and friends, they kept mentioning Georgia. So, I decided to flip a coin.

"First, I flipped Georgia against Clemson, three out of five. Georgia came up the first three times. Then I flipped Georgia against Southern Cal. The first two flips came out for Georgia, the third for Southern Cal, and the fourth for Georgia."

Walker still wasn't satisfied. He had his mother write the names of Southern Cal, Clemson, Alabama and Georgia on slips of paper and drop them in a bag. The first school Walker picked out of the bag three times, that's where he would go. And that's how Georgia "recruited" Walker.

Walker's favorite recruiter, he confessed, was the Marines. He was in ROTC in high school, and he wanted to join the Marines after graduation. "They offered a new change every day," he explained, "and would have helped me mature since people said I grew up too fast."

He bowed to pressure from his parents and friends and decided to attend college, thereby denying the Marines the next John Wayne. Georgia knew it had found something special right away when Walker led the Bulldogs to the national championship and finished third in the Heisman balloting as a freshman in 1980. Walker finished second in the Heisman race as a sophomore, by which time he had established himself as a world-class sprinter in track and field. He then won the Heisman as a junior after rushing for 1,752 yards. That effort gave him 5,259 yards over three seasons, making him the first junior in NCAA history to surpass the 5,000-yard rushing mark. He needed only 824 yards as a senior to break Tony Dorsett's career record.

But Walker turned his back on Georgia, the rushing record and a chance to become a four-time consensus All-America and a two-time Heisman winner by signing a three-year, $5 million contract with the New Jersey Generals of the United States Football League in 1983.

The imposing 6-foot-1, 222-pound running back led the USFL in rushing that year with 1,812 yards. Bothered by a shoulder injury in 1984, he rushed for 1,339 yards, caught 40 passes and scored a league-high 21 touchdowns. But the best was yet to come. In 1985, Walker rushed for 2,411 yards, thus breaking the pro season rushing record of 2,105 yards that Eric Dickerson of the Los Angeles Rams had set in the National Football League's 1984 season.

Walker doesn't regret his decision to leave college prematurely. "I'm happy," he said. "The NFL rule about not drafting underclassmen isn't a bad rule in some ways, but you have to think about the athlete, too. What if he gets injured his senior year? What will the NFL pay him then? The athlete should have the right to decide his future for himself."

Walker, a fifth-round pick of the Dallas Cowboys in the 1985 NFL draft, said he doesn't plan to play pro football for more than five seasons. "I enjoy football, but I'm not a fanatic about it," he said. "I'd like to try something else."

His dream, he added, is to become an FBI agent. Even though he was working toward completing his degree in criminal justice in the off-seasons, Herschel probably never will be able to wrap the requisite cloak of anonymity around his muscular frame.

# MIKE ROZIER
## Nebraska—1983

Mike Rozier and Archie Griffin were teammates briefly on the Jacksonville Bulls of the United States Football League in 1985. Asked what it was like playing alongside the only two-time Heisman winner, Rozier replied: "It's like any other thing. We don't sit back there counting our trophies."

As the Bulls' fullback, Rozier received the bulk of the ball-carrying responsibilities, and so Griffin, who was attempting a comeback after being released by the Cincinnati Bengals, retired after the fourth game of the season. Rozier was attempting a comeback of sorts, too, after a disappointing USFL rookie season with the now-defunct Pittsburgh Maulers. At Jacksonville, Rozier began to resemble the highly productive back who had rushed for 2,148 yards for Nebraska in 1983, averaging 7.8 yards per attempt.

Iron Mike became only the second college back to run for 2,000 or more yards in one season. (Southern California's Marcus Allen was the first.) The 5-foot-11, 210-pound I-back also was the second community college transfer to win the Heisman, following in the footsteps of O.J. Simpson. (Roger Staubach transferred to Navy after attending a military institute in New Mexico.)

Rozier was a good high school player in Camden, N.J., although not heavily recruited in the manner of a Herschel Walker. Nebraska was interested in Rozier, but his grades were not good enough to gain admission as a freshman. So, he spent one year at Coffeyville (Kan.) Community College, where he had an outstanding football season and brought up his grades before enrolling at Nebraska.

Over the next three years, he amassed 4,780 yards on the ground, and he scored 29 rushing touchdowns as a senior for an NCAA record.

"I never thought I'd get that far," Rozier said of his winning the Heisman, which he promised to cut up in the following manner: Nebraska quarterback Turner Gill would get the head, wingback Irving Fryar the arms, Rozier the legs and the Cornhuskers' offensive line the heart. Rozier wasn't held to his promise.

In its October 22, 1984, issue, Sports Illustrated reported that Rozier had admitted in a tape-recorded interview that he had signed with an agent and accepted the agent's money during Nebraska's 1983 season and that, before playing in the Orange Bowl, he had entered into a contract with the USFL's Maulers, a three-year, $3.1 million deal. Such actions, which were denied by the Maulers and an associate of Rozier's agent, were in violation of NCAA rules.

Rozier said he regretted the incident, while the Downtown Athletic Club was embarrassed by the revelation that it had, in fact, honored a professional football player—at least according to the NCAA's definition of the term.

After one year in Pittsburgh, Rozier reached a settlement on the final two years of his contract, freeing him to negotiate with Jacksonville. Then after one year with the Bulls, he signed a four-year contract with the Houston Oilers of the National Football League.

# DOUG FLUTIE
## Boston College—1984

The improbability of Doug Flutie's ascendancy into the record books and a nation's consciousness continues to swirl in his mind, along with the magic that made it all happen.

"I wanted to try and prove people wrong," he said. "I wanted to be the guy that did the impossible, the guy that no one expected to make it and then made it."

Flutie is 5-foot-9¾, too small, it seemed, to have set college football on its ear. The impossible dream for Flutie, it appeared in the beginning, was seeing over his offensive linemen in order to pass downfield. But pass he did, time after spectacular time, until he became the first major-college football player to throw for 10,000 yards (10,579) and compile 10,000 yards of total offense (11,317).

Jack Bicknell, who coached the amazing Flutie at Boston College and doesn't expect to coach anyone quite like him again, summarized the experience. "It was like a fairy tale," he said. "He's the kid like you read about in books."

The Magic Flutie. And his finest bewitching hour, make that six seconds, occurred on a 48-yard pass to Gerard Phelan with no time left to defeat Miami (Florida), 47-45, on November 23, 1984. Flutie's pass, which actually traveled 64 yards into the wind, left no doubt among football fans as to whom would win the Heisman, even though the balloting may have been over before that game.

"It was something so far out," Flutie said of winning the 50th Heisman. "It's something I never could have dreamed would happen."

Flutie also brought his school national rankings, national television appearances and bowl-game invitations.

All this Flutie-concocted attention paid off financially for Boston College, and for Flutie. Slightly more than a month after he led the Eagles over Houston in the Cotton Bowl, Flutie signed a six-year, $8.3 million contract with the New Jersey Generals of the United States Football League.

In April 1985, Generals Owner Donald J. Trump requested that other USFL owners help him pay Flutie's salary. The financial instability of the USFL has made the league's future, and Flutie's, uncertain, but the little quarterback still is in a state of awe over all that has taken place in his life.

"When I was younger," he said, "I idolized Bert Jones and Roger Staubach. But I never thought this would happen to me."

Flutie went to the White House to meet President Reagan after completing "The Pass" against Miami. Reagan then phoned Flutie after he won the Heisman. For an undersized football player, Flutie certainly travels in tall company.

*John W. Heisman, pictured here as coach of Pennsylvania in 1922, was athletic director of New York's Downtown Athletic Club when he died in 1936. He had coached at eight different colleges and was considered one of the top football innovators of all time.*